BUSINESS ACQUISITIONS
DESK BOOK
With Checklists and Forms
(SECOND EDITION)

BUSINESS ACQUISITIONS DESK BOOK

With Checklists and Forms

SECOND EDITION

F.T. Davis, Jr.

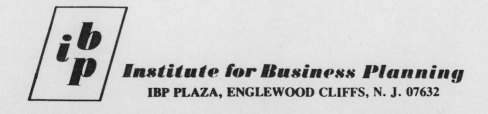

Institute for Business Planning
IBP PLAZA, ENGLEWOOD CLIFFS, N. J. 07632

© 1981

by F.T. Davis, Jr.

Second Printing ..... December, 1981

This publication is designed to provide accurate and authoritative information in regard to the subject matter covered. It is sold with the understanding
that the publisher is not engaged in rendering legal, accounting or other
professional service. If legal advice or other expert assistance is required, the
services of a competent professional person should be sought.

*—From a Declaration of Principles jointly adopted by a Commit-
tee of the American Bar Association and a Committee of Pub-
lishers and Associations.*

Library of Congress Cataloging in Publication Data

Davis, F. T.
    Business acquisitions desk book, with checklists and
forms.

    Includes index.
    1. Consolidation and merger of corporations--United
States. I. Title.
KF1477.D3 1981   346.73'06626   81-6464
ISBN 0-87624-049-X   347.3066626   AACR2

Printed in the United States of America
10-9-8-7-6-5-4-3-2

About the Author

F.T. Davis, Jr. received the Bachelor of Arts Degree from Princeton University, the Juris Doctor Degree from George Washington University, and the Master of Laws Degree from Harvard University. He is a member of the Georgia and District of Columbia Bars and is a partner in the Atlanta law firm of Hansell, Post, Brandon & Dorsey.

Introduction

Today's uncertain securities market, concerns about inflation, and the limited cash position of many businesses have caused many executives and their advisors to overlook the acquisition opportunities available. Opportunities lie both in acquisitions of publicly held corporations and of closely-held businesses.

Business Acquisitions Desk Book will serve not only as a refresher for the busy executive or professional as to the basic acquisition tools available under today's business conditions, tax laws, and securities laws, but will also discuss the techniques necessary to actually put together a profitable and successful acquisition.

All too often the busy executive planning or involved in a business acquisition has limited time to spend with his professional advisors such as lawyers and accountants. Discussions with these advisors are usually limited to the nuts and bolts of the particular transaction at hand, without a discussion of the big picture—the range of alternatives available—and their pros and cons. It is hoped that this book will help fill the gap between the executive's knowledge of business goals and the general direction desired, in the limited time available to professional advisors in which to discuss the broad range of alternatives available for the business transaction.

Too often in today's economy the business executive has so concentrated on the difficulties of his own business that he fails to see the once-in-a-lifetime opportunity available for acquiring new businesses and expanding present markets through acquisition techniques, often with minimum cost to the existing business.

Every type of transaction discussed in this *Desk Book* is based upon actual recent transactions and techniques. The transactions discussed can be profitable for both the acquiring and acquired business. For example, you will find a discussion of the actual type of transaction in which a business worth millions of dollars was acquired by payment of only $50,000 by the acquiring corporation, while the retiring owner of the business received several millions of dollars in cash at very favorable tax rates.

Recent tax law changes have shifted the ground rules on acquisitions and business ownership. New capital gains rates and corporate tax rates, as well as proposed tax changes, have made use of corporate vehicles for investment and acquisition even more desirable.

This *Desk Book* discusses a rarely used but important technique of exchanging entire businesses on a tax-free basis, eliminating capital gains taxes entirely. This technique allows a corporation to shift into entirely new markets, obtain much higher depreciation tax shelter, and modernize plant equipment at absolutely no tax cost at the time of exchange.

Until recently, many of the techniques and methods in this book were overlooked because of the easy accessibility of cheap borrowed money and the seemingly inexhaustible public markets for equity capital. The techniques are important in any type of market, but are absolutely essential in today's market, with high interest rates and volatile equity markets.

The new Installment Sales Revision Act of 1980 has made dramatic changes for acquisitions. This second edition shows how to use the new installment sales rules from both the buyer and sellers' standpoint. These rules are discussed in connection with tax planning for a "bootstrap" acquisition as well as other uses. The second edition sets out the fundamental points you will need to consider in any "leveraged buy-out." Among other new topics, SEC rules for small companies are covered. A new chapter (Chapter 6) has been added covering personal planning for the executive in acquisitions.

One final feature of the *Desk Book* should be mentioned. The Appendix contains examples of actual forms and documents of the type used in many of the transactions discussed in this *Desk Book*. In addition to the forms themselves, they are cross-referenced to major discussions in the text and also contain marginal comments which should be helpful to both the executive and the professional advisor planning similar transactions. Study of the forms will help the business executive and his professional advisors plan the acquisition from start to finish. Study of the forms provided in the Appendix, together with the analysis provided in the *Desk Book* itself, will help the busy executive understand such important provisions as accounts receivable warranties in acquisition agreements. All too often the importance of these strangely worded provisions does not come home to the executive until months after the acquisition itself.

This *Desk Book* does not attempt to explore all of the technical points which arise in any particular acquisition. Obviously, good professional advice is needed to plan and execute a successful corporate acquisition. Professional advisors have available to them, and can recommend to the busy executives, in-depth discussions of particular acquisition problems as well as the court cases and accounting board statements which govern these transactions.

Unfortunately, all too often, the busy executive is either given a quick and superficial general statement as to the rules which apply, or is plunged directly into detailed discussions of particular points, without ever being able to put the practical business questions in some type of framework. For the professional already familiar with the overview and details of acquisition problems, this *Desk Book* will serve as a ready reference.

This *Desk Book* is based upon the belief that there are unique acquisition and recapitalization possibilities in today's market. This book will provide the busy chief executive and his professional advisors with quick access to tried and tested tax-saving and money-making techniques used by today's knowledgeable business executive. The *Desk Book* will provide a quick refresher and checklist as well as a general discussion of acquisition possibilities in today's market.

After the *Desk Book* went to press, President Reagan signed the Economic Recovery Tax Act of 1981, lowering many tax rates and making several other changes to encourage investment. Effective July 1, 1981, the Internal Revenue Service also raised the minimum interest rate allowable on installment sales to 9%. Printing schedules have not permitted a revision of the examples or text to reflect the particulars of these changes. All of the techniques discussed in this Book remain valid, and many are even more attractive under the new rules. Some of the highlights of the new rules are discussed in a revised Section D of Chapter 2 of the Book.

The author gratefully acknowledges the help of the publisher for many useful suggestions, Mary Alice Trobaugh for her comments and assistance, my partners and clients for what they have taught me, and my wife, Win, for all of her help and patience.

Second Edition,
Atlanta
April, 1981

Partially Revised
August, 1981

F.T. Davis, Jr.

Table of Contents

Chapter 1

The Ground Rules
For a Tax-Free Acquisition

A. THE BASIC TAX-FREE ACQUISITION:
THE TAX-FREE CORPORATE REORGANIZATION

Planning for most acquisitions will involve consideration of provisions of the Internal Revenue Code that allow certain fundamental corporate changes without tax. While the eventual form of the acquisition may not be tax free, in most instances a tax-free reorganization must be considered as a possible alternative.

Normally, when property is sold or exchanged, a gain or loss is realized under federal income tax codes. By the same token, the Internal Revenue Code does not usually recognize and tax and "unrealized" gain.

> *Example:* The founder of a business corporation owning all of the shares of the corporation for which the original cost was $1,000, has no federal income tax to pay until he disposes of the stock, even though that stock now may have a fair market value of over $1,000,000. The stockholder may borrow, say, $500,000, secured by the appreciated stock, and still not pay any tax until he disposes of the stock during his life.

The Internal Revenue Code, provides a new tax "basis" for stock owned by a stockholder at his death, essentially avoiding any income tax with respect to lifetime appreciation for stock held at death. The Tax Reform Act of 1976 sought to eliminate this benefit, but the "stepped-up basis" was restored as a tax benefit by Public Law 96-223, which became effective April 2, 1980.

1

Example: The shareholder who had originally invested $1,000 and who dies with stock worth, say, $1,500,000, never pays any income tax with respect to the increase in the value of the stock during his life. Since the stock takes on a new basis in his estate, his executors may sell the stock for $1,500,000, and pay no capital gains tax whatsoever. However, if the shareholder had sold it one day before he died, there would have been a capital gains tax of approximately a half million dollars on the sale.

A tax-free corporate reorganization allows the shareholder during his life to exchange, under certain circumstances, interest in one business enterprise for interest in a combined business enterprise. It should be noted that any such tax-free reorganization type involves, at least theoretically, merely a *postponement* of taxes because the gain will be recognized if a sale of the stock eventually takes place. In practice, however, deferred taxes are often the equivalent of little or no taxes, and tax-free treatment is considered highly beneficial.

Early in the history of the federal income tax, Congress recognized that certain types of exchanges of property, in effect, left the owner in the same position as before, and should not give rise to tax.

Example: Someone invested $10,000 in a business corporation founded under New York law. Later the business grew and he decided to move the state of incorporation from New York to Delaware without any other change. The technical exchange of stock in the New York corporation for the stock of a Delaware corporation should not constitute a taxable transaction.

Similarly, it was established early that if the shareholders should decide to merge their corporation into a similar corporation so as to better compete, there should be no tax on the exchange of stock in the first corporation for the stock in the second corporation.

From these fundamental, and undoubtedly sound, principles, have grown one of the most complicated sets of rules in the present Internal Revenue Code. Provisions found in Section 354 through 368 deal with what tax practitioners call a "tax-free reorganization."

Each major type of tax-free reorganization should be considered before an executive can plan effectively for an acquisition.

1. The "A" Reorganization or Merger

The starting place for consideration of tax-free reorganization is the merger. A merger is simply a legal procedure which combines two corporations into one through certain technical steps which are authorized by statutes in the state (or states) in which the corporations were formed. In other words, just as state law provides that if certain steps are taken, a corporation will be created under the law, the laws of every state also provide a method for merging two corporations by following similar steps. These steps usually include the adoption of a resolution by the Board of Directors, then by the shareholders, and then the filing of certain certificates with the Secretary of State of the particular state as well as other technical procedures specified in the statutes. A typical merger statute (from Delaware) is found in Appendix A.

Section 368(a)(1) of the Internal Revenue Code specifies the type of corporate reorganizations which are tax-free for federal income tax purposes. The Internal Revenue Service Regulations, §1.368-1, state that for federal tax purposes "the term 'reorganization' and 'party to a reorganization' mean *only* a reorganization or a party to a reorganization as defined in . . . Section 368 . . ." (emphasis supplied).

Dealing specifically with the question of what is a "merger or consolidation" under §368(a)(1)(A), §1.368-2 of the Regulations states:

> The words "statutory merger or consolidation" refer to a merger or consolidation effected pursuant to the corporation laws of the United States or a state or territory or the District of Columbia.

With rising tax rates, it did not take alert executives and their professional advisors long to see that if the only requirement for tax-free treatment was to meet technical steps for a "merger" under state law, many transactions which were not really mergers could be cast as mergers to avoid the tax.

By the same token, it did not take the Internal Revenue Service or the courts enforcing the tax laws long to set up certain additional guideposts to reduce the use of statutory mergers for purposes totally outside of the scope of a combination of two businesses.

A careful study of the current Regulations of the Internal Revenue Service introducing the area of corporate reorganization will give the basic ground rules which apply to all sorts of reorganizations, and particularly to mergers. These Regulations include the following statements:

> . . . Under the general rule, upon the exchange of property, gain or loss must be accounted for if the new property differs in a material particular, either in kind or in extent, from the old property. The purpose of the reorganization provisions of the Code is to except from the general rule certain specifically described exchanges incident to such readjustments of corporate structures made in one of the particular ways specified in the Code as are required by business exigencies and which effect only a readjustment of continuing interest in property under modified corporate forms. Requisite to a reorganization under the Code are a continuity of the business enterprise under the modified corporate form, and [usually] a continuity of interest therein on the part of those persons who, directly or indirectly, were the owners of the enterprise prior to the reorganization. The Code recognizes as a reorganization the amalgamation . . . of two corporate enterprises under a single corporate structure if there exists among the holders of the stock and securities of either of the old corporations the requisite continuity of interest in the new corporation, but there is not a reorganization if the holders of the stock and securities of the old corporation are merely the holders of short-term notes in the new corporation. In order to exclude transactions not intended to be included, specifications of the reorganization provisions of the law are precise.

Both the terms of the specifications and their underlying assumptions and purposes must be satisified in order to entitle this taxpayer to the benefit of the exception from the general rule. Accordingly, under the Code, a short-term purchase money note is not a security of party to a reorganization, an ordinary dividend is to be treated as an ordinary dividend, and a sale is nevertheless to be treated as a sale even though the mechanics of a reorganization have been set up.

. . . A plan of reorganization must contemplate the bona fide execution of one of the transactions specifically described as a reorganization in §368(a) and for the bona fide consummation of each of the requisite acts under nonrecognition of gain as claimed. Such transaction and acts must be an ordinary and necessary incident of a conduct of the enterprise and must provide for continuation of the enterprise. A scheme, which involves an abrupt departure from normal reorganization procedure in connection with the transaction on which the tax is imminent, such as a mere device that puts on the form of a corporate reorganization as a disguise for concealing its real character, and the object and accomplishment of which is the consummation of a pre-conceived plan having no business or corporate purpose, is not a plan of reorganization.

(a) What Is The Difference Between a Merger and a Consolidation?

It should be noted in passing that the statute refers to a "merger or consolidation." The difference in the terms is generally of interest only to lawyers. A merger is a transaction in which one of the corporate parties (the "acquiring" corporation) absorbs another corporation (the "acquired" corporation) through technical statutory procedures. A consolidation, on the other hand, is a transaction in which a new corporation is formed and each of the constituent corporations ceases its own separate existence, all under similar technical statutory procedures.

As a practical matter, almost all "A" Reorganizations will be mergers. Consolidations are useful if there is to be a change in the state of incorporation of the resulting corporation, or if as a practical matter, there is some psychological advantage to be gained from neither of the corporations surviving, or if more than two entities are to be brought together and there is a fundamental restructuring in a totally new corporate framework.

For ease of reference in the rest of this book, we will simply refer to "merger" unless there is some particular and peculiar advantage in the use of a consolidation in the particular subject under discussion.

(b) What Are the Corporate Law Requirements?

A merger is in many ways the most sophisticated of corporate law transactions. Through certain proper incantations, meetings of shareholders or directors, adoption of elaborate plans of merger, and all but a tribal rain dance followed by a puff of green smoke, the filing of certain documents miraculously results, in the twinkling of an eye, in the combination of two business enterprises which up to that moment were entirely separate.. The filing of a piece of paper causes, as if by magic, the business combination. With the improbable stamping of a file clerk's stamp on a sheaf of papers, corporate rights and existences are radically modified. Although it may take months for a transfer agent to actually effect an exchange of certificates, and for clerks to change real estate titles and motor vehicles of record, the legal merger is usually effected by the filing itself.

Appendix A contains part of the statutory merger provisions of corporate laws found in the State of Delaware, which are similar to the laws found in most states. From a practical standpoint, the requirements involve the following formal steps:

1. The adoption of a "plan of merger" by a majority of the Board of Directors of the corporation. One plan of reorganization is set forth in the Appendix and should be studied by the executive to get a "feel" for the usual type of provisions in such a plan.
2. The plan of reorganization is then submitted to a specially called meeting of the shareholders of the corporation. In order for the plan to become effective, it must be approved, normally, by a majority of the shareholders of the corporation. Of course, there may be additional requirements peculiar to the particular corporation involved, such as approval by a group of preferred shareholders voting separately as a class, or approval by more than a simple majority of the shareholders.
3. After the directors and shareholders have approved the plan of merger, the corporation's lawyers will prepare forms of certificates or articles of merger which will be signed on behalf of the corporation and filed with the appropriate clerk.

As pointed out above, the filing itself is normally the act which actually effectuates the merger. There are provisions in most modern corporate statutes to allow some latitude as to the actual "effective date" to the merger. For instance, both Delaware statute and the Model Business Corporation Act would permit filing with the clerk during a particular month with the actual "effective date" of the merger postponed until the last day of the month. Such short delays are of great help to executives and the accountants for a company, since it is often possible to time the effective date to coincide with the end of the fiscal year of one or both of the constituent corporations.

It should also be noted that certain jurisdictions require additional formalities such as court orders before a merger is effective, but the modern trend is clearly towards a simple filing procedure after proper corporate steps are taken.

Example: Goliath and Little David Corporation both have fiscal years ending June 30th. They plan to merge. By scheduling the shareholders' vote on the merger in the middle of June, filing the papers with the clerk, and making the actual "effective date" June 30, the corporations will be able to use their regular year-end audited statements for purposes of their combined enterprise, and to start "clean" on July 1st with a new fiscal year for the merged corporation.

(c) What are the Tax Law Requirements?

As pointed out by the Regulations, it is absolutely mandatory that an "A" Reorganization comply with the applicable state merger statute. Without such compliance, the best intended reorganizations cannot qualify as an "A" Reorganization. As noted above, it took taxpayers, their advisors, and the Internal Revenue Service practically no time at all after the adoption of the forerunner of the present "A" Reorganization provision to learn that a transaction which technically followed the form of a "merger" could be in fact a sale of a business which was indistinguishable in its result from a taxable transaction. This caused the early overlay of additional requirements above mere qualification under a merger statute.

These additional requirements can generally be grouped around three rules:

1. business purpose,
2. continuity of business enterprise; and
3. continuity of ownership.

(i) Business Purpose: The "business purpose" doctrine started with the case of *Gregory v. Helvering,* decided by the U.S. Supreme Court in 1932 (293 U.S. 465). That case upheld the government's position that a reorganization which literally complied with the applicable state statute nonetheless was not a tax-free reorganization because the entire arrangement had no business purpose and was simply an elaborate scheme to provide a particular shareholder with a dividend.

As noted earlier, the Regulations (§1.368-1(b)) indicate that the purpose of reorganization provisions is to except from recognition of tax certain specifically described business combinations "required by business exigencies." The Internal Revenue Service now requires that corporations requesting an advanced ruling to the effect that a particular transaction constitutes a tax-free reorganization must include a statement of the "business purpose" of the transaction (Rev. Proc. 72-3, 1972-1, C.B. 105). See the Ruling Request in Appendix G for such a statement.

Appendix G also contains a recent "letter ruling" by the IRS under which a railroad and a natural resources transportation company were allowed to merge tax free in an "A" Reorganization. Note that as early as the fourth paragraph of the ruling, the IRS emphasizes the stated "business purpose"—to "unite geographically complementary systems and achieve substantial operating efficiencies and economies."

> *Example:* Shareholder owned most of the stock of two corporations, American and Cleveland. Cleveland conducted both a manufacturing and a jobbing business. American conducted its own jobbing business. Cleveland sold its manufacturing business and most of its tangible assets to Webster. American and Cleveland then merged. The IRS attacked the merger for lack of "business purpose" since Cleveland had sold many of its operating assets before the merger, although it kept its rights to jobbing customers and since there was a big operating loss carryforward involved. There was a "business purpose" in wanting to simplify record keeping and providing products for the jobbing business, and the taxpayer won. See *American Bronze Corporation v. Commissioner,* 64 T.C. 1111 (1975).

The question has sometimes arisen as to whether or not the business purpose referred to is the corporation's business purpose or the shareholder's business purpose. The Regulations quoted above, §1.368-1(b) and (c), indicate that the corporate business purpose is the test, but such cases as *Parshelsky's Estate v. Com'r,* 303 F.2d 14 (2d Cir., 1962) indicate that all of the actual business purposes must be considered, and that if the shareholder had a legitimate business purpose even though the reorganization was immaterial to the corporation itself, there would be sufficient business purpose.

(ii) Continuity of Business Enterprise: The same regulations, at §1.368-1(b), state that there must be "a continuity of business enterprise" in a tax-free reorganization. The courts have supported this rule. For instance, in *Standard Realization Co. v. Com'r,* 10 T.C. 708 (1948), the United States Tax Court found that a tax-free reorganization did not exist even though all of the outward requirements had been met because an acquiring corporation sold the acquired assets shortly after the transaction. The tax court judge stated:

> "The [Commissioner] argues that the plan . . . was not a 'plan of reorganization' . . . In [several cited cases] there was continuance of business by the [acquiring] corporation, and that fact was of crucial significance, for [as stated in an earlier case] . . . "the plan of reorganization must comprehend, and the new corporation created must when consummated, carry on in whole or in part the corporate business of the old corporation" . . .

After some vacillation, the Internal Revenue Service has decided that *some* of the business enterprise must be continued although it is not absolutely required that the surviving corporation engage in the *same* business as the acquired corporation. In December, 1979, the IRS published proposed regulations clarifying the continuity of business enterprise requirements. Proposed Regulation §1.368-1(d), states;

> "Continuity of business enterprise requires that the transferee either continue the transferor's historic business or use a significant portion of the transferor's historic business assets. The transferee is not required to continue the transferor's business. However, if that business is not continued, there must be significant use of the transferor's historic business assets in the transferee's business."

This concept of continuity enterprise has been taking shape over a number of years. For example, in *Beecher v. Com'r,* 221 F.2d 252 (2d Cir., 1955), the transfer of assets to a corporation was held to constitute a reorganization. There, the acquiring corporation continued some business with the assets acquired, but formed an entirely different business from that of the acquired corporation. The IRS had earlier agreed with that position in Rev. Rul. 63-29, 1963-1 C.B. 77, but in the new proposed regulations, examples indicate that continuity of business enterprise requires that the acquiring corporation continue at least *one* significant line of the acquired corporation's business.

The new proposed regulation indicates that, in applying the business continuity test, it is "not alone sufficient" that the acquiring corporation is in the same line of business as the acquired corporation, although the regulations concede that this "tends to establish the requisite continuity."

Here are some examples of how the new IRS proposals would work:

Example 1: Corporation P conducts three lines of business which are approximately equal in value. On July 1, 1981, P sells two of the businesses to a third party for cash and marketable securities. On December 31, 1981, P transfers all of its assets to Corporation Q solely in exchange for Q voting stock. Q continues the remaining manufacturing business of P without interruption. The continuity of business enterprise requirement is met because the IRS would hold that continuity of business enterprise requires only that Q continue *one* of P's three significant lines of business.

Example 2: Corporation R manufactures computers and Corporation S manufactures components for the computers. S sells all of its components to R. On January 1, 1981, R decides to buy components elsewhere. On March 1, 1981, S merges into R and R continues buying its components elsewhere but retains S's equipment as a backup source of supply. The use of the equipment as a backup source of supply constitutes use of a significant portion of the transferor's historic business assets thus establishing continuity of business enterprise within the IRS regulation. In other words, R is not required to continue S's business, but is merely required to use a significant portion of S's historic business assets.

Example 3: Corporation T is a manufacturer which, on January 1, 1977, sold all of its assets to a third party for cash and purchased a highly diversified portfolio of stocks and bonds. On July 1, 1980, T exchanges all of its assets with U, a mutual fund, in exchange for U stock. The continuity of business enterprise requirement established by the IRS regulations is not met because T's investment activity is not its historic business and the stocks and bonds which T acquired are not its historic business assets. The IRS has thus attempted to squelch the once popular sale of assets/investment in securities/merger with a tax-free bond mutual fund gimmick.

Example 4: Corporation V is a manufacturer of toys and Corporation W is a distributor of metal products. On January 1, 1981, V sells all of its assets for $100,000 in cash and $900,000 in notes. On March 1, 1981, V merges into W under a state law merger statute. The IRS regulations would hold that continuity of business enterprise was lacking in this case and the use of the sales proceeds in W's business was not sufficient to qualify under the continuity of business enterprise test.

Example 5: Corporation X manufactures farm machinery and Corporation Y operates a lumber mill. X merges into Y under a state merger law. Immediately after the merger, Y sells off X's assets and does not continue X's farm machinery manufacturing business. Continuity of business enterprise is lacking because neither the assets nor the business of X is continued.

(iii) Continuity of Ownership: One of the most important tests developed by the courts as applied to "A" Reorganizations is the requirement that a substantial portion of the stockholder's investment in both corporations continue in the surviving corporation.

In the early case of *Cortland Speciality Co. v. Com'r,* 60 F.2d 937 (2d Cir., 1932), there was an acquisition, but the shareholders in the acquired corporation received only cash and short-term promissory notes. Under most merger statutes, this is entirely permissible. The court held in *Cortland* that promissory notes, all of which would be paid out within 14 months, were not "securities" and therefore the exchange was not tax-free under the Internal Revenue Code.

The same question came before the Supreme Court of the United States in *Pinellas v. Com'r,* 287 U.S. 462 (1933). There the attempt was to have a tax-free reorganization when the shareholders of the acquired corporation received only notes payable four months after the reorganization. The Supreme Court stated that "the seller must acquire an interest in the affairs of the purchasing company more definite than that incident to ownership of its short-term purchase money notes" (p. 470).

Various courts have struggled since the 1930's to establish exactly what constitutes continuity of ownership. Perhaps the best statement was that of the Fifth Circuit in *Southwest Natural Gas Co. v. Com'r,* 189 F.2d 332 (5th Cir., 1951). There the Court stated:

> While no precise formula has been expressed for determining where there has been a retention of the requisite interest (there must be) a showing: (1) that the transfer of the corporation or its shareholders retained a substantial proprietary stake in enterprise represented by a material interest in the affairs of the transferee corporation, and (2) such retained interest represents a substantial part of the value of the property transferred. (p. 354).

The continuity of interest test requires that a substantial portion of the shareholders of the acquired corporation receive "securities" in the acquiring (or a related) corporation. Generally speaking, an equity interest may not be exchanged solely for debt interest if the transaction is to qualify as a tax-free reorganization. In the lead case of *LeTulle v. Scoffield,* 308 U.S. 415 (1940), the court stated:

> Where the consideration is wholly in the transferee's bonds, or part cash and part cash bonds, we think it cannot be said that the transferor retains any proprietary interest in the enterprise. On the contrary, he becomes a creditor of the transferee; and we do not think that the fact . . . that the bonds were secured solely by the assets of the transferor and that, upon default, the bondholder would retain only the property sold, changes his status from that of a creditor to one having a proprietary stake.

The present position of the Internal Revenue Service is that the continuity of the interest requirement is met when at least 50 percent of the value of all of the acquired corporation's stock is converted into a continuing stock interest. (See Rev. Proc. 66-34, 1966-2 C.B. 1232.)

Finally, there is the requirement that the interest continue for some time after the reorganization. In Rev. Rul. 66-23, 1966-1 C.B. 67, the Internal Revenue Service summarized the continuity of interest for ruling purposes to require that the shareholders of the merging corporation must retain a continuing interest through stock ownership in the acquiring corporation which is equal in value on the date of the reorganization to at least 50 percent of the value of all of the merging corporation's outstanding stock on the same date.

> *Example:* Corporation X and Y merge. Some shareholders of Y receive preferred stock of X. The IRS will probably require that the preferred stock cannot be redeemed by X sooner than five years after the merger. (See Rev. Rul. 78-142, 1978-1 C.B. 1111.)

2. The "B" Reorganization or Stock Swap

The second type of reorganization treated as tax free by the Internal Revenue Code is the acquisition of stock of one corporation in exchange solely for voting stock, the "B" Reorganization. Normally, such a transaction would take the form of the issuance of authorized but unissued shares of stock of the acquiring corporation to the shareholders of the acquired corporation in exchange for all of the stock of the acquired corporation. The net effect is that the shareholders of the acquired corporation become shareholders of the acquiring corporation and the acquired corporation becomes a wholly owned subsidiary of the acquiring corporation. The following diagrams shows a typical situation.

Step 1.

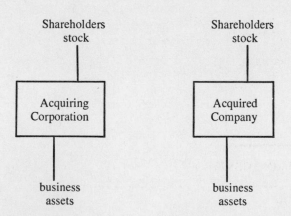

When the shares of the acquired corporation are held by a small group of shareholders, all of whom agree to the acquisition, and when the shareholders of the acquiring corporation do not mind the dilution of issuing additional shares, then the pattern outlined above can be followed with no real disadvantages, and can be the simplest of all types of reorganization. Merely adopting and carrying out a plan and exchange of stock is all that is required. Unfortunately, few situations are actually so simple.

Step 2.

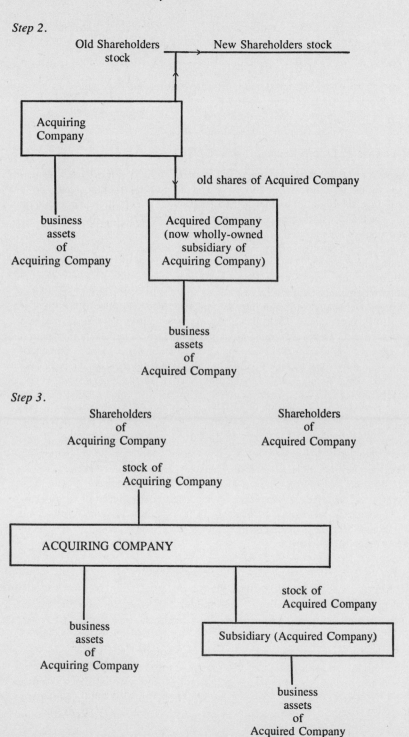

Step 3.

(a) Tax Law Requirements for a "B" Reorganization

The difficulties become apparent when the exact language of the statute is reviewed. Section 368(a)(1)(B) of the Code says that a tax-free "reorganization" means:

> The acquisition by one corporation in exchange solely for all or part of its voting stock (or in exchange solely for all or part of the voting stock of [its parent corporation]) of stock of another corporation if, immediately after the acquisition, the acquiring corporation has control of such other corporation . . .

The Regulations add the following discussion (§1.368-2(c)):

> In order to qualify as a "reorganization" under Section 368(a)(1)(B), the acquisition by the acquiring corporation of stock of another corporation must be in exchange solely for all or part of the voting stock of the acquiring corporation . . . and the acquiring corporation must be in control of the other corporation immediately after the transaction. If, for example, Corporation X, in one transaction exchanges nonvoting preferred stock or bonds in addition to all or part of its voting stock in the acquisition of stock of Corporation Y, the transaction is not a reorganization under Section 368(a)(1)(B). The acquisition of stock of another corporation by the acquiring corporation solely for its voting stock is permitted tax-free even though the acquiring corporation already owns some of the stock of the other corporation. Such an acquisition is permitted tax-free in a single transaction or in a series of transactions taking place over a relatively short period of time such as 12 months. For example, Corporation A purchased 30 percent of the common stock of Corporation W (the only class of stock outstanding) for cash in 1939. On March 1, 1965, Corporation A offers to exchange its own voting stock for all the stock of Corporation W tendered within 6 months from the date of the offer. Within the 6 months' period, Corporation A acquires an additional 60 percent of the stock of Corporation W solely for its own voting stock, so that it owns 90 percent of the stock of Corporation W. No gain or loss is recognized with respect to the exchanges of stock of Corporation A for stock of Corporation W. For this purpose, it is immaterial whether such exchanges occurred before Corporation A acquired control (80 percent) of Corporation W or after such control was acquired. If Corporation A had acquired 80 percent of the stock of Corporation W for cash in 1939, it could likewise acquire some or all of the remainder of such stock solely in exchange for its own voting stock without recognition of gain or loss.

(i) What Is "Solely" for Voting Stock? The easiest way to fail to meet the requirements of a "B" Reorganization is to give some other consideration, even a very small amount of cash to the acquired corporation's shareholders, or payment of some debt of those shareholders, in addition to voting stock. For instance, in the case of *Helvering v. Southwest Consolidated Corporation*, 315 U.S. 194 (1942), the Supreme Court held that there was "no leeway" in the requirement of "solely" for voting stock, and that warrants to purchase additional shares of voting common stock given to the shareholders of the acquired corporation, would make the entire transaction taxable. Another case, decided by the Tax Court in 1962, *Richard M. Mills,* 39 T.C. 393, held that even the payment of $27.36 incidentally as a part of a "B" Reorganization caused the entire transaction to be taxable.

In the real world of corporate acquisition, where there are often transfer taxes, attorneys' fees, accountants' fees, and financial advisors' fees of the shareholders of the acquired corporation which need to be paid, it is very easy to run afoul of the "solely" for voting stock requirement. In addition, the holders of 80 percent of the stock of the target corporation may not agree to the transaction. In an "A" Reorganization (statutory merger) unless the number of dissenting shareholders exceeds 50 percent, a dissenting shareholder will usually not cause a serious problem. In a merger, dissenting share-holders can be paid the cash value of their shares, and normally must be paid the cash value under state merger laws. However, if some of the shareholders are unwilling to accept the acquiring corporation's stock in a "B" Reorganization, any such payment as part of the reorganization itself kills tax-free treatment (Rev. Rul. 56-354, 1956-C.B. 206, and Rev. Rul. 57-114, 1957-1 C.B. 122). Some payment after the reorganization itself and not as a part of the plan of the reorganization may get by, but is very risky. Some cases have allowed a redemption by the acquired corporation of the stock prior to the exchange or a simultaneous purchase by the other shareholders (Rev. Rul. 68-285, 1968-1 C.B. 147, and *Howard v. Commissioner,* 238 F.2d 943 (7th Cir., 1956), but the risk is seldom worth the advantage, especially given the usual alternate possibility of structuring the transaction as a merger.

The courts continue to be strict in upholding the word "solely" in connection with the "B" Reorganization.

> *Example:* ITT wanted to acquire Hartford Insurance. It talked with Hartford management concerning the merger of the two companies but Hartford initially rejected the overtures. ITT then made cash purchases of Hartford stock and acquired about eight percent of the voting stock of Hartford for cash. Shortly thereafter, ITT and Hartford reached an agreement in principle to have a "B" Reorganization using an ITT subsidiary.
>
> The parties then sought and obtained a private letter ruling from the Internal Revenue Service which ruled that the transaction would qualify as a "B" Reorganization *provided* ITT first disposed of the eight percent stock it had acquired for cash to a third party. ITT then sold the stock to an Italian bank.
>
> When the Connecticut Insurance Commissioner raised some difficulties with the structure of the transaction, ITT recast the deal, made a voluntary tender offer to the shareholders of Hartford, and obtained the approval of the Connecticut Insurance Commissioner. More than 95 percent of Hartford's outstanding stock was tendered and exchanged for shares of ITT's $2.25 cumulative convertible voting preferred stock. The Italian bank, which ITT had conveyed its original eight percent interest, was among those tendering shares.
>
> In March, 1974, almost four years after consummation of the transaction, the IRS retroactively revoked its ruling approving the sale of Hartford stock to the Italian bank on the ground that the request on which the ruling was based had "misrepresented the nature of the proposed sale." The IRS then assessed tax deficiencies against many of the Hartford shareholders who had received the new ITT stock.
>
> After many court battles (which probably will eventually wind up in the Supreme Court) two Federal courts of appeal have held that the transaction *was taxable* because the acquisition of eight percent of the stock for cash violated the

"solely for voting stock" requirement of a "B" Reorganization. Because of the importance of this case, the complete decision of the court, *Heverly v. The Commissioner of Internal Revenue*, (3rd Cir.), decided March 25, 1980, is set out as Appendix B.

Additional real world hazards to the "solely" for voting stock requirement include the following:

(ii) Employment Agreements with Shareholders of the Acquired Corporation: A bona fide employment agreement with the shareholder of the acquired corporation or a subsidiary will normally be upheld. As a practical matter, it is often very difficult to separate negotiations concerning employment agreements from those concerning the acquisition of the corporation itself. The entire acquisition will be taxable if the employment contract is found to be a disguised payment for the acquired stock (Rev. Rul. 66-112, 1966-1 C.B. 68). The Internal Revenue Service has let it be known that it is very interested in reviewing employment contracts in such situations. (See 22 TAX LAWYER 196 (1968).)

(iii) Expenses: Before ruling that a transaction qualifies as a "B" Reorganization, the Internal Revenue Service normally requires that the shareholders themselves represent that they will pay their own portion of accounting expenses, commissions, attorneys' fees, and other reorganization expenses. In the absence of obtaining a specific ruling on such allocation from the National Office of the Internal Revenue Service, however, the door would seem wide open for an argument after the transaction as to whether or not the shareholders had paid their fair share.

Even with a ruling, the point is subject to scrutiny by the Internal Revenue Service to determine whether or not a fair portion has been paid by the shareholders. (See Bittker and Eustice, *Federal Income Taxation of Corporations and Shareholders*, 4th Edition, pp. 14–38.) As a practical matter, the shareholders of the acquired corporation are often very reluctant to use their own money to pay for such expenses when they have received no cash from the transaction, and have often received only shares of stock which are restricted as to transfer for a substantial period of time. It is possible to have the acquiring corporation agree to register the shares given in the transaction with the Securities and Exchange Commission or state securities administrator. Those expenses, which are normally considerable, may be borne by the acquiring corporation in maintaining an orderly market for its shares (Rev. Rul. 67-275, 1967-2 C.B. 142).

(b) Dividends

Occasionally it occurs to the shareholders of the acquired corporation that the acquiring corporation is obtaining surplus cash as part of the transaction, and the shareholders of the acquired corporation cause an extraordinary dividend to be paid by the target corporation shortly before the acquisition. If the dividend is part of the plan of reorganization, and if the dividends paid are not normal dividends, then the entire transaction may be treated as a taxable transaction (Rev. Rul. 70-172, 1970-1 C.B. 77).

(c) What Is "Voting Stock"?

It should also be noted that the requirement is for *voting* stock. This may be either existing common or preferred stock or a special class of stock created especially for the transaction, but the stock must have a vote. The stock may be either that of the acquiring corporation or of its parent under an amendment to this Section in 1964. Warrants, bonds, or convertible debentures won't qualify (*Helvering v. Southwest Consolidating Corporation,* 315 U.S. 194 (1942); Rev. Rul. 69-91, 1969-1 C.B. 106).

(d) What Is "Control" of the Target Company?

The statute requires that immediately after the reorganization, at least 80 percent of the total combined voting power as well as 80 percent of the total number of shares of all non-voting classes of stock must be owned by the acquiring corporation.

The 80 percent does not all have to be acquired at the time of the transaction, and the acquiring corporation can actually own a substantial amount of stock in the acquired corporation prior to the transaction, even if the stock may have actually been obtained for cash (Regulation §1.368-2(c), above). Also note that the acquisition may be a gradual one taking place over a "relatively short period of time" such as 12 months. This allows a public tender offer situation in which the acquiring corporation bids to exchange its voting shares for shares of the acquired corporation. Of course, any such tender offer must comply with stringent Federal securities laws, and a growing body of defensive state laws.

Also, control must reside in the acquiring corporation "immediately after" the transaction. Generally speaking, this means that 80 percent control must come to rest in a bona fide fashion in the acquired corporation. An acquisition followed by a sale of some or all of the acquired stock may result in a loss of "control" (*American Bantam Car Company,* 11 T.C. 397 (1948), affirmed, 177 F.2d 513 (3rd Cir., 1949).

(e) Compliance with Securities Laws

As in any acquisition transaction in which stock is exchanged or sold, careful attention must be given to securities laws and regulations both of the United States (such as, the Securities Act of 1933) and state laws (the laws directed at reducing the chance of the issuance to the public of bogus securities backed only by "blue sky"). The securities aspects of an acquisition are discussed in Chapter 2 and will not be repeated here.

(f) Planning Pointers for the "B" Reorganization

The most general comment concerning a "B" Reorganization is "avoid it if possible." There are simply too many restrictions imposed by the statute when compared with an "A" Reorganization to justify the use of a "B" Reorganization unless there is no reasonable alternative. There are two general exceptions:

(i) Use a "B" Reorganization when the transaction is so simple and clean that the advantages of avoiding merger statutes make a "B" Reorganization desirable.

Example: You and your associates are the sole owners of a corporation which operates a chain of grocery stores. The owner of an independent store in a small town wishes to affiliate his corporation with yours in order to gain diversity and liquidity for estate planning purposes.

The owner of the independent store will pay all of his own expenses. There will be no dividends paid to the independent owner prior to the reorganization. The independent owner is willing to receive voting common stock in your corporation and to hold a minority share of the corporation on the same terms as your associates, and subject to additional restrictions upon transfer required by securities laws and in order to assure continuing control within the management group. In such a business situation, shares of the common stock of your corporation may be exchanged for all of the outstanding shares of the independent grocer's corporation on a tax-free basis pursuant to a very simple written plan of reorganization.

After the acquisition, your corporation will have a wholly owned subsidiary consisting of the formerly independent store. Consolidated income tax returns may then be filed for future operating years with the new subsidiary so that, for most tax purposes, the corporations will be treated as one. The former owner of the independent store will have no tax at the time of the exchange and will carry over his tax basis in the shares which he formerly owned to the new shares.

(ii) Use a "B" Reorganization when you plan a public tender offer.

Generally, a tender grows out of plans by a larger corporation to acquire a corporation whose shares are relatively under-priced. There are required filings under Federal and state law prior to the tender offer and the tender offer may well generate a series of defensive lawsuits and administrative hearings.

Example: X Corporation believes that Y Corporation has three manufacturing plants that X could immediately use. Y stock is selling for two thirds of its book value. X offers to acquire stock in exchange for shares of X. X acquires the necessary 80 percent control after tender for shares of Y (and the other tests of the "B" Reorganization are met), the transaction, and the tendering shareholders of Y will realize no gain on the exchange. After the tender, Y will be at least an 80 percent owned subsidiary of X and should be entitled to file consolidated returns with Y.

Relatively new state laws allow hostile shareholders of the target corporation to stall or block take-over bids. A typical state anti-take-over statute is set out in Appendix C. Discussion of take-overs in detail is beyond the scope of this book. Obviously, no hostile take-over should be considered without careful study and advice from counsel familiar with the latest rules applicable to such corporate battles.

(g) Alternative to a "B" Reorganization—The Reverse Merger

It is usually possible to have the benefits of a "B" Reorganization without the liabilities by utilizing a "reverse merger." Anyone planning a "B" Reorganization should consider the reverse merger as an alternative prior to running the statutory gauntlet required of a straight "B" Reorganization.

A typical reverse merger could follow these steps:

1. The acquiring corporation would form a new wholly owned subsidiary.
2. The acquiring corporation would fund the new subsidiary with shares of the acquiring corporation itself.
3. A plan of reorganization and merger would be adopted by the new subsidiary corporation and the corporation to be acquired. Under the terms of the plan, the subsidiary corporation would merge *into* the corporation to be acquired, and upon the effective date of the merger, all of the shares of the acquired corporation will be *automatically* converted under state merger law into the shares of stock of the parent corporation held by the new subsidiary, and the subsidiary's shares will become those of the acquired corporations.

Most modern merger statutes allow this type of transaction, and as a result of those steps, the parent corporation then owns 100 percent of the outstanding stock of the acquired corporation while the dummy subsidiary corporation formed for the transaction has disappeared into the target company.

A diagram of the transaction would look like this:

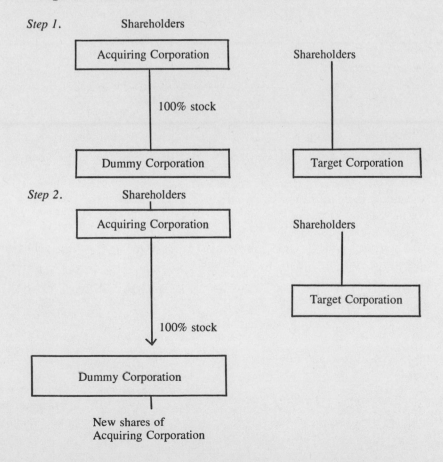

Step 3.

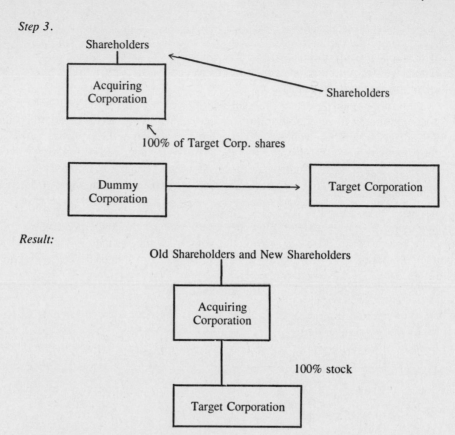

Result:

The reverse merger is usually treated as an "A" Reorganization under the Internal Revenue Code if:

1. A statutory merger takes place as part of the transaction;
2. Voting stock of the acquiring corporation is exchanged for 80 percent of all classes of stock of the acquired corporation; and
3. After the merger, the surviving corporation in the merger holds "substantially all" of the properties of both parties to the merger.

Forms of Agreement used in reverse merger are found in Appendix D.

Executives and their advisers should note that the field of reverse mergers is one which is under careful study by the Internal Revenue Service.

3. The "C" Reorganization or Assets Acquisition

The third type of reorganization treated as a tax-free transaction is the "C" Reorganization. A "C" Reorganization is defined as "the acquisition by one corporation, in exchange solely for . . . voting stock . . . of substantially all of the properties of another corporation . . ." (Section 368(a)(1)(C).)

The transaction often consists of nothing more than the issuance of new voting stock by the acquiring corporation to the target company itself in exchange for all of the target company's assets, subject to specified liabilities of the target company. Normally, the target company then liquidates and distributes the stock to its own shareholders. If properly planned, both the exchange of assets for stock and the liquidation of the corporation passing the stock through to the shareholders of the target company are tax free.

> *Example:* X Corporation agrees to acquire all of Y's assets in exchange for 500,000 new shares of X stock. After Y transfers its assets to X, it liquidates and distributes the new X stock to each of Y's shareholders.

The "C" Reorganization is greatly favored by the acquiring corporation because it is possible to specify exactly which liabilities are being assumed. In the merger transaction, all of the liabilities of the target company, as a matter of law, follow the target company's assets into the merged corporation. Of course, by a merger into a subsidiary corporation, the parent corporation itself can remain shielded from liabilities, but careful executives still prefer an assets acquisition, where possible, in order to provide the maximum type of protection against unforeseen liabilities.

A form of "C" Reorganization Agreement is found in Appendix E.

(a) Tax Requirements for a "C" Reorganization

(i) Voting Stock in a "C" Reorganization.

The use of "voting stock" has been discussed in connection with the "B" Reorganization. In a "C" Reorganization, the stock must be either the voting stock of the acquiring corporation or voting stock of its parent corporation.

A parent corporation is one that is in "control" of the subsidiary. Under §368(c) of the Internal Revenue Code, that means a corporation which owns at least 80 percent of the stock representing the voting power of the corporation and 80 percent of the total number of shares of all other classes of stock. The Internal Revenue Service interprets this to mean that parent corporation must own 80 percent of each class of stock of the subsidiary. (See Rev. Rul. 59-259, 1959-2 C.B. 115.)

> *Example:* X Corporation forms a new wholly owned subsidiary, A Corporation, and places 500,000 shares of X stock in A. A can exchange the 500,000 shares of X stock for all of Y's assets and still have the transaction treated as a "C" Reorganization.

There is an exception to the "solely for voting stock" requirement in a "C" Reorganization if the property for which voting stock was transferred has a value at least equal to 80 percent of the fair market value of all of the target company's property. Unfortunately, as discussed later, this exception is rarely of any use because of peculiar rules as to the assumption of liabilities by the acquiring corporation.

(ii) All Assets Must Be Acquired.

The second test is that "substantially all" of the target company assets must be acquired. The position of the Internal Revenue Service for ruling purposes is that there must be a transfer of the assets representing at least 90 percent of the fair market value of the net assets of the target company and a minimum of 70 percent of the fair market value of all of the assets held by the target company immediately prior to the transfer. (See Appendix E.)

As a practical matter, the safest plan is to seek to find some way to transfer all of the assets of the target company in order to avoid giving the Internal Revenue Service the opportunity to second-guess the transaction. Often valuation is less than a precise science, and the penalty for missing the "substantially all" test is to make the transaction taxable.

> *Example:* X acquires only one of five plants that Y owns for 100,000 shares of
> X stock. All five plants are comparable in size and value. Y then liquidates and
> distributes the 100,000 shares of X stock, the remaining four plants, and its other
> assets to Y's shareholders. Both Y and its shareholders must pay a capital gains
> tax because X did not acquire "substantially all" of Y's assets.

(iii) Assumption of Liabilities.

Assumption of some or all of the target company's liabilities is a routine part of a "C" Reorganization.

(iv) The 80 Percent Rule.

As mentioned earlier, voting stock need be given only for 80 percent of the fair market value of the assets in a "C" Reorganization. This rule on its face would allow the payment of 20 percent of the consideration in cash. In the real world of acquisitions, this is not usually true. In almost every "C" Reorganization, the acquiring corporation assumes some or all of the liabilities of the target company. If any liabilities are assumed, then the total amount of liabilities is treated as cash for the purposes of determining whether or not the 20 percent figure has been exceeded. (See §368(a)(2)(B).)

In other words, if no consideration is used other than voting stock, then liabilities in an unlimited amount may be assumed without jeopardizing the "C" Reorganization. If any cash or other consideration other than voting stock is used, then the liabilities assumed will normally make a "C" Reorganization impossible.

As a planning matter, in such a situation, an "A" Reorganization is often the answer since, as noted above, the IRS usually requires that only 50 percent of the value in an "A" Reorganization must be represented by stock.

(v) Cautions for "C" Reorganization.

The cautions mentioned earlier concerning the "B" Reorganization as to the expenses incurred in connection with the reorganization, employment contracts for officers of the target company, and other incidental matters, jeopardizing the "solely for voting stock" requirements, apply generally also in a "C" Reorganization.

(b) Use of "Contingent" Stock

In the course of negotiating the price in an acquisition transaction, often the acquiring and target companies will have different ideas as to the likely earnings of the target company for the foreseeable future after the acquisition.

The negotiating team for the acquiring corporation will often look to low past earnings and seek to set an average figure over a long number of years. On the other hand, the negotiating team for the target company will often point to the past few years which indicate an upward trend of earnings and attempt to project this trend into the future. Often this results in wide value differential for the stock of the target company.

A standard negotiating technique to avoid this impasse is to establish a base purchase value at the lower, average experience for a long number of years, with a contingent pay-out of additional shares in the event earnings exceed certain limits over a defined period years following the closing.

It is now well settled that, if properly executed, such a contingent stock provision will not jeopardize the tax-free nature of the transaction.

> *Example:* X agrees to acquire Y by merger in an "A" Reorganization. X issues Y shareholders 400,000 X shares at closing, and if Y's business nets an average of at least $800,000 in the next five years, Y shareholders will receive an additional 100,000 X shares in three years.

The Internal Revenue Service will now give ruling that the reorganization will remain tax free even though there is contingent stock. Favorable rulings will be issued if:

1. All of the stock will be issued within no more than five years;
2. There is a valid business reason for not immediately issuing all of the stock (and difficulty in valuing the stock is specifically considered as a good business reason);
3. The maximum number of shares which can be issued in any event is specified;
4. At least half of the maximum number of shares of each class of stock which can be issued in the reorganization is issued initially;
5. The right to receive the contingent stock is nonassignable; and
6. The stock to be received contingently is stock which would qualify for the reorganization if received initially. (See Rev. Rul. 74-26, 1974-2 C.B. 478.)

4. When Should You Get An IRS Advance Ruling?

The Internal Revenue Service will give written rulings in most situations as to the tax effects of particular proposed transactions. Clients often ask what the guidelines should be as to whether or not a ruling should be sought.

First, it must be recognized that a ruling will in most cases make the federal income tax treatment of a particular transaction certain. If all of the relevant facts are disclosed, and if the transaction takes place in accordance with those facts, the Internal Revenue Service will be bound by its ruling in the particular transaction involved.

Caution: All facts must be discussed. In the ITT case discussed previously, the IRS decided almost four years after the deal that it had been misled regarding certain facts. The IRS revoked its favorable ruling and assessed tax against many Hartford shareholders who thought the transaction was tax free.

Second, a ruling should be obtained unless there is some good reason not to. In other words, the tax effects of a transaction are so important in the real world, that the general policy should be to obtain a ruling.

Third, it should be realized that under the Tax Reform Act of 1976 (§120), all private tax rulings must be made available to the public (with names and other identification deleted). Procedures were also included to discourage contact of the IRS on behalf of a taxpayer by someone other than the taxpayer, and his tax advisor (*e.g.,* political influence attempts).

When should you *not* obtain a ruling?

1. When the transaction involves one of those areas in which the Service will not, as a policy matter, rule, such as a question involving the valuation of stock. These areas are set out in Appendix F.
2. When the timing of the transaction is absolutely critical and delay would be encountered with the Internal Revenue Service. Depending upon the load of the Internal Revenue Service at any particular time, it will usually take from three to six months to obtain a ruling. So-called "expedited" rulings can be obtained in as short a time as one month, but these are *very* rare indeed. Rulings which must go to more than one section of the National Office of the Internal Revenue Service may well take longer than the six-month period. If the transaction must be closed at the end of the fiscal year which occurs within five weeks, then a ruling will usually be out of the question.

   In Rev. Proc. 79-45, the IRS required that taxpayers fully explain the grounds for their position, and also call to IRS' attention *contrary* authority such as court decisions which would indicate that the ruling should *not* be given. The IRS later backed off that position, but the IRS will expect a fair presentation of all the authorities before IRS rules in a particular case.
3. If the transaction will take place whether or not a favorable ruling is obtained, *do not* seek a ruling. In other words, if you ask Papa and Papa says "No," then you are in a jam. Sometimes it is best not to ask Papa at all.

   Example: Y Corporation is going to merge with X for business reasons, regardless of the taxability of the transaction. Y may decide to structure the deal as a "clean" A Reorganization, and *not* seek an IRS ruling.

In some instances in which no ruling is to be sought, and the tax stakes are great, it will pay to use a recognized tax lawyer to give a written opinion as to the probable tax consequences of a particular transaction. Such an opinion is not only helpful in pointing out certain pitfalls which must be avoided in the transaction, but also may be persuasive to a Revenue agent later auditing the transaction.

Type of Transaction	Usual Consideration Received by Shareholder of Acquired Corporation	Usual Immediate Tax Consequences to Shareholder of Acquired Corporation	Usual Estate Effect on Shareholder of Acquired Corporation	Usual Continuing Credit Risk for Shareholder of Acquired Corporation	Usual Legal and Credit Risk to Acquiring Corporation
"A" Reorganization (merger), page 2	Stock + up to one-half cash	None, except to extent of cash "boot"	More estate liquidity	High	High
"B" Reorganization (stock swap), page 10	Stock	None	More estate liquidity	High	High
"C" Reorganization (assets), page 18	Stock	None	More estate liquidity	High	Average
Cash Sale or Redemption, page 25	Cash	Immediate capital gains	More estate liquidity	Low	Very high
Installment Sale or Redemption, page 25	Cash plus secured notes	Partially deferred capital gains	More estate liquidity	Average	Average
Annuity Sale or Redemption, page 115	Annuity contract	None, but deferred capital gains and ordinary income	Greatly reduced	Very high	High
Recapitalization, page 111	Preferred stock	None	Total estate tax often reduced by "capping" value of preferred	High	Low
Exchange, page 38	No change for shareholder, but corporate assets change	None	None	High	High

Detailed checklists for ruling requests have been issued by the IRS. Appendix F contains the checklist and guidelines for ruling on stock redemptions (Appendix F-2) and tax-free acquisitions (Appendix F-3). An actual request for ruling and portions of the ruling obtained in response are found in Appendix G.

B. REVIEW AND CHECKLIST FOR ACQUISITION ALTERNATIVES

The following chart provides a brief checklist for the planner of a corporate acquisition or its alternatives. It is merely a subjective view and makes certain basic assumptions about the usual form of a particular transaction. Discussion elsewhere in the Desk Book should be consulted for a more detailed analysis of the particular technique.

Chapter 2

Other Techniques and Considerations

A. THE INSTALLMENT SALE UNDER THE INSTALLMENT SALES REVISION ACT OF 1980

1. The Need for a Special Tax Rule

Tax laws ordinarily require that when property or cash is received for a particular asset such as all of the stock of a closely-held corporation, taxable gain is immediately recognized on the difference between what was paid for the asset and what was received for it. Obviously, the rule works well enough when an all cash payment is received in the transaction, because a portion of the cash may immediately be paid to the government at income tax time. A more difficult question arises when something other than cash, a promissory note for example, is received for stock. In that situation, special tax rules sometimes allow deferral of the tax until the note is actually paid.

2. The Law From 1954 to 1980

To help meet this need, Section 453 of the 1954 Internal Revenue Code specifically allowed the taxpayer to defer that part of a purchase price not actually received in cash upon the sale of corporate stock (or other capital assets), *provided* certain very strict tests were met. The primary tests were:

1. No more than 30 percent of the purchase price could be paid in cash in the year of sale;

2. The purchase price must be for a fixed amount payable in at least one installment in addition to the down payment;

3. The taxpayer must file a specific election in a particular manner to qualify.

3. The New Ball Game—1980

The Installment Sales Revision act of 1980 has greatly changed these rules to the general benefit of the taxpayer. No longer is it necessary to limit payments received in the year of sale to 30 percent. There no longer is a requirement that there must be a fixed amount payable in at least one installment in addition to the down payment, and no longer is a written election required to qualify.

These changes and other provisions are vitally important to business executives and their advisors. The new law will be discussed in some detail.

It should be noted, as a preliminary matter that what was Section 453 is now covered in three separate code sections, Section 453, Section 453A, and Section 453B. Code Section 453 will apply to sales of real property and business assets generally. Code Section 453A applies only to the special situation involving sales of personal property by dealers, and will rarely be involved in a business acquisition situation. Code Section 453B sets forth new rules applying to the disposition of installment obligations.

4. What Is An Installment Sale Under The New Law?

The new law defines "installment sale" simply as a disposition of real or personal property where at least one payment is to be received after the close of the taxable year in which the disposition occurs. This means that an "installment sale" no longer requires "installments." In other words, under the new law, *all* of the purchase price can be deferred to a more tax advantageous year. Under the pre-1980 law, an installment sale could occur only if some payment was made in the year of sale.

On the other side of the coin, there is no longer any restriction on the maximum amount which may be received in the year of sale (the old 30 percent trap).

5. Other Ground Rules Under the 1980 Act

The new act also makes the following key changes:

☐ There are special rules with respect to sales to members of families. Generally, the law now taxes the first seller in a family transaction when the second seller disposes of the property purchased.

> *Example:* Prior to the new law, some family sales were structured so that Father sold, say, stock in the family business, to Son for $1,000,000, $20,000 down and the balance at six percent over 12 years. Son then immediately turned around and sold the stock to a third party for $1,000,000, paid no tax (since his tax basis, the $1,000,000 purchase price from Father, was equal to the sales price). The IRS,

needless to say, vigorously fought this gimmick and sometimes lost. (See *Rushing v. Commissioner of Internal Revenue,* 441 F.2d 593 (5th Cir., 1971).)

As usual, as they say on Wall Street, "bulls get rich and bears get rich, but pigs get slaughtered." Congress changed the law in the 1980 Act.

☐ An installment sale can clearly be used with a tax-free like-kind property exchange and the like-kind property will not be treated as a payment for purposes of reporting profit under the installment sale portion.

☐ A contingent sales price, such as a sales price based upon future business profits or gross sales is now allowable. This is a key change for business acquisitions and is discussed in detail later.

☐ Distribution of installment sales obligations (such as notes from a purchaser of corporate assets) to shareholders in a liquidation of a corporation would not be taxed to its shareholders until payment is actually received on the installment obligation.

☐ No written election is required by the taxpayer, since installment treatment will be automatic unless there is an election not to treat the sale as an installment sale.

☐ Any deferred sale, including former "open" transactions where payment is uncertain (and, therefore, tax on it was deferred), will normally qualify for the new installment rules, even though both the payment amounts and dates, are contingent.

6. Using the New Installment Sales Rules in a "Bootstrap" Acquisition

Armed with the seller's desire to report the sale of stock of a corporation as an installment sale, the acquiring corporation can pay for an entire acquisition out of the earnings of the acquired corporation so that the acquisition pays for itself over a short period of years. This amazing result comes from the flexibility allowed under the new installment sales rules and the advantages to the seller in deferring income tax on the gain from the sale. An acquisition under the new rules is shown by the following example:

a) Magic Corporation was in the furniture business and had a successful track record.

b) Magic learned that the principal shareholder and officer of a similar corporation in a neighboring state planned to retire. Magic believed that a fair price for the Neighboring Corporation was $2,000,000 based upon net after-tax earnings of Neighboring of $400,000 per year ($800,000 pre-tax).

c) The owners of Neighboring Corporation were willing to sell for $2,000,000 but wanted to be assured of income over a period of years and also wanted to be able to spread the tax on the gain on their stock over several tax years.

d) Magic proposed to the shareholders of Neighboring that they sell all of their stock for $2,000,000, payable $200,000 down, with the balance over a nine-year period plus 8 percent interest per annum. The stock of Neighboring would serve as security for the notes.

e) Magic borrowed $200,000 from its bank and paid the Neighboring shareholder that amount, while delivering to the shareholders Magic's notes for the balance of $1,800,000. The notes were secured by all of Neighboring's stock.

f) Because of Magic's ability to buy more competitively, its business expertise, and its efficiencies of scale, the earnings of Neighboring Corporation increased $200,000 in the first year and 10 percent per year thereafter, before taxes.

Let's see how the arithmetic worked over a 10-year period (all figures are rounded and simplified for purposes of illustration):

At Closing:	Cash Paid Out	$200,000
	Net Cash In	-0-
	Bank Loan	$200,000

Year One:			
	Cash	(before tax)	$800,000
	Less:	(interest)	$144,000
		Balance	$656,000
		(corporate taxes)	328,000
	Net after tax		$328,000
	Less:		
	Principal payment to Neighboring shareholder		$200,000
	Net		$128,000
	Bank Loan Repaid with Interest		110,000
	Net Cash:		$ 18,000

Year Five:		
Cash Received	$1,171,280 ($800,000 + 10% × 4 years compounded)	
Less:	− 84,000 interest	
Balance	$1,087,280	
Less:		
Corporate Income Taxes	543,640	
Balance		$543,640
Less:		
Payments of Principal	200,000	
Net Cash		$343,640

Year Nine:		
Cash In	$1,886,358	
Less:		
Interest	16,000	
Net	$1,870,358	
Less:		
Corporate Income Taxes	935,179	
Balance		$935,179
Less:		
Final Payments of Principal	100,000	
Net Cash:		$835,179

Magic has repaid the bank loan since and has a very profitable corporation at absolutely no cost. The figures would obviously change depending upon the degree to which a buyer can make the business profitable and the length and interest rate of financing, but the same principle applies. Note that the Treasury Department from time to time specifies the minimum stated interest allowable to avoid "imputed interest." Even if the sale requires a higher rate of interest, say 10 to 12%, if some of the principal payments can be deferred until the later years (*e.g.*, interest only for five years), then the purchase is still very attractive.

7. Advantages to the Sellers

The transaction discussed above could also be of great benefit to the sellers. The sellers have received an income on their capital over a 10-year period, which has helped to fund their retirement with income from assets *prior* to recognition of capital gain. In other words, if the sellers had sold for cash and paid, say 30 percent of the sales price to the state and Uncle Sam as capital gains tax, the sellers would have had only $1,400,000 remaining to invest. Even if they could invest at a much higher interest rate, the sellers are better off making the sale, reporting it on the installment basis, and getting interest on what will eventually be Uncle Sam's money, all entirely legitimately.

Furthermore, the sellers have been able to spread their gain over 10 years. Since the "Alternative Minimum Tax" can apply to long-term capital gains in some tax situations, heavy capital gains realized in one year are sometimes penalized.

From the seller's standpoint, the Magic Corporation deal would be something along the following lines:

(Assume a tax basis for both sellers of $—0— and an ordinary marginal tax rate of 60 percent.)

At Closing:	$100,000 cash each
Sellers A and B Each	
Less Tax Each at 30%	
Capitan Gain (Fed. & State)	− 30,000
Net Cash:	$ 90,000 each
Year One:	$172,000 cash each
Less Tax Each:	
72,000 × 60%	43,200
(Ordinary Income-Interest)	
100,000 × 30% =	30,000
(Capital Gains-Principal)	
Net Cash:	$ 98,800 each
Year Nine:	$116,000 cash each
Less $16,000 × 60% =	− 9,600
Less $100,000 × 30% =	− 30,000
Net:	$ 76,400

8. Creative Planning of Installment Sales Under the 1980 Act

(a) No Cash Down Deals

Under the new rules, it is possible to give the seller no cash in the year of sale. This may be advantageous to sellers because they may have extremely high compensation income and be looking forward to retirement with an anticipation of being in a lesser tax bracket. The seller can sell the entire business, receive a note secured by a first mortgage on and security interest in all of the business assets, but defer payment until, say, January 2nd of the next year, giving the seller up to an entire year of use of the funds received the next January before paying personal income tax on the sale. The payments can be stretched out over a period of, say, 10 years so that the seller receives a steady stream of income, capital gain, and return of capital, allowing the seller to report the income at anticipated lower rates.

From the buyer's standpoint, there are obvious advantages in having no "front-end" payments, since the acqusition can often be designed so that the income from the business itself pays for all of the purchase price, especially where *no* down payment is required.

(b) Flexible Price Deals

Another creative device under the new rules involves a flexible acquisition price. Suppose that the parties are apart by $300,000 in the value of the business. The difference of opinion come from a question of projected sales of the business' products over the next five years. Under the new rules, installment sales treatment can be obtained. The purchase price would be set at a minimum of the buyer's top figure. An additional amount up to $300,000 would then be paid if, and when, sales by the company exceeded a certain amount in the first five years after the purchase.

While the Internal Revenue Service Regulations on the new act will not be adopted for some time, the congressional committee writing the act gave certain indications that the regulations will contain particular provisions helpful in the contingent sales area. The House Report on the Bill, H.R. 6883, gives executives and their advisors certain useful guidelines. Under these guidelines:

1. *Flexible sales where there is a stated maximum selling price*. The seller would be able to recover his tax basis related to the gross profit ratio determined by reference to the stated maximum selling price. Income from the sale would be reported on a pro rata basis with respect to every installment payment. Certain remote contingencies would not be taken into account unless they in fact occurred in the future, in which case the seller would reduce income by an adjustment.
2. *Flexible sales where no maximum selling price is set*. If there is a specific time set in the agreement (such as five years for payment), but there is no fixed amount, the taxpayer's basis will be recovered ratably over the fixed time period.

Example: Seller and Buyer have agreed on the purchase price in an assets transaction for everything other than certain sophisticated production machinery. If the production machinery can be utilized at 90 percent capacity over the next five years, then buyer is willing to pay a much higher amount for the equipment than if, as buyer projects, the machinery will only be used to 70 percent capacity.

Seller sells the real estate and all other assets except the equipment to buyer at the bargained price. Seller then sells the equipment to buyer for the right to receive $.25 per unit of output of the equipment over the next five years.

To see how this might work, assume that the equipment produces 1,000,000 units in the first year, 1,500,000 in the third year, 2,000,000 units in the fourth year, and 3,000,000 units in the fifth year. Seller has an $800,000 basis in the equipment. The seller might then report the sale along these lines:

	Cash Received	Seller's Tax Basis Allocated in That Year	Taxable Gain By Seller
1st year	$250,000	$160,000	$ 90,000
2nd year	$300,000	$160,000	$140,000
3rd year	$300,000	$160,000	$140,000
4th year	$500,000	$160,000	$340,000
5th year	$750,000	$160,000	$590,000

The Internal Revenue Service Regulations are expected to permit basis recovery over some reasonable period of time or basis recovery under the "income forecast" method. The House Committee specifically directs the Internal Revenue Service and its regulations to deal with a situation in which the amount payable to the seller is based on a declining percentage of the buyer's revenues. The regulations should prescribe rules which avoid, whenever possible, having an unrecovered basis for the seller after the final payment is received.

(c) Like-Kind Exchanges Permitted

The use of a tax-free like-kind property exchange is discussed later in this chapter. The 1980 Act liberalizes the old rule that had greatly limited the use of a like-kind exchange and an installment sale in the same transaction. Under the pre-1980 rule, when like-kind property was received along with cash and other property in an installment sale transaction, the like-kind property was considered part of the total "contract price" and as part of the "payment" under the old rules.

Under the new rules, like-kind property would be permitted to be received without recognition of gain and would not be treated as a payment. The gross profit on the installment sale portion would be based only on the amount of gain *recognized* in the exchange, and not on the recognized portion of the like-kind exchange.

The buyer would allocate tax basis first to the property received in the like-kind exchange, and any remaining basis would be allocated ratably among the installment obligations and any of the property which did not qualify for "like-kind" exchange (these changes are set forth in amended Code Section 453(f)(6), and Section 1031(d), and are discussed in the House Report at page 16).

These are important and far-reaching changes in the tax law. They give new opportunities to creative executives. Because the rules are so new, great care and study is required prior to any acquisition relying on the 1980 Act. To help in this study, Appendix H-1 sets out the Act itself, and Appendix H-2 contains the Joint Committee description and discussion of the proposal, and Appendix I sets out in full a business acquisition using installment sale treatment.

(d) Use of Installment Sales in Corporate Reorganizations

In a corporate reorganization, it is entirely possible to have part of the receipts treated as a tax-free exchange (*e.g.,* receipt of the other corporation's stock) while the amount of cash received is taxable "boot" (§356(a)). The 1980 Installment Sales Revision Act, §453(f)(6) applies more flexible rules where installment obligations are received as "boot" allowing installment sales treatment of "boot." See discussion of the Joint Committee on Taxation, Appendix H-2, Section II(G).

(e) IRS Requires Higher Minimum Interest on Installment Sales

As noted earlier, the Internal Revenue Service has proposed regulations, which when effective will apply retroactively to September 29, 1980, and which will require an interest rate of at least nine percent to be charged on all installment notes used to purchase property eligible for capital gains treatment. The old rules required at least six percent simple interest.

Under the new IRS rule, if at least a nine percent simple interest is not charged on an installment note, the Internal Revenue Service will constructively "impute" interest at ten percent compounded semi-annually. Assuming that the regulations will be adopted, the seller and buyer involved in an installment sales transaction, after September, 1980, should be sure to specify a nine percent simple interest per annum, if the lowest interest rate is desired.

B. AVOIDING CORPORATE TAX ON SALE OF A BUSINESS—§337

Normally, if a corporation sells its assets and then liquidates, the corporation will pay a tax upon the sale of its assets, and shareholders will pay a separate tax upon the liquidation of the corporation when they receive the proceeds of the sale in liquidation in exchange for their stock.

To avoid the double tax in such a situation, the Internal Revenue Code, §337, specifically provides that if a plan of liquidation is adopted and if the corporation distributes all of its assets (with provisions allowing a small reserve for pending claims), then the corporate tax upon sale of the assets may be entirely avoided. The shareholder still pays tax on the liquidation, but double taxation is avoided.

The rules under §337 are highly technical, but the two important points are that a plan of liquidation must be adopted, and all distributions must take place within 12 months after the date of the plan.

The new Installment Sales Revision Act of 1980 makes it possible for the first time to use an installment sale together with a 12-month corporate liquidation in a broad number of applications.

Under the old installment sales rules, if a liquidating corporation sold its assets for cash and installments and elected installment treatment for the sale, there was no benefit to the shareholders since the shareholders paid full capital gains tax when the corporation in turn distributed the installment notes to the shareholders in liquidation. This inequitable rule resulted in a number of inventive techniques by taxpayers to try and avoid the immediate tax on future payments. Most failed, all were complicated and risky.

Congress recognized the inequity of the old rule, and, as part of the Installment Sales Revision Act of 1980, provided new rules which are much more lenient for the selling shareholder. The new law includes the following points:

- ☐ The corporation now can elect installment sales treatment and distribute the installment obligations to the shareholder without triggering immediate tax to the shareholder.
- ☐ The shareholder now can report gain from the liquidation itself on the installment method, taking gain into account as the shareholder actually received payment under the installment note (new Code §453(h)(1)(A)).
- ☐ Since the sale of inventory (other than in a bulk sale) will not normally qualify for §337 benefits, any installment notes received with respect to the sale of inventory, not in bulk, would not qualify for installment treatment under the new law.
- ☐ Where there are several corporate tiers of parent and subsidiary corporations that are liquidated, the installment obligations may be passed through to the shareholders in certain circumstances (Code Section 453(h)(1)(E)).
- ☐ If a shareholder receives distributions in more than one taxable year, then the amount of gain and the basis that the shareholder has in his stock will be allocated among the various years' distributions.

Example: X is the sole shareholder of Alpha Corporation. He purchased the stock of the corporation some years ago for $200,000, and that amount is his adjusted basis. Alpha Corporation adopts a plan of liquidation in July of 1981 and sells all of its assets within 12 months for $1,000,000, $250,000 in cash and the balance in installment obligations.

When Alpha distributes the $250,000 in cash in December of 1981, X will report a gain of $50,000 ($250,000 cash received, less $200,000 basis in the stock).

In June of 1982, Alpha liquidates totally, and distributes the installment obligations. For 1982, X must recompute the gain reported in 1981 according to the installment sales rule for allocation of basis. The shareholder, in this case, would allocate 25 percent of the basis ($50,000) to the cash received in 1981, and 75 percent ($150,000) to the note received in 1982. X would have to file an amended return for 1981 to reflect the additional gain for that year.

Let's see how the new combination of §337 and the Installment Sales Revision Act could be used in an actual transaction:

☐ Wilson owns APEX Corporation, a manufacturer of fashion blue jeans. He purchased the stock of APEX 10 years ago for $100,000 and an agreement to continue to employ the firm's founder for five years. APEX has been highly successful but Wilson is now 63-years old and would like to find a purchaser.

☐ Johnson would like to purchase APEX for $2,500,000, payable $250,000 down, and the balance payable over 10 years at nine percent interest.

☐ Johnson wants to buy only the tangible assets of APEX along with its trademark "Ape Jeans," but not run the risk of purchasing any undisclosed liabilities that might be in APEX.

☐ Wilson believes that there are no undisclosed liabilities in his corporation, and wants to sell his stock, or at least structure the transaction so that he will be able to qualify for installment sales treatment and only pay tax when and if Johnson pays him.

☐ After much negotiation, the parties and their advisors decide that a creative use of §337 and the new installment sales rule can help the parties reach both of their primary goals.

☐ APEX adopts a plan of liquidation in February of 1981 under §337. In March of 1981, it enters into an agreement with Johnson to sell all of its assets, including its inventory in one bulk transaction for $2,500,000 payable $250,000 down, and the balance represented by a secured note of Johnson Corporation payable in equal annual installments over the next 10 years, with interest of nine percent.

☐ Even though APEX Corporation has long since depreciated its assets, it will pay no gain on the sale of its assets to Johnson Corporation (assuming no recapture of accelerated depreciation, LIFO inventory, or investment credit).

☐ After the closing of the transaction in 1981, APEX liquidates, distributes its cash and note to its sole shareholder, Wilson, and dissolves as a corporation.

☐ Wilson qualifies for installment sales treatment for the $2,500,000 which he has received from APEX. He will report his gain at capital gains rates over the next 10 years.

C. THE COVENANT NOT TO COMPETE

One of the hazards of purchasing a closely-held business is that the business and its shareholder are often intertwined. Many a hapless purchaser has acquired the rights to, say, a chain of delicatessens in a particular city, failed to reach any agreement with the owner that he will not go back into the business, only to find that shortly after the sale the former owner opens a competing delicatessen in the same town. The net result may be that the purchaser only bought half or less of the value he thought he was getting, because the customers of the old business remained loyal, not to the business, but to the former management.

In order to protect against such a problem, it is routine in the sale of a closely-held business for the purchaser to require that the owners of the business covenant not to compete with the business within a certain area for a certain period of time. It should be noted that the covenant not to compete offers a flexible tax planning tool.

As a general rule, the properly planned covenant not to compete will result in the purchaser being able to deduct all payments made to the seller for the covenant, and the seller will receive ordinary income. Because the seller is often retired and does not mind ordinary tax treatment in reasonable amounts each year, the benefits to the purchaser often far outweighs the detriment to the seller. In addition, if the seller becomes a consultant to the business for the period of the covenant, the payments to seller may qualify for the favorable "earned income" tax treatment and a maximum rate of 50 percent.

It is absolutely essential that the contract documents and the closing documents deal with the covenant not to compete as a separate matter and allocate specific payments for the covenant. If this is not done, the Internal Revenue Service may successfully contend that the amounts paid for the covenant are not deductible by the purchaser.

> *Example:* Forward Communications purchased a television station in Sioux City, Iowa for $3.5 million. The purchaser insisted upon the seller giving a covenant not to compete in television or radio broadcasting in the Sioux City area for five years. The contract was amended to include that covenant, but the purchase price remained the same.
>
> At the actual closing of the transaction, purchaser delivered a separate check for $250,000 to the seller and stated to the seller that the check represented the portion of the purchase price allocable to the covenant not to compete. The seller, apparently, did not either agree or disagree at the closing, but later treated the entire payment received as payment for capital assets.
>
> The Internal Revenue Service successfully prohibited Forward Communications from taking *any* tax deduction for the $250,000. The taxpayer contested the Internal Revenue Service's position but lost in the case of *Forward Communications Corporation,* decided by the Court of Claims in 1979 (608 F.2d 485). One lesson to be learned is that it is not enough to merely refer to a covenant not to compete in a sales contract. The parties must agree in the contract to allocate a particular, economically reasonable, portion of the purchase price, to the covenant, and then follow through with that concept in the closing documents.

D. THE NEW CAPITAL GAINS RULES—ACQUISITIONS AND THE ECONOMIC RECOVERY ACT OF 1981

The Economic Recovery Act of 1981 and the 1978 Revenue Act brought with them lower capital gains rates and other important changes. Congressional intent was to "unlock" capital which had been invested in businesses and elsewhere to help revitalize the economy.

This section will briefly discuss the capital gains and certain other provisions of the Economic Recovery Act of 1981.

1. Capital Gains

The 1981 Act lowered federal individual capital gains rates to a maximum of 20% for sales or exchanges after June 9, 1981. At the same time, for 1982 and later years, the maximum individual ordinary tax rate was set at 50%. The reduction of rates should make both the outright sale of a business more attractive, as well as sales over time because the tax on interest income is reduced.

2. Accelerated Cost Recovery Systems Provisions

The old law (which applies still for property placed in service before January 1, 1980) was designed to allocate depreciation deductions over the period the particular asset was used to produce income in a business. The 1981 Act establishes a new system, the Accelerated Cost Recovery System. The recovery periods for tangible property are 3, 5, 10 or 15 years (Economic Recovery Tax Act of 1981, Section 201f). In addition, Section 211 of the Act also allows an investment tax credit for qualified property. The upshot of these and other provisions is that a much greater tax deduction, and therefore tax "shelter", can be obtained by businesses as a result of capital expenditures. This allows a higher after-tax flow for the purchaser of a business to amortize debt growing out of a business acquisition.

3. The 1981 Act and Executive Estate Planning

The 1981 Act reduces estate taxes by setting in motion a gradual increase in the unified credit against estate and gift taxes. By 1986, up to $600,000 of an executive's estate is totally exempt from estate or gift taxes. Separately, effective January 1, 1982, there is an *unlimited* marital deduction, so that the executive may give gifts or transfers by Will in unlimited amounts to executive's spouse.

The annual gift tax exclusion is raised from $3,000 ($6,000 in a joint return) to $10,000 ($20,000 in a joint return). The planning opportunities from this are tremendous. For instance, an executive may now enter into a regular program of transferring up to $20,000 of stock in his business to his children each year tax-free. These transfers, carefully planned over a period of years, and eventually coupled with redemption and other techniques, can result in the effective transfer of a multi-million dollar business to the next generation, without incurring any transfer tax.

New incentive stock option provisions are also included in the new Act. Under these options there is generally no tax for key employees upon either the granting or exercise of the option. Instead, gain is recognized on a later sale of the stock, and gain is normally at capital gains rates (see new Section 422A of the Internal Revenue Code).

4. Other Provisions

Section 422 of the 1981 Act provides more flexibility for payment of estate taxes with respect to closely-held businesses in an estate (discussed in more detail in Section E of Chapter 7). Under the new provisions, effective January 1, 1982, amended Section 6166 of the Internal Revenue Code will apply if a closely-held business constitutes 35% of the decedent's gross estate. Payment of estate taxes with respect to the value of the closely-held business can be spread over 15 years, five years interest only, at a very low rate of interest (*e.g.* 4%).

The 1981 Act also provides more generous deductions for employer contributions to Employee Stock Ownership Plans to pay principal and interest on loans incurred to buy stock or other securities in the employer (see Section 333, 1981 Act).

Finally, the 1978 Act added an Alternative Minimum Tax which imposes an additional tax if a taxpayer has certain very high deductions and credits outside of the capital gain transaction in the same tax year. The Alternative Minimum Tax is a percentage (varying from 10 to 20 percent) of the excess (if any) of alternative minimum taxable income, over the regular tax.

In planning, it should usually be possible for the seller to avoid having an Alternative Minimum Tax when the business sale is the only unusual transaction in that particular tax year. Again, the flexibility involved under the new Installment Sales Revision Act, when combined with the new capital gains rules, should be kept in mind. In other words, the seller, by negotiating the year of payment of a particular installment should be able to place the capital gains in a year in which the Alternative Minimum Tax will not apply.

E. THE NEW WRITE-OFF OF ACQUISITION EXPENSES

Normally, costs incurred prior to the commencement of a business, such as acquisition costs, are non-deductible because they are not incurred in "carrying on of trade or business." These start-up costs historically were required to be capitalized for income tax purposes. Worse, they could not be depreciated or amortized because they had an "indefinite" useful life. In December, 1980, at the end of the 96th Congress, a new Code Section 194 was added to the Internal Revenue Code. Section 194 provides that start-up expenditures may be written off over a 60-month period. These "start-up expenditures" are any payments made in connection with "investigating the creation or acquisition of a trade or business, or creating a trade or business." They are limited to the type of expenditures which would be deductible by the business if it were already in existence, such as certain expenses for advertising, market surveys, training costs and professional services.

F. USING A TAX-FREE EXCHANGE IN A BUSINESS ACQUISITION

Most executives are familiar with the fact that if property is taken by the state by eminent domain, the owner may acquire new property and reinvest the condemnation funds, avoiding any tax. They are also familiar with the similar provisions involving the reinvestment in another home of the proceeds from sale of a residence. They are less familiar with another tax-saving provision found in §1031 of the Internal Revenue Code which allows an exchange of property held for productive use in a trade or business or for investment for another property of a "like kind" to be held for productive use in trade or business or for investment. The provisions of §1031 are most often used in exchanges of real property. The section has rarely been used or considered as a vehicle for exchanging entire businesses, although it appears that it might be very useful as an acquisition technique.

Section 1031 simply states that:

> No gain or loss shall be recognized if property held for productive use in trade or business or for investment (not including stock in trade or other property held primarily for sale, nor stocks, bonds, notes, choses in action, certificates of trust or beneficial interest, or other securities or evidences of indebtedness or interest) is exchanged solely for property of a like kind to be held either for productive use in trade or business or for investment.

Subsection (b) of the section states that if there is a tax-free exchange, but also other property or money ("boot") is received, then the gain is recognized only to the extent of the boot. Subsection (d) provides for a carryover basis for the assets exchanged.

The Regulations, §1.1031, add considerably to this skeleton statute. They provide that property held in a trade or business may be exchanged for property held for investment and vice versa. They also provide that the worlds "like kind" have references to the nature or character of the property and not its grade or quality. They specifically state that the fact that any real estate involved is improved or unimproved is not material, for that fact relates only to "the grade or quality of the property and not to its kind or class." The Regulations go on to state that a taxpayer may exchange property held for productive use in his trade or business such as a truck for a new truck or a passenger automobile for a new passenger automobile to be used for like purposes, or city real estate for a ranch or farm, or a lease with 30 years or more to run for fee simple title to improved or unimproved real estate, or investment property and cash for investment property.

One of the most difficult practical problems is the treatment of the assumption of liabilities in a §1031 exchange. The Regulations, §1.1031(d)-2, state that the amount of any liabilities assumed or to which the property is subject "is to be treated as money received by the taxpayer upon the exchange. . . ." Example (1) of the Regulations clarifies the computation:

> *Example (1):* B, an individual owns an apartment house which has an adjusted basis in his hands of $500,000, but which is subject to a mortgage of $150,000. On September 1, 1954, he transfers the apartment house to C, receiving in exchange therefore $50,000 in cash and another apartment house with a fair market value on that date of $600,000. The transfer to C is made subject to the $150,000 mortgage. B realizes a gain of $300,000 on the exchange, computed as follows:

Value of property received $600,000
Cash 50,000
Liabilities subject to which old
   property was transferred 150,000

    Total consideration received 800,000
Less: Adjusted basis of property
   transferred 500,000

    Gain realized 300,000

> Under section 1031(b), $200,000 of the $300,000 gain is recognized. The basis of the apartment house acquired by B upon the exchange is $500,000, computed as follows:

Adjusted basis of property
   transferred $500,000
Less: Amount of money received
   Cash.....................................$ 50,000
Amount of liabilities subject
   to which property was transferred $150,000
                                200,000

Difference 300,000
Plus: Amount of gain recognized
   upon the exchange 200,000

Basis of property acquired upon
   the exchange 500,000

1. Planning the Business Exchange

In 1957, a telephone company wanted to acquire another operating telephone company and at the same time dispose of its own operating subsidiary in a different location. The taxpayer requested the Internal Revenue Service to rule as to whether or not the provisions of §1031 covered an exchange of one telephone company's assets for the other's. The Internal Revenue Service ruled, in a published ruling (Rev. Rul. 57-365, 1957-2 C.B. 521), that where the parent company of the telephone system causes one of its operating subsidiary companies to exchange all of its assets, including both real estate and personal property (but not including inventory and securities) for all of the assets of another operating telephone company and an additional amount of cash to equalize the value, the exchange qualifies as an exchange or property of like kind within the meaning of §1031 on which gain would be recognized only to the extent of the cash received.

There would not seem to be any reason why this same technique could not be used by an acquiring company which wanted to upgrade a particular property by acquiring a larger property in exchange for the smaller property plus cash.

Similarly, a smaller company which had as its primary asset a plant used in its trade or business could apparently exchange the plant with the acquiring company for other real estate, whether improved or unimproved, which could be held for investment after the exchange rather than for use in the trade or business of the target company. It is also possible to combine a tax-free exchange under §1031 with an installment sale under §454. (See Rev. Rul. 65-155, 1965-1 C.B. 356 and the discussion of the Installment Sales Revision Act of 1980 at page 281.)

The three-party exchange technique was used in 1972 by Carroll Rosenbloom, the former longtime owner of the Baltimore Colts, when he acquired the Los Angeles Rams.

Let's look at the technique which Mr. Rosenbloom used, as reported in the press. (See *New York Times,* July 14, 1972, page 21, column 1.)

A Chicago businessman wanted to acquire the Colts which were owned by Mr. Rosenbloom. If Mr. Rosenbloom had sold the Colts, it was reported that there would have been at least $4,400,000 in capital gains taxes to pay. Instead, the Chicago businessman purchased all of the stock of the corporation which owned the Rams for approximately $19,000,000. Thereafter, Mr. Rosenbloom's corporation exchanged the assets of the Colts (including the franchise and player contracts) for the similar assets of the Rams. The swap apparently qualified as tax-free exchange of assets under §1031. Planning possibilities in such a transaction are obviously enormous and should be considered by any thoughtful executive as an alternative to more orthodox acquisition techniques.

2. Using a Three-Party Exchange

One of the secrets to successful exchanges in the real world is that one of the parties to the exchange does not have to own property to be exchanged at the outset of the transaction. In the Colts transaction discussed above, the eventual new owner of the Colts did not own the Los Angeles Rams at the time the parties started their discussions. Instead, the owner-to-be acquired the Rams in a straight purchase transaction.

Any exchange transaction is very temperamental and should be carefully studied by professional advisors. A ruling from the Internal Revenue Service also should be considered.

The three-cornered exchange, especially, requires meticulous planning. It is absolutely essential that the actual transaction followed be cast as an exchange rather than taking any shortcuts. For instance, while Rev. Rul. 57-244, 1957-1 C.B. 247 approves the use of three-cornered exchange, in the case of *Carlton v. The United States*, 385 F.2d 238 (5th Cir., 1967) the taxpayers lost because they shortcut the formalities. Instead of conveying title twice as is usually required to have a true three-party exchange, actual title went from the original owner to the eventual owner without the third party (who was purchasing the property to be used in the exchange) ever receiving the property.

Cases have held that it is also possible to exchange general partnership interests under §1031. See *Miller*, 63-2 U.S.T.C. ¶9606, U.S.D.C. (1963) and *R.E. Meyer Estate v. Commissioner*, 58 T.C. 311 (1973) (non acq.).

The Internal Revenue Service in 1975 approved a tax-free exchange of an existing factory and land for one constructed solely for the purpose of the exchange (Rev. Rul. 75-291).

3. Example of a Transaction Using a Tax-Free Exchange: The Recent TV-Radio Station Swaps

A good example of the use of tax-free exchange transactions can be found in the numerous recent swaps of TV and radio stations.

The Federal Communications Commission required certain corporations which own both newspapers and radio or TV stations in the same city to give up one or the other. Tax-free exchanges were tailor-made for such a situation since they allow a corporation to dispose of a television station in one city and acquire a television station in another city without incurring any capital gains tax on the disposition. In one well-publicized swap, the *Washington Post* and the *Detroit News* exchanged television stations so that, after the exchange, the *Post* owned WWJ-TV in Detroit, and the *News* owned WTOP-TV in Washington. Following the same pattern, the *Washington Star* exchanged WJLA-TV with Combined Communications for the latter's Oklahoma City station, KOCO-TV.

4. The New Installment Sales Revision Act and Like-Kind Exchanges

The Installment Sales Revision Act of 1980 gave new flexibility to like-kind exchanges. As has been noted above, if like-kind property is received plus other types of property or money, there is a tax imposed upon any gain represented by the money received and the fair market value of the other property (Internal Revenue Code §1031(b)).

Prior to the 1980 Act, when like-kind property was received, along with cash and installment notes, the like-kind property continued to qualify for nonrecognition treatment under Code §1031(b), but the value of the like-kind property was taken into account to determine both the contract price and the amount of payments received for purposes of the installment sales rules under §453.

The Installment Sales Revision Act of 1980 changed the rules and allowed greater flexibility. There are three principal new rules that affect like-kind exchanges:

1. The contract price, under the 1980 Act, does not include the value of the like-kind property received, but only the money and any other "boot" received (including the face amount of the installment notes) (Code §453(f)(6)(A));
2. The gross profit in most transactions involving a like-kind and an installment sale would be the amount of gain counting the installment note at its face value, but excluding the gain not recognized because of the exchange of like-kind properties (Section 453(f)(6)(B)); and
3. The like-kind property received would not be treated as a payment (Section 453(f)(6)(C)).

> *Example:* Jones Company, a partnership, exchanges its radio station in upstate New York, which has a basis of $400,000, for a radio station in northern Florida. The like-kind property involved in the transaction is worth $200,000, and there is a down payment of $100,000, with a balloon installment note due 12 months from closing in the amount of $700,000. The total deal is worth $1,000,000 to Jones. The basis which Jones had in the property swapped, $400,000, is fairly allocated $200,000 to the like-kind property received (based on its fair market value), and the remaining $200,000 to the installment transaction. The tax would be calculated as follows:

Contract Price	($1,000,000 less $200,000 like-kind property received)	$800,000
Gross Profit	($800,000 cash and notes less $200,000 basis allocated to cash and note)	$600,000
Gross Margin Ratio	($600,000/$800,000)	75%
Gain To Be Reported		
	A. Year of Sale (75% × $100,000 cash) $ 75,000	
	B. Next Year in Which Note is Paid (75% × $700,000) $525,000	
Total Gain Recognized		$600,000
Remaining Basis of Like-Kind Property	(the Florida radio station owned by Jones)	$200,000

G. A BRIEF LOOK AT CERTAIN SECURITIES RULES

Every executive should be familiar with the fact that any sale or exchange of stock or other securities is regulated by both state law and federal law. Generally speaking, both laws make it illegal to sell or exchange securities which have not first been registered with the state and the Federal Securities and Exchange Commission, unless a specific exemption for the transaction or security applies. The burden of finding an exemption lies on the one selling or exchanging the securities.

First, federal law exempts limited sale or exchanges by a corporation which is: (1) incorporated by and doing business in one state, and (2) which is offered and sold only to residents of that state. This is the so-called intrastate offering exemption (Securities Act of 1933, §3(a)(11)) and is fraught with a great many pitfalls. Second, federal law exempts offerings which do not involve a "public offering" of securities (§4(2)). This is often called the "private placement" exemption. From these two basic federal exemptions have grown certain rules of the Securities and Exchange Commission.

1. Rule 144

Rule 144 basically provides that anyone who acquires securities pursuant to the private placement exemption, from the issuer of securities, and who resells them after a two-year holding period through an unsolicited brokerage transaction and in limited amounts is not subject to the requirement of having to register securities. Rule 144 is applicable only to securities of an issuer which either is a reporting company under the Securities and Exchange Act of 1934, or which makes the same type of information publicly available. The Securities and Exchange Commission has recently published a detailed series of questions and answers clarifying many of the applications of Rule 144 (SEC Release No. 33-6099, August 2, 1979).

In 1978 and again in 1979, the SEC liberalized the sale of unregistered securities under Rule 144. The September, 1978 amendments more than doubled the volume of securities that can be sold under the Rule. The amendment provided that now the greater of one percent (1%) of the outstanding securities of the particular class sold *or* the average weekly trading volume during the four calendar weeks preceding sale, may be sold in any three-month period.

In 1979, the rule was liberalized further so that, three years after acquisition of restricted securities which are either listed on a stock exchange or in National Association of Securities Dealers' NASDAQ Quotation System for over-the-counter stocks, there is no limit to the amount an unaffiliated person may sell. For all other over-the-counter securities that make periodic reports to the SEC, the sales restriction terminates four years after acquisition.

Since the cost of full registration under the Securities Act remains high, Rule 144 is the basic "safe harbor" for minority shareholders in an acquired corporation who later wish to dispose of their stock, for venture capital corporations investing in small businesses, and for persons whose corporations are acquired by much larger corporations and who receive publicly traded securities in the large corporation.

2. Rule 145

Rule 145 requires that, usually, when a plan of a merger of other acquisition is submitted to shareholders of the target company, an "offer" occurs which brings into play the registration requirements of the Securities Act of 1933 unless an exemption applies. If no exemption applies, then a registration is required on a simplified Form S-14.

3. Rule 146

The SEC has provided in another rule, Rule 146 for a safe harbor as to small transactions which can qualify as "private placements." Basically, under Rule 146, if no more than 35 persons acquire the security and if all of the offerees either are capable of evaluating the merits and risks of the transaction or have an offeree representative who is capable of advising them in the evaluation and if resale of the securities is restricted, then the transaction will be treated as a private transaction not requiring registration. In an acquisition transaction where the target company is owned by a small group of people, Rule 146 is often used. If there is any question as to the sophistication of some or all of the shareholders of the target company, a professional such as an investment advisor or someone who regularly deals in securities is often designated as the representative to evaluate the financial and other information and to advise the shareholders of the target company as to the merits and risks of the securities of the acquiring corporation which they will be receiving.

Rule 146 also, in effect, requires that the issuer:

a) Determine that the person receiving the stock is acting for himself;
b) Place a legend on the stock certificate;
c) Flag the stock transfer records; and
d) Obtain an "investment letter" from the new shareholder stating that the shares will not be sold unless either registered or in an exempt transaction.

As a practical matter, most stock received in the acquisition of a closely-held business will be through use of the private placement exemption, and will be so-called "legend stock." That is, the certificates evidencing the shares will have a bold legend on their face to the effect that the stock has not been registered and may not be sold or exchanged until applicable laws and regulations have been met. In effect, the shareholder of the target company who receives such shares is probably locked in for at least a two-year period (under Rule 144). Since for tax reasons it is often important that the shareholders of the target company retain the stock which they receive to give a "continuity of interest," the legend often helps both the securities and tax aspects of the transaction.

This chapter does not attempt to go into any detail as to the myriad of securities regulations and laws which apply to most acquisition transactions. The executive should simply be aware that almost all acquisition transactions are subject to the securities laws and regulations and that an appropriate exemption or registration must be obtained. A copy of the chart used by certain members of the Securities and Exchange Commission Staff in comparing Rule 146 with rules exempting smaller transactions is set out in Appendix K.

4. Stock Issues for Small Companies

Sale of substantial amounts of shares either directly by a corporation or in a "secondary" offering by the controlling shareholder offers one alternative to an acquisition or merger. Unfortunately, the cost of a full S-1 registration with the SEC remains high when a relatively small amount is involved. A recent study by the SEC's advisory committee on corporate disclosure found that although the cost of a S-1 registration was $27 per $100,000 of sales for a medium-sized company, it was $1,849 per $100,000 of sales for a small company.

In addition to private placements, several specific SEC alternatives are available:

(a) Rule 240

This rule exempts offers and sales of securities if all of the following conditions are met:

1. The securities are not sold by advertising;
2. No commission is paid;
3. All securities sold (including any other offerings within 12 months) do not exceed $100,000;
4. There are less than 100 shareholders before and after the sale;
5. The securities are acquired for investment and not for resale; and
6. The issuer files a notice with an SEC Regional Office on Form 240.

As in all other situations where sales of securities are involved, state law must also be consulted and its requirements met.

(b) Proposed Rule 242

The SEC's new Rule 242 permits offers for sales of up to $2,000,000 of securities within a six-month period to an unlimited number of "accredited persons" (who each bought at least $100,000 of securities), plus up to 35 other "non-accredited" persons. If the sales were only to accredited persons, no particular disclosure information is required by the Rule. If non-accredited persons are involved, the issuer would have to furnish purchasers with disclosure information on a limited basis.

(c) Regulation "A" Exemption

Regulation "A" allows the sale, under a recent amendment, of up to $1,500,000 of securities during a 12-month period. The issuer, under Regulation "A", is required to file a notice with the SEC Regional Office and, if the amount of securities offered exceeds $100,000, an offering circular is required to be prepared and filed with the notice. Under Regulation "A", there is no requirement for *audited* financial statements if the issuing company is not a SEC reporting company. As a practical matter, however, state law or underwriters may require audited financials when Regulation "A" is used.

(d) Form S-18

A new and simplified registration form called the S-18 is available for corporations with assets of less than $1,000,000 and fewer than 500 shareholders, which are not subject to the SEC's continuous reporting requirement. The S-18 registration allows these corporations to raise up to $5,000,000 through the registration. The rules for an S-18 registration are more relaxed than under S-1. For instance, audited financial statements are required for only two years, rather than three as required under S-1, and the accounting standards are less stringent.

H. A BRIEF LOOK AT BULK SALES LAWS

The laws of almost every state contain a provision known as Article 6 of the Uniform Commercial Code. These are the "bulk sales laws," which are used to attack one specific form of commercial fraud which was defined by the drafters of the Act as follows:

> The merchant, owing debts, who sells out his stock in trade to any one for any price, pockets the proceeds, and disappears leaving his creditors unpaid.

To combat this problem, the Uniform Commercial Code simply provides that if there is any transfer in bulk and not in the ordinary course of the transferor's business of a major part of the materials, supplies, or other inventory or an enterprise whose principal business is the sale of merchandise from stock (including those who manufacture what they sell), then the transfer may be treated as though it did not take place for a period of at least six months after the transfer takes place or is discovered, unless the provisions of the Bulk Sales Article are followed. In other words, the creditor may sue the buyer of the goods.

The Bulk Sales Article does not apply to a new business which gives public notice of the transfer and which assumes all of the debt of the transferor so that the new business does not have an interest senior to the existing creditors of the old business.

To comply with the Bulk Sales Act, the following actions specified in §6-104 through §6-107 of the Uniform Commerical Code must take place:

1. The acquiring company must require the target company to furnish a list of existing creditors containing the names and business addresses of all creditors with the amounts of debt when known and the names of all persons who assert claims against the target company even if the claims are disputed. The list must be signed and sworn to by the target company. The responsibility for the completeness of the list rests on the target company and not on the acquiring company unless the aquiring company actually knows of discrepancies.
2. The parties prepare a schedule of the property to be transferred by the target company and both the schedule and the list of creditors are retained for six months after the transaction.

3. At least 10 days before the transfer of the property takes place, public notice is given, usually by publication in a newspaper and by mailing notice to each creditor. It is very important that notice be given to taxing authorities whether or not they appear on the list of creditors. See *U.S. v. Goldblatt Bros., Inc.,* 128 F.2d 576 (7th Cir., 1942). The notice states that a bulk transfer is about to be made and gives the names and business addresses of the acquiring and target company and states whether or not all of the debts of the target company are to be paid in full as they fall due, and, if so, where creditors should send their bills.

For planning purposes, the acquiring company should generally insist upon compliance with the Bulk Sales Act. Compliance is often a handy way in which to verify the accounts as stated by the target company. On the other hand, the target company (and occasionally the acquiring company) will not want to cause the disturbance of customers which often is the result of receiving the rather formal notice under the Bulk Sales Article.

I. A BRIEF LOOK AT TRADE REGULATION LAWS

Any person involved with acquisition should be aware of the existence of federal laws which prohibit certain acquisitions because of their anticompetitive effect.

A thorough discussion of these laws and rules is beyond the scope of this *Desk Book,* but the following observations may be useful:

1. Section 7 of the Clayton Act prohibits a corporation from acquiring stock or assets of another corporation where the effect of the acquisition may be to "substantially lessen competition or to tend to create a monopoly" in any line of commerce in any section of the country. Remedies for an acquisition or purposed acquisition in violation of Section 7 include injunctions against the acquisition, an order compelling divestiture of the property acquired or other interests, and additional remedies.
2. Sections 1 and 2 of the older anti-trust law, the Sherman Act, prohibit an acquisition when it constitutes a restraint of trade or the creation of a monopoly. Section 1 of the Sherman Act provides that every "contract, combination in the form of trust or otherwise, or conspiracy, in restraint of trade or commerce . . . is hereby declared to be illegal." Section 2 of the Sherman Act provides every "person who shall monopolize, or attempt to monopolize, or combine or conspire with any person or persons, to monopolize any part of the trade or commerce . . . shall be deemed guilty of a misdemeanor."
3. In addition, the Federal Trade Commission Act gives broad powers to regulate any competitive acquisitions affecting commerce to the Federal Trade Commission.

Antitrust practitioners divide corporate mergers into three types:

1. *Vertical Mergers* (that is, acquisition of suppliers or customers) which may tend to foreclose markets to competitors;
2. *Horizontal Mergers* (that is, between competitors) which may either give "monopoly" power or cause overconcentration; and
3. *Conglomerate Mergers* (that is between firms in different fields) which might remove potential competition or discourage competition by others because of the financial strength of the resulting firm.

In addition to the federal laws, there are laws in most states which could restrict mergers. Under federal law (the McCarran-Ferguson Act, 15 U.S.C. §1011f) states are given broad authority to regulate mergers involving insurance companies. There is similar authority in certain other areas in which the states have unique regulatory authority, such as wine and liquor businesses.

Pursuant to these statutory powers, there is no general requirement that notice be given to the Federal Trade Commission or the Justice Department prior to an acquisition or merger. However, acquisitions involving a certain size transaction, or involving certain industries such as the cement industry, the food distribution industry, or the grocery products manufacturing industry do require prior notice to the F.T.C. and the Department of Justice. The Hart-Scott-Rodino Antitrust Act of 1976 (15 U.S.C. 18a) tightened the existing rules. The Federal Trade Commission has published guidelines for mergers in such situations. In addition, it is possible to obtain from the Justice Department or the Federal Trade Commission certain pre-merger clearances.

The general guidelines for notification are triggered when one of the firms involved in a potential merger or acquisition has assets or annual sales of at least one hundred milion dollars and the other firm has assets or annual sales of at least ten million dollars.

The entire anti-trust and trade regulation area is complex and fast changing. All persons involved in acquisitions should be aware of the restrictions on any merger which could be anti-competitive and should seek the opinion of anti-trust counsel in the case of doubt.

Chapter 3

How To Find The Right Deal

A. GOAL ANALYSIS IN MERGERS AND ACQUISITIONS

Perhaps as many as one-half of the potential mergers and acqusitions never get farther than the casual talking stage simply because one or both parties do not utilize proper goal analysis. Goal analysis is familiar to most modern executives as part of the technique of "management by objectives," but it is seldom applied to the unfamiliar territory of mergers and acquisitions. For some strange reason, the corporation president, who has no difficulty at all seeing that a sales goal for each territory must be set and that the territorial sales managers must move towards that goal each year in order to reach larger business objectives, throws the book away when he seeks to acquire a new corporation in another sales territory, even though the potential acquisition will result in more sales than anything else the corporation might undertake.

1. How to Determine What You Really Want

The place to begin in merger and acquisition goal analysis is with your own goals. To simplify discussion, it is assumed that you are the acquiring corporation. If the acquiring corporation has not done its homework and does not know what points are absolutely essential to it and what points are negotiable business preferences, when the hard bargaining arrives and "make or break" decisions must be reached, there is no framework within which to make these decisions.

In a typical recent situation, Successful Corporation, manufacturer of an essential computer component, had an opportunity to acquire Target Company, a manufacturer of a computer terminal compatible with Successful's computer component. Successful's acquisition team, after a thorough study of Successful's general planning goals, determined the following needs for Successful which could be met by the acquisition:

1. Acquisition of a new, related product with anticipated sales effort efficiency.
2. Ability to bid on larger projects because of control of more components needed for the customer's complete computer installation.
3. Acquisition of more modern manufacturing facilities which can be modified to manufacture Successful's exisiting component as well as the new terminal. This would allow Successful to dispose of its present outmoded manufacturing facilities.
4. Acquisition of a research and development team which now works for Target Company.
5. Acquisition of a strengthened sales group in the northeastern United States presently working for Target Company.
6. Acquisition of the Target Company trademark and good will.
7. Acquisition of the services of the founder of Target Company at least for several years.
8. Shelter of some operating income through use of Target Company's loss carryovers.

Obviously, the goals list for any particular acquisition will vary and may include a variety of other goals. But the list should be forthright and include all goals which will in fact be important in the negotiations. For instance, if the acquiring company sets a goal of acquiring additional talent in the research and development field, it would be foolish to consummate an acquisition without adequate assurance that the research and development team would follow the acquired company.

After having established goals, it is then very important to set a priority for each goal. For instance, Successful Corporation rated the acquisition of the new plant of Target Company as a much more important goal than acquiring the founder of Target Company as a consultant for two years. Such a priority, clearly established prior to any serious negotiations, enables the acquiring company to better reach its important objectives in the heat of the actual negotiations.

2. How to Find Out What the Other Party Wants

Of equal importance with determining the goals of the acquiring corporation is an early determination of the goals of the Target Company and its owners.

The reasons given by the Target Company Board desiring the acquisition may or may not represent the true motivation for that corporation. The reasons given are often couched in terms of marketability of stock, broader capital base, greater marketing expertise. Hidden below such high-sounding goals may be such motivations as getting rid of a division or business which seems to have no hope for future profitability, providing a vehicle for firing a large number of incompetent staff persons without incurring that onus for present management, or providing some check upon incompetent second- or third-generation family management while diversifying the family fortune.

The importance of determining the true motivation is immediately apparent. If the motivation is stated to be "to provide estate liquidity," but the real motivation is to unload a "dog," such basic matters as the detailed nature of warranties by the seller and the desirability of basing part of the purchase price upon actual future earnings assume different degrees of importance.

Perhaps typical goals from the seller's standpoint (and this includes shareholders' and management goals) might include the following:

a) To sell at a price which seems to be greater than the present value of the business to its present owners.
b) To provide employment for present management over, say, five years.
c) To get rid of constant headaches in the shipping department caused by nepotism and an unwillingness to fire incompetent staff members.
d) To avoid future tangles with OSHA and other regulators who have been snooping around recently, and whose findings may require substantial future expenditures of capital.
e) To avoid investments of substantial capital in modernizing the old plant.
f) To convert unmarketable securities into marketable securities.
g) To provide liquidity for the estate of the principal owner.

3. How to Rank and Match Your Goals and His

After you have established your own goals and their relative priorities, and have collected as much information as you can concerning the other parties' stated and actual goals, you should then have a separate planning session with everyone assisting you on your side of the table. At this juncture, your lawyer, accountant, and other outside advisors should also certainly participate, so that the technical practicality of suggested proposals can be quickly tested.

Normally, goal analysis can be performed shortly before actual negotiations. Much of the data for the analysis which concerns the other party can be collected prior to face-to-face meetings. Also, since the parties themselves may not candidly admit particular goals or their relative priorities, to those on the other side of a deal, there is a constant need for feedback and re-evaluation of goals as negotiations progress.

One negotiation concerning the acquisition of a medium-size business continued off-and-on at a rather steady pace for more than two years before the goals of the parties and the possible framework for obtaining most of those goals was established. In a more typical case, the goals can be fairly well set after the first meeting of the principals, assuming proper background study.

Once goals and priorities are established, creative business planning can often meet various goals of the parties even though they at first seem inconsistent. Suppose that the acquiring corporation insists upon: (1) a minimum immediate cash outlay, (2) 100 percent control of the acquired corporation immediately, and (3) no dilution of control of the acquiring corporation by the existing shareholders. Suppose that the goals of the acquired corporation are: (1) liquidity, (2) participation in growth of the combined entity over at least a short-term period after the acquisition, and (3) prompt control in the event of serious mismanagement.

At first, such a list of goals would seem inconsistent if not directly contradictory. After these goals are communicated, a detailed planning session should be held. Such a session might result in a proposal to the acquired corporation along the following lines:

a) The acquiring corporation would create a new class of preferred stock, preferred as to dividends and upon liquidation, and which would have no vote unless a dividend was omitted or certain basic financial tests were not met.
b) The preferred stock would be callable or redeemable by the acquiring corporation after five years at the election of either the corporation or the shareholder at par value plus any accrued dividends.
c) Some of the stock would not be immediately delivered to the shareholders of the acquired corporation, but would be held in escrow and delivered only in the event certain levels of earnings were met by the separate corporation.

The solution met all of the goals of the acquiring corportaion in that: (1) no immediate cash payment was required and none would be required for five years, (2) the acquired corporation was immediately controlled, and (3) no voting control was given up unless serious defaults occurred in the payment of dividends. The acquired corporation's goals were met in that: (1) the stock acquired was marketable to a limited extent, cash payment in full was assured at the end of five years and in the meantime, dividends representing a return on capital would be obtained; (2) the escrow arrangement regarding the shares would allow the shareholders of the acquired corporation to share in the financial success of the business of the acquired corporation; and (3) immediate voting control would exist if the combined corporations got into serious financial difficulties and missed paying dividends. Best of all, the entire transaction could be structured as a tax-free merger with no immediate tax on the part of either the acquired or the acquiring group.

B. FINANCIAL ANALYSIS OF THE TARGET COMPANY

One of the basic considerations for the acquiring company is going to be the financial strength which the proposed acquisition will add to the resulting corporation. Early and continuing analysis of financial information by the acquiring corporation is absolutely essential. Prior to negotiations, the latest unaudited and audited balance sheets, profit-and-loss statements, and relevant schedules should be carefully analyzed. Important: Immediately prior to the closing of the transaction, the statements upon which the contracted warranties are to be made by the acquired corporation or its shareholders must be compared with the earlier figures and again carefully analyzed.

One of the frequent traps for an acquiring corporation is to base an entire series of negotiations and the deal itself upon outdated financial data and vague, "back of the envelope" type representations as to current sales and earnings. Suddenly, on the day of the closing, new financial data is presented and there is inadequate time to properly analyze it. Legally, the representations and warranties are usually based upon the papers presented at closing, and not on the tentative figures upon which early negotiations were based.

This section in no way attempts to give a complete discussion of accounting aspects of an acquisition transaction, rather it makes certain observations which are not always apparent in applying normal financial analysis techniques.

1. What You Should Know About the All-Important Balance Sheet

Just as the statement of profit-and-loss gives to management a moving picture of the operations of a business over a particular period (usually one year), the balance sheet gives an enlargement of a still photograph.

Reduced to its basic elements, the typical balance sheet would include the following information:

Balance Sheet of ABC Corporation December 31, 19 __
(Unaudited)

Assets			Liabilities and Net Worth		
Current Assets			**Current Liabilities**		
Cash	115X		Accounts Payable	175X	
Marketable Securities	200X		Notes Payable	50X	
Accounts Receivable	280X		Accrued Liabilities	220X	
Inventories	390X				
			Total Current Liabilities	445X	
Total Current Assets	985X				
Fixed Assets			**Long-Term Liabilities**		
Plant	900X		Mortgage Payable	100X	
Less Accumulated			Bonds	250X	
Depreciation	(400X)		Reserve	50X	
		500X	Total Long-Term		
			Liabilities	400X	
Furniture and Fixtures	200X		Total Liabilities	800X	
Less Accumulated			**Net Worth**		
Appreciation	(100X)		Common Stock	300X	
		100X	Paid-In Surplus	150X	
Real Estate			Retained Earnings	255X	
Held for Future Plan			TOTAL LIABILITIES	1,950X	
Development	100X		AND NET WORTH		
Other Assets	130X	830X			
Total Fixed Assets					
Prepaid Expenses	25X				
Goodwill	100X				
Unamortized					
Organization					
Expense	10X				
TOTAL ASSETS		1,950X			

Even a greatly simplified balance sheet is a very revealing document. A full audited balance sheet can be a gold mine of information. The sophisticated manager will look at the balance sheet itself briefly and then study the footnotes which appear on audited balance sheets. Normally, an audited balance sheet will have a legend at the bottom to the effect that "the accompanying notes are an integral part of the balance sheet." In fact, many managers say only half in jest, that if they only had time to read either the balance sheet or the footnotes, they would choose the footnotes. The reason is simple. Some footnotes merely contain facts which cannot handily be included in the balance sheet and which are supplementary in nature. Footnotes can be very important to management of the acquiring corporation even though they consist of entirely legitimate supplementary material, such as an explanation of depreciation policies for certain assets, or a further breakdown of certain categories such as "Other Assets." A final category of footnotes is the reason that a sophisticated manager jokingly might say that he would prefer to read the footnotes than the balance sheet if given the choice of one or the other. These footnotes represent the product of an often long and not always friendly battle between the independent auditors of the corporation and its management as to whether or not certain material matters should be disclosed in the balance sheet of the corporation.

Examples of this type of footnote would include an explanation of a reserve. Such reserves can often mask large, and in fact undetermined, liabilities of the corporation. Revaluation of assets could also be the subject of such a footnote, and could add an element of "blue sky" to an otherwise conservative accounting picture of the business enterprise, and could in certain instances magically transform a corporation with an earnings deficit into a corporation having a tidy surplus.

Reference to the above skeleton balance sheet gives the following food for thought:

Assets

Current Assets

Cash: Is this actually cash on hand (unlikely), or is it cash held in a checking account in a reputable bank? Is any of this cash held as compensating balances required to be held for loans at the bank, or is it freely usable for any purpose of the corporation? In an international business, it is important to determine whether or not the currency in which cash is held is United States dollars or some other currency, and whether in any event there is a currency valuation or restriction problem.

Marketable Securities: What are they? How are the valued? Are they subject to any restrictions on transfer? Are they pledged on any loans or other agreements? Why is the corporation holding them? Are they a possible surplus asset?

Accounts Receivable: This number may be the most worthless one in the group. You must analyze the aging of the accounts. You must also determine the credit worthiness of the customer, whether there are any known disputes, and what the past payment experience for those customers and the receivables generally has been. Customarily, there should be some reserve for non-collectible accounts set off against the gross figure.

Inventories: This covers a multitude of problems. Like receivables, a detailed schedule is required as well as a physical inspection of the inventories by someone very familiar with the business. If the business is a manufacturing business, the work in process and method of valuation of the work in process must be carefully studied. What is the age of the inventory, by category? What method of inventory valuation is used—LIFO, FIFO or some other system? What would the replacement cost of the inventory be? Is all of the inventory necessary and to what extent would it be replaced in a well-managed business? What is the historical cost of the inventory? Is the inventory physically held by the business without restriction or is it subject to financing arrangements such as field warehouses? Is it subject to additional freight costs?

Fixed Assets

Plant: What is the physical condition of the plant? Will it be useful to the combined enterprise? What is the cost of maintaining the plant and what are the taxes and related costs? How is the plant valued—cost, market, or replacement cost? What mortgages or other financial restrictions exist which might impede either a sale of the plant, additional financing to remodel the plant, or use of the plant by divisions of the combined businesses not presently occupying the plant?

Machinery and Equipment: What is the physical condition of the machinery? How much of it is really necessary for a well-run business? What replacement schedule is going to be required? How is the machinery and equipment valued for balance sheet purposes?

Depreciation: Never forget that depreciation is *not* an attempt by accountants to reflect present fair value of a particular physical asset. It is merely a systematic way of charging the historical cost of the asset over the asset's useful life. A misunderstanding of this accounting principle can be very costly. In other words, remember that assets are normally carried on the balance sheet of a corporation at the *lower* of historical cost or their present fair market value, less a charge against the historical cost, so that at the end of the useful life of the depreciable asset, the asset will have no value (or if it can be sold for salvage, only a residual salvage value). An asset shown on the books of the corporation costing $100,000 and held for 10 years may then be shown on the books of the corporation, depending upon the type of asset, to have a value of only $1,500, but may have an actual market value of $500,000.

Pre-paid Expenses: These normally include insurance premiums, and payments made for taxes, license fees, and similar changes which are normally not refundable or refundable only on a "short rate" basis. Are these of any value to the continuing enterprise? If so, what value?

Goodwill: In 999 cases out of 1,000, this item means almost nothing to the purchaser. It is normally the residue of a premium paid by someone in the past for a business over the value of its tangible assets. For the acquiring corporation's planning purposes, this figure should be totally omitted as it distorts surplus, book value of shares, and the assets being acquired. Courts have defined "goodwill" as simply value paid for a going enterprise which indicates the probability that customers will return to the same old place. Value obviously should be given to goodwill, but this should reflect itself more directly in the negotiation for purchase price, discussed elsewhere, rather than as part of the basic data upon which a purchase price is to be based, namely the balance sheet of the corporation.

Liabilities

Current Liabilities

Accounts Payable: What is the age of the payable? Are there any disputes as to amount? Are the accounts payable to corporations or other business entities affiliated with any of the owners of the present business? When are the payables due?

Notes Payable: What are they? What are they for? What are the precise terms of the notes? To whom are they payable? Is this merely the current portion of notes, the balance of which is shown as a long-term liability? Will a sale or merger of the business cause an acceleration of the note?

Other Accrued Liabilities: These are probably liabilities for wages and taxes and similar items. Does this include any change for accrued vacation and sick leave? The accounting profession has recently determined that accrued vacation and sick leave should usually be set out as a liability, but often no provision is made on the balance sheet. This may be a significant figure, and whether the figure is significant or not, an acquiring corporation which attempts to contradict employees' understanding concerning their accrued vacations and sick leave is asking for serious employee relations difficulties. If the acquisition is to take place in the middle of a fiscal year, or at a time in which there may be accrued vacation or sick leave rights which carry over, you have a very interesting point of negotiation.

Long-Term Liabilities

Mortgage Payable: Look at an actual copy of the mortgage and note. Is there any signed loan agreement affecting the deal? What is the mortgage for? What is the amortization schedule of the note? Is the mortgage at a favorable rate? Will a sale or merger of the business cause an acceleration of the mortgage? If not, would a ltater sale of the particular property mortgaged to a third party as part of a restructuring of the corporation's assets cause an acceleration of the mortgage note?

Other Long-Term Liabilities: This is a catch-all, watch it. Get a detailed breakdown of these as well as the maturities. This can hide and lump together debts maturing one year and one day from the date of the balance sheet and debts maturing 99 years from the date of the balance sheet. There is obviously a vast operational difference. Again, get the documents themselves and determine any peculiarities of the loans. Don't rely upon hearsay or summaries. Often the existing management itself doesn't know of all of the provisions of old loan agreements and notes.

Remember also that there are sometimes liabilities which may not be reflected on the balance sheet. A lease of plant equipment may or may not be treated for balance sheet purposes as a purchase of the equipment or plant. There may be a large number of contracts involving substantial sums of money which are not shown as liabilities for accounting purposes, but which are practical liabilities of the business. A long-term contract to supply a raw material to a third party at a specified price may become an enormous liability. The day after the date of the balance sheet, the corporation may have been sued for $10,000,000. Depending upon the facts, the acquiring corporation will certainly want to take those kinds of liabilities into account. The day after the balance sheet an OSHA inspector may have insisted upon some changes in order to reduce sound in the plant which would cost $5,000,000 (or, which in fact may be technologically impossible at any cost). Smoke ou these types of liabilities early. What about agreements with labor unions? If there are none, have there recently been activities seeking to organize employees? Are there environmental problems? Are there zoning problems? If the business is an international enterprise, are there political and currency problems?

Net Worth

Common Stock: This is simply an historical item stating what portion of the initial or subsequent capital of the corporation was paid for the par value of the stock or its equivalent. The item is sometimes important insofar as it may limit technical recapitalization possibilities. It is of essentially little worth in valuing the company.

Paid-In Surplus: Under most corporate laws, this is technically "Capital Surplus." Normally it is the amount paid in "over and above" the par value for stock issued by the corporation. It can also arise as a result of certain transactions such as a revaluation of corporate assets. It is of some technical importance in the event of a recapitalization, but of little importance in valuing the business.

Retained Earnings: This is simply what's left over. If the corporation doesn't have any, that's of some importance. If it does have some, that in and of itself has little meaning.

2. How to Analyze and Project Cash Flow

One fundamental and continuous management decision is how to deploy existing cash and the determination of needs for new cash. It is absolutely essential that the acquiring corporation obtain a very good approximation of the cash flow requirements.

Cash flow is related to the concept of net income, but deals particularly with actual cash generated. For instance, a charge of $750,000 for depreciation of buildings, machinery, and equipment in a particular year is considered an actual charge against operating income, but would not reduce the cash available at the end of that year. Therefore, cash flow does not include any reduction with respect to depreciation or amortization. By the same token, capital expenditures which would not be charged against income, such as the purchase of a new piece of machinery or equipment for $300,000, obviously have a direct effect on available cash.

In a day in which much higher debt leverage exists in many corporations than was thought prudent in earlier times, it is very important that cash flow projections include a complete analysis of debt servicing and repayment schedules. In addition to existing debt amortization, there may be the amortization by the business of debt generated in the acquisition itself.

As a rule of thumb, a proper acquisition will usually be capable of carrying all of its existing and projected cash flow needs and retiring all acquisition debt within a five- to 10-year period.

Always remember that the cash flow projections are not merely an extrapolation of past earnings and cash requirements into the future, but will reflect new management policies. To a certain extent, there may be great economies as a result of the acquisition. On the other hand, standards of machinery and building maintenance, compensation, and other items may rise and create additional demands on cash flow.

All of this must be thoroughly analyzed and meticulously set down on an accounting spread sheet over a period of at least 10 years following the proposed acquisition.

Almost any target business will use the accrual basis of accounting as opposed to the cash basis. One of the first steps in developing the cash flow projections for the target company is to convert the important accrual basis accounts to a projected cash basis. The two accounts that normally have the most significant effect on the accrual basis of accounting are the accounts receivable and the accounts payable of the business.

In studying the balance sheet of the target company, a charge was made against the total amounts of receivables for non-collectibility. In preparing the cash flow statement, in effect, a charge is also made against the receivables for the anticipated delay in payment of those receivables.

In analyzing the cash flow from net receivables, the first step is to determine the average number of days required in the particular business for the collection of an account receivable. Assume that analysis of the target company shows that its receivables are paid, on the average, on the fiftieth day after billing. The second step is to determine the amount of one day's sales by simply dividing the net sales for the month or year or projected period by the number of days involved. The historical income statement will give a very good idea of what these sales have been. Management acumen will be needed to project what the sales will be after the acquisition. Having cranked in the projection of sales and the accounts receivable, management of the acquiring corporation will then be able to calculate the end-of-the month balances for the target company.

Having calculated the projected outstanding balance for receivables, it is then a simple matter to take the beginning balance for each month less the balance at the end of the month to determine an approximation of the monthly collections of accounts receivable by month. Such a month-by-month projection might show that collections of receivables will be down in the month of May and up in the month of October. A less detailed, but nonetheless essential calculation for receivables on a quarterly or annual basis should be performed for the entire 10-year period.

Detailed schedules need to be then made showing the relationship between purchase of inventory or raw materials and payment for such purchases. This schedule is very similar to that used for a calculation of receivables. It might look something like this:

Inventory and Raw Materials Acquisition and Accounts Payable

Month	Raw Materials Acquired	Other Inventory Acquired	Accounts Payable
JAN.	432,612	120,600	712,419
FEB.	305,436	93,068	945,602
MAR.	372,810	112,614	814,312
*			
*			
*			
DEC.	412,604	114,312	633,623

The actual schedule should be expanded by adding to the monthly needs for cash anticipated, such as payments for labor, manufacturing expense, other expenses such as advertising, taxes, utilities, and various services.

Finally, there should be added to the disbursements side of the analysis, anticipated payments for new fixed assets, payment of debt, and payments on leases and other contracts.

The entire result will be a projected cash flow statement which would include items such as:

Cash Sources:
1. Accounts Receivable Collected.
2. Other Income Such as Rent.

Cash Uses:
3. Payments for Purchases.
4. Payments for Labor and Services.
5. Payments for Raw Materials.

6. Payments for Other Inventory.
7. Payments for Other Expenses.
8. Payments for Fixed Assets.
9. Payments of Existing Accounts Payable.
10. Payments to Amortize Debt.
11. Payments on Leases and Contracts.
12. Payments of Taxes.

These items should be broken down month by month.

The same process should then continue through each of the 10 years immediately following the proposed acquisition. Obviously, the projection is more indefinite as the time after the proposed acquisition draws on.

The cash flow analysis will tell management of the acquiring corporation at least two things:

1. Does the acquisition probably make sense from a cash standpoint, projected over a reasonable period of time?
2. How shall it best structure any payments of acquisition debt, interest, or dividend over the 10-year period following the acquisition?

As to the first question, if the proposed acquisition is going to call for a serious commitment of cash by the acquiring corporation, not only over the short term, but over the medium range of, say, 10 years, this will have to be carefully weighed. There is usually little justification for an acquisition which continues to be a cash drain on the acquiring corporation. Short-term (*i.e.*, one or two years) cash drains are often the reasons for some of the best target companies being available. Medium, and certainly long-term cash drains, are the hallmark of the worst acquisitions ever made.

The structuring of acquisition debt amortization, interest, and any dividends, can be readily suggested after a careful cash flow analysis. If the cash flow is going to be very "tight" within the first few years after the acquisition, but then a combination of increased projected sales and economies is projected to put the business in a strong cash flow position, the management for the acquiring corporation might consider an interest-only debt acquisition deal with payments at the *end* of the first and second years, and with amortization of the debt only after the projected positive cash flow time arrives.

3. The Earnings Crystal Ball

Having developed figures as to estimated sales, costs of goods sold, gross profit margins, and debt amortization costs, these figures should then be carefully run through a future "pro forma" profit-and-loss statement for a period of 10 years to determine, with the highest accuracy possible, whether or not the proposed acquisition is going to be profitable for the acquiring company.

Such a statement requires a complete and realistic projection of gross sales for the target company throughout the period. The least useful type of sales projections are based strictly upon past performance. It is safe to assume that the acquiring company is going to add something new to the equation, and, for better or worse, the target company after acquisition will probably not remain static. Also, something more is required than a mere mechanical projection of the acquiring corporation's sales experience to the target company, since here again, the target company's experience is going to continue to have some effect upon future sales.

A more scientific method of calculating the sales increases is by a detailed breakdown by units or areas and a projection based upon those, tested against the unit or area experience of both the acquiring and the target company.

The accounting profession is currently wrestling with changing concepts of depreciation, and with inflation accounting. Particular industries also undergo sudden changes in accounting which can dramatically affect reported earnings. When insurance companies changed accounting methods a few years ago "earnings" were directly affected, but actual income often remained the source. When Union Carbide changed its accounting by increasing equipment depreciation life, capitalizing construction financing costs, and flowing-through investment credits, it was estimated that its 1980 earnings would increase over 70 percent, solely because of these accounting changes. The accounting basis for present, past, and future earnings must be carefully studied, and fully understood in any acquisition.

4. Book Value

The most useless standard bench-mark for determining the value of a target company is unadjusted "book value." This is nothing more than dividing the number of shares outstanding of a particular corporation into the total net worth of the company (that is, stated capital, capital surplus, and earned surplus). Many corporations' stocks have sold well below unadjusted book value just before they have filed for reorganization under the Bankruptcy Act.

On the other hand, one element of a valid test for the amount which can be profitably paid for a target company is the "adjusted book value." Adjusted book value reflects the actual present value of all assets, and all liabilities, as discussed earlier. Assets which have a fair market value greatly in excess of the value shown on the books, such as an old plant which has been fully depreciated on the books, but which has many useful years left and a high replacement cost, are adjusted to these new values. After these and other adjustments are made, the resulting "adjusted book value" can then constitute one element in determining the proper fair market value for the target company's shares.

5. Unneeded Assets—How to Plan for the Future

No financial analysis of the target company is complete unless a realistic appraisal of surplus assets is made. Very often the target company will hold real estate, or excess inventory, or excess machinery which will no longer be required after a merger or combination. A realistic cash value valuation of these assets when disposed of over a reasonable period of time, such as one year after the acquisition, is essential.

In making plans for such possible disposition of surplus property, careful attention must be given to the provisions of any existing loan agreements or other restrictive contracts. Often these will prohibit the disposal of certain major assets. One possibility is a reworking of these agreements based upon a stronger resulting company after the merger, but this type of decision should be made only after at least a tentative agreement to the plan has been arrived at with the lender involved.

There may be other practical problems which should be considered prior to a determination that property is surplus. For instance, there may be labor agreements which would hamper the combination of production facilities or the elimination of certain plants. Even if such agreements may not prohibit these things on their face, it is wise to consult labor counsel for the company if there seems to be any possibility that there may be an objection by the collective bargaining representative of the employees of the target company to any such disposition of assets.

In ABC Company's balance sheet discussed earlier, the management of the acquiring company determined that the "Real Estate Held for Future Plant Development" was readily marketable. The price which could be obtained upon sale of the land could more than pay for carrying the first three years' payments in an installment note purchase of the entire ABC Company. It goes without saying that if there are certain assets which the acquiring corporation plans to dispose of, the acquisition agreement must not seriously restrict the disposition of these assets.

6. The Advantages of Calculating Both Your Deal and His

In almost every serious acquisition, management for the acquiring corporation gives careful attention to the benefits of its own deal to their company. The really sophisticated acquiring corporation will also be thoroughly familiar with the transaction from the viewpoint of the shareholders of the target company. In negotiations, this is often critical in order to strike a workable bargain.

For instance, management of the acquiring corporation might see a particular transaction this way: average five years' past earnings, after tax—$200,000 per year; average five-year predicted earnings using better management techniques—$300,000 per year; proper multiple for target company prior to merger—six times earnings; proper multiple for combined corporations, with better management and more marketable security—10 times earnings; book value for all shares of the corporation outstanding as shown on the company's books—$900,000; and adjusted book value—$1,200,000.

The deal might look something like this:

Target Company's Deal

Value based on existing operations:	$ 200,000.00
	× 6
	$1,200,000.00
Stated Book Value:	+ 900,000.00
	$2,100,000.00
	÷ 2
Fair Market Value =	$1,050,000.00

Acquiring Corporation's Deal

Value based on projected operations:	$ 300,000.00
	× 10
	$3,000,000.00
Adjusted Book Value:	+ 1,200,000.00
	$4,200,000.00
	÷ 2
Value to Acquiring Corporation =	$2,100,000.00

The implications for the acquiring corporation (and the acquired corporation) at the bargaining table are obvious. It is amazing how seldom both sides really do their homework and examine a deal through the eyes of the other side.

Also, when calculating the other person's deal, serious consideration should be given to particular needs of the other side. For instance, if the deal is to be a tax-free merger, it is important to know whether or not marketability of the new shares is of critical importance. Do the shareholders of the acquired corporation have in their mind a bailout at some point in either the immediate or medium-term future? If so, the creation of special classes of stock, limitations on registration rights, and the breadth of market in the acquiring corporation's traded shares are all going to be of great importance. The importance of these features may translate themselves into a smaller "price" for the target company.

On the other hand, often the shareholders of the target company will want to have a firm income stream over some period of time (*e.g.,* in the retiring principal shareholder situation). They may wish to have a moderately high degree of safety, plus a steady stream of income. This situation often lends itself to the payment of a relatively low permissible interest in an installment sale plus principal payments to each shareholder in amounts calculated so as to realize only part of the gain in the early years.

The possibilities for meeting particular needs and goals sought by the target company (or for that matter the acquiring company) are indefinite. To create a workable deal in your particular situation, it is absolutely essential that, early in the deal, management use a sharp pencil not only on its own company's deal, but also the other party's deal.

C. TACTICS AND PLANNING IN THE BUSINESS ACQUISITION

1. Importance of Analyzing the Parties' "Needs"

Attempting to negotiate a business acquisition without consideration of the needs and goals of the other party to a negotiation is like hiking through a swamp when one could follow a well-marked trail. Either route may have difficulties. One may not reach the end of the journey safely in any event. But if the goal is to get from Point A to Point B, needlessly tramping off into a swamp is foolish.

The understanding of the other partys' needs is absolutely essential in any type of negotiation. On a recent thoughtful analysis of an international crisis, Professor Roger Fisher, who teaches international negotiation at Harvard Law School, indicated that the United States was making two errors, reacting rather than acting positively and ignoring the interests of our adversaries. Professor Fisher then stated the rule, which applies as much to business as to governmental negotiation:

> The cure . . . is to understand our interests and those of our adversary, and then to find measures that will solve their problems in a way that solves ours . . .

This basic principle of negotiation applies not only to business negotiation, but to international and other negotiations. President John Kennedy once reviewed a book on military history and distilled the following formula for negotiating:

> Keep strong if possible. In any case, keep cool. Have unlimited patience. Never corner an opponent, and always assist him to save face. Put yourself in his shoes—so as to see things through his eyes. . . .

There are two separate levels of needs of the other party which must be understood in negotiation. The first has already been discussed in the section on Goal Analysis. These are the more or less rational goals of the other party in the transaction. They may not be articulated. They may even be contradictory, but they tend to have a rational as opposed to emotional basis. These must be determined by use of a careful scouting report as well as a constant and perceptive use of feedback during negotiations.

An example of this type of need or goal would be the need to assure continued employment until retirement age for the founder of the business which was the target company in the acquisition. Again, the need itself has two separate elements—one is the need for an income on which to live, the second is the need to retain a visible management role. Other typical needs or goals would include concern for the welfare of the employees of the business, concern for the community in which the business is located, concern that the current quality of the product is maintained, and concern that the same philosophy of management be followed.

At a separate level are the motives which directly affect the particular person doing the negotiation for the target company. Gerard I. Nierenberg, in the *Art of Negotiating* (Hawthorne Books, 1968), quotes Professor Maslow of Brandeis University and indicates that there are seven categories of needs which are basic factors in human behavior:

   (i) Physiological needs;
  (ii) Safety and security needs;
 (iii) Social and belonging need;
 (iv) Esteem needs;
  (v) Needs for self-actualization;
 (vi) Needs to know and understand; and
(vii) Aesthetic needs.

Professor Maslow's findings are also discussed in Dale Carnegie and associates, *Managing Through People* (Simon and Schuster, 1975).

In the merger or acquisition negotiation, these types of needs are a big ingredient. It will be helpful to look at each of these "needs" more closely.

(i) Physiological Needs. More negotiations have been won by "fanny fatigue" than anyone would care to admit. There comes a point in any negotiation, once the basic commitment has been made to negotiate and to attempt to strike a deal, at which medium-sized negotiating points become inconsequential. Take the normal question in a business negotiation concerning the time provided in the acquisition agreement for the warranties of the target company to expire. The target company, naturally, would like to hold the period of warranty to the shortest possible time. The goal of the acquiring corporation is to extend the warranties period to the full limits allowed by applicable statutes of limitation. Suppose that X Company has been negotiating to acquire Widget Company over a period of several months. Suppose that all major points of the deal have been resolved except the length of warranty and whether or not 90 or 120 days after the closing will be given in which to collect receivables before a charge for uncollectibility is made against the price. The odds are better than 80 percent that, if the decision is placed by the acquiring corporation at the end of a long negotiating session and after clear demonstration of good faith and reasonableness on other points, the target company will trade the time of its warranties for the time to collect accounts receivable, although the time to collect accounts receivable is almost meaningless (that is, the difference between 90 and 120 days) while the time for the warranty is very substantial (for instance, whether or not the time for making warranty extends past the time when the Internal Revenue Service would have an opportunity to audit the target company and propose tax adjustments). Timing and a dedicated use of "fanny fatigue" make the difference.

(ii) Safety and Security Needs. It is a rare situation in which successful negotiations in an acquisition can take place when the negotiator for the target company has the impression that immediately after the closing he will be fired. The acquiring company

has very little control over the negotiator chosen by the target company, but if in good faith the acquiring company does intend to continue the employment and position of the negotiator after the acquisition, and does see an important role for the regotiator and his colleagues in the combined operation, this should certainly be made known, at least indirectly to the negotiator.

At an even more elementary level, the initial negotiation upon which the determination is made essentially to strike a deal or forget it, should be made in a quiet and serene location after all sides are well-fed and unhurried. This is just the reverse of the "fanny fatigue" technique. In other words, when the "basic deal or no" is at stake, the negotiator for the other side should feel totally safe, secure, and unhurried. When the commitment has been made and your position is basically strong, and details are involved, time, pressure, and fatigue may work in your favor.

(iii) Social and Belonging Needs: The negotiator for the other side should be convinced that he will personally belong and be appreciated in the new organization, and that his colleagues and the enterprises they have built in the target company will be part of a continuing team.

(iv) Esteem Needs: This is obvious but very frequently overlooked. To offer to hire the founding president of the target company for a period of five years after the acquisition as an assistant vice president of the acquiring company at a salary of $100,000 per year, has less chance of being accepted by the founding president than an offer to hire the same person for a period of five years as *president* of the Widget Division or subsidiary at a salary of $65,000.

(v) Needs for Self-Actualization: This involves the need to recognize one's potential. Perhaps the most concrete example of the fulfillment or non-fulfillment of this need in negotiations concerning acquisitions is the ability of the acquiring corporation to visualize and meet not only the personal needs of the individual negotiators on behalf of the target company, but also their perception of the needs of the target company itself. Negotiations should recognize the target company's potential and its likelihood of greater success as part of a merged organization than as a continuing separate entity.

(vi) Needs to Know and Understand: These needs are universal. Meeting these needs involves communication and patience and lack of a condescending attitude. In the first instance, it is absolutely essential that your own negotiating team have good communications and that everyone understand the basic position of your organization. Otherwise there is a tendency on the part of individual members of a negotiating team to take inconsistent positions and reduce the negotiating position to the lowest common denominator. It is also important that the true position of your entity be successfully communicated to the other side.

Many acquisitions fail because the position of one party, which if properly explained to the other side would have been acceptable, is not explained or is explained in a manner leading to untrue conclusions or in a threatening fashion. If you want to seek a business acquisition negotiation break down promptly, let the negotiator for the acquiring company indicate that there is going to be ruthless elimination of jobs and existing management in the acquired company. Strangely enough, this is true even if the negotiators for the target company recognize the need for elimination of unnecessary personnel, and even though the probability of this happening can be inferred from a total unwillingness on the part of the acquiring corporation to give any type of employment contracts or assurances. A simple (but true) statement that "we never enter into employment contracts in this type of acquisition," is usually acceptable. But a direct statement to the effect that many "heads will roll shortly after the closing" is nearly always fatal to negotiations. In fact, if such a direct statement is not fatal, the acquiring corporation itself should have second thoughts. In other words, the loyalty of the neogtiating teams to their organization, and perhaps the loyalty of the personnel throughout the organization is brought into question.

(vii) Aesthetic Needs: Finally, Maslow considers aesthetic needs. One may simply observe that a negotiation in a bare room with a bare light bulb on a three-legged stool brings different assumptions and results than a negotiation in a well-lighted, comfortable conference room with a minimum of distractions. One could also note that many a target company has lost a favorable acquisition because its plants or warehouses or offices were "dirty" or "disorganized." It is amazing how often a spotless plant, even with antiquated machinery, creates a favorable impression on the most hard-nosed and sophisticated inspectors.

2. The Scouting Report—Use of Available Public History

Behind every good business acquisition negotiation is a thorough scouting report. Sources for the report are infinite—these include financial publications, local papers, financial reporting services, SEC Forms 10K, and professional investigations.

It hardly needs to be said that it is critically important in negotiating to know of the past and recent problems and successes of the other side. Is there a cash crunch? Is there a cash surplus? Are the personnel well-qualified by background and training? Is the company respected in its geographic community and its business community? Is the product respected? What type of consumer comments have been obtained? What type of labor relations history or reputation is there? Have there been past or recent scandals of a type that would undermine the integrity of the business, financial or otherwise? Are there any known idiosyncrasies or difficulties of the proposed members of the negotiating team for the other side? What is the age and background of the principal officers and negotiators?

Let's put it this way. If you are playing in a sandlot football game, scouting will be either non-existent or primeval. There may be some vague idea that you must know if your opponent has a 7-foot end or a 300-pound tackle, but basically, the scouting report and the game take place simultaneously. In high school or college, if the game is a serious one, there will be an exchange of game films and a careful study, at least from secondary sources, of the strengths and weaknesses of the opponent. For an important professional game, especially one such as the Super Bowl, there is a thorough review of all game films, there are first-hand scouting reports obtained from recent games, public statements as to injuries, and an endless study of plays and defensive signals. All of these are carefully analyzed. Treat your business acquisition negotiation as the Super Bowl. It is too important to be relegated to the sandlot.

D. CARE AND FEEDING OF LAWYERS AND ACCOUNTANTS

The executive will find himself or herself associated with at least two peculiar species of advisors throughout the process of negotiating and closing the business acquisition. These are the lawyer and the accountant. Both can perform services of enormous value in the transaction. In fact, only the most foolhardy business would attempt an acquisition without their services at some point in the transaction.

1. What a Lawyer or Accountant Can't Do—The Executive's Responsibility

There are two primary ways to err in the use of lawyers and accountants in an acquisition. The first is to fail to use them at all, or to give them such a minor, technical role that they are simply asked, say, to determine whether a written agreement would be legally binding, or whether financial statements seem to be internally consistent. At the other extreme, and far more common for the small or medium-sized acquisition, is too much reliance on professional advisors in areas which are essentially business areas.

Perhaps it is because a good acquisition lawyer will have experience in acquisitions much more frequently than such an executive. Perhaps it is because the lawyers tend to talk in incomprehensible language, and the accountants in incomprehensible figures. In any event, it is absolutely essential for the business leader directing either the acquiring or target corporation's negotiations to determine his organization's business goals independently of his professional advisors, and for the executive to remain totally in charge of the tough business decisions throughout the acquisition process. For instance, it would be up to the professional advisors to indicate that a certain structuring of an acquisition transaction could give rise to accelerated income tax deductions for the enterprise by increasing depreciation and other expenses. It would be up to the business leader to determine whether or not such reduced federal income taxes would be more desirable than higher profits to report to shareholders.

It would be up to the professional advisors to indicate the legal effect of entering into a five-year employment agreement with the chief executive officer of the target company. It would be up to the business leader of the acquiring corporation to determine whether or not such an agreement would be wise, not only economically, but in view of possible changes which might be required in order to integrate the target company into the larger organization.

2. The Proper Use of the Lawyer

Having said all that, the lawyer familiar with business acquisition matters can still be of invaluable service if properly utilized. To the corporate acquisition department of a large business which is involved in many acquisitions every year, the lawyer undertakes very specific services such as drafting the basic agreement and any letter of intent, suggesting the actual form of the acquisition from a standpoint of legal and tax considerations, as well as the preparation and closing of the acquisition documents themselves. To the small or medium-size company which is generally unfamiliar with the details of an acquisition, the lawyer may also serve as a valuable guide to the entire process by raising planning questions to be answered by management or other professional advisors, and by suggesting techniques for management in structuring their transaction.

Again, there can be either an under-use or an over-use of lawyers by executives. Under-use is a failing normally associated with either the very small transaction, or the very large organization which attempts to perform the legal function "in-house" as much as possible.

A typical "under-use" telephone conversation might go this way:

Corporate President: Mr. Jackson please. . . . Bill, this is Sam Wilson with Consolidated Widgets.

Lawyer: Sam, How are you?

Corporate President: Fine. Say, Bill, I'm not calling you about those wills that Mary and I have been studying for the last couple of years. We still want to get those executed someday, but just haven't had a chance. I'm calling to see if you would be able to give us a hand with a merger.

Lawyer: Tell me something about it.

Corporate President: You are probably familiar with Ajax Corporation which is located about 40 miles down state. They are the fifth largest manufacturers of widget gauges in the country. We've had a very pleasant relationship with them over the years and know their product quite well. I've played golf with their president almost every good weekend for the last five years. We've pretty well agreed on the details, but I'd like you to look at the deal from our side.

Lawyer: Sure. When shall we get together?

Corporate President: Well. I've got a contract their lawyer has drawn up that I think sets out the deal we've agreed to. It isn't very long or complicated and I was wondering whether or not I could see you this afternoon.

Lawyer: I'm sorry, but I have a closing in another transaction which is
                               scheduled for this afternoon and may run on into this evening.
                               Could we get together first thing tomorrow morning?

Corporate President: Well, I suppose so, but that doesn't leave us much time. We had
                               hoped to be able to sign the agreement tomorrow afternoon
                               because their fiscal year ends this week and we'd like to close
                               then.

While the above conversation may be somewhat extreme, it does represent an
all-too-frequent, and all-too-unsophisticated view held by some corporate management
of the role of a lawyer in an acquisition. Obviously, the fundamental parameters of the
transaction have already been set, and any negotiating to be done will be done from a
posture of nit-picking and delay. The lawyer is relegated to the role of proofreader for the
other side. One of the most valuable tools, that of preparing the first draft (especially for
the acquiring corporation), has already been discarded. Of course, the selling side
usually wants a very brief agreement. Of course, warranties will be held to a minimum
"in order to keep the agreement short." Of course, they will use the "best financial
statements available" rather than a stub audit.

At the other extreme, the conversation may go something like this:

Corporate President: May I speak to Mr. Jackson please?
                               Bill, this is Sam Wilson over at Consolidated Widgets.

Lawyer: Hello Sam.

Corporate President: Sam, we are thinking about looking at one or two businesses to
                               acquire and wonder if you would be able to help out.

Lawyer: Sure, tell me something about them.

Corporate President: Well, we've got a list of 10 or 15 businesses and we'd like you to
                               draw us up an acquisition agreement which we might be able to
                               use. We plan to have a business strategy meeting with our de-
                               partment heads Wednesday of next week at 9:00 a.m. and hope
                               you can join us then.

Here, the basic business determination as to whether or not an acquisition is even
desirable has not been made. To ask a lawyer to draft an agreement in such a situation is
like asking a good architect to draft plans and specifications for a house, without
specifying the lot, location, materials, or cost. It can be done, but it is probably
meaningless.

What is the proper use of the lawyer? Obviously, the use is going to depend to some extent on the recent familiarity of the executive with acquisition matters, as well as the in-house capability of the particular client. If the acquiring corporation has a full-time legal staff and a separate merger and acquisition department, the utilization of outside counsel can be greatly reduced. Interestingly enough, lawyers in private practice dealing with acquisition matters are invariably used in an acquisition by a sophisticated acquisition department, because an independent lawyer and his firm can give advice which simply has a different perspective than that of the business organization itself, despite fine legal qualifications of the staff.

The proper use of the lawyer in a business acquisition, in a typical case, should probably involve the following steps:

a) If the client has not been involved recently in acquisition matters, there should be a preliminary discussion session in which the executive's acquisition team becomes generally familiar with the acquisition process, its possibilities, the trade-offs involved in any deal, and the time schedule.

b) The executives themselves should then prepare scouting reports and do the necessary analysis, perhaps assisted by brief meetings with the lawyers or several telephone discussions.

c) After the basic homework has been done and the decision to pursue the acquisition further has been made, the executives should make initial contact with the target company, without the lawyer (except in extreme situations, such as when the target company is already involved in a legal proceeding such as reorganization under the Bankruptcy Act, anti-trust litigation, or a bitter estate dispute).

d) The executive should then indicate to the lawyer the outlines for the deal. Nothing should be signed that is not drafted by the lawyer. The lawyer, if it is desired by the two corporations, can then prepare a brief letter of intent setting out the outlines of the business transactions. A typical form of letter of intent is found in Appendix M. At this stage, further conferences may be held between counsel and the management personnel themselves in order to discuss and weigh various legal trade-offs which will assume greater proportions in the final transaction. For instance, the pros and cons of any covenant not to compete should be discussed and decided at this stage, before even a letter of intent is executed.

e) After the letter of intent is executed, there should be a meeting involving, for the first time, lawyers, accountants, and negotiating teams for both the acquiring and target companies. At this meeting, the basic ground rules for the transaction should be set forth.

f) Your lawyer should then prepare the acquisition agreement and submit it with comment and revision to the other side's lawyer. A typical agreement for a cash sale of a business appears as Appendix J.

g) Conferences should be held either between the lawyers, or if the business points are involved, with the entire negotiating team, to iron out the final draft of the agreement.

h) Necessary accounting and business determinations before the closing should be

made, and necessary approval (if required) from regulatory authorities such as the
SEC and FTC should be obtained.
i) The closing should be held under supervision of your counsel.

There it is. There may be variations, and there undoubtedly will be. But it is
amazing, how many proper business acquisitions follow almost to the letter the foregoing chart. If you follow such a chart as a basic guideline, you should be able to
properly utilize your lawyer.

3. The Proper Use of the Accountant

Much of the investigation and many of the warranties involved in any acquisitions
transaction will be based upon accounting figures. Any particular accountant may be of
value to the advisor as to many different areas of the acquisitions transaction, but the
essential roles for the accountant are twofold. First, the accountant should advise and
assist with an analysis of the other company's financial information. Second, the
accountant should prepare "pro forma" accounting information; that is, profit-and-loss
statements and balance sheets based upon the assumption that the acquisition had already
taken place. No matter how much one studies operating and balance sheet figures, until
they are actually combined on paper, the impact of the acquisition will be difficult, if not
impossible, to assess.

The accountant is the proper person to at least supervise the analysis of financial
data provided by the other company. Accountants are in a position to calculate or
approximate the effect of the accounting assumptions made and methods elected by the
other party's accountant in preparing the financial statements furnished to you. Since
accounting remains almost as much of an art as a science, it is not only comforting but
often essential to have your own expert interpret the other side's financial data.

In preparing pro forma statements (as well as actual statements after the acquisition), the accountants will normally focus on two chief sub-areas: (1) the comparability
of the accounting data, and (2) the rules to be followed in accounting for the particular
business combination.

John L. Harvey in "Accounting to Merge By" in *Management Guides to Mergers*
(Wiley-Interscience: New York, 1969) lists the following areas which normally are
involved in adjustments in order to make accounting comparable:

1. Inventory and Asset Valuation (*e.g.*, FIFO or LIFO method for inventory valuation).
2. Research and Developments Cost (*e.g.*, capitalized or expensed).
3. Pension Plans (*e.g.*, is there any actuarial deficit?).
4. Executive Incentive Plans (*e.g.*, possible future dilution of stock through stock
   option exercise).
5. Income Taxes (*e.g.*, are any deferred?).
6. Extraordinary Items (*e.g.*, does income include unusual items such as the sale of an
   investment or other items not related to the operations of the business?).

Perhaps the most fundamental technical determination to be made by the accountant in an acquisitions transaction is whether or not the acquisition will qualify for "a pooling of interest" treatment. There are two fundamental ways to treat a corporate acquisition for accounting purposes: (1) "purchase" or (2) "pooling."

In the actual business world, it is more customary to think of an acquisition as a "purchase." That is, the acquiring corporation acquires a particular group of assets which constitute a complete business enterprise. If accounting treatment follows that philosophy, then the value of what is paid for the asset (*e.g.,* stock, other securities, cash) is allocated among the various assets purchased and those assets are then shown on the books of the acquiring corporation. One very practical effect of using the "purchase" method is that, almost certainly, there will be a premium over the market value of tangible assets paid for the business enterprise. If there is, this premium will be allocated to intangible assets, and if there are no intangible assets having determinable lives (such as a patent), then the entire surplus value will be lumped into an asset known as "goodwill." As discussed earlier, goodwill, in this context, boils down to a "soft" figure equal to whatever is left over and cannot be allocated to other assets. The bad news is that accountants will amortize the entire "goodwill" figure in present-day acquisitions over no less than a 40-year life. Therefore, at least 2.5 percent (1/40) of this figure will be charged each year against income of the corporation after the acquisition.

Even if all of the purchases were allocable to particular assets, this will often mean a write-up of the value of those assets for book purposes, and the write-up will itself often create heavy depreciation charges which will be charged against book income. The words "book income" should be emphasized because, unless the transaction is a taxable one for the acquired corporation or its shareholders, the depreciation will not offset income for income tax purposes, since the Internal Revenue Service will not recognize a higher tax basis of those assets.

Because of disadvantages in using the "purchase" method, the acquiring corporation will seek to have the acquisition treated as a "pooling of interest." This simply means that the businesses are treated as though they are in fact a combination of two going enterprises. In a pooling, the assets, liabilities, net worth, income, and losses of each enterprise are combined. Assets will have the same value on the new balance sheet as they had on the old balance sheet, generally speaking. This treatment can give almost miraculous results to an income statement, especially on a per-share basis.

The use of pooling is now very restricted by the accounting profession, but it can be used if certain criteria are met. These include:

a) Each combining company has been autonomous for at least two years and is independent;

b) The combination takes place according to a plan and within one year after the plan is initiated;

c) Only ordinary voting common stock is used;

d) No distribution or recapitalization of either corporation has taken place within two years;

e) No unusual acquisition of treasury stock for the combination takes place;

f) The target company's shareholders' relative ownership remains the same;

g) No stock voting rights of the target shareholders are restricted; and

h) The combination is resolved at the closing and no contingent stock is used. (See SEC Accounting Release No. 146M.)

A good accountant is absolutely essential in analyzing the transaction. Such an accounting adviser can often point out new accounting trends. These might include:

1. Advice on the preparation of financial statements for a closely-held concern short of a full audit. Effective July 1, 1979, the American Institute of Certified Public Accountants adopted new standards which allow an accountant to say more than was previously allowed in the letter accompanying financial statements that have not undergone an audit. In many cases, the accountant can perform or supervise many of the same tests which would be required in an audit, but eliminate such time consuming procedures as an independent verification of assets and liabilities. The accountant can advise as to the desirability within a particular business of the use of such financial statements instead of a full audit.

   There are two standards short of a full audit now allowed by the AICPA. The first is called "Compilation." This means that the CPA puts information furnished by the client corporation into financial statement form without verifying it. The other is called "Review." In a "Review," the CPA not only places the information in financial statement form, but also makes inquiries of management and performs certain analysis to obtain "limited assurance" that no material changes are required.

   A recent study by a national accounting firm (see September 12, 1980, *Daily Report for Executives,* p. K–1) determined that bankers were accepting the new, limited financial statements from about 25 percent of their previously audited small customers. Where the size of the loans are not too large, and the capital structure seems basically sound, existing small business bank customers should certainly explore the less expensive "Review" or "Compilation" statements.

2. The accounting professional can advise as to the effects of the new Financial Accounting Standards Board requirements (effective for fiscal years ending after December 25, 1979) for accounting adjustments to reflect the impact of inflation on financial statements.

3. The Financial Accounting Standards Board has recently proposed that, effective June 15, 1980, there would be specific criteria for recording pre-acquisition contingencies of purchased businesses, with rules as to whether such contingencies were recorded as part of the acquiring corporation's purchase price or as elements of post-acquisition net income.

4. Timing and Homework—How to Avoid Unnecessary Professional Time and Expense

Appraisal, accounting, and legal expenses in any acquisition transaction can be substantial.

On the one hand, it is penny-wise and pound-foolish to get a poor appraisal, or utilize poor accounting assistance, or rely upon poor legal advice and draftsmanship in order to save a few dollars. On the other hand, even with corporations having large in-house professional departments to provide most of these services, there can be an inordinate waste of time by overutilizing professionals. After all, the executive is the captain of the acquisition ship and must choose the destination, course, and speed. The professionals in an acquisition are, depending upon the particular stage, either the chief engineer or the pilot, but the basic decisions are for the captain.

What should the corporate official charged with the responsibility for a particular acquisition do to properly utilize professionals?

In the first place, the corporate official should be generally familiar with the professional principles to be applied. A review of pertinent sections of this and other guidebooks to acquisitions is a logical starting place before any major acquisition. The corporate official should understand that the different professionals involved in a transaction will bring different concepts to the transaction.

For instance, take the concept of price or value. Obviously, an appraiser is the expert in this area. It should be his job to determine the "fair market value" of particular assets or groups of assets. By "fair market value" he means that price which a willing buyer and a willing seller, both under no compulsion to buy or sell, would pay for the particular asset. On the other hand, accountants will consider the asset "value" to be reflected on the books to be the lower of cost or market. By this the accountant means the lower of either the historical asset cost, less depreciation, or the present fair market value of the asset. In inflationary times such as these, this usually means that the book value of an asset will be well below the present fair market value. The lawyer's view of value is still different. The acquisitions lawyer will approach the matter often from the standpoint of the planned use of the particular asset by the acquiring corporation and the method of use to seek to assure that this "value" will remain available for the acquiring corporation. For instance, of what "value" is the wrong kind of inventory, accounts receivable to be collected only by losing the customer, or real estate which cannot be used or sold in the current economic climate?

The same type of situation can arise in many other areas of any acquisition. In addition to these differences in professional approach, it must be understood that the function of the professionals varies greatly. An appraiser is theoretically a dispassionate official giving an outside view of a determinable result. That is, an appraiser views himself in the same light as a surveyor. The surveyor simply marks off what is there, using established professional rules and measurements.

An accountant views himself usually as performing somewhat the same function in that a certified public accountant is theoretically an outside person applying impartial "generally accepted accounting principles" to the books of accounting of the business. When the certified public accountant for the other corporation provides you with his certificate and financial statements, his role is that of an independent professional. In addition to that impartial function, of course, accountants in fact have broad leeway in the principles to be applied, and may suggest entirely legitimate methods of accounting and treatment which will, in fact, cause differences in results.

The lawyer is certified as an "officer of the court" by a particular state or other governmental entity, and is limited by historical, ethical, and legal principles. On the other hand, the lawyer is, in both theory and practice, an advocate and extension of his client. Within the bounds of propriety, it is not up to the lawyer to draft a contract equally favorable to all parties and to the public, it is up to the lawyer to prepare a contract most favorable to this client. An ethical, competent acquisitions lawyer will not take advantage of less experienced counsel on the opposite side of a transaction, but he will attempt to translate relative bargaining strength into the acquisitions structure and documents. For instance, warranties in an acquisitions may well reflect the relative enthusiasm and bargaining strength of the parties in the deal.

Unless the executive charged with directing an acquisition understands these differences in functions and approaches of the various professional advisors, meetings with the professional are apt to be punctuated with "Why don't you guys get your act together?" and "Can't you guys agree on anything?"

Given an understanding of the difference in role, here are some random suggestions that the busy executive should keep in mind in dealing with professionals:

1. Ask the lawyer "What's the worst that can happen?"—This will probe possibilities which may not have occurred to the executive, but which the lawyer may assume the executive realizes. For instance, the "ironclad" note secured by a mortgage may be deferred indefinitely or even be entirely wiped out in a later bankruptcy proceeding.
2. Ask the accountant "What other financial information do we need?"—Often there will be subschedules, working papers, tax returns, and detailed books and records which will be available for the asking, and which will allow you and your accounting advisor to determine more clearly the correctness of financial statements furnished by the other party.
3. Ask the appraiser "What are the details of each 'comparable sale'?"—One method of determining the fair market value of an asset is to look at a series of sales of properties which are "comparable" to the property involved. Often, if there has not been much recent sales activity, these sales are anything but "comparable." A sale six years ago may not reflect the current situation at all. This does not mean that the appraiser is doing a poor job. It simply means that he has very rough guideposts to use. You should know this.
4. Where possible consider the following rules when utilizing professionals:
    a) If the professional is called in for a specific part of the project, such as an appraisal: first make sure that you have done your homework in understanding the professional principles involved; second, assemble all of the data which you have available for the professional; third, define the problem as precisely as possible for the professional; fourth, give the professional a reasonable amount of time in which to work—don't ask an appraiser to complete his appraisal in three days unless there is literally no other possibility; and fifth, stay out of the way and let the professional do his work.
    b) If the professional involved is more concerned with the acquisition transaction as a continuing matter, such as the accountant or the lawyer: first, do your homework and understand the principles which he will probably apply—for

instance, review the tax effect of various types of reorganizations, review the securities effects, review the accounting effect in broad outline; second, contact the professional early in the game and get *preliminary* advice—the hazard here is that the professional will not be brought in soon enough to help the actual overall structuring of the deal; third, after the professional has given basic direction to the transaction, do not utilize the professional for purely business portions of the negotiations.

In this intermediate stage of negotiations when general levels for compensation for a continuing executive are decided, particular relationships with customers are discussed, and inspection of manufacturing plants takes place except in the rarest of circumstances, a few meetings with, or telephone calls to, the professional are much more effective (and much less costly) than asking, say, the lawyer to attend detailed sessions reviewing inventory control procedures.

Finally, when the basic transaction has been molded through long discussions, allow a day or so to completely brief your counsel and accountant on the entire transaction before putting your counsel at the negotiating table to work with you in hammering out a final legal document. All too many transactions involve a more or less lifeless form-book type agreement without any feel of the underlying particular business acquisition involved. Such agreements usually indicate either that many matters of substance were never discussed by the business executive or there exist many oral "side agreements" which will come back to haunt business executives (and their counsel) for years.

There was a recent transaction in which the agreement contained a rather specific provision about reimbursement for a particular cost to be incurred by the acquiring corporation for one year after the closing. The agreement had been hammered out in frantic hours just before the signing. Even though top executives of the corporation involved had been thoroughly briefed by the attorneys and their own fellow executives as to the contract provisions, it became apparent a few months after the closing that top executives of the acquiring corporation were preoccupied with other business decisions at the time. The contract simply didn't reflect their interpretation of the "handshake" side deal. The result was misunderstandings and strained interpretations of the clear words of the agreement for more than a year after closing.

To summarize, do not attempt to save a few dollars by avoiding use of lawyers, accountants, appraisers, and other professionals as required, but do them and your treasurer the courtesy of doing your homework first, and using professionals not to make decisions, but to advise you in your decisions, so that your transaction can be as rewarding and surprise-free as possible.

Chapter 4

How To Negotiate
And Evaluate Your Deal

A. NEGOTIATING THE DEAL

Most Americans are uncomfortable in negotiation. What is a well-conditioned instinct in the Mideast or South America, the art of negotiation is normally a painfully learned alien art to most Americans. The reason can be summed up in one word—impatience. The same qualities which are so admirable in building a business and building a nation, qualities such as drive, determination, decisiveness and, yes, even impatience, become strongly negative factors in most negotiations for business acquisitions.

In the first place, there is almost a natural rhythm to any transaction as important as buying or selling a business.

> *Example:* Swartz has a successful office supply business in the capital city of his state. He wants to acquire a similar business for cash or cash and notes in the principal southern city in the state. Southern Office fills the bill perfectly. It has a similar philosophy of management, it is successful, it is ideally located, and it has an appropriate share and reputation in its community.
>
> As a strategic matter, Swartz is much better off making a simple, unanxious inquiry at some appropriate time of the management of Southern Office to the effect that "When you think it would be to your advantage to sell, I certainly hope you will talk with us, since we have the same philosophy of business." The odds are, that a patient, long-term, strategic move will eventually result in some discussions, perhaps even serious negotiations over the course of years for the acquisition of Southern Office.
>
> On the other hand, a direct, impatient, and anxious approach to Southern Office, "We'll give you $1,000,000 for your business if we can acquire it before

the end of the month,'' will rarely result in positive negotiations, at least in the absence of some strategic intelligence indicating that the timing is right.

Suppose that Southern Office has just had a record sales year on the heels of constantly expanding sales and profits and that things look even rosier for the next three years. Suppose further that the head of Southern Office's children have been with Southern Office several years and are now clearly showing an ability to handle the business and have an interest in gradually acquiring the founding shareholder's shares. Suppose further that, after many years of toiling in the organization, the President of Southern Office has just learned that he will, in two years time, be elected as the national head of the independent office supply organization (provided that his firm is still independent).

All of the signals are wrong—the family, the financial, and the personal. All indicate that this is not the time to make the best deal with Southern Office. In fact, unless someone offers a disproportionately high deal, it is very unlikely that Southern Office can be acquired.

Although the point is quite simple, it is often overlooked. As Ecclesiastes said, ''There is a time and a season for everything.'' Spend your valuable negotiating time and resources where they are most likely to pay off, and to fit in with your own strategic plan.

Before considering the letter of intent and other steps in actually realizing your deal, it might be well to consider a few tactical negotiating points, and even a few thoughts on the nuts and bolts of negotiation.

In the past few years, there have been several good books and seminars on negotiation in general, and negotiation in the business context in particular. One of the best has already been mentioned, Nierenberg's *The Art of Negotiating*. This has now been updated and is available in paperback under the title *Fundamentals of Negotiating* (Hawthorn Books, 1973).

Most successful negotiations for business acquisitions will have three common points:

1. Common and conflicting goals of the parties to the negotiation;
2. A need for a non-zero sum result; and
3. Imperfect information.

These three points are important enough to consider further.

1. Common and Conflicting Goals

We have already discussed the need for analysis of not only your goals but also the other side's goals in Chapter 3. This cannot be overemphasized. The greatest difference between an expert in business acquisition negotiations and a novice is that the expert carefully analyzes goals and plans the negotiation. This does not mean that everything goes strictly according to schedule, nor that all of the expert side's goals are reached. It simply means that the expert has a plan. It means that the expect recognizes the priority of goals so that, in the midst of negotiation, the expert knows where he is going.

2. Non-Zero Sum Results

In any successful negotiation, both parties must feel that they have "won" something. A zero sum game in sociology is a fairly complicated concept which often boils down to the fact that, for every advantage to one side, there is an equal and opposite disadvantage to the other side.

In the world of sports, for instance, bridge is a zero sum game. There are 13 tricks to be won. Every trick taken by one side is not taken by the other side. On the other hand, golf is not a zero sum game. There are winners and losers, but no absolute or finite number of strokes (as anyone who has seen my golf game can readily attest).

> *Example:* Knowing that a successful negotiation must involve a "win" by both sides, a negotiator may use the "Big Pot" technique. Suppose that A wishes to acquire the target company for $1,000,000 cash. If A opens negotiations by stating his goal directly to the seller, and if the $1,000,000 really is the highest possible figure from A's standpoint, the setting for a zero sum game has been created. If A finally purchases the business for $1,050,000, no matter how fair the price is, A will feel that he has "lost." On the other hand, if the seller, who wanted to obtain $1,000,000 for the business, opens negotiations with a "Big Pot" price of $1,200,000, and only finally reluctantly agrees to A's price of $1,000,000 both A and seller will have "won." The seller will have gotten the price he wanted, A will have gotten the price he wanted, and A will feel much more inclined on the course of the negotiations to accommodate seller on various "minor" points such as the closing date, or the seller's retaining certain assets.

3. Imperfect Information

In any business acquisition negotiation, there is always insufficient and imperfect information. Satchel Paige is said to have stated the rule: "It's amazing what you can observe if you just look." In negotiation, it's amazing what you can learn if you just listen.

If you are the buyer, ask youself why, really, is the seller interested in selling? How competent, really, are the middle-level managers in the business? How strong, really, is seller's customer list? Has seller recently lost or is seller about to lose an important customer? Is it likely that seller's manufacturing equipment will become obsolete or of less value because of recent technical developments unknown to the buyer? The list is infinite. The impact is important.

Simply, stated, the basic tactic in business acquisition negotiations is to only give information in exchange for other information or some other advantage. Remember, we are not talking here about full disclosure of all relevant facts, which will obviously be made at or prior to the closing of the transaction. That must occur. What we are talking about, is the flow of information in the course of determining whether or not there is going to be a deal. In general experience, once there is agreement as to a deal, only some major new bit of information will have the effect of terminating the deal.

Often minor or even peripheral information can have a substantial effect on the

81

negotiation of a deal. For instance, under the "Pareto Principle," it is generally true that 80 percent of the substantive negotiation takes place in the last 20 percent of the time actually alloted for negotiation. For this reason, such simple facts as the other party's expectation as to the time to be allotted to this particular negotiation can be important in "pacing" concessions and offers.

Example: The negotiating team for acquiring corporation has arrived in your city to negotiate the purchase of your business. They have already completed inspection of the plants and most of the time-consuming preliminaries. Included in the group are the top officers of the purchaser. They have no other purpose in being in your city other than negotiating this deal.

They indicate to you only a casual interest in acquiring your business. You learn that they have made *two* nights' reservations in the hotel in your city and do not have plane reservations until the following day. A safe working assumption is that they seriously want to acquire your business, that their first offer will not be their last, and that you can anticipate, and pace the negotiations over a two-day period.

Before leaving the subject of negotiations, we should consider the difference between an "impasse" and a "deadlock." Any serious negotiation will hit certain impasses. A good negotiator will seek to avoid actual deadlock, unless the deal has in fact become undesirable, or is uneconomic or expendable at that point. It should be noted, that a feigned "deadlock" is an old negotiating technique used when there is a disproportionate bargaining power, but this tactic can usually be recognized fairly easily.

In most business acquisition negotiations, there are numerous "impasses" on minor and major items. An impasse simply means that no further progress can be made on one particular issue at that time. A skilled negotiator will make note of the impasse and the relative positions of the parties, and simply move on to negotiating another point, leaving the impasse for negotiation at a more appropriate time.

Example: In the negotiations of the deal set forth in the "Pro-Seller Stock Purchase Agreement" shown in Appendix I, an impasse was reached with respect to the giving of absolute warranties by the sellers. Purchaser simply went on to negotiate other parts of the transaction, and then returned to certain representations which were absolutely essential from the purchaser's standpoint (such as warranties concerning valid corporate organization and the stock ownership of the corporation). The selling shareholders then injected the concept of "several" (not joint) liability for each shareholder if any loss occurred as a result of the breach of a warranty. Sellers still declined to give certain warranties. The sellers then directed the negotiations to other parts of the transaction. Later, they returned to discuss certain parts of the warranties (*e.g.*, payment of all taxes) that the buyer wanted, and injected the concept of limiting warranties "to the best knowledge of the stockholders."

Buyer finally accepted this view with respect to certain warranties and rejected it as to certain other warranties. Sellers were still adamant on particular points and again directed the negotiations to other issues. After several further impasses on the warranties point, the provisions set out in Articles 5 and 8 of Appendix J were agreed upon.

The net result was:

- ☐ "Several," but not joint, liability;
- ☐ Some absolute warranties (*e.g.,* stock ownership), and some "best knowledge" warranties (*e.g.,* title to property); and
- ☐ A carefully negotiated time limit, dollar limit, and notice procedures in case any warranties were claimed to have been false.

In fact, in the transaction represented by Appendix J, because of these provisions and the careful negotiations, the sellers never had their purchase price reduced, although, in fact, the market for the company's product seriously declined shortly after the transactions closed, and although certain minor pre-existing problems (which were unknown to the sellers) did appear after the closing.

In summary, patience, planning, and careful use of negotiating tactics and basic human courtesy will lead to successful business acquisition.

B. LETTERS OF INTENT

1. Do You Need a Letter of Intent?

Custom and practice in business acquisitions decrees that after there is the handshake on the deal, the parties then execute a more or less meaningless document known as the "letter of intent." From a legal standpoint, the letter of intent is (or should be) meaningless. It is simply a statement of what the parties intend to do provided that they are able to "sell" the transaction to their boards of directors, provided a legal agreement acceptable in all its terms can be drawn, provided financing can be obtained, provided state securities regulators approve, provided Federal regulators approve, and provided that a myriad of other contingencies are met. A typical form of "letter of intent" appears in Appendix M.

Most lawyers would advise their clients to avoid any letter of intent because there always exists some possibility that through misunderstanding and reliance, one party will later claim damages if the deal flies apart. On the other hand, the carefully drawn letter of intent makes it clear, in fact probably states on its face, that it is in no way legally binding.

All in all, a letter of intent may prove to be a very useful practical document if it is carefully drawn and recognized for what it is. The real purpose of the letter of intent is to serve to memorialize the business essentials of a trade which has been "morally" struck. The terms in no way are legally binding and are certainly subject to renegotiation if the circumstances change. However, as a practical matter, if the letter of intent indicates an exchange ratio of three A Corporation shares for each B Corporation share, or states that the assets will be purchased for $2,000,000 payable 10 percent down and the balance over five years at 12 percent interest, there is great moral suasion in later negotiation to abide by these terms. In other words, the parties are psychologically committed to those essential terms, and from a practical standpoint will go to some lengths and suffer some economic and practical advantages in order to carry out those terms.

Since the letter of intent is drawn up based on the terms reached by the principal negotiators for both sides, it serves the very practical purpose of a joint memorandum to other negotiators, lawyers, and professionals who will be working on the transaction as to these essential terms. It is amazing how frequently misunderstandings as to essential terms arise if the exact language of the terms is not mutually set down. In other words, if each party to a negotiation prepares its separate memorandum of the essential terms, each is likely to emphasize certain terms and de-emphasize certain other terms, leading to useless and time-consuming further negotiation by subordinates.

2. Timing and the Letter of Intent

There is one practical disadvantage to the letter of intent. The rules governing securities of publicly held corporations usually require that once the essential terms of a transaction are agreed to in principle, as by letter of intent, there must be a public announcement. The public announcement is intended to protect those trading in the securities of either corporation from trading when others have the "inside information" concerning the transaction. The rule is generally a beneficial one, but there is always the risk that just as much harm can result from too early an announcement of a very tentative deal as from too tardy an announcement of a transaction. The executive, particularly, must consult with his lawyer in advance of any letter of intent if publicly traded securities are involved in either of the corporations.

Another corollary of the rule requiring announcement of the transaction for a publicly held corporation as soon as there is a letter of intent is the effect upon employees of the acquired corporation. Employees almost always exhibit some natural nervousness when an acquisition is involved if they are employed by the target company. It is absolutely critical that uncertainty be removed as far as possible. Simultaneously with the execution of the letter of intent, and press announcement, a carefully worded announcement should also be made to all employees and labor unions which represent employees, to avoid the circulation of misinformation. More about this later.

It goes without saying that bankers and others vitally interested in the financial health of the business will also have been informed promptly. Bankers hate to be among the last to know, for both practical and psychological reasons.

To summarize, the question of timing is simply one of planning and common sense. A well-thought out schedule might look something like this:

Monday—Terms of the agreement discussed earnestly and tentatively resolved.
Tuesday—Draft of letter of intent prepared in form acceptable to both parties.

Wednesday—Tentative approval of banker, board of directors, and other key persons.

Thursday—Simultaneous public announcement, announcement to employees, and execution of letter of intent.

C. "KICKING THE TIRES"

1. How the Pro's Do It

Most people when asked to state what distinguishes the professional business acquisitions executive from the unsuccessful amateur will state that it involves patience in searching for just the right company. While this is indeed one of the hallmarks of the professional, actual experience indicates that it is a much later stage of the transaction at which the pro's really show their stuff. This is the critical stage (the earlier, the better) either before or after the letter of intent or initial contract when the books of the other company are completely opened, and the final evaluation is made as to whether or not the transaction is to take place. The contract will undoubtedly set out certain standards and representations which must be met. The time to determine whether or not these representations are true, to the extent possible, is *before* the closing, not afterwards.

The acquiring company must have an acquisitions team which will visit *every* facility of the target company and study their day-to-day operations thoroughly. The professional acquisitions person will trace the processes involved time and time again: Where is the inventory stored? Is there another warehouse? Who owns the trucks? What kind of common carrier transportation service is available? What do the people on the loading dock say about the service? What kind of damaged freight claims do we have? How old is the machinery? How well-maintained is the machinery? What do the union leaders think of employee morale? What does middle-management think of the target company and the proposed acquisition? What are the backgrounds and capabilities of middle-management?

The professional acquisitions person will find out the answers to these and many similar questions before the closing. The questioning will not be done in an offensive or meddling way. The questioning will be done in a systematic and meticulous way which is not disruptive of the target company's business.

Medical science relies heavily upon new, sophisticated x-ray, radio wave, and radioactive material scanning techniques which are fed into a computer. A composite of millions of bits of information can reconstruct a three-dimensional picture which can be used by a trained radiologist to determine exactly what the interior of a particular organ looks like. The same technique is used by the professional acquisitions person. Bits and pieces of information gathered from inside and outside of the company during the critical and investigation stage prior to closing gives to the acquisitions team a composite picture showing the weak and strong points of the company *prior* to the closing.

2. Do Your Own Homework

It is amazing how frequently the acquisition team for the acquiring corporation will have not fully done its homework. They will not have obtained the 10-K and other reports filed with the SEC prior to serious negotiations concerning the target company. They will not have obtained all of the annual reports and other information sent to the shareholders and others, freely available, concerning the target company. They will not have obtained samples of each of the products of the target company and checked with applicable state and Federal regulatory officials to determine whether or not there have been an undue number of complaints or whether there are any pending actions concerning the paricular company.

Real estate records are generally open for all to examine to determine exactly what mortgages lie against the company's real property, and whether the property is owned or leased. Uniform Commercial Code financing statements are available at offices of Secretaries of State or at the county courthouses to show exactly what secured financing exists. Local business libraries and newspaper "morgues" normally contain indexes which catalog all published articles relating to a particular company over the past several years.

All of this data should be assembled as a preliminary matter in a notebook on the target company. This data should be carefully studied by the acquisitions committee before any overture is made to the target company itself.

3. How to Solve the Delicate Problem of Publicity and Present Employees

As mentioned earlier, nothing makes present employees of the companies involved in an acquisition, particularly the employees of a target company, more nervous than to first learn of the acquisition through the public press or some rumor. Like it or not, the medium is in some special way the message for the employee. If a public medium is used rather than a direct announcement to the employees themselves, the employees get the unmistakable message that their jobs are unimportant or in jeopardy, or both. Obviously, nothing makes for poorer employee morale than uncertainty concerning continued employment.

As soon as the letter of intent is executed, and simultaneously with any public announcement, the employees and any collective bargaining representatives at each location for the target company should be personally told of the proposed transaction in a very general way. The points, similar to the following could be emphasized:

1. The final agreement has not been executed;
2. The transaction will result in a stronger company and more opportunity for each of them through broader markets for the product.
3. It is the present plan to continue business operations much as they have been under the present company; and
4. If reasonably certain, the tentative closing date for the transaction.

Obviously, no statement should be made that is not absolutely true. Also, obviously, no statement should be made that is unnecessarily alarming or inflammatory. The format used should not be a question-and-answer session but simply an announcement. Supervisory personnel should be briefed carefully first, and all of their own questions should be answered so that they will be able to spread the word on a person-to-person basis to the rank-and-file employees.

After the closing, it is imperative that top management of the acquiring corporation visit as many locations in the target company as possible to assure employees of the continuation of beneficial policies and to welcome them into an enlarged and better organization. Many an acquiring corporation chief has neglected this important step to his sorrow. Employees who do not feel they are part of a team will have poor morale and poorer productivity. It is absolutely essential that lines of communications be kept open at the time of any acquisition.

In a recent airline acquisition, steps similar to these were carefully followed. In addition, a middle management was systematically brought to the home office of the acquiring corporation and thoroughly informed of the policies and philosophy of the acquiring corporation. In other words, they were "sold" on the new company. It is no accident that a persistent flood of complaint letters to regulatory authorities concerning the acquired corporation for years prior to the acquisition became an even larger torrent of *complimentary* letters a few months after the acquisition. Acquiring corporation executives remain amused at the stream of compliments for the "new" personnel. They were the same people—they just had different motivations, and a thorough employees information program was used as part of the acquisition.

4. Getting the "Feel" of the New Business—The "Go" or "No-Go" Signal

After all of the homework has been done, and after all of the tires have been kicked, after your accountants and other professionals have presented to you the relevant data and it has been analyzed, there should be a top-level strategy session held with your entire acquisition team. Insofar as possible, the routine questions relating to mechanics of closing, particular contract provisions, and operational questions not concerning the acquisition, should all be ruled out of order for the meeting. The sole purpose of the meeting should be to obtain a consensus as to whether or not the acquisition makes sense.

Unscrambling a bad acquisition is an almost impossible task. Simply electing never to break the egg is a much simpler process. The acquisition team should review the revised financial data including the adjusted balance sheet and cash flow statement as well as the pro forma projection. Labor relations experts should estimate the compatibility of the target company's labor policies and labor force with that of the acquiring company. Lawyers should report on the legal risks remaining in the contract. Facilities experts should report on the physical condition of the plant and equipment. When all of these pieces and the other parts of the acquistion tableau are in place, then each executive member of the acquisitions team should independently make his "go" or "no-go" list. This list is simply a statement of the pros and cons of the acquisition as he sees it.

A typical "go" or "no-go" statement (shown here in abbreviated form) might look like the following:

Go or No-Go Acquisition Statement Proposed Acquisitions of Little David Corporation

Positive	Negative
Good physical plant	History of poor labor union relations with
Modern machinery	contract negotiations in progress at
Geographical area compatible with ours	present time.
Product compatible with ours	Poor cash flow, would be a drain on cash flow
	for next three years.
	Federal agency is in process of investigating
	industry and has questioned safety
	of one of the principal products of target
	company.

Each of the sheets can then be combined and a composite "go" or "no-go" schedule made. The pro's and con's can then, in a concrete fashion, be hashed out and discussed.

At the end of the conference, the chief executive on the acquisition team should make a firm decision. If the decision is "no-go," that should be communicated immediately to the necessary parties. Some of the best and wisest acquisition decisions relate to acquisitions which are never made. It is much easier not to make a bad deal than to spend millions in time and effort trying to save it.

If the signal is "go," all members of the acquisition team must swing in 100 percent behind the transaction to make it a success.

D. RECENT LEVERAGED BUY-OUT STRATEGIES

The techniques discussed throughout this book have been used by business executives and corporations with great success over the past ten years.

1. How Does It Work?

The leverage buy-out transaction usually involves a purchase of a business with its own assets. The "leverage" comes from the fact that certain payments for the business are made to the seller (or, alternatively, to a lender) from the actual earnings of the acquired business.

> *Example:* Some years ago, Rollins purchased Orkin Exterminating Company. The transaction, from the seller's standpoint, was a sale involving over $50,000,000 in cash paid over a short period of time. From the purchaser's standpoint, the cash flow of the purchased Orkin's businesses more than paid

back all of the purchaser's bank loans in the first five or so years after the acquisition. In other words, Rollins owned the businesses (which became a major building block of a diversified corporation) and paid literally *nothing* for the business, other than what the businesses themselves produced over the first few years of ownership.

2. What To Do

☐ Find a business that is cash-rich, generates a heavy cash flow, or is selling for less than its asset value.

☐ Estimate, conservatively, the cash flow which can be obtained from the business over a period of, say, the next five years.

☐ Remember, that cash flow may be greater for a purchaser than it is for the present business if techniques such as increased depreciation can be used because of obtaining a new tax basis for the purchased assets.

☐ Obtain a preliminary indication that a banker, insurance company, or other source will finance the transaction for you if certain conditions are met.

☐ Negotiate with the present owners or management, either for a sale on an installment basis, or for new equity shares in your present company, or for cash.

☐ If the purchase is to be on an installment basis or for cash, make the necessary arrangements with your lender and close the transaction.

☐ If you correctly calculated the deal and do a good job managing the business, after five to ten years you should own the business free and clear, have fully paid off the seller, and should have a good source of cash flow to be used for further acquisitions.

> *Example:* A former sales and marketing manager for International Telephone and Telegraph Corporation purchased Syracuse China Corporation from IT&T by putting together a group of investors, $350,000 of his own cash, and borrowing the rest. At the time he purchased the deal, the business had $16 million of sales and no profits. Good management and hard work turned the business into a very profitable one. In a few years, the executive sold his 25 percent interest in the company for $4 million, cash, and received an employment agreement naming him as chief executive officer at a substantial salary (see *Forbes*, July, 1978, cover story "Do You Sincerely Want To Be Rich?").

Attention to the business and financial sections of your local newspaper, and a reading of business periodicals such as *The Wall Street Journal, Business Week, Forbes, Barron's, Fortune,* as well as specific industry publications, (such as *Editor & Publisher,* in the newspaper field) will give the executive an up-to-date view on current trends and techniques.

> *Example:* A leading weekly business periodical recently described a successful leverage buy-out this way:

"It was a rags-to-riches story . . . ORICO, newly emerged from Chapter XI bankruptcy proceedings, boasted little more than a pile of debt, a huge tax-loss carryforward and 2400 shareholders who hadn't seen their stock trade in over two years. Sargent, by contrast, was making money. It boasted $4 million cash in the till and borrowings represented only 27 percent of equity. Yet ORICO last January wound up raising $39.1 million to take over Sargent, merging the latter into a [new corporation]. Today, renamed Sargent, its stock trades again on the Pacific Coast Stock Exchange, where it recently changed hands around four."

"What helped breathe new life into ORICO was the use of an old financing technique that's enjoying fresh popularity these days—the leverage buy-out. Simply put, it involves the purchase, typically of a seasoned enterprise, private or public, for cash. The buyers attempt to minimize their equity investment by use of bank loans and other forms of debt to effect the acquisition. . . ." (*Barron's*, September 24, 1979).*

Example: A few years ago, Trend Carpet Mills learned that Champion International Corporation wanted to sell its north Georgia manufacturing business because of a series of losses. An alert investment banker put together the following deal:

- ☐ He acquired a publicly traded corporation which had few assets or liabilities but which had a $13 million tax loss carryforward. The public corporation had a negative net worth and its 800,000 shares were selling at $.12 each. He purchased 300,000 new shares for $.25 a share, paid $15,000 down, and the balance over a period of four years.
- ☐ He acquired Trend, which had a modern plant and $64 million in net assets for a $54 million purchase price payable $30 million in cash, $16 million in notes, and $8 million in preferred stock.
- ☐ Two life insurance companies put up $16 million of the $30 million cash and a New York bank provided a revolving credit based on accounts receivable of about $14 million.

The road to a successful leverage buy-out is often bumpy. Executives who practice the art probably look at 20 to 50 businesses for every one which becomes a serious acquisition target. Unfortunately, many executives use hunches instead of market research, or confuse their own hobbies and predilections for general consumer trends. Any successful acquisition involves patience, careful financial analysis, knowledge of the business, the market, and the geographic area. It involves knowledge of acquisition techniques, careful financial planning, and wise use of professional advisers.

---

*Barron's, "High-Wire Finance Leverage Buyouts Offer Plenty of Reward, Risk," Steven S. Anreder, September 24, 1979, page 4, Copyright 1979, Dow Jones & Company, Inc. (used by permission).

Chapter 5

Closing
And Follow-Up

A. THE CLOSING

1. The Importance of a Final Strategy Meeting

Just as the investigatory or "kicking the tires" stage of the acquisition ended with a final meeting at which the "go" or "no-go" signal was given, the closing stage of the transaction should end with a final strategy meeting immediately prior to the closing. At this meeting, the entire acquisitions team should be present and a complete review of the contract and all of the schedules must be held on an item-by-item basis.

Ideally, the final strategy meeting will be held two days before the final closing. It should take several hours and should result in a checklist of the specific final questions to be answered prior to the execution of the documents at the closing.

2. The Preliminary Closing

In order to avoid a chaotic situation which is bad, not only on the digestion of all parties, but also often results in important details being overlooked, an entire day or afternoon should be set apart in the conference room in which the closing will take place for a preliminary closing. It is not necessary for all of the members of the acquisition team to be present, but it is important that the closing attorneys for each side, and a representative of management be present.

Each document and schedules to be executed or initialled should be carefully set out in the order in which it will be executed. The text of each copy and the clarity of each of the copies to be signed can be verified. Each place where a signature is to appear should be carefully flagged and a detailed closing agenda prepared. All schedules must be prepared in legible form and with the necessary number of copies, and set out on the closing table. If the contract and the actual closing documents are executed simultaneously, this is doubly important.

When all of the documents have been set out and verified by the parties, the closing room should then be locked and left until the closing to be held the next morning.

3. Typical Checklist for Acquisition Closing

Each closing is different, but a typical closing checklist might include the following:

1. Time, date and place of closing.
2. Full names of persons to be present as principals and representatives of all parties.
3. Corporate documents with respect to target and acquiring corporation:
   a) Certificate of incorporation.
   b) By-laws.
   c) Good standing certificates and tax status certificates showing good corporate and tax "housekeeping" in accordance with state records.
   d) Certificates of authority for all states where the target corporation is qualified to transact business.
   e) Certificates showing location or delivery of complete minute books and stock records of the acquired corporation.
4. List of shareholders and addresses.
5. Authorizations:
   a) Incumbency certificates showing names, corporate titles, and signatures of corporate officers.
   b) Certified copy of resolutions of the Board of Directors.
   c) Certified copy of resolutions of the Shareholders.
6. Financial statements—this should either be a summary or, better, full copies of the audited financial statements of both corporations for the past five years, along with a letter showing transmittal of auditors' letters to management for the past five years, auditors' inquiry letters and replies for the past five years.
7. Tax returns—there should be a transmittal showing delivery to the acquiring corporation of all returns for all open years along with any related audit and revenue agents reports or waivers of statutes of limitations.
8. Contracts and agreements:
   a) All loan agreements.
   b) All material contracts.
   c) All leases.
   d) All deeds.
   e) All non-competition, employment, or secrecy agreements.
   f) All agreements concerning membership in trade associations.

g) All guarantees.

h) All union agreements.

i) All pension plans and actuarial reports or profit-sharing plans and agreements or other employee benefit agreements.

9. Miscellaneous.

   a) Description of any material licensing agreements.

   b) Description of any material insurance contracts.

   c) Description of any material litigation pending or threatened or administrative proceedings pending or threatened.

   d) Any lists of patents, trademarks, or copyrights.

   e) Title reports and Uniform Commercial Code searches.

10. Acquisition agreement or plan of merger.

11. Any employment agreements.

12. Any stock escrow agreements.

13. Any specific indemnification certificates or representation certificates.

14. Any necessary consents of assignments.

15. Any necessary resignations of directors or officers.

16. Legal opinion.

17. Bank confirmations, checks, receipts, or official certificate showing effectiveness of merger.

It is strongly suggested that early in the pre-closing preparations, a draft Closing Memorandum detailing each document be prepared. As in the checklist above, the Memorandum will use a series of letters and numbers so that each document will be assigned a specific designation (*e.g.*, the Good Standing Certificate in the State of Ohio might be Document C(4)). A form of Memorandum of Closing is set out in Appendix N.

Counsel for both the acquiring and target corporation can agree on these documents, their order, and their designations. Prior to closing, as the documents are assembled, they can be dropped in a separate file folder with the same designation. At the pre-closing and closing, these folders will greatly expedite the location of the necessary documents.

After the closing, one of the counsel, probably for the acquiring corporation, should retain enough duplicate sets of documents so that the Closing Memorandum, followed by the documents in proper order (after recording, for those documents which need to be recorded or filed) can be bound in a volume. The author has found this practice to be invaluable, not only in setting out the documents in a logical way, but allowing them to be referred to years after the closing.

4. How to Avoid Losing $40,000 at the Last Minute

Especially in a transaction in which the closing of the final written contract and the signing of the transfer documents take place simultaneously, it is very easy for the acquiring company to make a mistake. It is mandatory that there be sufficient time between the preliminary closing and the final closing for the acquisition team to deliberately review each of the documents with a special emphasis to the schedules. There have been too many medium- and large-sized acquisitions which resulted in $20,000, $40,000, or $200,000 losses to the acquiring company simply because adequate time was not allowed for the review of all of the schedules upon which the legal transaction took place.

For instance, it is customary, as noted above, to have a detailed schedule showing all suits and threatened lawsuits against the target company. All too often this schedule does not appear until the last minute. It is only then that management for the acquiring company learns that there is a substantial EEOC matter pending against the company. Needless to say, a loss of the matter could result in serious financial and other costs to the target company in the future. All too often, the matters raised do not rise to the magnitude which would warrant the calling off of the deal. If careful time for review of these schedules and deliberation as to their possible effects on the transactions is not allowed, it is very easy for the acquiring corporation, faced with the loss of an acquisition or the "swallowing" of a recently disclosed liability, to simply go ahead and swallow a $40,000 or $50,000 potential claim at the last minute.

Proper scheduling and examination of these matters by the acquisition team can avoid such a costly decision by allowing time for further systematic negotiation on particular problems found.

5. If You Don't Know, Ask

One of the best rules in all phases of an acquisition is to ask if you have any doubts. This is especially true in the critical days immediately prior to the closing. Many a chief executive of an acquiring corporation has learned to his sorrow that a new and obscure footnote which appears suddenly on the financial statements of the target company prior to closing has meant a major shift in one of the product lines. Many an attorney for an acquiring corporation has learned to his sorrow that a brief, two-lined reference to a letter threatening an investigation in a schedule of potential litigation has signaled the start of a most costly battle with the United States Department of Justice.

> *Example:* A recent transaction involved the purchase of a closely-held corporation owning timberland. The corporation's books were maintained on a cash basis and its accounting statements were unaudited. One factor in the purchase price was the anticipated income stream from cutting the mature timber on the corporation's land. Income for the corporation showed steady increases over the past five years, but careful reading of one footnote in each of the first three of those five years showed that the income did not take into account a larger purchase of timber at the end of the sixth year preceding closing, which had been paid for in that year, but which represented timber cut in the fifth, fourth, and third year before closing.

In that case, an alert executive asked about the footnote and was told by the seller the details of that peculiar transaction. The purchaser was then able to more accurately reflect the income pattern. If you don't know, ask.

It is up to the principals and attorneys for the target company to disclose all necessary information requested. It is the responsibility of the acquiring corporation to ask the necessary questions, and if the responses are not complete or satisfactory, to seek clarification before the closing.

B. FOLLOW-UP

1. Importance of Coordination with Your Accountant

As soon as ink is set to paper and the closing party is over, you should put your accountant to work. Have your accountant physically separate all transactions which occurred before and all those transactions which occurred after the closing. If possible, have all books of account closed with respect to the operation before the closing. Have your accountant and accounting personnel explain to personnel of the target company your systems of control and the keeping of accounts.

It is almost impossible to reconstruct a jumbled mess which will exist if no clear accounting lines are drawn immediately after the closing. There have been several instances in which poor accounting practices made it impossible to enforce warranty provisions set out in a carefully drawn acquisitions contract.

2. The All-Important Follow-Up Schedule

As in any modern management process, there must not only be detailed planning, but there must also be a coordinated follow-up and implementation program.

Nowhere is this more important than in your acquisition transaction. At a minimum, your follow-up schedule should include the following:

a) Necessary accounting steps to separate old and new operations.
b) Changing all bank accounts and access to safe deposit boxes.
c) Changing necessary corporate officers and by-laws.
d) Changing employee benefit packages such as health insurance and retirement benefits.
e) Notifying tax authorities of the transaction.
f) Obtaining transfer of necessary state accounts such as unemployment insurance.
g) Issuance of joint press releases.
h) Meeting with new employees.
i) Implementation of training program for management of target company.

j) Follow-up on contractual matters such as collection of accounts receivable and preparation of inventories.

3. How to Break the News to New Employees and Keep Their Goodwill and Loyalty

A poor first step with new employees after the acquisition will take years to remedy. A well-thought out announcement to new employees can build employee loyalty and goodwill.

One of the most successful methods of dealing with new employees is for the chief executive officer of the acquiring company himself to appear before as many groups of employees and management personnel for the acquired company as possible, to explain in simple fashion the goals and intentions of the acquiring company. In the first place, such an appearance creates an opportunity for the new employees to discover that the chief executive officer of the acquiring company does not in fact have horns and a long tail. Secondly, it allows the chief executive officer to explain in direct language that the employees' jobs are not in jeopardy (assuming that is the case). Lastly, it allows the executive of the combined company to appear with the old management and give a visible impression of continuity which words on a printed page can never do.

4. Press Releases That Solidify Your Company's Standing

As pointed out earlier, it is a very good idea for press releases after an acquisition to be joint press releases. The watchwords are brevity, optimism, and harmony in any press release.

The release should be drawn well before the preliminary closing and should be initialed by the appropriate members of the acquisition team of both parties. At a minimum, these points should usually be included:

a) The names of the announcing executives. In other words, "President Smith of Little David Corporation today announced," etc.
b) A precise but non-technical mention of the transaction. In other words, if the transaction was an acquisition of assets, it would suffice to say that all of the business and assets of Little David were acquired by Goliath, etc.
c) A statement as to the continuing operation of the acquired company as a separate corporation, division, or whatever the case may be.
d) A statement as to the great benefits to the public, employees, and stockholders from the transaction.
e) Generally, no mention of the acquisition price or the nuts-and-bolts details of the transaction.
f) A flowery, enthusiastic, and optimistic statement by first one president and then another as to the wonderful nature of the transaction and the hopes for the future.

Chapter 6

Personal Planning for
The Executive in Acquisitions

Whether the executive in the acquired corporation is the corporation's founder, a minority shareholder, or a professional manager with no direct ownership stake in the business, the acquisition will have a profound effect on the executive's business life. These same concerns are important also to the executives of the *acquiring* corporation because personnel of the acquired corporation are a vital asset, often the most important part of the acquisition.

A. HOW THE FOUNDING EXECUTIVE CAN AVOID LOSING CONTROL OF THE CORPORATION

The problem of acquisition is especially acute for the founding executive who has, almost literally, a paternal interest in the business enterprise. Very early in the negotiations concerning the merger, the founding executive must make clear his wishes as to his own continued employment as well as that of key corporate family members. Employment contracts must be incorporated into the acquisition agreements if continued employment is essential. Nevertheless, it is always a wrenching experience for the founder of a corporation to lose the absolute control which goes with owning a majority of the stock.

A typical situation for the founding executive might involve an agreement under which he would continue to remain as the chief executive officer of the corporation for three years after the merger, and would have a seat on the acquiring corporation's board. This arrangement allows for an orderly transition into the new management team while giving the acquiring corporation's board the direct benefit of the founder's wisdom. A typical employment agreement is set out in Appendix O. Each employment agreement should be tailor-made for the particular executive's situation. Key factors which should be included are:

☐ *The Length of the Agreement.* From the executive's standpoint, an agreement without a fixed term offers very little protection. Under most states' laws, an agreement without a term may be construed to be an agreement terminable at will, or an agreement to employ for the period of compensation (*e.g.*, if the executive is paid so many dollars per month, the employment agreement will be construed as an employment for a minimum period of one month).

☐ *The Duties To Be Performed By The Executive.* It is usually the law that a corporation may bind itself to have certain duties performed by an executive, although only the board of directors, annually, can legally elect an executive to a particular office, such as that of President. Note that in the employment agreement set out in Appendix O (Paragraph number 1) the executive insisted that his officer (Chairman of the Board) be designated, even though this portion of the employment agreement might not have been fully enforceable. The real protection for the executive under that agreement was that the executive "shall not be expected to perform duties substantially different from those performed by [the executive] prior to [the closing]." The executive in Appendix O had not been directly in charge of the day-to-day operations of the corporation and wanted to preserve his flexible personal schedule, while providing a clear period of transition for the firm acquiring his corporation.

An executive who had been the chief executive officer of a corporation might want his employment agreement to describe his duties as "those normally performed by the chief executive officer of the corporation." The Treasurer or chief financial officer might want to describe his duties as "having primary responsibility for the financial operation of the corporation, and having duties customarily performed by the chief financial officer of the corporation."

Remember, that while it is often technically and legally impossible for a public corporation to bind itself to elect the executive to a particular office, and while these restrictions flow through to boards of directors of closely-held or subsidiary corporations, most modern corporation statutes allow for shareholder agreements, which may legally provide in detail for the management of a closely-held corporation. Such a management agreement might be used by the executive as an adjunct to the particular executive's employment agreement where the executive is going to be a principal shareholder of the new corporation, but not the majority shareholder.

☐ *Restrictions On The Executive During And After Employment.* From the corporation's standpoint, there will often be an insistence upon a noncompetition agreement during and after employment. Additionally, the corporation may claim ownership of trademarks, patents, and copyrights produced by the executive during his employment, and may claim protection of customer lists and trade secrets.

Many of these restrictions are not unreasonable and, in fact, will be absolutely required by many larger corporations, especially those in scientific or technical fields. From the executive's standpoint, care should be taken to exclude *existing* trademark, patent, and copyright property owned by the executive, and not being purchased by the acquiring corporation, as well to narrow the geographic scope and time of post-employment restrictions.

☐ *Compensation.* The compensation should, from the executive's standpoint, be stated for as long a period of time as is reasonable, certainly annually (*e.g.,* "Executive shall be paid $_____ per year, payable in twelve (12) equal installments on the last day of each calendar month.") A more difficult part of the agreement, and one which, strangely enough, is often simply finessed, is a clear description of the bonus arrangement for the executive. If it is tied to a formula or certain goals, or even certain goals to be mutually agreed to annually, this should be spelled out in detail in the employment agreement.

☐ *Termination.* The date and manner of termination should be provided. The executive should try to obtain the legal right to have a statement of cause presented if he is to be terminated for cause, and the right to appeal that statement or cure the cause.

If the executive's compensation is a material inducement to the acquisition itself, the executive should insist upon the absolute right to payment (or liquidated damages) for a minimum period of time, even if the board of directors should fire the executive.

☐ *Fringe Benefits and Reimbursement for Expenses.* If profit-sharing or pension plans, medical plans, life insurance plans, or any other fringe benefits are specifically granted the executive, these should be spelled out in the agreement. The method and standards for reimbursing the executive's expenses on behalf of the corporation should also be spelled out.

☐ *Other Miscellaneous Provisions.* The executive may want to provide that the duties shall be performed only in one geographic area (presumably, his home location), and that disputes would not be brought into court immediately but would be arbitrated through the American Arbitration Association in a particular location. The executive may also want to spell out his right to hire and fire certain key associates and support personnel, and any right of access to particular officers and the board of directors.

If the founder, or the second-generation executive in an acquired corporation, can candidly admit that he will not be happy as a member of the larger management team with a smaller voice, it is often best to provide for a brief (perhaps one year) transition period, and for the executive then to enter into an entirely new business which does not compete with the old. Some of the most satisfied business executives involved in the sale of an oldtime family business, have been those who determined prior to any acquisition agreement that they will not remain with the new corporation beyond a specific period of time, and then entered an entirely new business field or devoted themselves to one or more pet civic projects, or entered public service.

B. HOW THE MINORITY SHAREHOLDER/MANAGER CAN PROTECT HIS INTEREST IN THE CORPORATION

Perhaps the most difficult position to protect in a business enterprise is that of the longtime minority shareholder. With 20/20 hindsight, such individuals would undoubtedly say that the best general rule was never to become a minority shareholder in a closely-held business enterprise. Perhaps the second best bit of hindsight would be for the minority shareholder to have insisted upon certain specific protections at the time of his initial investment in the corporate enterprise. These protections might have included a provision prohibiting merger or other acquisition without an extraordinary majority of shares in the corporation. For instance, the holder of 31 percent of the stock of a closely-held business could insist that the charter of the corporation require the vote of at least 70 percent of the outstanding shares or common stock prior to any merger or other acquisition (and, of course, appropriate protections against dilution of percentages of ownership).

In addition, the minority shareholder might insist upon a "buy or sell" agreement. Such an agreement could provide that any shareholder in a corporation owned by a small number of shareholders may at any time elect to either buy out all of the other shareholders or sell his own shares. Normally, the shareholder taking the initiative specifies a price and terms for the shares involved and gives an option to be exercised within 30 to 60 days by the other shareholders to either sell their shares on the specified price or terms, or to collectively buy the shares of the stockholder who initially named the price and terms. A typical buy/sell agreement appears as Appendix P.

The practical effect of such an arrangement is to give a minority shareholder a clear voice in all major corporate actions, including proposed acquisitions. That voice, of course, can be translated into protection for the executive's employment after the acquisition itself.

In addition to pre-planning to protect the position of the minority shareholder, there is a growing body of law to protect minority shareholders when they are treated unfairly by the majority in an acquisition.

Although it is beyond the scope of this *Desk Book,* there is a growing body of law which indicates that the same price should normally be offered to the minority shareholders as to the majority shareholders. That is, the majority should not be paid a premium for their "control." The directors of the corporation, normally consisting of many of the majority shareholders, have a special fiduciary duty towards the minority shareholders to protect their interests. If they fail to protect the interests of all shareholders, they may be liable for damages to the minority.

C. THE PROFESSIONAL MANAGER

The professional manager may, in fact, be the founding shareholder, or may be a minority shareholder, but is used here to refer to any business executive whose role in the corporation is more that of a manager than investor.

In the large organization, more and more attention is being paid to the effect upon corporate changes of all types upon business executives. For instance, shortly after American Telephone & Telegraph Co. started to implement recent sweeping internal reorganizations, medical directors throughout the Bell System reported finding higher levels of anxiety among employees coming in for routine physicals. As a result, a large number of Bell System companies started or expanded programs to help employees cope with change in the workplace and with the stress that accompanies change. Bell started a series of seminars to help key executives deal with the stress of change and new position. The stress of corporate changes is not limited to small business executives.

From the standpoint of the executive in the acquired corporation, there are a few ground rules:

☐ *Remain flexible*. Remember that the acquiring corporation doesn't really know what the roles of key executives are in the acquired corporation until after the merger and after experience with the strengths and weaknesses of the entire management team.

☐ *Be a producer and have a positive attitude*. Often executives of the acquired corporation unnecessarily put a "chip on their shoulder," which causes unnecessary strife with their counterparts in the acquiring corporation.

☐ *Learn all you can* about the acquiring corporation, its management, and their personalities. Find out what has actually taken place in its previous acquisitions.

☐ *Consider obtaining an employment contract* as part of the acquisition. Your bargaining position prior to the acquisition may be strong enough to assure such a contract.

☐ *Check any stock options which you may have* to see what the effect of the acquisition will be on them. Obtain the advice of your lawyer.

The other side of the coin is the need to keep key managers on the team for the acquiring corporation. A recent friendly merger involved the acquisition of Microdot, Inc., by Northwest Industries, Inc. after a hostile takeover attempt by another corporation was successfully avoided. Less than a year after the friendly acquisition, the founding President of Microdot resigned. When a *Business Week* reporter asked him to sum up his reasons for leaving, the founding President responded "I just wasn't used to having a boss."

Studies have indicated that there are certain instances in which it is easier for management to become part of the new team. These include:

☐ When the corporations continue to be distinct, separate operations, especially where different geographic areas or product lines are involved. It is much more difficult when there is an immediate attempt made to integrate the two operations. For instance, the integration of PanAmerican World Airways, Inc. and National Airlines, Inc. is a very difficult merger from a personnel standpoint since, at all levels, from top executives through pilots to support personnel, the new corporation sought an immediate integration raising questions of seniority, personnel practices and other potential management nightmares.

☐ When there is great incentive for the acquired corporation to participate in the merger, such as upon the death of the founding shareholder or of a key executive. In other words, the acquired corporation is in many ways incomplete from a personnel standpoint and needs the support of certain personnel of the acquiring management team in order to make a whole management structure.

☐ When the acquired corporation is very small and it obviously benefits from the depth and management expertise available to its executives in the new structure.

A leading business magazine recently conducted an indepth study of the problems of business executives after mergers and noted that the management team of the acquired company is often more important to the success of the enterprise than the financial statements or physical assets. The study noted that many executives involved in acquisitions believe that once a merger is finished they can make the acquisition palatable to the key executives.

The study found that if the managers of the acquired corporation were allowed to continue on much as they did before, they were likely to remain with the new enterprise. The Coca Cola Company, among others, was found to hold meetings at the acquired corporation's headquarters to give a psychological lift to the new managers. Both specific support assistance to the newly acquired managers and a certain amount of "ego-massaging" was found to be very beneficial.

Personnel relations, especially at the key executive level, will become more important in the 1980's in any business acquisition. It is important for key executives, in both the acquiring and acquired corporation, to realistically deal with, and plan for, the changes that will come with the acquisition. With proper planning, the acquisition can be not only a business success, but an opportunity for personnel growth for all of the key executives involved.

D. PERSONAL WEALTH PLANNING IN AN ACQUISITION

The present tax laws favor certain types of income and certain types of wealth accumulation. For instance, income earned by an individual generally is taxed at a maximum federal income tax rate of 50 percent, capital gains are taxed at a usual maximum of 28 percent, while income from dividends is taxed at a rate of up to 70 percent. Ownership of real estate, and machinery and equipment used in a business is tax-favored through depreciation, amortization, and investment tax credits, which can shelter all or almost all of the income from those assets in the early years of ownership. Of course, one of the most heavily favored tax incentives is that given to small business held in corporate ownership form.

Throughout this *Desk Book,* many of those advantages have been made clear. From the standpoint of the individual executive and his own estate growth, such factors as: an effective corporate tax rate of 26.75 percent on the first $100,000 of net income each year; the ability to build up a tax-free corporate retirement plan, much of which can escape estate tax at the executive's death; and the ability to use a closely-held corporation to acquire a business and pay for both principal and interest on such acquisition by using dollars never taxed individually to the executive, are among advantages which accrue to the executive attempting to build a personal estate today. The balance of this chapter will explore some of these wealth-building techniques.

Reducing Individual Taxes

As a general rule, the executive in an acquisition should consider retaining capital assets (*e.g.*, stock in the acquiring corporation) which should appreciate over the years, and will eventually be taxed at a very favorable rate, if at all. Now that individual tax rates for "earned" income do not exceed 50 percent (and there are now proposals to reduce the maximum below that percentage) the executive should maximize the amount of cash compensation paid as salary. Of course, there are certain fringe benefits which can be received by the executive tax free, and these should be utilized where available and appropriate (*e.g.*, the executive may receive a $50,000 group term life insurance policy tax free, and other additional life insurance coverage at reduced tax costs). Income from dividends and interest is the least favored income under the present tax laws.

Personal Ownership of Real Property

In a closely-held business sale, it is often possible for the executive to personally retain ownership of real property such as a plant building or machinery and equipment used in the business. The plant or the machinery and equipment can then be leased to the operating corporation at a fair rental, and the cash paid by the corporation for rent is both deductible to the corporation and, often, sheltered from income tax in the hands of the individual. Let's look at an actual example.

> *Example: Here's an example of how the executive can retain ownership of real property for maximum benefits in an acquisition.* Smith Company is a successful manufacturer of hunting clothing. Its business has been growing and it needs an additional capital base. Jones Company, a large publicly-held corporation, has negotiated with the Smith brothers (owners of all of the stock of Smith Company) for a tax-free merger under which the Smith brothers would receive stock of Jones Corporation.
>
> Jones Corporation is only willing to proceed with the acquisition if additional plant capacity near the existing Smith Company plant can be assured. The Smith brothers know of an available plant which is vacant and tied up in extended

court proceedings. They make an offer to purchase the plant over a period of 10 years at a favorable interest rate, which is accepted by the court. They then lease the plant to Jones for a 10-year period at a fair rental, subject to rental increases based upon reappraisal every three years of the fair rental value of the building. In simplified form, here's how the transaction works:

```
Purchase price of plant building  ........................$250,000.00
    Amount paid down ...............................25,000.00
    10 year note at 9 percent...........................$225,000.00
    Monthly note payments  ..............................2,850.20
    Deductible interest portion
    of the monthly payment (for
    the first payment; this will
    gradually decline as the 10
    year period progresses) ..............................1,687.50
    Starting monthly rent (net
    for plant) ...........................................3,000.00
    Rental average over 10-year
    period (3 year adjustments) ..........................4,250.00
    Annual depreciation (20-year
    remaining life, straight line,
    $220,000 allocated to plant)  .......................11,000.00
```

Executive Benefits:

1. Owns plant free and clear after 10 years (value of $648,435 if 10 percent, compounded, increase in value each year);
2. Net cash plan averaging about $1,400 per month ($4,250 average rent, less $2,850 note payment);
3. Tax deductions of $11,000 per year depreciation, plus the interest portion of the note payment.

This example was possible because the corporations involved authorized the executive (in fact, the acquiring corporation required the executive) to obtain additional plant capacity. The executive was able to purchase the plant at a bargain rate and with bargain financing because of the court proceeding, and because there were no other competing buyers for that particular plant. The Jones Corporation was willing to enter into the net lease arrangement because the fair value of the plant to the corporation was at least the stated monthly rental. Care must be taken in any of these transactions so that the Internal Revenue Service will not contend that the payments were in fact merely disguised dividends. To help avoid this problem, you should make sure that there is a genuine economic benefit to each party in the transaction.

Similar arrangements are possible with new or used machinery and equipment, with the executive not only obtaining the benefits of fast tax write-offs, but also obtaining investments credits in certain circumstances.

Use of the Personally Held Corporation Itself
for Tax Benefits

Let's look at a few of the benefits of the small business corporation, many of which are discussed in greater detail in other parts of the book:

1. A pension or profit-sharing plan can be utilized to build up a healthy retirement benefit for the employees of the corporation. Not only is the corporation entitled to deduct from its taxable income amounts contributed to the qualified plans, but the plans themselves are entirely tax free, allowing earnings to compound for the executive's and other employees retirement. These retirement benefits can, in certain circumstances, be passed on to the executive's beneficiaries entirely free of estate tax. In a world inhabited by an estate tax with rates up to 70 percent, this is a substantial benefit.
2. The corporate form itself is a major advantage from the executive/investor's standpoint. In the first place, the investor's other assets are legally insulated from the liabilities of the corporation. That is, the corporation stands as a separate legal entity, and creditors of the corporation must, generally, look only to the corporate assets and not to the executive/shareholder's personal assets for satisfaction of their debts. The tax advantage is more subtle. The corporation conducting an active business is entitled to accumulate as many assets and as much of its earnings as are reasonably required to conduct its business, and reasonably anticipated expansion of the business.

   Example: A corporation which was started by the executive long ago with a capital of $50,000, can conduct an active business with assets of $50 million, and the executive will never have paid any personal income tax on the increased value. If the executive either holds onto his stock until death, or exchanges his stock for stock in a publicly held corporation in a tax-free merger, no capital gains will be paid with respect to the increased value. These are intentional benefits granted under our tax laws to encourage the accumulation of risk capital and for entrepreneurs to continue to take risks and to provide the base for the nation's economic growth.

On a smaller scale, a corporation is able to accumulate up to $150,000 in earnings even without a specific reasonable need for the accumulation before being required to pay any dividends. Corporations are able to invest in other corporate stock and to pay tax only on 15 percent (or less) of the amount of the dividend received. Since the corporate tax rates are lower than the individual tax rates, income retained in the corporation is, in a sense, "sheltered" for the individual owning stock in the corporation.

Under the present tax law, the first $25,000 of a corporation's ordinary taxable income is taxed at a rate of 17 percent, the next $25,000 at a 20 percent rate, the next $25,000 at a 30 percent rate, the next $25,000 at a 40 percent rate, and amounts over $100,000 at a 46 percent rate. For a small corporation, having taxable income of $75,000 after expenses, (which, of course, include payment of the executive/shareholder's salary) the effective federal tax rate is only slightly more than 22 percent.

Corporate Ownership

The corporate form of ownership is very advantageous to the executive in an installment sale acquisition of a business. If an individual personally buys the stock of a new corporation, the interest paid on the installment debt is deductible, but the principal must be paid out of after-tax dollars. If, on the other hand, the individual's wholly-owned corporation purchases the new corporation's stock on the installment basis, the principal amounts can often be received by the acquiring corporation tax free, so that the principal payments are made with pre-tax dollars.

> *Example: Here is an example of how maximum tax benefits can be achieved in an acquisition.* X is the sole shareholder of X Corporation, a small manufacturing business is California. X wishes to acquire on the installment basis all of the stock of Z Corporation, a similar manufacturing operation in Texas for a $2 million purchase price, payable $200,000 down and the balance over 12 years at 9 percent interest in equal monthly payments of $20,484.54, principal and interest.
>
> If X Corporation acquires the Z Corporation stock, and Z Corporation pays X a dividend sufficient to pay the principal and interest on the Z notes, X will pay ordinary income tax (perhaps at a 70 percent rate) on the dividends, and will only be able to deduct the interest portion of the payments.
>
> If, on the other hand, X causes his X Corporation to purchase the Z stock on the same terms, X Corporation will be entitled to receive dividends from Z Corporation at no federal tax. This is because if X and Z file consolidated federal income tax returns, there is no tax on dividends paid from one member of such a consolidated group to another. (There are also other provisions which allow tax-free transfer of dividends even without consolidated returns.) Z Corporation may pay to X Corporation dividends in the full amount necessary to amortize the acquisition note which X Corporation has given to the previous owner of Z Corporation. Interest on note to the seller is still deductible to X Corporation. If the previous owner of Z Corporation insists upon it, it is even possible for X, the individual, to guarantee X Corporation's note, while X Corporation pays off the acquisition debt itself.

This chapter has highlighted some of the many aspects of personal planning for the executive involved in any corporate acquisition transaction. The corporate executive, especially the executive who is a substantial shareholder in one of the corporations involved in a corporate acquisition, should consider obtaining his own *personal* tax and legal advice from his own personal advisor, so that the transaction can be carefully structured to provide maximum tax and other benefits to the executive.

Chapter 7

Alternatives to Acquisition in Today's Market

Any acquisition must be carefully tested against the available alternatives. Alternatives for the acquiring company include expansion into new markets and new products without acquiring an existing company in those markets. This chapter will concentrate upon the alternatives for the target company. Often some of the best acquisitions for the target company are those to which the chief executive says "No thanks."

A. RECAPITALIZATION

1. How to Use a Recap to Transfer Corporate Control

One of the leading causes of a business seeking to be acquired is the need to provide liquidity and increased income for the business' founder. Often there are successors in the business who are capable of continuing the business but who lack the capital base necessary to buy out the founder. Often a carefully planned recapitalization can meet the needs of the new managers and the founding owner at the same time.

A typical situation might be a medium-size manufacturing company having a net after-tax earnings of $150,000 per year. All of the stock is owned by the founder who has no descendants interested in actively participating in the business. A management group of three executives is capable of running the business but does not have the ability to raise the $1,500,000 necessary to pay the fair value for the founder's stock.

In this situation, the founder might allow the three key employees to purchase for cash $30,000 of the common stock of the company. At the same time, the founder might convert his common shares into $1,500,000 worth of voting preferred stock paying a dividend of $80,000 per year with a provision for redemption in five years at $1,500,000 payable $150,000 down and the balance represented by notes of the business (either secured by all of its assets or the endorsement of its three common shareholders) in nine annual installments of $150,000 principal, plus interest at the rate of 9 percent per annum.

The net result of the transaction will be to provide an immediate income through dividends to the founding shareholder and give him voting control of the business for the next five years. No income tax will be payable on the conversion of the common stock of the founder into preferred stock since it should qualify as a recapitalization and therefore a tax-free reorganization under the Internal Revenue Code. At the end of five years, the total redemption of the founder's shares should qualify as an installment sale so that gain will be payable by the founder at capital gains rates over a period of 10 years.

For the remaining key employees, they will have acquired a business for a total investment of $30,000, and the business will have paid for itself over a 15-year period. Through a mutual buy-sell agreement among themselves, the key employees can assure a fair price for their stock in the business and an orderly transfer of control in the future should one of them die or decide to leave the business.

2. How to Provide for the Heirs of a Deceased Shareholder

One of the most difficult decisions any business executive has to face is providing in a fair manner for the heirs of a deceased business partner. Often a recapitalization can provide in a tax-saving manner a fair and workable solution.

A typical situation involved the two equal owners of a prosperous middle-sized retail business in the midwest. One of the owners died unexpectedly at the age of 55 leaving a widow and two college age children. The after-tax net income of the business had been approximately $130,000, for many years, but no dividends had been paid, and these funds had been plowed back into the business capital. Since both of the founding shareholders drew adequate salaries, there had been no pressure for dividends.

The immediate needs of the widow and family of the deceased shareholder were for increased income since the salary was no longer available. On the other hand, there was a desire to retain a continuing ownership interest in the business in the event the children of the deceased shareholder wished to become active in the business after they graduated from college.

The solution was to create a new class of preferred stock. All of the shares of this deceased shareholder were converted into those shares of stock. Immediately, a dividend of $50,000 per year became payable on the stock. A unique feature of the preferred allowed it to be converted at any time within seven years after the date of issue into common shares. The conversion ratio was based on a prearranged formula relating to earnings and net worth of the business at time of conversion. If no conversion took place, the stock provided that it must be redeemed in the seventh year for 20 percent cash and the balance in notes payable over the following five years.

This unique arrangement allowed for immediate income to the family of the deceased shareholder while at the same time permitting re-entry into the business in a common stock ownership format if the family wished. By providing for a formula conversion, the interest of the continuing common stockholder was also met, since the value of his common stock would, presumably, increase in value each year, and therefore the percentage of ownership of the business represented by the preferred stock would decrease. This decrease in value was offset by the $50,000 per year in cash paid as a dividend on the preferred stock.

Although the corporation now paid the dividend with after-tax dollars (compared with the pre-tax salary dollars formerly paid to the deceased shareholder), all of the parties found that their goals were met in a reasonable way.

3. How to Separate Security from Growth Potential—The "Freeze" Technique

Another situation often confronting the owner of a business is a desire to transfer the ownership of the business to a second or third generation while at the same time preserving reasonable income for the founding generation and minimizing unified estate and gift taxes.

From the business standpoint, it is often very important that the founding owner of the business have his income protected for the founder's lifetime (and that of his immediate family) while minimizing inflationary growth from an estate standpoint. This has given rise to various techniques usually lumped under the term "the estate freeze."

The basic concept is that the income and capital base of the founder is placed in a preferred position, which not only gives a preference in the event of liquidation and as to income, but also provides a "cap" for future inflationary growth. This is especially useful if the other owners of the shares which have the growth potential, as well as the business risks, are family members or are valued employees to whom the founder would probably wish to leave the business in the founder's will. The technique has become so common that one accountant refers to his founder clients as "Eskimos" because they are all frozen.

Let's look at one example to see how the technique might work and could be used as an alternative to the sale of a family business.

> *Example:* One typical and successful export business owner discovered a way to affect a "transfer" to his children without the payment of any gift or estate taxes.
>
> All of the stock of the export corporation was owned by the founder who had a son and daughter both of whom were active in the business. The income of business over the past five years had consistently been between $25,000 and $50,000, net of taxes, but new markets which the son or daughter had planned for the business could increase net income to the $150,000 to $300,000 range within

two years. A carefully thought out recapitalization plan avoided a potentially serious estate tax problem.

Since the average net income of the business had been $35,000 a year for the past five years, and since businesses of that type normally sold for 10 times after-tax earnings, the parties determined that the fair market value of the business was then $350,000. The father created a new class of preferred stock which paid a dividend of $35,000 per year and which was redeemable at any time after five years for $300,000 payable 20 percent down and the balance over five years at 9 percent interest. The 100 shares of common stock which were still held by the father were given outright to the son and daughter. No gift tax was payable because of the use of the father's and mother's annual joint $6,000 gift tax exemption to each of the children, coupled with a portion of their joint unified estate and gift tax credit. The son and daughter immediately entered into a buy-sell arrangement between themselves to provide for the orderly transfer should one of them die or decide to leave the business.

When the father died some years later, the total value of the stock in the company in his estate was the $300,000 preferred stock. The common stock had grown in value to about $2,000,000 by that time, but the children owned the common stock at no cost in either cash outlay or estate taxes. Other assets of the father's estate provided for the widow.

Let's see how much estate tax was saved without use of the freeze technique:

Father had other assets which were worth $2 million at the time of his death, and which were left to his widow. The stock in the business which was worth $350,000 in our example above, had grown to a value of, say, $2 million at the time of the founder's death.

Estate tax on $2 million: $780,800

Let's see how it worked with the freeze technique:
Other assets value: $2,000,000
Value of Preferred Stock: 300,000
Total taxable estate: $2,300,000
   Less ½ marital
   deduction (remainder
   in trust for widow
   and children) $1,150,000
Balance as taxable estate.......................$1,150,000
Estate Tax $407,300
Savings through use of "freeze"
technique: $373,500

4. Caution Concerning Recapitalization and Subchapter S

Many smaller corporations elect to pay tax only at the shareholder level through a "Subchapter S" election. One of the requirements of a Subchapter S Corporation is that it have only common stock. Most recapitalization of Subchapter S Corporations will "kill" the election when the recap takes place because some preferred stock will be issued. This possible disadvantage must be carefully weighed whenever a Subchapter S Corporation is involved.

B. THE PRIVATE ANNUITY AS AN ALTERNATIVE TO SALE

One of the least-understood and least-used tax planning alternatives to acquisition available in connection for a closely-held business is the private annuity.

The private annuity involves the sale or redemption of stock in a closely held corporation, not for cash, but in exchange for a contract to pay a certain amount to the selling party for the rest of the selling party's life. Because tax rules usually require that this type of contract be unsecured, the private annuity lends itself to use only in situations where there is a great deal of confidence between the parties. Its ideal application is among parents, their children, and their closely-held corporation.

Properly executed, a private annuity transaction can have the following tax results:

1. No estate taxes upon the death of the transferring individual with respect to the property transferred;
2. No immediate tax to the transferring individual;
3. Immediate, unfettered ownership of the property by the acquiring individual; and
4. Payment of regular amounts of money at favorable tax rates to the transferring individual for the rest of his life.

1. How to Use a Private Annuity to Transfer Corporate Control

As pointed out earlier, the usual goals which lead the founder of a business to consider its sale to an outsider include a desire for estate liquidity, increased income, and reduction of estate taxes. Each of these goals may often be met by use of a private annuity instead of a sale or merger. The private annuity, properly planned, can result in an immediate increased income to the founding shareholder, an effective transfer of property to another generation of family members or to employees, favorable tax treatment for amounts received by the retiring founding shareholder, and a total elimination of any estate taxes with respect to the shares held by the founding shareholder.

These same benefits to the founding shareholder also operate as benefits for the new shareholders, whether they are family members, long-time key employees, or new purchasers of the business.

A typical transaction involving the use of private annuity to transfer a multi-million dollar regulated business was handled as follows:

Step One: The founding shareholder, through a regular program of lifetime gifts over the years, gave a substantial number of shares of the common stock of the corporation to his wife and three children. Under the Tax Reform Act of 1976, an amount of stock having a value of about $175,000 plus $6,000 per individual donee could be transferred at one time without any gift tax (see Act §2001).

Step Two: The husband entered into a redemption agreement with the corporation under which the corporation agreed to redeem all of the husband's remaining shares of common stock on a specified date. The contract provided that part of the redemption price was to be paid in cash at the closing and part by an unsecured private annuity contract. The annuity contract provided for the payment of an annuity to the husband for his life in equal quarterly installments.

Since it was important that the redemption price for the stock be the actual fair market value of the stock, the corporation used an independent appraiser to give a written opinion as to the value of the stock being redeemed. Having made that determination, tables issued by the Internal Revenue Service were used to give the amount of each quarterly payment under the annuity agreement. As required by IRS Regulations, the husband's rights under the annuity contract were *not* subordinated to claims of other creditors of the corporation and were not secured.

Step Three: A favorable private ruling was obtained from the National Office of the Internal Revenue Service prior to the redemption. Since the law in the private annuity area is fast changing, and since acceptable alternative courses of action (such as an installment sale redemption) were available, the parties decided that a ruling would be desirable.

In order to obtain the Ruling, and to assure beneficial tax treatment, certain additional steps were required:

a) At closing, the husband had to agree to resign as a director, officer, and employee of the corporation and file an agreement to the effect that he would not become a director, officer, or employee of the corporation for at least 10 years. This type of agreement was necessary to avoid "attribution" of the shares still owned by the children and wife back to the husband. If their shares had been "attributed" to the husband, the entire redemption payment would be treated as a dividend, and ordinary income. Section 302(c)(2)(A)(iii) of the Internal Revenue Code and Section 1.302-4 of the Regulations spell out how to file such an agreement.

b) A statement had to be made that there was no obligation of any kind on the part of any of the remaining shareholders to purchase the father's stock, and that no remaining shareholder would be personally liable, either directly or as a guarantor, for the annuity obligations.

c) The corporation had to state in writing that the husband had no option to acquire any further shares of the corporation's stock, and that the corporation did not plan to borrow any money for the redemption.

The balance of the transaction was worked out as follows:

Step Four: The closing was held, the father's stock was redeemed, and the annuity payments started.

Step Five: IRS allowed payments to the husband under totally separate existing agreements between the husband and the corporation, such as pension agreements and leases of personal and real property to the corporation to continue.

The benefits of the transaction included:

a) The husband obtained cash from the corporation at capital gains rates by having some of his stock redeemed outright.
b) The husband was assured of income for life. The payments under the private annuity were favorably taxed: part was tax-free as a return of capital, part as ordinary income as an interest factor, and the balance as a capital gain, under the formula set out in Ruling 69-74(1969-1 C.B. 43).
c) No gain or loss was recognized by either the children or the wife on redemption of the husband's stock.
d) When the husband died some years later, the private annuity was given a zero value, and no Federal estate taxes were paid with respect to the annuity.

A Ruling Request and Form of Ruling obtained from the Internal Revenue Service in a similar situation appears in Appendix G.

2. How the Private Annuity Cuts Estate and Income Taxes

Use of a private annuity transaction should avoid any future estate taxes with respect to the property transferred. The closing of the private annuity transaction passes legal title to stock (or other assets involved) to the other party. When an annuity is exchanged for stock, the old stock certificates are transferred and delivered with executed stock powers attached, and, if a sale is involved, new certificates are issued and the old certificates are cancelled. If the value of the stock equals the value of the annuity and other consideration received at the time, the stock is removed from the transferor's taxable estate and therefore should not be taxed upon the transferor's later death. Since the annuity expires at death, it is not taxed either.

Example: You are the founder of a business which you estimate is now worth $350,000, but which will grow rapidly in value because of inflation and other factors over the next 10 years. You sell the stock in the business to your son, who is an active manager in the business, for $350,000, represented by a private annuity. You receive payments every year between the time of the sale and your death.

At death, other assets in your estate are worth $2 million, the value of the interest which you sold to your son was also worth $2 million. To simplify the calculation, it is assumed that your spouse does not survive you.

Estate tax *without* any private annuity:

Other assets:	$2,000,000
Value of business stock	$2,000,000
Total:	$4,000,000
Estimated estate tax:	$1,880,800

Estate tax *with* private annuity:

Other assets	$2,000,000
Private annuity (ends at death and not included in estate)	—0—
	$2,000,000
Total estate tax	$ 780,800
Savings through use of private annuity:	$1,100,000

Three pitfalls must be avoided or the stock will still be taxed at the death of the former shareholder. These pitfalls involve transfers "in contemplation of death" (§2035), transfers with a "retained life interest" (§2036), and transfers "taking effect at death" (§2037).

(a) Contemplation of Death Transfers

Under the Tax Reform Act of 1976, IRC §2035 provides that any transfer for less than full consideration taking place within three years of the transferor's death will be included in the transferor's estate. A specific exception is found in §2035 itself for any asset which was disposed of in "a bona fide sale on adequate and full consideration." Since any transfer from an individual is potentially subject to inclusion if death occurs within three years, it is important to build a record in every private annuity transaction showing that the annuity and the shares exchanged for it had the same value. It is critical that the fair market value of the shares or other property transferred be determined at the time of transfer, and that the tables suggested in the Internal Revenue Regulations to determine the value of the annuity itself be used. If these two steps are taken, no successful attack under §2035 should be possible by the Internal Revenue Service.

(b) Retained Interest Transfers

Section 2036 of the Internal Revenue Code includes in an estate property to which the decedent retained a life interest when he died. For instance, it is clear that a transfer of the stock of a closely-held corporation to a son, where the transferor-father retained the right to vote the stock and receive all dividends paid with respect to the stock during the father's life, would constitute a transfer with a retained life interest. The full market value of the stock would be includable in the taxable estate of the father upon his death.

In order to avoid an attack by IRS based on this theory in a private annuity transaction, it is very important that the annuity agreement and all of the documents relating to the transaction make it clear that the transferor has absolutely no interest whatsoever in the stock transferred after the date of transfer. The payments under the annuity should be determined only with reference to the value of the stock or other property transferred, or the underlying operations of the corporation. In other words, the annuity should and must be a simple contractual obligation of the person granting the annuity (*e.g.*, the son) without future reference to the property transferred (*e.g.*, the stock or future corporate earnings or dividends).

(c) Delayed Transfers

Section 2037 includes in a person's gross estate property transferred by a transaction not taking effect until death. If a private annuity were issued not for stock itself, but merely for a promise to transfer the stock later upon death, the stock would remain taxable in the transferor's estate. For this and other reasons, it is unwise to issue a private annuity secured by the transferred stock of the corporation or any of the assets of the corporation. The transferring party must instead rely upon the integrity of the person or corporation issuing the annuity and general contract rights.

Besides estate tax savings, an unsecured annuity issued by a person or corporation which doesn't regularly issue annuities is given special benefits under the income tax law.

The current position of the Internal Revenue Service with respect to payments under a private annuity provides that a portion of each payment received under a private annuity constitutes a return of capital, a portion constitutes capital gain, and a portion constitutes ordinary income. These rules are set out in Revenue Ruling 69-74 (1969-1 C.B. 43).

3. Questions to Ask Before Using a Private Annuity

The first question to ask in planning for any private annuity is whether the business facts are favorable for such an annuity. For instance:

a) Is the transferor willing to totally divest himself of any interest in the property transferred (*e.g.*, the family business)?
b) Is the transferee (*e.g.*, the child) trustworthy and capable of managing the property (*e.g.*, running the business)?
c) Are there assets in the transferor's estate which are adequate to take care of other members of the transferor's family (*e.g.*, the wife and other children) as well as the transferor, independent of the annuity?
d) Is there a serious estate tax problem, absent the annuity transaction?

First, is the transferor ready to retire absolutely from the business involved? Unless he is, in all probability there cannot be a successful annuity transaction. More annuity transactions falter on this point than any other. Normally, in order to obtain capital gains treatment, as pointed out earlier, it will be necessary for the retiring shareholder to have no further interest in the corporation (other than as a noteholder) for at least the next ten years (IRS Code §302(c)(2)(A)).

Second, what is the reliability of the transferee? It is the height of business folly (even though, arguendo, good "tax planning") to transfer the business to a ne'er-do-well sibling, or to a person who has not exhibited the necessary business ability and experience to manage the property successfully. If management ability doesn't remain in the business, the desired transfer to the next generation will be thwarted because of the likelihood of financial difficulties for the business enterprise. Also, the economic base, the business, which constitutes the base of the annuity payment, will be weakened.

Third, most annuity transactions will have serious practical difficulties if the property transferred is the principal asset owned by the transferor. From a practical standpoint, the economic risk of the transferor is great because of a lack of both diversification and control. Even if the transferor is willing to assume the economic risk, the transaction may prove unfair to other siblings not involved in the transaction and to the spouse if there is a default in the annuity payments.

Last, if there is not a serious estate tax problem (or some other compelling reason for considering the private annuity transaction) the private annuity should not be seriously considered. It is a fairly complicated transaction with the best of plans subject to some risk and tax attack, and is usually not worth the effort and risk unless the potential estate tax savings are substantial.

4. Planning a Private Annuity Redemption

A frequent use of a private annuity transaction involves the redemption of the stock of a corporation owned by a founding shareholder, so as to leave the remaining stock in the corporation in the hands of the children, spouse, or key employees.

Euripides Corporation was founded 40 years ago by one individual who owned, until recently, all of the shares of the stock of the corporation. The corporation is very successful financially and has provided a good living and dividends for the founder's two sons, his only children. One of the sons now serves as the Executive Vice President and Production Manager and the other as Vice President and General Sales Manager.

Over the years, the founder has made it a policy of annually giving stock worth $6,000 to each of the sons and to his spouse. The present stock ownership of the corporation is as follows: Founder, 1,000 shares, Son John, 100 shares, Son Patrick, 100 shares, Wife Ruth, 100 shares. Total outstanding, 1,300 shares.

After careful study, the board of the corporation decided that the corporation should redeem all of the 1,000 shares of stock owned by the founder in exchange for an annuity issued by the corporation itself and payable over the remaining life of the founder. The founder was 65 years of age and his wife is 62.

The first hurdle met by the board was to make sure that the redemption was not treated as a dividend to the founder. If the proper steps were not taken, all amounts received could be treated as ordinary dividend income and there would not even be a tax deduction for the amounts paid by the corporation. The rules with respect to redemptions of stock are set out in §302 of the Internal Revenue Code. As a practical matter, the board discovered that the only rule set out in §302 which was of any use was the provision in

§302(b)(i)(C) that the redemption would not be treated as a dividend if it constituted a *complete* termination of all of the founder's ownership of stock in the corporation.

The rule was further complicated by the fact that a "complete termination of interest" under §302 means a complete termination of the interest of not only the particular shareholder involved, but also of those closely related to him. In fact, the rules technically reach the individual, his parents, grandparents, children, grandchildren, spouse, controlled corporations, controlled partnerships, and any trust or estate for any of their benefit. The board found that the stock owned by the sons and the spouse could be "attributed" to the founder so that, absent a special provision in the statute, the proposed redemption would not be a complete termination of the founder's interest. Fortunately, §302(c) provides an exception which has strict requirements but which solved the board's problem. Section 302(c) provides that if all of the stock actually owned by the founder was redeemed, and if the founder entered into a written contract filed with his income tax return under which he agreed that for 10 years after redemption he would not acquire any interest in the corporation whether as director, stockholder, or otherwise, then, no "attribution" would be applied in that situation and a "complete termination" of his interest existed.

By use of annuity redemption, the remaining shareholders in effect "acquired" the interest of the founder and yet were able to let the corporation itself pay for the acquisition by redeeming the founder's 1,000 shares for a private annuity contract issued by the corporation.

5. Cautions Concerning Private Annuity Transactions

The successful annuity requires thoughtful planning.

It is important to the retiring shareholder that the remaining stock of the corporation, or at least stock holding voting control, remain in trustworthy hands, because the private annuity depends upon its unsecured contractual nature for its important income tax benefits. It is important that shares of stock in the corporation be placed, either through purchase or gift, in the hands of trustworthy family members or other trustworthy individuals well before the time for use of the annuity becomes desirable.

C. THE EMPLOYEE STOCK OWNERSHIP AS AN ALTERNATIVE TO ACQUISITION

1. Background to ESOP: The Pension or Profit-Sharing Plan

Most retiring owners of a business want to provide for their own estates. Just as important to most business founders is the recognition that it is good business to allow long-term employees to participate in the growth of capital of a business. Unfortunately, it is a rare business which has rank-and-file employees who can make any significant contribution in cash to the firm's capital, or who care to risk after-tax dollars to obtain a small fractional interest in their employer corporation.

The usual way to provide retirement security for long-time employees is the pension or profit-sharing plan. Before looking at the relatively new concept of the ESOP, a brief look at these two traditional plans will be helpful.

Pension and profit-sharing plans enable an employer corporation to establish a plan and separate trust and to contribute an amount each year to the trust and to obtain an immediate tax deduction. Normally, the employee will not be charged with the receipt of any income for the employer's contribution to the plan in then-current year, but will be taxed only after retirement when he receives payments from the Trust. Under §1512 of the Tax Reform Act of 1976, and other statutes, there are special tax benefits available as to pension and profit-shring plan lump sum benefits received.

A "pension plan" is technically a plan under which contributions are made by the employer whether or not the business is profitable in a particular year. The employee is entitled to receive, upon retirement, certain pension benefits. Pension plans may be either "fixed benefits" plans (that is, designed to give a specified benefit of, say, X dollars per month for life, upon retirement) or a "money purchase" plan (under which the amount of the employer's *contribution* is fixed, and the amount of the retirement benefit itself depends upon the actual investment and actuarial experience of the plan).

The "profit-sharing plan" is another method of providing a retirement benefit for employees. Although the tax laws allow the receipt of amounts contributed to a profit-sharing plan as early as two years after the contribution, a profit-sharing plan has traditionally been used to defer payment until after retirement because of the tax advantage to the employee, and the desirability of having some retirement benefit for the employee. A profit-sharing plan differs from a pension plan in many respects, but one of the most significant is that contributions are normally payable only from net profits of the employer.

An employer corporation may contribute up to 25 percent of the amount of its payroll for covered employees to a pension plan or a combination of separate pension and profit-sharing plans. A profit-sharing plan, alone, can receive up to 15 percent of such amount. Investments of pension plans and profit-sharing plans funds are generally restricted to the type of investment suitable for an independent trustee. The operation of these plans as well as their requirement of "vesting" and forfeiture is governed by the Employees Retirement Income Security Act of 1974 (known as "ERISA"), which has had a major impact on all retirement plans.

2. Requirements for an ESOP and a TRASOP

Against the background of the usual pension and profit-sharing plan, there have existed for many years certain other types of plans. One of these, called the Employee Stock Ownership Plan (or ESOP), has characteristics which make it an ideal corporate planning tool in many situations. An ESOP is similar to a profit-sharing plan, except that contributions to the plan in any year are *not* limited to profits, and all of the plan assets may (and usually must) be invested in the employer corporation's own stock. Like other retirement plans, contributions to an ESOP may be made by the employer in cash or in property (which can include newly issued stock of the employer). These characteristics, along with some creative planning, allow the ESOP (and the associated trust which holds the assets for the plan, called the Employee Stock Ownership Trust, or "ESOT") to be utilized to create a much larger retirement benefit for employees than other types of plans under certain circumstances, while at the same time greatly improving the cash flow of the employer. Before looking at some of the planning possibilities for an ESOP, a more detailed look at the ground rules for an ESOP is in order.

Section 401 of the Internal Revenue Code sets out requirements for the qualification of a retirement plan's trust as a "qualified" trust, and specifically says that such a trust must form a "part of a stock bonus, pension, or profit-sharing plan of an employer." The Internal Revenue Regulations, §1.401-(b)(1)(iii) defines a stock bonus plan as follows:

> A stock bonus plan is a plan established and maintained by an employer to provide benefits similar to those of a profit-sharing plan, except that the contributions by the employer are not necessarily dependent upon profits and the benefits are distributable in stock of the employer company. For the purpose of allocating and distributing the stock of the employer which is to be shared among his employees or their beneficiaries, such a plan is subject to the same requirements as a profit-sharing plan.

The Revenue Act of 1978 contains definitions of an ESOP in §409A which it added to the Internal Revenue Code. This and other sections indicate that an ESOP may be a qualified stock bonus plan or money-purchase pension plan. It is assumed that the plans will normally be a stock bonus plan. The Code requires that such a plan to constitute an ESOP must be an individual account plan, and must be designed to invest primarily in qualifying employer securities. An individual account plan is one in which each participant has his own individual account maintained, and benefits under the plan are based solely on the amount in each individual participant's account. It is possible for an ESOP to use certain types of employer debt obligations but normally the benefits to both the employees and the employer will be maximized if common or preferred stock is used. Section 409A(h) and IRS Regulations make use of voting common stock as to which the employee beneficiary will have a "put" upon distribution, desirable for the funding of most ESOT's (see Reg. §54.4975-7).

Unlike almost any other type of qualified plan, there are no requirements for "diversification" of plan assets for an ESOP, and therefore the plan's assets may consist solely of one class of stock in one corporation (*i.e.*, the employer). Furthermore, stock may be held by ESOP even though a "reasonable return" is not made on the investment (Rev. Rul. 69-65, 1969-1 C.B. 114). Put differently, the employer stock contributed to an ESOP need not produce any specific amount of income; that is, the employer need not pay any specific amount of dividends on the stock, or perhaps, any dividends at all.

Since distributions are made from the ESOP to the employee directly in employer company stock, there is no need normally for an ESOP to have much liquidity, unlike normal pension or profit-sharing plans.

As mentioned above, the ESOP may receive tax deductible contributions from the employer even in years in which there is no profit (unlike the profit-sharing plan). Section 401(a)(3)(A) provides that the maximum contribution in any one year to an ESOP is 15 percent of the total participant's compensation, plus a carryover for previous years of the plan in which the 15 percent maximum deduction was not fully utilized, up to a maximum amount of 25 percent of participant's compensation in any one year. The employer's contribution may be the employer's stock, cash, or other property. Normally, other property is not utilized in planning for an ESOP because, if it has appreciated, a capital gain would be recognized by the employer corporation at the time of the contribution (Rev. Rul. 73-345, 1973-2 C.B. 11). The employer stock alone is deductible at a fair market value without any regard to the corporation's basis for the stock (which is normally zero).

In 1971, the Internal Revenue Service published a ruling stating that a trust forming a part of a qualified plan usually is not prohibited in borrowing the funds to purchase employer securities.

The Tax Reduction Act of 1974, the Tax Reform Act of 1976 and the Revenue Act of 1978 give an added bonus for use of an ESOP of a special type and enables the employer corporation establishing such as ESOP (called a "TRASOP") to take an 11 percent investment tax credit rather than 10 per cent investment tax credit otherwise applying.

3. How to Use an ESOP as an Acquisition Alternative

The unique characteristics of the ESOP have great potential in creating an alternative to an acquisition. Certain possible uses will be outlined here, but the possibilities are limited only by the imagination of the executive and his professional planners.

(a) One-Shot Generation of Liquid Capital

The Federal Internal Revenue laws allow a corporation to obtain a refund of federal income taxes previously paid by carrying back a tax loss to offset taxable income in prior years. The ESOP created the possibility of generating a tax loss growing out of a deduction to the Employee Stock Ownership Trust in a year in which there are no taxable profits for the corporation. The ESOP also allows a contribution to be made, as discussed above, in stock of the corporation rather than in cash or other property.

These three attributes can be tied together in order to obtain a substantial cash tax refund without any offsetting drain on the cash flow of the corporation.

For instance, Alhambra Corporation has a payroll of $5,000,000 per year. For each of the past five years, it has paid $500,000 in federal income taxes. In the present year, because of market conditions, it anticipates no taxable income and the payment of no federal income taxes. It has been anticipating borrowing from its primary lenders in order to help improve short-term liquidity.

The ESOP provides an alternative for Alhambra's current liquidity needs.

After a thorough economic analysis, Alhambra Corporation adopts an ESOP and establishes a trust for the benefit of its employees. It contributes to the trust authorized, but previously unissued shares of the corporation itself, which have a fair market value of $750,000, equal to 15% of Alhambra's payroll. Since Alhambra Corporation had no net taxable income for that year, there is now created a $375,000 ($750,000 × 50% effective state and federal corporate tax rate) tax loss which can be carried back to the preceding year to reduce income taxes which were paid. For instance, if taxable income in the preceding year had been $1,000,000 resulting in the payment of a tax of about $500,000, the carryback would cause taxable income for the preceding year to be reduced to $250,000 ($1,000,000 less $750,000) with a corresponding tax refund of almost $375,000, payable in cash by the United States Government to the corporation shortly after the filing of the necessary returns and claims for refund.

In a given case, that $375,000 could be the difference between having to merge into a larger corporation or being able to maintain the corporation as an independent, closely held corporation.

(b) Estate Liquidity Through Use of ESOP

An ESOP is also often a valuable method to create estate liquidity. Obviously, the techniques set forth in Section 1 above could generate necessary liquidity to enable an installment purchase or lump sum purchase of stock from a deceased shareholder. As discussed later in this chapter the tax code provides for an installment purchase of closely-held corporation's stock over a 15-year period in certain circumstances, and some deferral estate taxes over that same period.

More directly, a pattern along the following lines could be used:

The founder of Family Corporation owns 25 percent of its stock while his wife and children own the balance of the shares. The family members are the corporate officers and there is a payroll of $5,000,000 per year, with federal corporate taxes of $1,000,000 per year. The corporation has good credit and a sound business but no excess of cash from which a stock redemption could be made at the present time. The value of the deceased shareholder's shares is $2,000,000. The corporation establishes an ESOP. The ESOP borrows $2,000,000 from the corporation's banker backed by the guarantee of the corporation and an undertaking to pledge shares of stock to be purchased by the ESOP. The terms of the loan from the bank require principal payments of $200,000 per year for 10 years, plus interest at the rate of 10 percent per year.

The bank makes the loan to the ESOP, and the ESOP purchases all of the shares of stock of the deceased shareholder for the $2,000,000 in cash. At that point, the ESOP owns the stock, the estate of the deceased shareholder has $2,000,000 in cash, the bank has the stock as collateral.

Each year for 10 years, the corporation takes a tax deduction and contributes in cash the sum of $200,000 plus the accrued interest on the bank loan to the ESOP, taking a tax deduction for the entire amount. The ESOP takes those funds and pays them to the bank so that at the end of the 10 years, the loan is completely repaid. The corporation has obtained the deduction for the *full* amount of the loan to be paid over time (rather than merely interest costs as in the normal redemption), all of the stock has stayed within the control of the present shareholders and employees, and the estate has immediate cash.

(c) Use of ESOP to Finance a New Plant

Capital Corporation needs to finance a new plant and warehouse at a total cost of $4,000,000. It does not wish to issue stock outside of the corporate shareholder and employee family. With an ESOP it is possible for Capital Corporation to pay for the entire plant and warehouse with after-tax dollars.

The method used by Capital Corporation is the following:

Capital forms an ESOP which acquires a commitment from a life insurance company for a loan of $5,000,000, to be secured by shares of stock of Capital Corporation and a new plant to be built by Capital Corporation, along with Capital's guarantee.

ESOP then purchases from Capital shares of Capital having a fair market value of $5,000,000 for $5,000,000 in cash. Capital Corporation then pays $5,000,000 for the new plant to a third party.

Annually, Capital Corporation contributes to the ESOP the amount of $750,000 (15 percent of its payroll) which entitles it to a tax deduction in that amount. The ESOP uses those funds to retire the principal and interest of the life insurance company loan.

The net effect of this transaction is that the Capital Corporation has its new plant, its eligible employees have shares of stock of Capital Corporation worth $5,000,000, Capital Corporation has received tax deduction for amounts equal to both the principal and interest of the loan, and the lender has received payment of the loan in full.

4. Caution in Use of an ESOP

The use of an ESOP for corporate purposes as outlined in this chapter is a relatively recent development. It is particularly important that the executive's professional advisors thoroughly review any proposed use of an ESOP to make certain that it will qualify under fast-changing tax and securities statutes and regulations for the benefits sought. Valuation of the ESOP's stock is often a difficult task in a closely-held corporation, and state and federal securities laws must be observed.

Particular attention would be given to the fact that new stock issued to an ESOP will dilute the equity ownership of the other shareholders. The Revenue Act of 1978, §409A(e) *requires* that the employee/beneficiaries of the ESOP be allowed, in most circumstances, to direct the vote of the shares held for them. This will usually have little effect in a closely-held corporation, because of the founding family of the corporation will be careful not to place in the ESOP shares which could actually affect control. It is possible, however, that the shares held in ESOP will have a practical effect in the case of a merger or other transaction involving the corporation which requires a shareholder vote.

Example: Little David Corporation has 43 percent of its stock held by the founding family, 25 percent of its stock held in an ESOP, and the balance of the shares of stock held by several large unaffiliated shareholders. The founders very much wish the corporation to participate in a merger. Since a greater than 50 percent vote is required under most merger statutes in favor of the merger, if the unaffiliated outside shareholders oppose a merger, the actions of the individual employees in directing the ESOP to vote their respective shares, will be critical to the outcome of the merger.

D. FRANCHISING AS AN ALTERNATIVE TO ACQUISITION

Franchising can often be an alternative to acquisition for potential acquiring and acquired corporations.

For the potential acquiring corporation, it can be a means of rapid growth, without the need to accumulate enormous amounts of capital or to bear all of the market risks. A typical situation might involve a corporation with a unique system for repair of automobile transmissions. Rather than acquiring transmission shops throughout the country, or establishing a number of branches, the company could offer independent business executives the opportunity to share in the trademark, techniques, and equipment on a franchise basis. This might call for initial payments upon the opening of each franchise location, and the payment of percentage gross revenues throughout the entire business operation.

For potential target corporations, franchising can offer an opportunity for capital growth and the benefits of being affiliated with a larger corporation, without some of the disadvantages. A corporation which has a successful business which has reached the present limits of growth under its capitalization should consider not only the possibilities of new investors and being acquired by a corporation with a larger capital base, but also the possibilities of expanding its business by franchising techniques and know-how in order to participate in diverse geographic growth.

Example: Algonquin Corporation has a very successful fast-food restaurant in a California city. The founder has operated the restaurant for more than 20 years and does not wish to invest more capital in expanding the business. A group of potential purchasers of the business contact the founder and suggest that the founder sell his shares.

One real alternative to a sale or other acquisition transaction for the founder, would be for the founder to license the trademarks, recipes, and other trade secrets to the persons who wish to acquire the business. Founder will retain his existing business, the persons who wish to acquire the business will be free to open additional businesses in the same format and under the same trademark in other geographic areas, and founder, or his business, will be entitled to substantial income, not only as "start-up" payments for each new business location, but also as continuing percentage licensing royalties (perhaps 4 percent of all gross sales) for as long as the franchises are operated. The potential purchasers get what they wished, the know-how, trademarks, goodwill, and skill of the founder's business for a small "front-end" payment. Founder retains his business and reaps the benefits of future growth, without any additional new capital commitments.

Most franchises which are offered today are subject to the Federal Trade Commission rules concerning franchise disclosure (16 C.R.F. §436 *et seq.*), and many states have even stricter acts. See Appendix Q for FTC Franchising Rules. Basically, these rules which became effective in late 1979, require that a Disclosure Statement be furnished to each prospective franchisee at an early date and, normally, ten days prior to the execution of any franchise agreement. The FTC Disclosure Statements require detailed financial information on the franchisor and on any agent or territory operator for the franchisor. The information includes names and addresses of the closest existing franchisees as well as extensive information concerning the franchise agreement itself.

E. LIBERALIZED ESTATE TAX PAYMENT PROVISIONS AS AN ALTERNATIVE TO ACQUISITION

To the extent that a proposed acquisition is chiefly motivated from a desire to increase estate liquidity for one or more key shareholders, consideration should be given to special provisions in the Internal Revenue Code allowing deferred payment of estate taxes with respect to closely-held businesses in certain situations.

As an incentive to encouraging continued family ownership of small and medium-sized businesses, the Internal Revenue Code contains two specific provisions which allow estate taxes to be paid over a period of time. The first of these can be a real bonanza for a medium-size business because it allows, in effect, four percent 15-year financing for the first $345,800 of estate taxes owed with respect to a qualifying business. Not only that, but there can be terms of interest only for the first five years.

This is the way that Section 6166 works:

☐ *Qualifying Business.*
The value of the interest in the closely-held business must exceed 65 percent of the adjusted gross estate. A qualifying "closely-held business" may be a corporation carrying on a trade or business, or even a proprietorship or partnership if:
1. At least 20 percent in value of the voting stock or ownership of the business is included in the gross estate, and
2. The business has 15 or fewer owners.
Interests held by a husband and wife as joint tenants, tenants by the entirety, or tenants in common, are treated as being owned by one shareholder or partner and there are rules for property owned by estates and trusts set out in the statute.
☐ *Interests in Two or More Closely-Held Businesses.*
Interests in two or more closely-held businesses are treated as a single closely-held business if the decedant's gross estate included more than 20 percent of the total value of each of such businesses. This is not merely an estate tax deferral provision,

but is really an asset which every owner of a small or medium-size business may have in his or her estate and should carefully consider.

Another provision, Section 6166A, grants a 10-year extension of time for payment at an interest rate which is presently set at 12 percent by the Internal Revenue Service, with more liberal qualifying rules. In order to qualify, the value of an interest in a closely-held business included in the estate must exceed either:

1. 35 percent of the value of the gross estate; or
2. 50 percent of the taxable estate.

Example: Wilbur Wilson owns all of the common stock of Wilson Corporation, which is now worth about $2 million. The other assets in his adjusted gross estate are worth less than $1 million. Here's the way Wilson's estate plan (simplifed) might use Section 6166:

Value of Wilson Corporation	
Stock	$2,000,000
Value of Other Assets	1,000,000
Value of Adjusted Gross Estate	$3,000,000
65 percent of Adjusted Gross Estate	$1,950,000

Wilson Corporation's stock exceeds 65 percent of the adjusted gross estate, and therefore qualifies since 100 percent of the value of the voting stock of the business is included in the gross estate and the business has only one owner. Assuming no marital deduction:

Cash estate tax payable in Wilson's estate if §6166 *not* elected:	$1,290,800
With §6166 election, cash payable:	$ 905,000

Balance of $385,800 payable in a 15-year note, four percent interest, interest only for the first five years.

Chapter 8

A Brief Look At
Acquisitions in the 1980's

Where acqusitions will head in the 1980's is more a task for a soothsayer than a lawyer/adviser. But since many of the business, legal, accounting, and tax trends are already established for the acquisitions of the 80's, it is possible to make some educated guesses:

☐ Tight money and high interest rates will lead to more self-financed acquisitions. Faced with the high prime rates of the early 1980's, many executives will opt for a leveraged, "boot-strap" deal from the seller.

☐ In inflationary times, the start-up costs of a new enterprise will often greatly exceed the cost of acquiring assets through the merger route. This means that there are many acquisition bargains for the sophisticated and knowledgeable executive. While there are disadvantages, there are enormous potential advantages to the acquisition of an existing corporation to expand product lines or geographic areas or to add additional plant capacity when faced with rapidly escalating construction and machinery costs.

☐ More and more entrepreneurs will use a successful business as a basis for a "mini-conglomerate" to build personal fortunes and to diversify holdings.

☐ Among publicly-traded corporations, there will be a return to more traditional agreements submitted through corporate channels to the shareholders for approval, rather than cash tender offers furnished by bank loans.

☐ There should be an increase in the protection of the rights of minority shareholders in buy-out situations.

☐ More foreign buyers will participate in United States corporate takeovers, and United States business executives will pay more attention to the possibilities of acquisitions of foreign subsidiaries to develop growing markets.

☐ More and more commercial banks will establish or enlarge departments of corporate finance, not only place securities privately, but also to plan mergers and acquisitions for bank customers.

☐ At the federal level, regulations may discourage acquisitions by very large corporations. At the state level, regulations may require more of a waiting period before consummating mergers.

☐ More employees and executives will become owners of corporations for which they work, especially where potential bankruptcy or plant dislocation seems probable. In addition, new devices, such as ESOP's, will give more executives a stake in their corporation.

☐ More and more useful and publicly available financial information will be contained in corporate financial statements. Part of this will come as a result of the changes decreed by the Financial Accounting Standards Board Rules adopted in December, 1979. These rules will cause many annual reports to have supplemental footnotes which will indicate substantial upward adjustments and depreciation. These footnotes will reflect depreciation based upon replacement costs rather than historical costs. These reports will also show the increase in the value of inventory, property and plant held during the year, as well as adjusting dividends, on a historical basis, for inflation.

☐ A trend toward divestitures by publicly held corporations. As more emphasis is placed on strategic planning and immediate earnings for these corporations, more slow growth divisions will be offered for sale. These are often excellent buys for the knowledgeable executive in a closely-held business.

The skilled executive or professional advisor who has familiarized himself with techniques like those described in this *Desk Book* will be ready for the tremendous opportunities which are available for creative business acquisitions in the 1980's. Let's review some of those techniques:

☐ The classic tax-free acquisition techniques, the "A", "B", and "C" Reorganizations which involve no substantial cash outlay for the acquiring corporation, a largely tax-free transaction for the target corporation, and often the opportunity to become holders of a publicly traded security for the holders of a formerly closely-held enterprise. Diversification of risk and growth potential are provided without recognizing capital gains.

☐ The flexible installment sale under the Installment Sales Revision Act of 1980. This allows postponement of tax on the part of the seller, and the potential for buying a business with its own earnings for the purchaser. The 1980 Act has made this useful tool even more flexible for creative acquisitions in the 1980's.

☐ The tax-free exchange provides a tool that will be even more useful in the 1980's. Regulated businesses such as radio stations may be required to divest other regulated enterprises in certain markets. The tax-free exchange of one station for a station in another market is a natural technique for this situation.

☐ Use of a creative mixture of business, tax, and negotiating techniques can often make the "impossible deal." Buyer and seller are $500,000 apart. The reason is a difference of opinion as to the earnings potential of the target company over the next five years. Creative negotiating on the part of the buyer will fix the price at the *buyer's* price, but allow the seller to "earn out" additional stock *if* earnings reach the seller's estimate in the next five years.

☐ The founding father of a successful business enterprise, at age 65, is becoming more and more concerned about estate taxes. He very much wants to leave the business to his son and daughter, both of whom are active in the business, but he realizes that estate taxes will be enormous. He realizes that even without real growth, if inflation continues, steeply graduated estate tax rates will drive the cost of transferring his interest in the business to the next generation higher and higher.

Rather than seeking a merger with a larger corporation in order to acquire a market for the shares of stock, the founder might consider "freezing" the value of his shares. This will allow his son and daughter to purchase (or be given) controlling common shares in the corporation. The value of the founder's stock will be reduced at his death, and estate taxes will be slashed. As another option, the founder might consider a private annuity with his son and daughter, completely eliminating any estate taxes on his shares of stock in the business.

In summary, acquisition opportunities (and alternatives to acquisition opportunities) will be great in the 1980's. Acquisitions will be based upon more and better information than ever before. New techniques will evolve to meet the fast-changing needs of both sellers and buyers.

Those involved in acquisitions in the 1980's can profit from Emerson's observation that "This time, like all times, is a very good one if we but know what to do with it." It is hoped that your acquisitions in the 1980's will be fruitful and rewarding, and that this *Desk Book* will help you better recognize the opportunities in acquisitions today, and what to do with them.

Appendix

Appendix A

Excerpts from
Typical Merger Statute
(Delaware Code, Title 8,
Section 251)

See discussion beginning page 4

Merger or consolidation of domestic corporations.—(a) Any two or more corporations existing under the laws of this state may merge into a single corporation, which may be any one of the constituent corporations or may consolidate into a new corporation formed by the consolidation; pursuant to an agreement of merger or consolidation, as the case may be, complying and approved in accordance with this section.

(b) The board of directors of each corporation which desires to merge or consolidate shall adopt a resolution approving an agreement of merger or consolidation. The agreement shall state: (1) the terms and conditions of the merger or consolidation; (2) the mode of carrying the same into effect; (3) such amendments or changes in the certificate of incorporation of the surviving corporation as are desired to be effected by the merger, or consolidation, or, if no such amendments or changes are desired, a statement that the certificate of incorporation of one of the constituent corporations shall be the certificate of incorporation of the surviving or resulting corporation; (4) the manner of converting the shares of each of the constituent corporations into shares or other securities of the corporation surviving or resulting from the merger or consolidation, and, if any shares of any of the constituent corporations are not to be converted solely into shares or other securities of the surviving or resulting corporation, the cash, property, rights, or securities of any other corporation which the holders of such shares are to receive in exchange for, or upon conversion of such shares and the surrender of the certificates evidencing them, which cash, property, rights, or securities of any other corporation may be in addition to or in lieu of shares or other securities of the surviving or resulting corporation; and (5) such other details or provisions as are deemed desirable, including, without limiting the generality of the foregoing, a provision for the payment of cash in lieu of the issuance or recognition of fractional shares, interests, or rights, or for any other arrangement with respect thereto, consistent with the provisions of Section 155 of this title. The agreement so adopted shall be executed in accordance with Section 103 of this title. Any of the terms of the agreement of merger or consolidation may be made dependent upon facts ascertainable outside of such agreement, provided that the manner in which such facts shall operate upon the terms of the agreement is clearly and expressly set forth in the agreement of merger or consolidation.

(c) The agreement required by subsection (b) shall be submitted to the stockholders of each constituent corporation at an annual or special meeting thereof for the purpose of acting on the agreement. Due notice of the time, place, and purpose of the meeting shall be mailed to each holder of stock, whether voting or nonvoting, of the corporation at his address as it appears on the records of the corporation, at least 20 days prior to the date of the meeting. At the meeting the agreement shall be considered and a vote taken for its adoption or rejection. If a majority of the outstanding stock of the corporation entitled to vote thereon shall be voted for the adoption of the agreement, that fact shall be certified on the agreement by the secretary or assistant secretary of the corporation. If the agreement shall be so adopted and certified by each constituent corporation, it shall then, in addition to the execution required by subsection (b) of this section, be executed, acknowledged, and filed, and shall become effective in accordance with Section 103 of this title. It shall be recorded in the office of the Recorder of the County of this state in which the registered office of each such constituent corporation is located; or if any of the constituent corporations shall have been specially created by a public act of the Legislature, then the agreement shall be recorded in the county where such corporation had its principal place of business in this state. In lieu of filing and recording the agreement of merger or consolidation, the surviving or resulting corporation may file a certificate of merger or consolidation, executed in accordance with Section 103 of this title, which states (1) the name and state of incorporation of each of the constituent corporations, (2) that an agreement of merger or consolidation has been approved, adopted, certified, executed, and acknowledged by each of the constituent corporations in accordance with this subsection, (3) the name of the surviving or resulting corporation, (4) the amendments or changes, if any, in the certificate of incorporation of the surviving corporation that are to be effected by the merger or consolidation, or, if none, that the certificate of incorporation of one of the constituent corporations, naming it, shall be the certificate of incorporation of the surviving or resulting corporation, (5) that the executed agreement of consolidation or merger is on file at the principal place of business of the surviving corporation, stating the address thereof and (6) that a copy of the agreement of consolidation or merger will be furnished by the surviving corporation, on request and without cost, to any stockholder of any constituent corporation.

(d) Any agreement of merger or consolidation may contain a provision that at any time prior to the filing of the agreement with the secretary of state, the agreement may be terminated by the board of directors of any constituent corporation notwithstanding approval of the agreement by the stockholders of all or any of the constituent corporations.

(e) In the case of a merger, the certificate of incorporation of the surviving corporation shall automatically be amended to the extent, if any, that changes in the certificate of incorporation are set forth in the agreement of merger.

(f) Notwithstanding the requirements of subsection (c), unless required by its certificate of incorporation, no vote of stockholders of a constituent corporation surviving a merger shall be necessary to authorize a merger if (1) the agreement of merger does not amend in any respect the certificate of incorporation of such constituent corporation, (2) each share of stock of such constituent corporation outstanding immediately prior to the effective date of the merger is to be an identical outstanding or treasure share of their surviving corporation after the effective date of the merger, and (3) either no shares of common stock of the surviving corporation and no shares, securities, or obligations convertible into such stock are to be issued or delivered under the plan of merger, or the authorized unissued shares or the treasury shares of common stock of the surviving corporation to be issued or delivered under the plan of merger plus those initially issuable upon conversion of any other shares, securities, or obligations to be issued or delivered under such plan, do not exceed 20 percent of the shares of common stock of such constituent corporation outstanding immediately prior to the effective date of the merger. No vote of stockholders of a constituent corporation shall be necessary to authorize a merger or consolidation if no shares of the stock of such corporation shall have been issued prior to the adoption by the board of directors of the resolution approving the agreement of merger or consolidation. If an agreement of merger is adopted by the constituent corporation surviving the merger, by action of its board of directors and without any vote of its stockholders pursuant to this subsection, the secretary or assistant secretary of that corporation shall certify on the agreement, that the agreement has been adopted pursuant to this subsection and that, as of the date of such certificate, the outstanding shares of the corporation were such as to render this subsection applicable. The agreement so adopted and certified shall then be executed, acknowledged, and filed and shall become effective, in accordance with Section 103 of this title. Such filing shall constitute a representation by the person who executes the agreement that the facts stated in the certificate remain true immediately prior to such filing. (§ 251, as amended by L. 1967, c. 186, § 16; L. 1969, c. 148, § 22; L. 1970, c. 421, §§ 8, 9; L. 1971, c. 235, § 5; L. 1974, c. 437, §§ 12, 13, and 14.)

Appendix B

Case Discussing "Solely for Voting Stock Requirement of 'B' Reorganization"

See discussion beginning at page 12.

Arden S. Heverly, et al. v.
Commissioner of Internal Revenue,
_____ F.2d _____ (3d Cir., 1980)

Author's Note: This case re-affirms the
rule that only voting stock may be used
in a "B" Reorganization

Before Aldisert, Weis and Higginbotham, Circuit Judges.

OPINION OF THE COURT

Aldisert, Circuit Judge: The major issue presented by these consolidated appeals from the United States Tax Court and the United States District Court for the District of Delaware is whether the use of consideration other than voting stock is allowable in a tax deferred stock for stock reorganization as defined in § 368(a)(1)(B) of the Internal Revenue Code, 26 U.S.C. § 368(a)(1)(B). In the vernacular, the question is whether "boot" may be used in a clause B corporate reorganization. Both courts below agreed with the taxpayers that other consideration is allowable so long as "control" of the target corporation is obtained "solely for . . . voting stock," and thus allowed them to defer recognition of their gain under § 354(a)(1), 26 U.S.C. § 354(a)(1). We hold that, in a stock for stock transaction in which control is achieved, the acquiring corporation may exchange no consideration other than voting stock to effect a tax deferred clause B reorganization. We therefore reverse.

I. The facts have been detailed in the trial court opinions, *Reeves v. Commissioner* [CCH Dec. 35,870], 71 T.C. 727,728-31 (1979), and *Pierson v. United States*, 472 F. Supp. 957,958-60 (D. Del. 1979), so we need not elaborate them at length. The transaction at issue involved the acquisition of stock in Hartford Insurance Company by International Telephone and Telegraph Corporation. ITT first made overtures to the management of Hartford in 1968, suggesting either an acquisition of Hartford by ITT or merger of Hartford into ITT. Hartford rejected these immediate proposals, but apparently gave no definitive veto to a future amalgamation. ITT subsequently purchased for cash, in two block transactions and various open market transactions, approximately eight percent of Hartford's outstanding stock.

In December 1968, ITT proposed merger terms to Hartford, leading to a provisional agreement on April 9, 1969, to merge Hartford into a wholly owned subsidiary of ITT. The Antitrust Division of the Department of Justice commenced litigation to enjoin the merger in August 1969, but its motion for preliminary injunction was denied in October 1969. On October 13, 1969, the Internal Revenue Service issued a private letter ruling advising ITT and Hartford that

139

the proposed merger would be within § 368(a)(1)(B) if ITT unconditionally divested itself of the Hartford stock it had previously purchased for cash. On October 21, the IRS ruled that ITT's proposed sale of the stock to Mediobanca, an Italian bank, would constitute an unconditional disposition, and ITT consummated the sale.

Although ITT overcame the obstacles erected by the Antitrust Division and the IRS, and obtained approval for the transaction from the Hartford and ITT shareholders, the merger fell through when the Connecticut Insurance Commissioner withheld his approval. ITT and Hartford then proposed an offer to the Hartford shareholders of ITT stock for their Hartford stock. The Connecticut Insurance Commissioner ultimately approved this plan, and ITT submitted the exchange offer to the Hartford shareholders on May 26, 1970. By June 8, 1970, over ninety-five percent of the Hartford shares, including those held by Mediobanca, had been tendered.

In March 1974, the IRS, alleging misrepresentations in ITT's application for the private letter ruling regarding the sale of Hartford stock to Mediobanca, retroactively revoked its ruling that deemed that sale an unconditional disposition of the stock. The effect of the revocation, according to the IRS, was to disqualify the transaction from treatment under clause B and thus to preclude tax deferral of the gain realized by the Hartford shareholders when they exchanged their Hartford stock for ITT stock. The Service reasoned that clause B allows no consideration other than voting stock, and that the purchase for cash of eight percent of Hartford stock by ITT precluded treatment of the transaction under clause B. As a result, the Service assessed tax deficiencies against the former Hartford shareholders, including the appellees here.[1]

II. In the trial courts, taxpayers sought deferral of their gain under § 354(a) of the Internal Revenue Code, 26 U.S.C. § 354(a), arguing that they participated in a corporate reorganization. They rely on § 368(a)(1)(B), which defines "reorganization" as an acquisition, solely for voting stock, of stock of another corporation, if the acquiring corporation is in "control" of the other corporation immediately after the exchange.

The two courts below granted taxpayers' motion for summary judgment, though on somewhat different grounds. Before both courts, taxpayers asserted alternative grounds for summary judgment. They argued initially that the cash purchases of stock by ITT in 1968 were not part of the same "plan of reorganization" as its acquisition of ninety-five percent of Hartford's stock in 1970. The requirement that the exchange be "solely for voting stock" was thus fulfilled because the prior cash purchases should not be considered. Their alternative argument was that even if the cash purchases were part of the plan of reorganization, they constituted a separate "transaction" from the exchange of stock for stock. Under their interpretation, clause B requires only the acquisition of "control" of the target corporation "solely for . . . voting stock" of the acquiring corporation. Thus, ITT's acquisition was within clause B because the stock transaction gave it "control" of Hartford. Both courts accepted the second argument and, concluding that it was fully dispositive, declined to address the first argument.

A. The appeal from the tax court emanates from a case styled *Reeves v. Commissioner* [CCH Dec. 35,870], 71 T. C. 727 (1979), which held that ITT's acquisition of more than eighty percent

---

[1]The appellees from the Tax Court, at appeal No. 79-1985, successfully contested the following deficiencies:

Docket No.	Party	Deficiency Assessment
4953-74	Arden S. and Sophia S. Heverly	$ 2,192.81
6153-74	Edna L. Boyer, Deceased, represented by John H. Bozic, Jr., Executor	13,202.00
6187-74	Katherine D. Harvey	41,454.28
8602-74	John J. and Agnes C. DeFraine	1,684.74

The appellee from the district court, John Lewis Pierson, at appeal No. 79-2192, recovered a judgment refunding $3,683 already paid plus statutory interest.

of Hartford's stock in a single transaction satisfied the "solely for voting stock" requirement of clause B, regardless of the cash exchanges. *Id.* at 741-42. In an opinion announcing the decision of the court,[2] Judge Tannenwald began his analysis with an observation that the legislative history underlying § 368 is inconclusive on this issue. *Id.* at 732 (citing *Turnbow v. Commissioner*, 368 U.S. 337, 344n. 8 (1961). He distinguished *Helvering v. Southwest Consolidated Corp.*, 315 U.S. 194 (1942), in which the Supreme Court held that an earlier version of the reorganization section dealing with both stock for stock and stock for asset exchanges allowed no consideration other than voting stock, because it involved an asset acquisition, not a stock acquisition. He also noted that *Southwest Consolidated* addressed a situation in which voting stock represented only sixty-three percent of the total consideration. 71 T. C. at 734-35.

Judge Tannenwald distinguished other decisions by grouping them into two categories. The first category included decisions in which the control requirement could be met only by taking into account prior acquisitions. In this category he grouped *Lutkins v. United States*, 312 F.2d 803 (Ct. Cl.), cert. denied, 375 U.S. 825 (1963), *Commissioner v. Air Reduction Co.* 130 F.2d 145 (2d Cir.), cert. denied, 317 U.S. 681 (1942), and *Pulfer v. Commissioner*, 43 B.T.A. 677 (1941), aff'd 128 F.2d 742 (6th Cir. 1942) (per curiam). 71 T. C. at 736. The second category of decisions involved single transactions in which more than eighty percent of the target corporation's stock was acquired but both voting stock and other consideration was used in the acquisition. 71 T. C. at 736. Included in this category were *Turnbow v. Commissioner* [62-1 USTC ¶9104], 368 U.S. 337 (1961), *Mills v. Commissioner* [CCH Dec. 25,753], 39 T. C. 393 (1962), rev'd, 331 F.2d 321 (5th Cir. 1964), and *Howard v. Commissioner* 24 T. C. 792 (1955), rev'd on other grounds, 238 F.2d 943 (7th Cir. 1956). More specifically, "[i]n *Mills* and *Turnbow*, *each shareholder* whose stock was being acquired *got cash*." 71 T. C. at 736. In addition, "*Howard* is factually distinguishable . . . because some stockholders involved in the one exchange transaction . . . received cash." *Id.* at 737. Judge Tannenwald concluded that neither category should apply to a situation in which ITT obtained "control" of Hartford by giving only ITT shares for Hartford shares in exchanges clearly separable from concurrent cash exchanges.

As support for his conclusion that clause B is undeserving of a "pervasively rigid interpretation," Judge Tannenwald noted that legislative amendments of clause B indicate a continuing congressional concern that courts were interpreting the "solely" requirement too rigidly and that the IRS had issued numerous rulings allowing technical exceptions to that requirement. *Id.* at 740. He also noted that a strict construction of "solely for . . . voting stock" would create such "odd results" as making some transactions that initially complied with clause B retroactively taxable if additional shares were acquired for nonstock consideration. *Id.* at 740-41. The court concluded:

> We are not unaware of the conceptual difficulties involved in determining what is "the acquisition" for purposes of a (B) reorganization and that an argument can be made that separating out the 1970 exchange begs the question, or to put it another way, assumes the issue which requires decision. But we do not see the situation in this light. The facts of the matter are that the 1970 exchange, standing by itself, satisfied in every way the literal requirements of section 368(a)(1)(B) and that neither legislative nor judicial history nor policy requires that that exchange (involving in excess of 80 percent of Hartford's stock) not be separated from the other acquisitions of Hartford stock by ITT for cash, at least for the purpose of disposing of the legal issue raised by petitioners' second contention. We take this position with full knowledge that, for the purpose of disposing of that contention, on this motion for summary judgment, we must assume that the pre-1970 cash purchases were part of the "plan of reorganization." But our position, simply stated, is that, in the context of this case, such assumption is of no consequence because the prior purchases are irrelevant.

---

[2]Four judges joined the plurality opinion, two judges concurred in the result, and five judges dissented. See note 4, *infra*.

Id. at 741 (footnote omitted).[3] Two judges concurred and five judges dissented.[4] The Commissioner has appealed the Tax Court decision.[5]

B. The district court blazed a somewhat different trail. Judge Schwartz also concluded that prior decisions did not foreclose a result favorable to the taxpayers. He dealt at length with *Southwest Consolidated*, noting that it was decided under the Revenue Act of 1934, which treated stock acquisitions identically to asset acquisitions. 472 F. Supp. at 962. But subsequential changes in the reorganization statute have, he reasoned, destroyed that decision's precedential value. *Id.* at 963. The *Air Reduction* and *Howard* decisions, emphasizing the identity between stock and asset acquisitions, relied on *Southwest Consolidated* to disallow consideration other than voting stock in stock acquisitions. Judge Schwartz found *Air Reduction* unpersuasive because it failed to give a reasoned elaboration for its conclusion. 472 F. Supp. at 962-63. Although Judge Schwartz recognized that the ninth circuit had examined the legislative history of clause B in *Turnbow*, he noted that the court's inquiry did not determine whether "solely" permits consideration other than voting stock, "but rather was aimed at demonstrating that there was *some* limitation on the presence of boot." *Id.* at 965. Similarly, he noted that in *Mills v. Commissioner* [64-1 USTC ¶9474], 331 F.2d 321 (5th Cir. 1964), the fifth circuit addressed an issue other than the "solely" requirement in concluding that cash payments for fractional shares were not "consideration" in the sense prohibited by clause B. 472 F. Supp. at 965. Finally, he disapproved *Lutkins v. United States* [63-1 USTC ¶9252], 312 F.2d 803 (Ct. Cl.), cert. denied, 375 U.S. 825 (1963), because it relied entirely on *Southwest Consolidated* and *Howard* as the rationale for disallowing cash in a stock for stock exchange. 472 F. Supp. at 965-66. He interpreted the Supreme Court's decision in *Turnbow* as expressly reserving the issue. *Id.* at 966.

After concluding that no prior decisions were of precedential value, Judge Schwartz analyzed the legislative history of clause B. He noted that the ninth circuit's analysis of the legislative history in *Turnbow* hinged on its assumption that the amendment to clause C allowing some

---

[3]Taxpayers reassert before us their argument, which the Tax Court accepted in the language quoted in text, that even if the cash purchases and the stock for stock exchange were part of the same "plan of reorganization," they were not part of the same "transaction" and thus deserve separate analysis under clause B. The majority of the tax court, two concurring judges and five dissenting judges, rejected this argument as a distinction without a difference. See 71 T. C. at 743 (Scott, J., concurring); *id.* at 744 (Quealy, J., dissenting); *id.* at 745 n. 1, 749-51 (Wilbur, J., dissenting). We agree. To allow taxpayers to sever their acquisitions into separate "transactions" would lead far beyond the result taxpayers seek in this case, tax deferral when at least eighty percent of the target's stock is acquired for the acquiring corporation's stock. It would also render application of the "creeping control" amendment in clause B almost a matter of caprice: Some exchangers would be aggregated to allow deferral, while others would be severed to allow deferral. Recognition of such a distinction not only seems trivial, but would come at great cost to predictability in structuring transactions under clause B. Only through litigation could a corporation determine whether its exchanges would be aggregated or severed.

[4]Judge Scott, joined by Judge Irwin, concurred, arguing that the Tax Court's decision in *Howard* was indistinguishable and should have been expressly overruled. 71 T. C. at 742-44. Judge Quealy's dissent rejected the plurality's "nebulous distinction" of prior decisions, and concluded that the law under clause B is too well settled to justify a change. 71 T. C. at 744. Judge Wilbur, joined by three other judges, relied on prior decisions in dissent, repudiating the distinctions used by the plurality. 71 T. C. at 745-49. He also emphasized the disadvantages of upsetting a settled interpretation of clause B, 71 T. C. at 749, and criticized the majority for implicitly separating the cash purchases from the stock for stock exchange, *id.* at 749-51. When the case was decided, the Tax Court had one vacancy due to the retirement of Judge Raum. Four judges, Judges Drennen, Fay, Goffe, and Hall, did not participate.

[5]The Commissioner has also appealed to three other courts of appeals: the first, fourth, and ninth. Those appeals are still pending. *Chapman v. Commissioner*, No. 79-1336 (1st Cir., argued Nov. 7, 1979) (before Coffin, C. J.,Bownes, J., and Clark, J.); *Reeves v. Commissioner*, No. 79-1438 (4th Cir., argued Feb. 6, 1980) (before Haynsworth, C. J., Bryan, J., and Russell, J.); *Coffen v. Commissioner, appeal docketed*, No. 79-7278 (9th Cir. June 18, 1979).

nonstock consideration in asset acquisitions necessarily implied an intent not to allow other consideration in stock acquisitions. He rejected this assumption, however, because Congress may have been unaware of a settled judicial interpretation of clause B when it amended clause C. Instead of relying on specific citations to the legislative history, he relied on the "principal policy underlying the statutory scheme—that of facilitating corporate reorganizations," and noted that allowing some consideration other than voting stock in clause B reorganizations would be advantageous in effecting reorganizations. *Id.* at 973. He also analogized clause B to clause C, noting that "[i]f Congress was content to permit up to twenty percent boot in a (C) reorganization, it must be assumed *a fortiori* that an equivalent amount of boot was permissible in a (B) reorganization, absent a clear rule to the contrary of which Congress must have been aware."*Id.* at 973 (footnote omitted). Finally Judge Schwartz reasoned that allowing consideration other than voting stock under clause B would, in view of the "creeping control" amendment to clause B in the 1954 Code, create a "well-ordered universe" in the reorganization sections of the Internal Revenue Code. *Id.* at 974 (quoting Merritt, *Tax-Free Corporate Acquisitions—The Law and the Proposed Regulations*, 53 Mich. L. Rev. 911, 933 (1955)). These considerations, he concluded, dictated a construction of clause B that allows up to twenty percent nonstock consideration so long as the acquiring corporation acquires at least eighty percent of the target corporation's stock solely for its own voting stock.

III. After a detailed review of prior decisions, the legislative history, and the policies underlying the reorganization section, we conclude that the interpretation urged by the Commissioner is essentially correct. At the outset we emphasize the burden the taxpayers must shoulder in overturning a construction of the statute that has prevailed in both judicial opinions and tax planning for almost fifty years. Were we clearly convinced that this prevailing interpretation is incorrect, we would not hesitate to adopt the construction advocated by the taxpayers. But their argument, under close examination, implicitly assumes that the prevailing statutory construction is so irrational that the Commissioner must affirmatively justify it. Not only do we disagree with the assumption that disallowing nonstock consideration under clause B is irrational, but we note that the taxpayers have subtly attempted to shift their burden of overturning a settled construction of the statute back to the Commissioner. Quite apart from the reasons below, which indicate that consideration other than voting stock has no place in stock for stock acquisitions, we fundamentally disagree with taxpayers' implicit assumption that the settled construction of the statute, in an area in which stability is of considerable importance, should be accorded little or no deference.

IV. Because this case presents an issue of statutory construction, "the starting point must be the language of the statute itself."*Lewis v. United States*,—U.S.—, 48 U. S. L. W. 4205, 4207 (Feb. 27, 1980) (citations omitted); see also *United States v. DiSantillo,* No. 79-1524, slip op. at 13 (3d Cir., filed Feb. 7, 1980). Under the statutory schema the general rule is that any gain[6] on the sale or exchange of property must be recognized. At the time of the transactions under consideration here, this rule appeared in § 1002 of the Internal Revenue Code, 26 U. S. C. § 1002: "Except as otherwise provided in this subtitle, on the sale or exchange of property the entire amount of the gain or loss, determined under section 1001, shall be recognized." Taxpayers argue that their exchanges are within an explicit exception to § 1002, however, because § 354(a) of the Code provides that "[n]o gain or loss shall be recognized if stock or securities in a corporation a party to a reorganization are, in pursuance of a plan of reorganization, exchanged solely for stock or securities in such corporation or in another corporation a party to the reorganization." If a valid reorganization occurs, any consideration other than stock or securities received by shareholders is subject to recognition in the amount of the gain realized, but the gain recognized will not exceed

---

[6]At the time of the exchanges, "gain" was defined in § 1001. Section 1001(c) referred to § 1002 for the general rule regarding recognition of gain. Section 1001 was amended in 1976 to incorporate § 1002 into § 1001(c), which now states: "Except as otherwise provided in this subtitle, the entire amount of the gain or loss, determined under this section, on the sale or exchange of property shall be recognized." 26 U.S.C. § 1001(c). This change in the placement of the recognition requirement has effected no substantive change.

the amount of nonstock consideration received. § 356(a) of the Internal Revenue Code, 26 U.S.C. § 356(a). See *Turnbow v. Commissioner* [62-1 USTC ¶9104], 368 U. S. 337, 344 (1961).

The linchpin of taxpayer's argument, therefore, is that the acquisition of Hartford stock by ITT was a valid reorganizataion as defined in § 368(a)(1) of the Code, 26 U.S.C. § 368(a)(1). Specifically, they rely on clause B, which defines a reorganization as

> the acquisition by one corporation, in exchange solely for all or a part of its voting stock (or in exchange solely for all or a part of the voting stock of a corporation which is in control of the acquiring corporation), of stock of another corporation if, immediately after the acquisition, the acquiring corporation has control of such other corporation (whether or not such acquiring corporation had control immediately before the acquisition). . . .

§ 368(a)(1)(B) of the Internal Revenue Code, 26 U.S.C. § 368(a)(1)(B). The section defines "control" as "the ownership of stock possessing at least 80 percent of the total combined voting power of all classes of stock entitled to vote and at least 80 percent of the total number of shares of all other classes of stock of the corporation." *Id.* at § 368(c). The parties agree that ITT obtained the requisite amount of Hartford stock to achieve "control" under this definition. They also agree that if the transaction satisfies clause B, the taxpayers received stock from a "party to a reorganization" in exchange for their stock in a "party to a reorganization." See *id.* at § 368(b). Thus, the dispute centers on the language in clause B requiring that one corporation acquire "solely in exchange for all or part of its voting stock . . . stock of another corporation if, immediately after the acquisition, the acquiring corporation has control of such other corporation. . . ."

Taxpayers argue that the acquiring corporation must obtain "control" of the target corporation "solely for . . . voting stock," and that consideration other than voting stock is permissible under clause B if this precondition is met. The Commissioner disagrees, arguing that the acquiring corporation must obtain "control" in a transaction in which it exchanges voting stock and no other consideration. We conclude that no clear resolution of these competing arguments is apparent on the face of the statute. We must therefore analyze the widest range of available materials to derive an answer. This perforce makes our task exhaustive and requires an opinion that is more lengthy than we would prefer. But this task is necessary here because, as a reviewing court, we must examine and evaluate prior judicial constructions, the legislative history, the policies represented by each term in the statute, and the relationship of clause B to the overall statutory schema.

V. Our analysis of the judicial history of clause B must begin with the Supreme Court's decision in *Helvering v. Southwest Consolidated Corp.* [42-1 USTC ¶9248], 315 U.S. 194 (1942). That case arose under § 112(g)(1) of the Revenue Act of 1934, 48 Stat. 680, 705, the relevant portion of which stated:

> (1) The term "reorganization" means . . . (B) the acquisition by one corporation in exchange solely for all or a part of its voting stock: of at least 80 per centum of the voting stock and at least 80 per centum of the total number of shares of all other classes of stock of another corporation; or of substantially all the properties of another corporation.

See 315 U.S. at 196. It bears emphasis that the 1934 Act combined both assets acquisitions, now in clause C, and stock acquisitions, now in clause B, in one clause, treating them identically. The district court recognized this identical treatment. 472 F. Supp. at 962.

In *Southwest Consolidated*, the creditors of Southwest Gas Utilities Corporation had reorganized it under a plan approved by the Delaware chancery court to assure optimal payment of their claims. They formed a new corporation, Southwest Consolidated, to which the assets of the old corporation were transferred for a package of 49,300 shares of common stock, 2,760 Class A warrants, 18,445 Class B warrants, and a cash payment directly to non-participating security holders of $106,680. The fair market value of the assets at the time of the exchange was $1,766,694.98. The controversy arose when the new corporation tried to use the old corporation's basis in the assets, about $9,000,000, to compute gains and losses. The Court held that the transfer of assets had been a recognition transaction outside the reorganization definition in § 112(g)(1)(B), thereby precluding use of the higher carry-over basis of the old corporation. 315 U.S. at 199.

A. The proper interpretation of *Southwest Consolidated* has caused great controversy between the parties in this case. Taxpayers distinguish it in two ways, arguing first that it involved an assets acquisition, not a stock acquisition. They argue second that the holding of the decision is that thirty-seven percent nonstock consideration coupled with sixty-three percent stock consideration fails to qualify as a stock for assets acquisition. ITT, they emphasize, acquired only eight percent of Hartford's stock for nonstock consideration, much less than the thirty-seven percent involved in *Southwest Consolidated*. The Commissioner relies primarily on the Court's statement that ''Congress has provided that the assets of the transferor corporation must be acquired in exchange 'solely' for 'voting stock' of the transferee. *'Solely' leaves no leeway*. Voting stock plus some other consideration does not meet the statutory requirement.'' 315 U.S. at 198 (emphasis added). We agree with the Commissioner's interpretation, although we will respond more directly to the arguments presented by taxpayers.

1. The Court's decision in *Southwest Consolidated* is relevant to this case even though it involved an asset acquisition. The statute it was construing, the Revenue Act of 1934, treated asset and stock acquisitions identically. Even though subsequent amendments to both clauses have indicated congressional recognition of important differences between asset and stock acquisition, no such recognition was present in the 1934 Act, and we conclude that the Court's construction of the solely for voting stock requirement for assets acquisitions was equally applicable to stock for stock transactions. There was no explicit statutory distinction *ipsissimis verbis*, and we find no express language in the Court's opinion suggesting the presence of one. In addition, the taxpayers' argument with respect to *Southwest Consolidated* is somewhat disingenuous: They distinguish the leading Supreme Court decision on the solely for voting stock requirement because it was an asset acquisition case, even though at that time, in 1942, both stock and assets acquisitions were treated identically. Yet later, in an attempt to incorporate the apparently greater flexibility of the present version of clause C into clause B, they argue that Congress in 1954 could have intended no difference between the two transactions when it amended clause C but failed to amend clause B. We refuse to accept this best-of-both-worlds interpretation, and conclude that at the time it was decided, *Southwest Consolidated* served as the authoritative construction of statutory language describing both stock and assets acquisitions.

2. The second distinction urged by taxpayers concerns the amount of nonstock consideration involved in *Southwest Consolidated*. Beginning with the total asset value of $1,766,695, they compute the nonstock consideration as follows:

Cash	$106,680
2,760 Class A warrants at $29	80,040
18,445 Class B warrants at $25	461,125
	$647,845

See *Reeves v. Commissioner*, 71 T. C. at 735 n. 8. The ratio of nonstock to total consideration was thirty-seven percent. Thus, by combining the cash transferred, about six percent of the total consideration, with the stock warrants, about thirty percent of the total consideration, taxpayers conclude that *Southwest Consolidated* dealt with such an extreme situation that it is of little value in a close case such as this. But there is no indication in the Court's opinion that it was influenced by the *combined* value of the nonstock consideration. Indeed, the Court dealt with the cash and the warrants separately, arguably in the form of alternative rationales.[7] See 315 U.S. at 199–201. With respect to the six percent cash exchanged the Court emphasized that

---

[7] The Tax Court itself has deemed them alternative rationales, explaining in *Mills v. Commissioner* [CCH Dec. 25,753], 39 T. C. 393, 398 (1962), *rev'd on other grounds*, [64-1 USTC ¶9474] 331 F.2d 321 (5th Cir. 1964): ''The Supreme Court held that the $106,680 was other consideration and *alternatively* that certain warrants issued were also not voting stock.'' (emphasis added).

> [t]he rights of the security holders against the old corporation were drastically altered by the sale made pursuant to the plan. The sale not only removed the lien from the property and altered the rights of security holders in it; it also limited and defined the rights of the individual creditors if they elected to take cash rather than participate in the plan.

Id. at 199 (citation omitted); see also *id.* at 200. The Court also emphasized the devastating effect of the warrants on the transaction. See *id.* at 201.

But most persuasive in response to the taxpayer's second argument is the Court's clear statement that " '[s]olely' leaves no leeway. Voting stock plus some other consideration does not meet the statutory requirement." *Id.* at 198 (citation omitted). Although a large amount of nonstock consideration was at issue in *Southwest Consolidated,* the precept announced by the court was much more inclusive. In Pound's trichotomy,[8] the Court *interpreted* the statutory precept as "leav[ing] no leeway." It then *applied* that precept to the specific facts, which, as taxpayers note, clearly dictated the Court's result. We cannot regard either step as unnecessary to the decision.

B.   Other decisions relevant to this issue are not controlling precedents in this circuit, but are influential to the extent that their reasoning is persuasive. Unfortunately, few courts have fortified their conclusions on this troublesome issue with a reasoned elaboration. Several courts rely exclusively on *Southwest Consolidated.* See *Commissioner v. Air Reduction Co.* [42-2 USTC ¶9598], 130 F.2d 145, 148 (2d Cir.) *cert. denied,* 317 U.S. 681 (1942); *Howard v. Commissioner* [CCH Dec. 21, 163], 24 T. C. 792, 804 (1955), *rev'd on other grounds,* [57-1 USTC ¶9232], 238 F.2d 943, (7th Cir. 1956); *Howard v. Commissioner* [57-1 USTC ¶9232], 238 F.2d 943, 946–47 (7th Cir. 1956) (citing legislative history to establish that acquisitions of stock and acquisitions of assets were intended to be treated alike, and then relying on *Air Reduction*); *Lutkins v. United States* [63-1 USTC ¶9251], 312 R.2d 803, 805 (Ct. Cl.), *cert. denied,* 375 U.S. 825 (1963); *cf. Mills v. Commissioner* [CCH Dec. 25,753] 39 T. C. 393, 400 (1962) (relying on *Southwest Consolidated* in strictly construing "solely" and holding that no *de minimum* rule applies under clause B), *rev'd* 331 F.2d 321, 323, (5th Cir. 1964) (Maris, J., sitting by designation) (citing *Southwest Consolidated* to demonstrate that no consideration other than voting stock is allowable under clause B but concluding that cash payments for fractional shares are not "consideration" for purposes of the "solely for . . . voting stock" requirement).

In *Commissioner v. Turnbow* [61-1 USTC ¶9148], 286 F.2d 669 (9th Cir. 1960), *aff'd in part,* [62-1 USTC ¶9104] 368 U.S. 337 (1961), the ninth circuit examined the legislative history behind clause B. It found that Congress had added the solely for voting stock requirement, as an alternative to complete elimination of these types of reorganizations, to preclude tax deferred treatment for transactions that were actually sales but that were structured as reorganizations. 286 F.2d at 673. Quoting the Senate Finance Committee Report, S. Rep. No. 558, 73d Cong., 2d Sess. 17 (1934), reprinted in 1939-1 C. B. (pt. 2) 586, 598–99,[9] which accompanied the Revenue Act of 1934, the court concluded that the congressional purpose could best be effected by allowing no nonstock consideration under clause B. The court also noted that a construction of clause B allowing nonstock consideration so long as eighty percent of the target corporation's stock was acquired solely for stock would render a subsequent amendment to clause C superfluous. See §

---

[8]Dean Pound wrote:

Supposing the facts to have been ascertained, decision of a controversy according to law involves (1) selection of the legal material on which to ground the decision, or as we commonly say, finding the law; (2) development of the grounds of decision from the material selected, or interpretation in the stricter sense of that term; (3) application of the abstract grounds of decision to the facts of the case. Pound, *The Theory of Judicial Decision,* 36 Harv. L. Rev. 940, 945 (1923).

[9]It will be noted that the proposed amendment requires that *** the acquisition, whether of stock or of substantially all the properties, must be in exchange solely for the voting stock of the acquiring corporation. 286 F.2d at 673 (quoting S. Rep. No. 558, 73d Cong., 2d Sess. 17 (1934), *reprinted in* 1939-1 C. B. (pt. 2) 586, 598–99).

368(a)(2)(B) of the Internal Revenue Code, 26 U.S.C. § 368(a)(2)(B).[10] That amendment allowed, within strict limits, consideration other than voting stock in clause C transactions. If the language in clause B could be interpreted to allow nonstock consideration, the court reasoned, the identical language in clause C could be similarly interpreted. Because that interpretation of clause B would have rendered the amendment to clause C unnecessary, the court concluded that the effort of Congress in amending clause C demonstrates that clause B does not allow nonstock consideration. 286 F.2d at 674.[11]

Taxpayers question the *Turnbow* decision, arguing that it assumes improperly that Congress intended clause B to allow only voting stock as consideration. By structuring its analysis around subsequent amendments to clause C, which had already been construed in *Southwest Consolidated,* and then comparing clause B, which had not been authoritatively construed at the time of the 1954 amendment,[12] the ninth circuit, according to the taxpayers, "begged the question." Equally probable, they contend, is a congressional intent to amend clause C to conform it to clause B. We have no small difficulty with taxpayers' indictment of *Turnbow,* because they rely on the dissimilarity of clauses B and C to distinguish *Southwest Consolidated,* but emphasize a latent congressional purpose to keep them identical through the amendments to clause C. Nevertheless, we will not rest our analysis totally on either the ninth circuit decision in *Turnboq* or the Supreme Court's decision in *Southwest Consolidated.* We turn to our own independent analysis of the legislative history.

VI. The reorganization provisions of the Internal Revenue Code have developed over the lifetime of the Code as Congress made revisions to accommodate legitimate business needs. Provision for deferred tax treatment of reorganizations first appeared in the Revenue Act of 1918, c. 18, 40 Stat. 1057, 1060, § 202(b), which stated in relevant part:

> [W]hen in connection with reorganization, merger, or consolidation of a corporation a person receives in place of stock or securities owned by him new stock or securities of no greater aggregate par or face value, no gain or loss shall be deemed to occur from the exchange, and the new stock or securities received shall be treated as taking the place of the stock, securities, or property exchanged.

See H. R. Rep. No. 1037, 65th Cong., 2d Sess. 44–45 (1918), reprinted in 1939–1 C. B. (pt. 2) 130, 132. In 1921, Congress replaced this section with a more sophisticated treatment,[13] but retained the requirement that the shareholders in the reorganization exchange receive "in place of any stock or securities owned by [them], stock or securities in a corporation a party to or resulting from such reorganization." § 202(c)(2) of the Revenue Act of 1921, c. 36, 42 Stat. 230. The Conference Report to the House, H. R. Rep. No. 486, 67th Cong., 1st Sess. 17 (1921), reprinted

---

[10]Section 368(a)(2)(B) appears in note 25 *infra.*

[11]When the Supreme Court affirmed the ninth circuit's decision in *Turnbow,* the parties assumed the validity of the ninth circuit's decision that nonstock consideration is impermissible under clause B. See 368 U.S. at 341.

[12]Taxpayers' analysis assumes that Congress was unaware of, or implicitly disapproved of, the decision in *Commissioner v. Air Reduction,* 130 F.2d 145 (2d Cir.), *cert. denied,* 317 U.S. 681 (1942).

[13]The relevant portion of the Act provided: [e]ven if the property received in exchange has a readily realizable market value, no gain or loss shall be recognized—

(2) When in the reorganization of one or more corporations a person receives in place of any stock or securities owned by him, stock or securities in a corporation a party to or resulting from such reorganization. The word "reorganization," as used in this paragraph, includes a merged or consolidation (including the acquisition by one corporation of at least a majority of the voting stock and at least a majority of the total number of shares of all other classes of stock of another corporation, or of substantially all the properties of another corporation) recapitalization, or mere change in identity, form, or place of organization of a corporation, . . . Revenue Act of 1921, c. 136, 42 Stat. 227, 230, § 202(c).

in 1939–1 C. B. (pt. 2) 206, 209, noted that the Act "provides that the property exchanged shall consist only of stock or securities. . . ."

When Congress amended the reorganization provisions in 1924,[14] the statute became amenable to undesirable interpretation. Although Congress intended no radical change in meaning from the prior Act,[15] *see* H. R. Rep. No. 179, 68th Cong., 1st Sess. 13 (1924), reprinted in 1939–1 C. B. (pt. 2) 241, 251, it soon realized that the change had enhanced the prospects for tax avoidance. By 1934,[16] Congress had become concerned that the reorganization provisions were being abused. The House Report on the 1934 Act illustrates this concern:

> The reorganization provisions have been in effect for many years, having been adopted in substantially their present form in 1924. They state in detail how each step of a reorganization should be treated for tax purposes. The policy was adopted of permitting reorganizations to take a wide variety of forms, without income-tax liability. As a result, astute lawyers frequently attempted, especially during the prosperous years, to take advantage of these provisions by arranging in the technical form of a reorganization, within the statutory definition, what were really sales.

> * * *

> [T]he definition of a reorganization has been restricted so that the definition will conform more closely to the general requirements of corporation law, and will limit reorganizations to (1) statutory mergers and consolidations; (2) transfers to a controlled corporation, "control" being defined as an 80 percent ownership; and (3) changes in the capital structure or form of organization.

> By these limitations the committee believes that it has removed the danger that taxable sales can be cast into the form of a reorganization, while at the same time, legitimate reorganizations, required in order to strengthen the financial condition of the corporation, will be permitted. Furthermore, the retention of the other reorganization provisions will prevent large losses from being established by bondholders and stockholders who receive securities in a newly reorganized enterprise which are substantially the same as their original investments.

---

[14]Section 203(h)(1) of the Revenue Act of 1924, c. 234, 43 Stat. 253, 257, § 203(h)(1), stated:

(1) The term "reorganization" means (A) a merger or consolidation (including the acquisition by one corporation of at least a majority of the voting stock and at least a majority of the total number of shares of all other classes of stock of another corporation, or substantially all the properties of another corporation), or (B) a transfer by a corporation of all or a part of its assets to another corporation if immediately after the transfer the transferor or its stockholders or both are in control of the corporation to which the assets are transferred, or (C) a recapitalization, or (D) a mere change in identity, form, or place of organization, however affected.

[15]The Senate amended the House version to include within its terms the case of a transfer by a corporation of all or a part of its assets to another corporation if immediately after the transfer the transferor or its stockholders, or both, are in control of the corporation to which the assets are transferred. This is a common type of reorganization, and clearly should be included within the reorganization provisions of the statute. S. Rep. No. 398, 68th Cong., 1st Sess. 17 (1924), *reprinted in* 1939-1 C. B. (pt. 2) 266, 278. The change was reflected in 203(h)(1)(B) of the statute. See note 14 *supra*.

[16]The Senate proposed an amendment in the Revenue Act of 1926 that would have allowed a corporation owning at least a majority of the voting stock and at least a majority of the total numbers of shares of all other classes of stock of another corporation to distribute that stock to its own shareholders without requiring the recipients of the stock to recognize gain. "This is done on the theory that there is no actual income to the distributee until he sells the stock, since his interest in the assets is exactly the same as it was before." S. Rep. No. 52, 69th Cong., 1st Sess. 16 (1926), *reprinted in* 1939-1 C. B. (pt. 2) 332, 345. The amendment failed. H. R. Rep. No. 356, 69th Cong., 1st Sess. 30–31 (1926), *reprinted in* 1939-1 C. B. (pt. 2) 361, 362 (House conference report). The failure of this amendment demonstrates the importance of a reorganization transaction to the statutory schema providing tax deferral.

H. R. Rep. No. 704, 73d Cong., 2d Sess. 14 (1934), *reprinted in* 1939-1 C. B. (pt. 2) 554, 564. Though sympathetic to the concern about tax avoidance, the Senate restored the stock and assets acquisition provisions with a significant modification:

> Your committee is in complete agreement with the purposes of the House bill which aim at tax-avoidance schemes in this connection. However, some modifications are recommended in order to bring about a more uniform application of the provisions in all 48 of the States. Not all of the States have adopted statutes providing for mergers or consolidations; and, moreover, a corporation of one State cannot ordinarily merge with a corporation of another State. The committee believes that it is desirable to permit reorganizations in such cases, with restrictions designed to prevent tax avoidance. Consequently, the committee recommends the insertion in the House bill of an addition to the definition of the term "reorganization" as follows:
>
> "(B) the acquisition by one corporation in exchange solely for its voting stock: of at least 80 per centum of the voting stock and at least 80 per centum of the total number of shares of all other classes of stock of another corporation; or of substantially all the properties of another corporation;"
>
> The committee believes that these transactions, when carried out as prescribed in this amendment, are in themselves sufficiently similar to mergers and consolidations as to be entitled to similar treatment. It will be noted that the proposed amendment requires that (1) the acquiring corporation must obtain at least 80 percent of the voting stock and at least 80 percent of the total number of shares of all other classes of stock of the other corporation, instead of only a majority as provided by the present law; and (2) the acquisition, whether of stock or of substantially all the properties, must be in exchange solely for the voting stock of the acquiring corporation.
>
> Your committee approves the retention of the exchange and reorganization provisions with these changes.

S. Rep. No. 558, 73d Cong., 2d Sess. 16–17 (1934), *reprinted in* 1939-1 C. B. (pt. 2) 586, 598–99. The House acceded to the Senate provision. H. R. Rep. No. 1385, 73d Cong., 2d Sess. 21–22 (1934), *reprinted in* 1939-1 C. B. (pt. 2) 627, 632 (House conference report). This version of the statute was before the Supreme Court in *Southwest Consolidated*.

Congress amended the reorganization section in the Revenue Act of 1939 by separating the treatment of stock and asset acquisitions, placing them in clause B and clause C respectively.[17] In explaining a change in the assets acquisition definition that allowed acquiring corporation to assume the transferor's liabilities, thereby overruling *United States v. Hendler*, 303 U.S. 564 (1938), the House Report stated:

> The definition of "reorganization" as contained in section 112(g)(1) of the Internal Revenue Code is amended by section 213(b) of the bill. Clause (B) of this definition now provides that in order for the transaction to constitute a reorganization, the acquisition of properties therein described must be in exchange *solely* for voting stock. Section 213(b) provides that if the corporation acquiring the properties assumes liabilities of the party from whom the properties are acquired, or takes the property subject to a liability, such assumption of liabilities, or taking subject to a liability, shall be disregarded in determining whether the properties are received in exchange solely for voting stock.

---

[17]As amended, § 112(g)(1) stated in relevant part:

(1) The term "reorganization" means . . . (B) the acquisition by one corporation, in exchange solely for all or a part of its voting stock, of at least 80 per centum of the voting stock and at least 80 per centum of the total number of shares of all other classes of stock of another corporation, or (C) the acquisition by one corporation, in exchange solely for all or a part of its voting stock, of substantially all the properties of another corporation, but in determining whether the exchange is solely for voting stock the assumption by the acquiring corporation of a liability of the other, or the fact that property acquired is subject to a liability, shall be disregarded, . . . Revenue Act of 1939, c. 247, 53 Stat. 862, 870, § 213(b).

H. R. Rep. No. 855, 76th Cong., 1st Sess. 19 (1939), *reprinted in* 1939-2 C. B. 504, 519. As noted earlier with respect to the *Southwest Consolidated* decision, stock and assets acquisitions had been treated identically in the 1934 Act. Thus, when Congress stated in the House Report that "for the transaction to constitute a reorganization, the acquisition of properties therein described must be in exchange *solely* for voting stock," it was inferentially referring to stock acquisitions as well. We deem the report's emphasis of "solely" to be significant evidence of congressional understanding of this section.

In 1954, Congress amended clause B to eliminate uncertainty about "creeping acquisitions." Before the amendment, a corporation that had previously acquired stock of the target corporation could not avail itself of clause B if it owned more than twenty percent of the target's stock. The amendment corrected this problem by requiring the acquiring corporation to hold control "immediately after the acquisition," "whether or not [it] had control immediately before the acquisition." Internal Revenue Code of 1954, Pub. L. No. 83-591, 68A Stat. 1, 120, § 368(a)(1)(B). See S. Rep. No. 1622, 83d Cong., 2d Sess. 273 (1954), *reprinted in* [1954] U.S. Code Cong. & Ad. News 4621, 4911.[18] In 1964, Congress again amended clause B to allow the acquiring corporation to use either its own stock, or the stock of a corporation controlling it, in exchange for the target corporation's stock. Revenue Act of 1964, Pub. L. No. 88-272, 78 Stat. 19, 57, § 218(a). Neither the legislative history of the 1954 amendment, nor that of the 1964 amendment, is directly helpful in addressing the issue before us. See S. Rep. No. 830, 88th Cong., 2d Sess. (pt. 2) 227 (1964), *reprinted in* [1964] U.S. Code Cong. & Ad. News 1868, 1898.[19]

This review of the legislative history fails to provide a conclusive answer to the question presented in this case. Nevertheless, we deem several developments influential to and supportive of our ultimate decision. First, as originally enacted in 1918, the provisions dealt exclusively with the receipt by shareholders of stock or securities for their own stock or securities. Congress altered this treatment in 1924 by removing the explicit requirement that the exchange involve only stock or securities, but later realized allowing other consideration had promoted tax avoidance. Thus, in 1934 Congress added the "solely for . . . voting stock" requirement, and has retained it until the present day without relevant modification to clause B. We construe this action in adding and

[18]Taxpayers rely heavily on the Senate Report's statement that "[u]nder section 112(g)(1)(B), of existing law, one corporation can acquire *enough stock* of another to get control of the second corporation solely for its own voting stock tax free." S. Rep. No. 1622, 83rd Cong., 2d Sess. 273, *reprinted in* [1954] U.S. Code Cong., & Ad. News 4621, 4911 (emphasis added). The amendment allowing "creeping control" centered on corporations already owning over twenty percent of the target's stock, and that were thus unable to acquire the requisite amount of stock ("enough stock") for control. In this context, we do not read the statement as support for taxpayers' argument that only eighty percent of the stock acquired must be acquired for voting stock; Congress instead was emphasizing that less than eighty percent was available for the acquiring corporation to acquire.

[19]Taxpayers isolate a statement in the legislative history of the 1964 Act as support for their argument, considered below, that clause B should be treated like clause C insofar as nonstock consideration is concerned:

"[T]he 1954 code permits tax-free reorganizations in the case of the exchange of the parent's stock for the assets of a corporation acquired by the subsidiary. However, a similar result is denied where the subsidiary acquires the stock of the other corporation in exchange for the stock of its parent corporation. Since Congress has considered the "continuity of interest" rule satisfied in the case of asset acquisitions, there seems to be no reason for not applying the same rule to stock acquisitions, since there is little in substance to distinguish an asset acquisition from a stock acquisition." S. Rep. No. 830, 88th Cong., 2d Sess. (pt. 1) 83, *reprinted in* [1964] U.S. Code Cong. & Ad. News 1673, 1755. That Congress found "little in substance to distinguish an asset acquisition from a stock acquisition" for purposes of allowing an acquiring corporation to use its parent corporation's stock does not imply that no differences exist for purposes of allowing nonstock consideration. See page 36–39 [CCH p. 83,761] *infra*.

retaining the voting stock requirement as a conscious decision by Congress to foreclose other consideration.

In addition, when Congress legislatively overruled the *Hendler* decision by amending clause C in 1939, it recognized that asset acquisitions, which were being separated from stock acquisitions for the first time, allowed only exchanges "*solely* for voting stock." We think the simultaneous separation of the transactions and amendment of the asset acquisition provision, without altering the stock acquisition provision, demonstrates congressional recognition of differences between the two transactions. It also indicates, though perhaps not conclusively, an intent to leave the "*solely* for voting stock" language unaffected as it applied to stock acquisitions.

Finally, the rather frequent amendments to the reorganizations provisions imply close congressional supervision and awareness of their use and abuse. This close supervision makes us even more wary of taxpayers' assertion of "implicit" amendments to clause B by amending clause C.

We now examine the policies at work in the reorganization provision in an attempt to effectuate a rational operation of the schema.

VII. Taxpayers submit essentially two policy arguments supporting their construction of clause B. First, they argue that the voting stock requirement appears in the statute to assure a "continuity of interest" between the pre-transaction equity holders of the target corporation and the post-transaction equity holders. Sufficient continuity of interest is retained, they argue, if voting stock of the acquiring corporation is exchanged for a control, or eighty percent, block of the target corporation's stock. They conclude that the voting stock requirement and the control requirement are interrelated, in effect meaning, that an acquisition, solely for voting stock, of control of the target corporation is within clause B.

Their second argument is that clause B, under the construction urged by the Commissioner, fails to conform to the general legislative schema. Taxpayers note that in both clause A and clause C reorganizations, Congress and the courts have allowed certain amounts of nonstock consideration. To disallow consideration other than voting stock in clause B, they argue, would impose a degree of inflexibility on stock for stock transactions that is totally unjustified in view of congressional intent to make the other reorganization provisions flexible. They conclude that this court should not adopt a construction that would impute such an allegedly irrational result to Congress.

We must analyze these arguments cognizant that Congress has provided tax deferral for reorganizations as a matter of legislative grace, and that strict compliance with the statute is necessary regardless of our agreement or disagreement with the conditions imposed. See *Lutkins v. United States* [63-1 USTC ¶9252], 312 F.2d 803, 805 (Ct. Cl.), *cert. denied*, 375 U.S. 825 (1963). As Justice Harlan wrote for the Court in *Commissioner v. Gordon* [68-1 USTC ¶9383], 391 U.S. 83 (1968):

> Section 355 provides that certain distributions of securities of corporations controlled by the distributing corporation do not result in recognized gain or loss to the distributee shareholders. The requirements of the section are detailed and specific, and must be applied with precision. It is no doubt true, as the Second Circuit emphasized, that the general purpose of the section was to distinguish corporate fission from the distribution of earnings and profits. However, although a court may have reference to this purpose when there is a genuine question as to the meaning of one of the requirements Congress has imposed, a court is not free to disregard requirements simply because it considers them redundant or unsuited to achieving the general purpose in a particular case. Congress has abundant power to provide that a corporation wishing to spin off a subsidiary must, however bona fide its intentions, conform the details of a distribution to a particular set of rules.

Id. at 91–94 (footnote omitted). Thus, although Congress may have engaged in legislative overkill to meet potential exigencies, we as a court must be reluctant to impose our own standards of strict rationality onto the statutory schema.

A. Although we agree that the continuity of interest doctrine is reflected in the voting stock requirement of clause B, we do not agree that a necessary relationship must exist between that requirement and the control requirement. The continuity of interest requirement is of judicial origin and applies throughout the reorganization provisions. One of the first statements of the doctrine was by Judge Augustus Hand in *Cortland Specialty Co. v. Commissioner* [3 USTC ¶980], 60 F.2d 937 (2d Cir. 1932), a case arising under the 1926 Act and involving a transfer of assets from one corporation to another in exchange for cash and notes. *Id.* at 938. Although the acquisition of assets provision of the 1926 Act did not explicitly impose a voting stock requirement, the court noted that "[r]eorganization, merger, and consolidation are words indicating coporate readjustments of existing interests. They all differ fundamentally from a sale where the vendor corporation parts with its interest for cash and receives nothing more." *Id.* at 939. In specific application to the reorganization statute, Judge Hand explained:

> When describing the kind of change in corporate structure that permits exemption from these taxes, section 203 does not disregard the necessity of continuity of interests under modified corporate forms. Such is the purpose of the word "reorganization" in section 203(b)(3) of the act, 26 USCA § 934(b)(3), where a corporation exchanges its property "solely for stock and securities." Such also is the nature of the "merger or consolidation" described in subdivision (h)(1)(A) where a corporation acquires a majority of the stock of another, and such is the nature of the "reorganization" described in subdivision (h)(1)(B) of section 203, 26 USCA § 934(h)(1)(B), where a corporation transfers assets to another corporation, and the transferor, or its stockholders, immediately thereafter are in control of the transferee. The words "A recapitalization," in subdivision (h)(1)(C) of section 203, 26 USCA § 934(h)(1)(C), and "A mere change in*** form *** of organization, however effected," in subdivision (h)(1)(D) of section 203, 26 USCA § 934(h)(1)(D), involve the same idea.
>
> When subdivision (h)(1)(A) included in its definition of "merger or consolidation" the "acquisition by one corporation of *** substantially all the properties of another," it did this so that the receipt of property by the corporation surviving the merger might serve to effect a reorganization as does an acquisition of stock. Each trasaction presupposed a continuance of interest on the part of the transferor in the properties transferred. Such a limitation inheres in the conventional meaning of "merger and consolidation," and is implicit in almost every line of section 203 which we have quoted.

60 F.2d at 940. The Supreme Court adopted Judge Hand's analysis in *Pinellas Ice Co. v. Commissioner*, 287 U.S. 462, 470 (1933), and applied it in several cases thereafter. See, *e.g.*, *Helvering v. Alabama Asphaltic Limestone Co.*, 315 U.S. 179, 182–83 (1942); *LeTulle v. Scofield*, 308 U.S. 415, 420 (1940); *Groman v. Commissioner* [37-2 USTC ¶9533], 302 U.S. 82, 89 (1937); *Helvering v. Minnesota Tea Co.*, 296 U.S. 378, 385 (1935); *John A. Nelson Co. v. Helvering*, 296 U.S. 374, 377 (1935). In a case involving a statutory merger and arising under the Revenue Act of 1938, this court applied the doctrine to disallow tax deferral even though the literal terms of the reorganization provisions had been met. *Roebling v. Commissioner*, 143 F.2d 810, 812 (3d Cir.), *cert. denied*, 323 U.S. 773 (1944). When it added the solely for voting stock requirement in the 1934 Act, Congress recognized the developing case law in this area and approved it.

> The courts have shown a commendable tendency to look through the mere form of the transaction into its substance. The Supreme Court has indicated that the broad principle underlying these sections is that no taxable profit is realized from a reorganization, if no money passes and if the changes in corporate organization are essentially changes only in form, with the stockholders continuing their former interest in the original enterprise.

H. R. Rep. No. 704, 73d Cong., 2d Sess. 13 (1934), *reprinted in* 1939-1 C. B (pt. 2) 554, 564.[20] In *Southwest Consolidated* the Supreme Court recognized that, with the addition of the solely for voting stock language, "[t]he continuity of interest test is made much stricter." 315 U.S. at 198. In addition, under acts prior to that passed in 1934, courts had held that long term bonds and preferred stock, not just voting stock, satisfied the continuity of interest requirement. See *John A. Nelson Co. v. Helvering,* 296 U.S. 374, 377 (1935) (preferred stock and cash for assets); *Scofield v. LeTulle,* 103 F.2d 20, 21–22 (5th Cir. 1939) (long term bonds), *rev'd on this issue* [40–1 USTC ¶9150], 308 U.S. 415, 420–21 (1940). Although Congress ratified the continuity of interest doctrine, it tightened it by disallowing nonvoting stock and bonds and by raising the level of continuity required. We conclude that the requirement in clause B that the exchange by solely for voting stock incorporates the continuity of interest doctrine, an important aspect of any tax deferred reorganization.

Our disagreement with taxpayers lies in our perception of the policy promoted by the control requirement. "Control," we think, is important to another aspect of a reorganization, the requirement that the corporation undergo some change in form or structure. As the second circuit noted in *Cortland Specialty Co. v. Commissioner* [3 USTC ¶980], 60 F.2d at 940, "[r]eorganization presupposes continuance of business under *modified corporate forms,*" (emphasis added); cf. *Scofield v. San Antonio Transit Co.,* 219 F.2d 149, 154 (5th Cir.) (corporate shell from which creditors had removed all assests "could not be recast into a new and modified form in the sense contemplated" by the asset acquisition provision), cert. denied, 350 U.S. 823 (1955).

As an example of the importance the control requirement carries, we note that had ITT acquired less than eighty percent of Hartford's stock, the transaction would have been taxable, even if ITT had met the solely for voting stock requirement. Even though the continuity of interest would have been complete, with all Hartford shareholders retaining at least an indirect interest in Hartford, the modification of the corporate structure would have been insufficient to allow tax deferred treatment. Judge Augustus Hand examined a similar situation in *Heberlein Patent Corp. v. United States,* 105 F.2d 965, 968 (2d Cir. 1939). The case arose under the 1928 Act analogue to what is now clause D, § 368(a)(1)(D) of the Internal Revenue Code, 26 U.S.C. § 368(a)(1)(D), which required a transferor of assets to perceive stock representing control of the transferee. The transferor obtained less than eighty percent of the transferee's stock, and therefore the exchange was taxable. See also note 18 *supra.*

We therefore reject taxpayer's argument that the voting stock requirement necessarily relates to the control requirement. Instead, we deem the stock requirement to have been directed to preserving continuity of interest, whereas the control requirement assures some modification, albeit slight, of corporate form. This divergence of policies served by the respective provisions reestablishes their independence, see also S. Rep. No. 558, 73d Cong., 2d Sess. 16–17 (1934), reprinted in 1939-2 C. B. 586, 598–99, and undermines taxpayers' attempt to intergrate them both into the continuity of interest requirement. Although both requirements are perhaps high for purposes of the policies they serve,[21] we must defer to the congressional decision on each.

---

[20]The House Report on the 1934 Act recommended elimination of the stock and assets acquisition provisions, and the Senate added the voting stock requirement. The Senate, however, added the requirement in response to what it felt were the legitimate concerns of the House. S. Rep. No. 558, 73d Cong., 2d Sess. 16-171 (1934), *reprinted in* 1939-1 C. B. (pt. 2) 586, 598–99.

[21]We note that the eighty percent requirement for control may also be criticized as too high for its purpose, because votes of less than eighty percent of the shares are necessary to accomplish any transaction under state corporation law. See. *e.g.,* ABA-ALI Model Bus. Corp. Act §§ 59(c) (majority vote required to amend articles of incorporation) and ¶3.03(4)(b) (listing states requiring more than a majority); 73 (majority vote required for merger or consolidation) and ¶3.03(4)(b) (listing states requiring more than a majority); 79 (majority vote required to dispose of assets other than in the regular course of business) and ¶3.03(4)(d) (listing states requiring more than a majority) (2d ed. 1971).

B. Taxpayers note that in other transactions covered by different clauses of the reorganization provisions, Congress has allowed consideration other than voting stock. Judge Schwartz relied on clause A[22] and, more heavily, on clause C.[23] Although Congress initially treated assets and stock acquisitions identically, we conclude that significant differences in the nature of the transactions justify the disparate treatment currently provided in 368(a).

1. In a statutory merger or consolidation, the corporations affected must submit the proposal to their shareholders and obtain an extraordinary majority before the transaction can be completed. Although taxpayers are correct that some nonstock consideration can change hands in a merger or consolidation qualifying under clause A, courts have applied the continuity of interest requirement to those transactions to limit the exchange of such consideration. See *Roebling v. Commissioner* [44-2 USTC ¶ 9388], 143 F.2d 810, 812 (3d Cir.), cert. denied, 323 U.S. 773 (1944). But the most important difference between the two types of transactions is that a statutory merger or consolidation effects a complete change in corporate structure by its very nature, whereas a stock acquisition will only effect a structural change if the acquiring corporation obtains sufficient stock. Even then alteration is less radical, because the acquired corporation continues to exist as a subsidiary of the acquiring corporation. Shares in the merging corporation are exchanged, essentially, by operation of law rather than by shareholder choice, as in the stock acquisition. All these aspects of mergers or consolidations—substantial corporate formalities, judicial application of a limited continuity of interest requirement, radical change in corporate structure, and automatic conversion of shares—distinguish them from stock acquisitions, and could be a basis for congressional allowance of nonstock consideration in those transactions.

2. Taxpayers, and the district court, rely more heavily on the analogy to clause C. We once again note significant differences between the two transactions and conclude that Congress could have consciously drawn legitimate distinctions. To effect an acquisition of assets under state corporate law, either by explicit requirement or as a matter of practical necessity, the acquiring corporation must make some provision for the creditors of the transferor corporation. See U. C. C. §§ 6-105, 6-106. Although the assets on which those creditors have based their extensions of credit are removed to a different business context, the transferee corporation is usually not liable, absent its agreement, for the debts of the transferor corporation. See, e.g., *United States v. City of Palm Beach Gardens,* 466 F. Supp. 1155, 1163 (S. D. Fla. 1979); see also *Kemos, Inc. v. Bader,* 545 F.2d 913, 915 (5th Cir. 1977) (cash purchase); *Drug, Inc. v. Hunt,* 35 Del. 339, 358–62, 168 A. 87, 94–95 (1933) (stock for assets; acknowledging the principle but holding that transferee had

---

[22]Section 368(a)(1)(A) defines "reorganization" as "a statutory merger or consolidation."

[23]Section 368(a)(1)(C) defines "reorganization" as:

(C) the acquisition by one corporation, in exchange solely for all or a part of its voting stock (or in exchange solely for all or a part of the voting stock of a corporation which is in control of the acquiring corporation), of substantially all of the properties of another corporation, but in determining whether the exchange is solely for stock the assumption by the acquiring corporation of a liability of the other, or the fact that property acquired is subject to a liability, shall be disregarded. . . .

Also applicable to Clause C is § 368(a)(2)(B):

(B) Additional consideration in certain paragraph (1)(C) cases.—If—

(i) one corporation acquires substantially all of the properties of another corporation.

(ii) the acquisition would qualify under paragraph (1)(C) but for the fact that the acquiring corporation exchanges money or other property in addition to voting stock, and

(iii) the acquiring corporation acquires, solely for voting stock described in paragraph (1)(C), property of the other corporation having a fair market value which is at least 80 percent of the fair market value of all of the property of the other corporation, then such acquisition shall (subject to subparagraph (A) of this paragraph) be treated as qualifying under paragraph (1)(C). Solely for the purpose of determining whether clause (iii) of the preceding sentence applies, the amount of any liability assumed by the acquiring corporation, and the amount of any liability to which any property acquired by the acquiring corporation is subject, shall be treated as money paid for the property.

agreed to assume liabilities, producing a *de factor* merger); *Husak v. Berkel, Inc.*, 234 Pa. Super. 452, 456–57, 341 A.2d 174, 176–77 (1975). Nevertheless, secured creditors may have a contractual veto over the transaction by refusing to allow the transfer of their collateral; unsecured creditors must also be considered. See U. C. C. § 6-106. Recognizing that the inability to provide for creditors of the transferor corporation under clause C would emasculate the usefulness of that provision, Congress amended the provision in 1939 to allow the acquiring corporation to assume the transferor corporation's liabilities. This amendment was a response to *United States v. Hendler* [38-1 USTC ¶9215], 303 U.S. 564 (1938), which held that assumption of the transferor's liabilities violated the solely for voting requirement. The House Report said:

> The recent Supreme Court case of *United States v. Hendler* [38-1 USTC ¶9215], (303 U.S. 564 (1938) has been broadly interpreted to require that, if a taxpayer's liabilities are assumed by another party in what is otherwise a tax free reorganization, gain is recognized to the extent of the assumption. In typical transactions changing the form or entity of a business it is not customary to liquidate the liabilities of the business and such liabilities are almost invariably assumed by the corporation which continues the business. Your committee therefore believes that such a broad interpretation as is indicated above will largely nullify the provisions of existing law which postpone the recognition of gain in such cases.

H. R. Rep. No. 855, 76th Cong., 1st Sess. 19 (1939), reprinted in 1939-2 C. B. 504, 518–19. In contrast, a stock acquisition does not, by itself, affect the assets of the acquired corporation; it merely changes the distribution of equity interests in the target corporation, which becomes a subsidiary of the acquiring corporation.

The provision allowing cash or other property in a clause C transaction was added in 1954. Internal Revenue Code of 1954, Pub. L. No. 73-591, 68A Stat. 1, 120–21, § 368(a)(2)(C). Contrary to what taxpayers argue, this provision, § 368(a)(2)(B), does not allow substantially more flexibility in clause C transactions than in clause B transactions. If cash or other property is given, the liabilities assumed by the acquiring corporation must be included in the total twenty percent allowable nonstock consideration, whereas the assumption of liabilities need not be counted against the solely for voting stock requirement if no nonstock consideration is exchanged. Thus, since provision must be made for creditors, and since rarely will the transferor corporation have less than twenty percent of its asset value encumbered by liabilities,[24] the apparent permissibility of cash or other property under clause C is almost inevitably illusory. We believe Congress was fully aware of, and probably intended, this limitation on nonstock consideration under clause C. See S. Rep. No. 1622, 83rd Cong., 2d Sess. 274–75, reprinted in [1954] U.S. Code Cong. & Ad. News 4621, 4913.

The negative relationship of liabilities assumed to cash or other property in an assets acquisition strongly indicates that the allowance of cash or other property under clause C was also intended to allow accommodation of creditors, just as was the provision for assumption of liabilities. But because provision for creditors is of minimal concern in a stock acquisition, this rationale has no relevance to clause B.

We conclude, therefore, that disallowance of nonstock consideration under clause B is not offensive to the statutory schema. Indeed, in view of ths substantive distinctions among the various transactions covered in § 368, disallowance of nonstock consideration under clause B is perfectly justifiable, if not clearly desirable. We thus reject the analysis of the district court, which reasoned

---

[24]Data collected by the Federal Trade Commission and reported in aggregate form by industry group indicate that the percentage of total liabilities to total assets exceeds twenty percent, and generally is close to forty percent, for every industry group. FTC, Quarterly Financial Report for Manufacturing, Mining, and Trade Corporations 22-81 (3d Qtr. 1978) (table presentation). Although some individual corporations within the groups could have a lower ratio, the data demonstrate that corporations generally have too much debt, relative to assets, for the cash allowance in clause C to be used with any frequency.

that allowing cash in a clause B reorganization would promote a "well-ordered universe" under § 368.

VIII. Taxpayers have failed to convince us that the interpretation of clause B that has prevailed for almost fifty years is inconsistent with the legislative intent or with sound policy. Rather, our survey of the relevant materials indicates that the settled interpretation best effectuates legislative intent and tax policy. We therefore reverse both lower courts.

The other argument presented by taxpayers as an alternative basis for affirmance is that the cash purchases by ITT in 1969 were not part of the "plan of reorganization" through which the exchange offer was made in 1970. Neither court below considered this argument. Because these cases come before us on appeals from entry of summary judgment, which requires a determination that there are no genuine issues of material fact, see Fed. R. Civ. P. 56(c), we deem it unwise for an appellate court to address this issue until it has been considered by the courts below. We therefore remand this issue for consideration in the first instance by the trial courts.

Accordingly, the decision of the Tax Court appealed at No. 79-1985 and the judgment of the district court appealed at No. 79-2192 will be reversed and the causes remanded for further proceedings consistent with the foregoing.

Appendix C

Typical State Statute on Corporate Take-Overs

1977 Georgia Laws, page 649f (Chapter 22-19 of the Georgia Business Corporation Code, as amended). See discussions at page 16.

CHAPTER 22-19. CORPORATE TAKEOVERS

22-1901 Definitions

As used in this Chapter, unless the context otherwise requires, the term:

(a) "Equity security" means any of the units into which the proprietary interests in a domestic or foreign corporation are divided or any security convertible into any such unit or any warrant or right to subscribe for or purchase any such unit.

(b) "Person" means any individual, corporation, partnership, limited partnership, syndicate, joint-stock company, unincorporated organization, trust, estate or association.

(c) "Offeror" means a person who, directly or indirectly, makes any takeover bid, and includes all persons acting jointly or in concert for the purpose of making a takeover bid. "Offeror" does not mean

(1) any person, including any bank or broker-dealer, lending funds to an offeror in the ordinary course of its business;

(2) any bank, broker-dealer, attorney, accountant, consultant, or employee solely because such person furnishes information or advice to or performs ministerial duties for an offeror; or

(3) any broker-dealer who acts as dealer-manager or in some similar capacity in connection with such takeover bid; provided in the case of (1), (2), and (3) above, such person does not otherwise participate in the takeover bid.

(d) "Associate" of a person means

(1) any corporation or other organization of which such person is an officer or general partner

157

or is directly or indirectly the beneficial owner of 10 percent or more of any class of equity securities or other proprietary interests in such organization;

(2) any trust or other estate in which such person has a substantial beneficial interest or as to which such person serves as a trustee or in a similar fiduciary capacity; and

(3) any relative or spouse of such person, or any relative of such spouse, who has the same home as such person.

(e) "Offeree" means the record holder of equity securities which an offeror acquires or offers to acquire in connection with a takeover bid.

(f) (1) "Takeover bid" means

(A) the offer to acquire or the acquisition of any equity security of an offeree company, by means of a tender offer or request or invitation for tenders, if after the acquisition thereof the offeror, together with its associates, would be directly or indirectly a beneficial owner of more than ten percent of any class of the outstanding equity securities of the offeree company, or

(B) the offer to acquire or the acquisition of any equity security of an offeree company by any means other than a tender offer or request or invitation for tenders as contemplated by (A) above, if prior to such offer or acquisition the offeror, together with its associates, is directly or indirectly the beneficial owner of more than ten percent of any class of equity security of the offeree company and such acquisition, together with all other acquisitions by such offeror and its associates within the 12-month period immediately preceding the date of such offer or acquisition, would constitute more than two per cent, of any class of equity security of the offeree company.

(2) With respect to conduct of the type specified in sections 22-1901 (f)(1)(A) and 22-1901 (f)(1)(B), a takeover bid shall not include, for the purposes of this Chapter, an offer to acquire, or the acquisition of, any equity security of an offeree company pursuant to:

(A) an offer or offers made to not more than 15 offerees during any period of 12 consecutive months;

(B) an offer made on substantially equal terms to all shareholders of the class of equity securities of the offeree company to which the offer relates and as to which the offeree company, acting through its board of directors, has, prior to the time that such offer is first made, recommended acceptance to such shareholders, if the terms thereof, including any inducements to officers or directors of the offeree company and any of their associates that are not available to all shareholders, have been disclosed to all shareholders;

(C) an offer by a corporation to acquire its own equity securities or the equity securities of its subsidiary corporation as defined in section 22-102 (c); or

(D) an offer to exchange the securities of an issuer for equity securities of an offeree company where the securities proposed to be issued are registered pursuant to the Federal Securities Act of 1933, as amended, or the Georgia Securities Act of 1973 [Chapter 97-1], in connection with such exchange offer.

(E) (i) an offer by a person to exchange securities for, seek to acquire, or acquire in the open market or otherwise, any voting securities of a domestic insurer or of a person controlling a domestic insurer if such person making the offer is subject to the requirements of section 56-3403 of the Georgia Insurance Code relating to acquisitions of or mergers with domestic insurers, or

(ii) an offer by a person to merge with a domestic insurer or with a person controlling a domestic insurer if such person making the offer is subject to the requirements of section 56-3403 of the Georgia Insurance Code relating to acquisitions of or mergers with domestic insurers.

(3) With respect solely to conduct of the type specified in section 22-1901 (f)(1)(B), a takeover bid shall not include, for the purposes of this Chapter, an offer to acquire, or the acquisition of, any equity security of an offeree company pursuant to an offer made by (A) a person who is an officer or director of the offeree company or who, together with his associates, is directly or indirectly the beneficial owner of more than 50 percent of the outstanding equity securities of the offeree company, or (B) any relative or spouse of such person, or any relative of such spouse, who has the same home as such person.

(g) "Offeree company" means a corporation having 100 or more holders of record of its equity securities and whose equity securities are the subject of a takeover bid, which (1) in the case of a domestic corporation has either its principal office in this State or significant assets in this State, or (2) in the case of a foreign corporation has both its principal office in this State and significant assets in this State.

(h) "Broker-dealer" means any person engaged, directly or indirectly, as agent, broker or principal, in the business of purchasing, offering, selling or otherwise dealing or trading in securities for the account of others or for his own account. "Broker-dealer" shall include "dealer" and "salesman" as such terms are defined in sections 97-102 (a)(5) and 97-102 (a)(15) respectively of the Georgia Securities Act of 1973.

(i) "Commissioner" means the Commissioner of Securities of this State.

22-1902 Registration of Takeover Bids

(a) It shall be unlawful for an offeror to make or continue to make a takeover bid or to acquire any equity security pursuant to a takeover bid, unless such takeover bid is the subject of an effective registration statement under this Chapter. Before a registration statement can become effective under this Chapter, the offeror shall file such a statement with the commissioner containing the information prescribed in subsection (b) of this section, shall comply with the other requirements as set forth in said subsection (b) and the requirements set forth in subsection (c) and, not later than the date of such filing, shall send a copy of such statement by certified mail to the offeree company at its principal office.

(b) In the case of an offeror which is a corporation, the registration statement shall be executed by the offeror in the manner provided in section 22-104(c), and in the case of all other offerors, as prescribed by the commissioner. The registration statement shall be filed with the commissioner on forms prescribed by the commissioner. The registration statement shall be accompanied by a consent to service of process properly executed by each person who may be deemed an offeror in the form specified in section 22-1908 and by the filing fee specified in section 22-1909 (a). The registration statement shall contain the following information and such additional information as the Commissioner by rule or order shall prescribe:

(1) The identity, business or occupation, background and address of the principal place of business of each person who may be deemed an offeror as defined in section 22-1901 (c);

(2) The amount of equity securities of the offeree company beneficially owned by each offeror and its officers and directors and by each associate of such offeror and of its officers and directors, the amount of equity securities acquired during the last 12 months by each such person and the consideration paid therefor, and the amount of equity securities of the offeree company which each such person has a right to acquire directly or indirectly, together with the name and address of the principal place of business of each such person;

(3) The source and amount of funds or other consideration used or to be used in acquiring any equity securities of the offeree company and, if any part of such funds or other consideration is or will be borrowed or obtained from any other person, a description of the transaction and the names of the parties thereto, except that where a source of funds is a loan made in the ordinary course of business by a bank, if the person filing such statement so requests, the names of the bank shall not be made available to the public;

(4) A statement of any plans, intentions or proposals which the offeror has to liquidate the offeree company, relocate any operations of the offeree company, sell any of its assets, effect its merger or consolidation, or make any other material changes in its business, corporate structure, management or personnel;

(5) All material information as to any contracts, arrangements or understandings, either in existenace or proposed, which the offeror has with any person with respect to the takeover bid or with respect to any equity securities of the offeree company, including any employment or management contracts with existing management or proposed between the offeror and the existing

management of the offeree company, transfers of any equity securities, joint ventures, loan or option agreements, puts and calls, guarantees of loans, guarantees against loss, guarantees of profits, division of losses or profits, or the giving or withholding of proxies, naming the person or persons in each instance with whom such contracts, arrangements or understandings have been or are proposed to be entered into;

(6) (A) All material information concerning the organization and operations of any offeror which is a corporation, partnership, business trust or association, including the year, form and jurisdiction of its organization, a description of the business done by each such offeror and any material changes therein during the past three years, a description of each class of such offeror's capital stock and its long-term debt, a description of the location and character of the principal properties of the offeror and its subsidiaries, a description of any pending legal or administrative proceeding to which the offeror or any of its officers, directors or associates is a party and which is material to an offeree's consideration of the offer, the names of all directors and executive officers of the offeror and their material business activities and affiliations during the past three years.

(B) Copies of its consolidated balance sheet as of the end of its most recent fiscal year and, if the date of filing the registration statement is more than 90 days after the end of its most recent fiscal year, a consolidated balance sheet as of a date not more than 90 days prior to the date the registration statement is filed, statements of income and source and application of funds for each of the three full fiscal years preceding the date the registration statement is filed and for the interim period, if any, between the end of the most recent fiscal year and the date of the most recent balance sheet being filed, together with statements of income and source and application of funds for the comparable interim period in the prior year. All such statements shall have been prepared in accordance with generally accepted accounting principles consistently applied. All statements covering fiscal years shall be certified by an independent public accountant duly registered and in good standing as such under the laws of the place of his residence or principal office and all interim statements shall be certified by the chief accounting or finanical officer of the offeror.

(7) All material information concerning the identify and background of any offeror, other than an offeror referred to in paragraph (6) above, including the material business activities and affiliations of each such offeror during the past three years, a balance sheet of the offeror as of a date within 90 days of the filing of the registration statement certified by the offeror or an independent public accountant, and a description of any pending legal or administrative proceedings to which the offeror or any of such offeror's associates is a party and which is material to an offeree's consideration of the offer.

(c) At the time of filing the registration statement, the offeror shall file with the commissioner and shall also mail to the offeree company by certified mail three copies of any written materials proposed to be used in connection with the takeover bid in the form proposed to be published, used or sent to offerees. Such material shall include all advertisements, circulars, letters or other materials of the offeror soliciting or requesting the acceptance of the takeover bid. All such material published, sent or delivered to offerees shall contain all material terms of the proposed takeover bid, including the information required by paragraphs (1), (2), (3), (4) and (5) of subsection (b) and shall state the registration statement filed by such offeror under this Chapter is on file at the office of the commissioner and that upon request, the offeror will promptly forward to any offeree copies of such registration statement and the materials required to be filed under this subsection (c), as such statement or materials may be amended or supplemented from time to time, at no expense to such offeree.

(d) The commissioner may require the offeror to file any other documents, exhibits and information that he deems material to the takeover bid, and he may permit the omission of any of the information specified in subsection (b) if he determines that such information is not required for the protection of offerees or is unreasonably burdensome on the offeror. The commissioner may by order summarily delay the effective date of the registration statement if he determines that the registration statement does not contain all of the information required, or that the offeror has not filed all of the materials required to be filed under subsection (c), or that any solicitation materials proposed to be published, delivered or sent to offerees do not meet the requirements of subsection (c) or do not provide for full and fair disclosure to offerees of all material information concerning the takeover bid, subject to the right of the offeror to a hearing as provided in section, 22-1907 (b) of this Chapter.

(e) A registration statement filed under this Chapter shall become effective at 3:00 p.m. 10 full business days after the date of filing the registration statement with the commissioner unless delayed by order of the commissioner, or unless prior thereto the commissioner calls a hearing with respect to the takeover bid that is the subject of such registration statement. The commissioner shall call a hearing if so requested by the offeree company, acting through its board of directors, by a written request filed with him not later than 4:00 p.m. on the seventh full business day following the date of filing of the registration statement. If a hearing is called, the registration statement shall not become effective until it is declared effective by order of the commissioner. Notwithstanding the foregoing, if, at any time prior to the date upon which any registration statement under this Chapter would otherwise become effective under this section, any other offeror shall file a registration statement under this Chapter with respect to a takeover bid for any class of equity securities of the same offeree company, the effective date of any prior registration statement shall be postponed until such prior registration statement is declared effective by order of the commissioner or until earlier of (1) the effective date of the subsequent statement, (2) the date of withdrawal of the subsequent statement, or (3) the date of denial of effectiveness of the subsequent statement.

(f) Any hearing called by the commissioner under this section shall be held within 20 days of the date of filing of the registration statement under subsection (b), and any determination made following the hearing shall be made within 30 days after such filing, unless the commissioner by order extends such time periods for the convenience of the parties or for the protection of offerees in this State. If, following the hearing, the commissioner finds that the registration statement does not contain all of the information required to be included therein or that the solicitation materials proposed to be published, delivered or sent to offerees do not meet the requirements of subsection (c) or fail to provide for full and fair disclosure to offerees of all material information concerning the takeover bid, he shall by order deny effectiveness of the registration statement, without prejudice to any subsequent filing of a registration statement by such offeror. If he finds that the registration statement contains all of the information required to be included therein and that the solicitation materials proposed to be published, delivered or sent to offerees meet the requirements of subsection (c) and provide for full and fair disclosure to offerees of all material information concerning the takeover bid, he shall by order promptly declare the registration statement effective.

(g) Upon the occurrence of any event which causes any registration statement filed under this Chapter or any materials required to be filed under subsection (c) to become materially inaccurate or incomplete, the offeror shall file with the commissioner an appropriate amendment to such registration statement or shall appropriately amend or supplement its filing of such materials, and not later than the date of such filing shall send a copy of such amendment or such amended or supplemental materials by certified mail to the offeree company at its principal office and to any offeree to whom such materials have previously been delivered. The commissioner shall have the power to issue an order summarily causing any registration statement to cease being effective if he shall find that such registration statement or any materials required to be filed under subsection (c) in connection with such registration statement are, for any reason, materially inaccurate or incomplete.

(h) It shall be unlawful for any person to make any representation to any person that the filing or effectiveness of registration statement or the registration of any takeover bid under this Chapter, or the existence of any exemption from the registration requirements of this Chapter, means that the commissioner has passed in any way upon the truth, completeness, or accuracy of any such registration statement, the merits of any takeover bid or exempt transaction, or has recommended or given approval to any takeover bid or exempt transaction. Any solicitation materials sent to offerees in connection with a takeover bid registered under this Chapter shall contain the following legend on the cover page thereof in bold face print or capital type:

THIS TAKEOVER BID HAS BEEN REGISTERED WITH THE SECURITIES COMMIS-SIONER OF THE STATE OF GEORGIA. THE SECURITIES COMMISSIONERS HAS NOT PASSED UPON THE MERITS OF THE TAKEOVER BID AND DOES NOT IN ANY WAY ENDORSE OR RECOMMEND THE ACCEPTANCE OR REJECTION OF THE TAKEOVER BID.

22-1903 Solicitations and Communications

(a) Copies of all advertisements, circulars, letters or other materials of the offeree company, soliciting or requesting the acceptance or rejection of the takeover bid, shall be filed with the commissioner and sent to the offeror not later than the time copies of such solicitation materials are first published, used or sent to offerees.

(b) No solicitation or communication by offeror or an offeree company to an offeree in connection with a takeover bid shall make any false statement of a material factor or omit to state a material fact necessary in order to make the statements made, in the light of the circumstances under which they are made, not misleading. The commissioner may by rule or order prohibit the use of any solicitation material deemed by him materially false or misleading.

22-1904 Limitations on Offerors

No offeror shall make a takeover bid of the type specified in section 22-1901 (f)(1)(A) if he beneficially owns, directly or indirectly, five percent, or more of any class of the equity securities of the offeree company, any of which were purchased within one year before the proposed takeover bid, unless the offeror, before making such prior purchase, or before the 30th day following the effective date of this Chapter, whichever is later, made a public announcement of his intentions or the lack thereof with respect to changing or influencing the management or control of the offeree company and filed with the commissioner and with the offeree company a statement specifying such intentions or the lack thereof and containing such additional information as the commissioner may by rule prescribe.

22-1905 Fraudulentand Deceptive Practices or Manipulative Acts

(a) It shall be unlawful for any offeror or offeree company, or an officer, director or associate of an offeror or offeree company, or any broker-dealer acting on behalf of any offeror or offeree company to engage in any fraudulent, deceptive or manipulative acts or practices in connection with a takeover bid.

(b) Any broker-dealer who knowingly acts on behalf of an offeror in connection with any offer to acquire or any acquisition of any equity security of an offeree company pursuant to takeover bid which is not the subject of an effective registration statement under this Chapter shall be deemed to have engaged in a fraudulent, deceptive or manipulative act or practice.

22-1906 Administration

This Chapter shall be administered by the commissioner, who shall have the same powers and authority with respect to this Chapter as are vested in him under sections 97-110 and 97-111 of the Georgia Securities Act of 1973, with respect to such Act.

22-1907 Hearings

(a) Any formal hearing held pursuant to the provisions of this Chapter shall be conducted in accordance with the provisions of section 97-116 of the Georgia Securities Act of 1973.

(b) Where the commissioner has issued an order summarily delaying the effective date of a registration statement under section 22-1902 (d), he shall promptly send to the offeror a notice of opportunity for hearing as to whether the registration statement and other materials filed by the offeror comply with the requirements of this Chapter.

22-1908 Consent to Service

Where a consent to service of process is required under this Chapter, such consent to service of process shall be in the form prescribed by the commissioner, shall be irrevocable, and shall provide that actions arising out of or founded upon the acquisition or offer to acquire any securities in violation of this Chapter may be commenced against the person executing such consent in any court of competent jurisdiction and proper venue within this State by the service of process or pleadings upon the commissioner. Service of any such process or pleadings in any such actions against the person who has filed a consent to service with the commissioner shall, if made upon the commissioner, be by duplicate copies, one of which shall be filed in the office of the commissioner and the other shall immediately be forwarded by the commissioner by registered mail to the person against whom such process or pleadings are directed at his latest address on file in the office of the commissioner.

22-1909 Fees and Costs

(a) The commissioner shall charge a filing fee of $250 for any registration statement filed by an offeror in connection with a takeover bid of the type specified in section 22-1901 (f)(1)(A), a filing fee of $50 for any registration statement filed by offeror in connection with a takeover bid of the type specified in section 22-1901 (f)(1)(B), a filing fee of $20 for any statement of intent filed by an offeror as specified in section 22-1904 and may charge a fee which shall not exceed $50 for any amendment to a registration statement or statement of intent previously filed under this Chapter.

(b) Upon filing an application with the commissioner for hearing under this Chapter the requesting party shall pay to the commissioner a fee of $250 and shall deposit with the commissioner such sum, not to exceed $2,500, as the commissioner may require to defray the costs of such hearing.

(c) Upon the conclusion of any hearing held pursuant to this Chapter, the expenses reasonably attributable to such hearing shall be charged to and allocated between the offeror and offeree companies in such manner as the commissioner shall by order provide.

22-1910 Injunction and Prosecution of Violations

Whenever it may appear to the commissioner, either upon complaint or otherwise, that any person has engaged in, or is engaging in, or is about to engage in any act or practice or transaction which is prohibited by this Chapter or by any rule, regulation or order of the commissioner promulgated or issued pursuant to any section of this Chapter or which is declared to be unlawful under this Chapter, the commissioner shall have the power and authority to act, at his discretion, in the manner specified by section 97-113 of the Georgia Securities Act of 1973: Provided that in addition to the power and authority conferred by such section 97-113, the commissioner may apply to any superior court of competent jurisdiction in this State for an order requiring the rescission of any purchases of securities determined to be unlawful under this Chapter or any rule or order hereunder and provided further that the right to a hearing provided for in section (a)(1) of such section 97-113 shall refer to the right of hearing provided for in section 22-1907 (b) of this Chapter.

22-1911 Venue

For purposes of venue for any civil or criminal action under this Chapter, any violation of this Chapter or of any rule, regulation or order promulgated hereunder shall be considered to have originated, to have been committed and to have accrued, in addition to, and not in limitation of any other counties that may be prescribed by reason of other laws, (a) in any county in which any act was performed in furtherance of the transaction which violated the Chapter, (b) in the county of any violator's principal place of business in this State, (c) in the county of the offeree company's principal place of business in this State, and (d) in any county in which any violator had control or possession of any proceeds of said violation or of any books, records, documents or other materials or objects that were used in furtherance of said violation.

22-1912 Criminal Penalties

(a) Any person who shall wilfully violate any provision of this Chapter in connection with a takeover bid of the type specified in section 22-1901 (f)(1)(A) shall be deemed guilty of a felony and upon conviction thereof shall be punished by a fine of not more than $5,000 or imprisonment of not less than one and not more than five years, or both.

(b) Any person who shall wilfully violate any provision of this Chapter in connection with a takeover bid of the type specified in section 22-1901 (f)(1)(B) shall be deemed guilty of a misdemeanor and upon conviction thereof shall be punished by a fine of not less than $500 nor more than $1,000, or by imprisonment for not more than 180 days, or both.

(c) Nothing in this Chapter shall limit any statutory or common law right of the State to punish any person for violation of any provision of any law.

22-1913 Civil Liabilities

(a) Any offeror who purchases an equity security in connection with a takeover bid not in compliance with this Chapter shall be liable to the person selling the security to him, who may sue in any court of competent jurisdiction to recover the equity security, plus any income received by the offeror thereon, upon tender of the consideration received, or for damages. Damages are the excess of the value of the equity security on the date of purchase or its present value, whichever is greater, over the present value of the consideration received for the equity security. Tender shall require only notice of willingness to pay the amount specified in exchange for the equity security. If such suit be successful, in whole or in part, the court may award such person reasonable attorneys' fees.

(b) Every person who directly or indirectly controls a person liable under subsection (a) shall also be liable jointly and severally with and to the same extent as such person, unless the person liable hereunder proves that he did not know, and in the exercise of reasonable care could not have known, of the existence of the facts by reason of which the liability is alleged to exist. Contribution shall be allowed as in cases of contract among the several persons so liable.

(c) No action may be maintained to enforce any liability created under this Chapter unless brought within one year after the discovery of the violation or after such discovery should have been made by the exercise of reasonable diligence. In no event, however, shall any action be brought to enforce a liability created under this Chapter more than three years after the date of the violation.

(d) The rights and remedies under this section are in addition to any other rights or remedies that may exist at law or in equity.

22-1914 Reciprocity

Regardless of whether an offer or acquisition is subject to the provisions of this Chapter, the commissioner shall have the authority to apply for appropriate relief to any superior court of competent jurisdiction to enjoin the offer to acquire, pursuant to a tender offer or invitation for tenders, or the acquisition of any equity securities of a corporation or other issues or securities, if such offer or acquisition is the subject of any temporary or permanent administration or judicial order restraining or enjoining such offer or acquisition under any act or law of any other state which is substantially similar to this Chapter.

22-1915 Application of Chapter

(a) This Chapter shall apply to an offeree company (1) in the case of a domestic corporation only if such offeree company is a corporation for profit organized under the provisions of the Georgia Business Corporation Code or under any prior general corporation law of this State and (2) in the case of a foreign corporation only if such offeree company is a corporation for profit organized under laws other than the laws of this State for purposes similar to the purposes for which corporations for profit are organized under the provisions of the Georgia Business Corporation Code.

(b) This Chapter shall not apply (1) to any offeree company having fewer than 100 holders of record of its equity securities, or (2) to any offer or acquisition which requires a prior approval by vote of the holders of at least a majority of the outstanding equity securities of the offeree company pursuant to its charter or articles of incorporation or the applicable corporation statute.

Appendix D

Tax-Free Merger Plans Using "Reverse" Merger and New Dummy Corporation

Appendix D-1 is an actual agreement used in a tax-free reorganization in which an insurance company formed a holding company. Because it was important that the insurance company remain qualified in the various states, a reverse merger form was used.

Note that this particular plan does not include any warranties or provisions as to counsel's opinion at closing. This is because the particular transaction involved in this plan was the creation of an insurance holding company, and there were really no adverse parties involved in the transaction. If, instead, the transaction had been a merger of two unrelated corporations, substantial warranties of the type found in the agreement and plan of reorganization for a "C" Reorganization, found in Appendix D-2, would have been included.

Appendix D-2 is a recent agreement involving the acquisition of a United States insurance holding company by the subsidiary of a foreign corporation for cash. The reverse merger technique was used in order to compel all of the public shareholders of the insurance holding company to accept cash, if a majority of the holders of shares approved the transaction.

Appendix D-3 is an agreement used in the recent formation of a bank holding company for a medium-size, publicly-held state bank. Use of the reverse merger technique allowed the existing bank charter to remain intact, while the public shareholders of the bank were "moved up" to a position of becoming shareholders of the new holding company. The bank then was left as a wholly-owned subsidiary of the new holding company.

See discussion beginning at page 16.

Appendix D-1

PLAN OF MERGER AND REORGANIZATION AGREEMENT

The parties should be precisely specified and given a short designation to be used throughout the rest of the agreements.

THIS PLAN OF MERGER AND REORGANIZATION AGREEMENT ("the Plan") is made among AMERICAN, INC. a Kansas corporation ("American"), HOLDING COMPANY, INC., a Kansas Corporation ("Holding Company"), and 252, INC., a Kansas Corporation ("252").

WHEREAS, American was chartered by the Secretary of State of Kansas in the year 19_____, and it has a maximum authorized capitalization of 3,000,000 shares of common stock of the par value of $1.00 per share of which 2,000,000 shares are issued and outstanding; and

The purpose of the "Whereas" clauses is simply to set the purpose of the agreement. Normally, these clauses do not have any operative legal effect, but in the case of disputes they are often used by courts to search out the intention of the parties in case there should prove to be an ambiguity in part of the operative portion of the agreement.

WHEREAS, Holding Company was chartered by the Secretary of State of Kansas, on March 1, 19_____, and it has a maximum authorization capitalization of 5,000,000 shares of common stock of $1.00 par value, of which 2,000,000 shares are issued and outstanding and held by its wholly owned subsidiary, 252; and

WHEREAS, 252 was chartered by the Secretary of State of Kansas, on January 24, 19_____, and has a maximum authorized capitalization of 10 shares of $100 par value common stock all of which is outstanding and held by Holding Company; and

WHEREAS, the boards of directors and a majority of the directors of American, Holding Company, and 252, deemed it desirable and in the best interest of their respective corporations and their stockholders, that 252 be merged into American under and pursuant to the provisions of Kansas statutes and as a "Reorganization" within the meaning of §368 of the Internal Revenue Code of 1954;

The "Now, Therefore" clause simply recites the consideration and purpose of the agreement and starts the operative portion of the agreement.

NOW, THEREFORE, in consideration of the premises and of the mutual agreements, covenants, and provisions herein contained, and for the purpose of prescribing the various terms and conditions of said merger, and the mode of carrying the same into effect, pursuant to the laws of the state of Kansas or not inconsistent herewith, the said parties under their respective corporate names and seals have agreed and do hereby agree as follows:

The type of transaction should be precisely stated as soon as possible, and as briefly as possible.

1. Merger

252 shall merge into American, and American shall continue as the surviving corporation.

2. Terms of Merger

In order to comply with the statute and to memorialize the intention of the parties, the precise terms of the merger should be set forth in some detail.

Here we have the reverse merger because the existing corporation to be acquired was merged with the new "shell corporation" which was called 252, Inc., and the acquired corporation survived.

An effective date should be specified. Here it is the date of filing with the Secretary of State. It would be possible to delay the date to the end of the month if the actual filing time could not be controlled.

The exchange of shares under the merger spelled out.

It is often desirable to provide for the mechanics of stock certificate transfer. Often the old certificates remain outstanding for years although they represent interests in the merged corporation.

(a) American shall be the surviving corporation and the corporate identity, existence, purposes, powers, franchises, rights, and immunities of American shall continue unaffected and unimpaired by the merger, and the provisions of the present charter and by-laws of American shall remain unchanged and shall continue as the charter and by-laws of American, the continuing corporation resulting from this merger, and it shall be governed by the laws of the state of Kansas. The directors and officers of American shall remain unchanged by the merger.

(b) The corporate identity, existence, purposes, powers, franchises, rights, and immunities of 252 shall be merged into American, and American shall be fully vested therewith.

(c) The separate existence of 252 shall cease at the effective date, whereupon American and 252 shall become a single corporation.

(d) The merger of 252 into American shall be effective ("effective date") as of the close of business on the day that the Articles of Merger are filed with the Secretary of State of Kansas. Upon filing, and by virtue of such filing, all property of 252, both real and personal, tangible and intangible, and all debts of 252 and obligation of 252, without further act or deed, shall be possessed by and vested in American.

(e) Upon the effective date, the holder of such common share of American will become the holder of one common share of Holding Company for each share held of American. Each holder of a qualified or restricted or other stock option for common shares of American will become the holder of a similar stock option for the same number of shares of Holding Company common stock. Such Holding Company options shall supersede the American options and shall have substantially the same terms, conditions, and values as the options of American, and the price of the Holding Company shares purchasable under the American options previously held. On the effective date, the present stock certificates of American shall be deemed to be Holding Company certificates, but Holding Company may call upon all of American's common stock shareholders to call their certificates representing American shares it exchange for appropriate Holding Company certificates.

The directors have approved the transaction at the time the plan and agreement is executed, but the stockholders' approval remains for a later date.

3. Stockholders' Approval

The directors of each of the parties hereto hereby authorize and direct the officers of each of the parties to submit this Plan for approval to the stockholders of each such corporation at a regular or special meeting to be called and held, all in accordance with the laws of Kansas and the respective charter and by-laws of each corporation, as quickly as may be practicable after execution hereof, and to take such other actions as they may deem desirable to effectuate the merger.

4. Mode of Effecting

Certain corporate house-keeping details should be specified so that clerical confusion will be minimized after the merger.

The name, Articles of Incorporation, officers, and directors of the surviving corporation, American, shall remain unchanged on the effective date, and American's registered office and principal place of business in the state of Kansas shall remain at 3340 Bigtree Avenue, N.W., Clayton, Kansas, and the registered agent shall be its president, who presently is W. Hillard Greene, at such address, but the board of directors may from time to time appoint any qualified person or entity as registered agent, or designate another registered office and principal place of business. The maximum number of shares of capital stock with par value authorized to be outstanding at any one time shall remain 3,000,000 shares of common stock at par value of $1.00 per share. The manner, terms, and basis of converting the shares of capital stock of each merging corporation shall be as aforesaid: that is, on the effective date, each shareholder of American shall become a shareholder of an identical number of shares of Holding Company and Holding Company shall become the sole shareholder of American. All such exchange of shares shall be automatic on the effective date. The shares presently issued and outstanding of Holding Company held by 252 shall become the shares held, after the effective date, by the shareholders, of American immediately prior to the effective date. The shares of 252 held by Holding Company immediately prior to the effective date shall become all of the outstanding shares of American upon the effective date.

5. Approval

The provisions for a meeting of the stockholders is not only a statutory requirement, but to include the procedure for approval in some detail in the agreement serves as a handy checklist for the corporate secretary in calling the meeting.

After approval at the meetings of the stockholders of each corporation, of which meetings, not less than 20 days before such meeting, notice of the time, place, object, and that one of the purposes is to consider the proposed Plan of Merger shall be given or waiver thereof obtained in accordance with Kansas law and the terms of the charter and by-laws of each of the respective corporations to each stockholder of record, on the record date hereinafter specified, whether entitled to vote at such a meeting or not. The record date for each corporation shall be at the close of business 30 days before said meetings. Any notice so given shall contain a clear and concise statement that if the Plan of Merger is effective, shareholders dissenting therefrom are entitled, if they file a written objection to such Plan before the vote of the shareholders is taken thereon and comply with further provisions of Kansas law regarding the rights of dissenting shareholders, to be paid the fair market value of their shares. A copy of this Plan, together with a copy of the most recent annual balance sheet and any available annual profit-and-loss statement for each of the merging corporations, shall accompany such notice. At said meeting, said Plan shall be voted on in person or by proxy and if the Plan shall be approved by the affirmative vote of the holders of a majority of the shares entitled to vote thereon, then that fact shall be certified by the secretary of each corporation under the seal of each corporation, and a petition shall then be presented by the merging corporations to the Secretary of State of Kansas, or other duly authorized official of said state, attaching to said petition a copy of this Plan and appropriate Articles of Merger and any other documents required by law, with the certificates thereon of the secretaries of the merging corporations certifying as to the fact of the adoption of this Plan by such respective majorities.

Even though the merger has the effect of transferring all property, there is a considerable period of time after the merger in which record transfers must take place for motor vehicle and other such property.

6. Further Instruments and Clarification

When requested by American, 252 will execute and deliver all such instruments as may be deemed necessary or desirable to confirm to the surviving corporation title to the property of 252 and to carry out the intent and purposes of this Plan.

There should be a provision for modification of the agreement to take care of minor contingencies which could arise between stockholder approval and the actual effective date.

At any time before or after approval and adoption by the respective stockholders of the parties to this Plan, this Plan may be modified in matters of form, or supplemented by additional agreements, articles, or certificates, as may be determined by a majority of the board of directors of all such constitutent corporations to be necessary, desirable, or expedient to clarify the intention of the parties hereto or to effect or facilitate the filing, recording, or official approval of this Plan and the consummation of the merger and reorganization herein contemplated, in accordance with the purpose and intent of this Plan.

7. Abandonment of Merger

There should always be a "kickout" provision in case some unforeseen circumstance, such as a shareholder's lawsuit or an antitrust action should arise.

This Plan may be terminated and the merger provided for hereby abandoned by the majority vote of the entire board of directors of any of the parties hereto at any time prior to the effective date.

IN WITNESS WHEREOF, each of the parties hereto has caused this Plan to be executed on its behalf by its president, its corporate seal to be affixed hereto, and all to be attested by its secretary, this _____ of May, 19_____.

AMERICAN, INC. ("American")

[Corporate Seal]

By: _____

Attest: President

_____

Secretary

The precise corporate names should be used. Normally the method of signing should be by the president with the corporate seal affixed and the seal and signature attested to by the corporate secretary. Of course, there will also be in the record appropriate resolutions adopted by the board of directors authorizing the president to execute the agreement on behalf of the corporation.

HOLDING COMPANY, INC. ("Holding Company")

[Corporate Seal]

By: _____

Attest: President

_____

Secretary

252, Inc. ("252")

[Corporate Seal]

By: _____

Attest: President

_____

Secretary

APPENDIX D-2

AGREEMENT AND PLAN OF MERGER

The parties are the public corporation, the acquiring corporation, and the new "dummy".

AGREEMENT AND PLAN OF MERGER, dated March 5, 1980 among Financial Inc., a Georgia corporation ("Financial"), MEV Corporation, a Delaware corporation ("Mev"), and Frederick Corporation a Georgia corporation ("Subsidiary II").

Recitals

The authorized capital stock of Financial consists of 10,000,000 shares of Common Stock, $1.00 par value per share ("Financial Common Stock"), of which 2,439,344 shares are issued and outstanding, and 1,000,000 shares of Preferred Stock, no par value, none of which is issued or outstanding.

The respective Board of Directors of Financial, Mev and Subsidiary II have, by resolutions, duly approved and adopted this Agreement, and the Boards of Directors of Financial and Subsidiary II have directed that it be submitted to the stockholders of Financial and Subsidiary II, respectively, for approval.

At the Effective Time of the Merger (as defined in Section 1.1) of Subsidiary II and Financial pursuant to the terms hereof (the "Merger"), the outstanding shares of Subsidiary II Common Stock will be converted into shares of Financial Common Stock, with Financial being the surviving corporation in the Merger, and all shares of Financial Common Stock issued and outstanding immediately prior to the Effective Time of the Merger (other than shares held by Mev, Subsidiary II or any affiliate of Mev or Subsidiary II) will be cancelled and the holders thereof will be entitled to receive in exchange for each such share of Financial Common Stock $55.00 in cash.

In consideration of the mutual benefits to be derived from this Agreement and the representations, warranties, conditions, covenants and agreements hereinafter contained, Financial, Mev and Subsidiary II agree as follows:

175

Article I

General

1.1. *Execution, Filing and Effectiveness.* Subject to the provisions hereof, this Agreement shall be executed by each of Financial, Mev and Subsidiary II and on or prior to the Closing Date (as defined in Article VI hereof) Articles of Merger ("Articles of Merger") shall be executed by Financial and Subsidiary II and delivered to the Secretary of State of the State of Georgia for filing, as provided in the Georgia Business Corporation Code, as soon as practicable on the Closing Date. The Merger shall become effective as of the time of delivery of the Articles of Merger to the Secretary of State for filing (the "Effective Time of the Merger"). At the Effective Time of the Merger the separate existence of Subsidiary II shall cease and Subsidiary II shall be merged with and into Financial (Subsidiary II and Financial are sometimes referred to herein as the "Constituent Corporations" and Financial is sometimes referred to herein as the "Surviving Corporation").

Since a public corporation was involved a paying agent was required to distribute cash for shares.

1.2. *Delivery of Cash.* Mev agrees that in connection with the closing of the Merger it will cause Subsidiary II to make adequate provision to assure that the cash to which holders of Financial Common Stock shall be entitled pursuant to this Agreement will be provided as and when required.

Article II

Effect of Merger on Capital Stock of the Constituent Corporations, Certificate of Incorporation, By-Laws, Officers and Directors of the Surviving Corporation

2.1. *Conversion of Shares.* The manner and basis of converting the shares of each of the Constituent Corporations and the consideration which the holders of such shares shall receive are as follows:

(a) *Subsidiary II Common Stock.* Each of the shares, $1.00 par value per share, of Subsidiary II Common Stock issued and outstanding immediately prior to the Effective Time of the Merger shall, by virtue of the Merger and without any action on the part of the holder thereof, be converted into one share of Financial Common Stock.

(b) *Financial Common Stock.* Each of the shares of Financial Common Stock issued and outstanding immediately prior to the Effective Time of the Merger (other than shares of Financial Common Stock to be cancelled as set forth in Section 2.1(c) and (d) shall, by virtue of the Merger and without any action on the part of the holder thereof, be converted into and shall represent the right to receive $55.00 in cash.

(c) *Shares Held by Mev or an Affiliate of Mev.* Any shares of Financial Common Stock held by Mev, Subsidiary II or any affiliate of Mev or Subsidiary II immediately prior to the Effective Time of the Merger shall, by virtue of the Merger and without any action on the part of the holder thereof, be cancelled.

(d) *Financial Treasury Shares.* Any shares of Financial Common Stock held at the Effective Time of the Merger in the treasury of Financial shall, by virtue of the Merger and without any action on the part of Financial, be cancelled.

2.2 *Mechanics of Exchange.* (a) Mev shall authorize The First National Bank of _____ to act as Exchange Agent hereunder (the ''Exchange Agent'') and shall authorize a bank in Atlanta, Georgia to act as a Paying Agent hereunder (the ''Paying Agent'').

(b) On or prior to the Closing Date, Mev shall cause Subsidiary II to deliver (or make adequate provision to deliver) to the Exchange Agent the cash payable in exchange for shares of Financial Common Stock pursuant to Section 2.1.

(c) Each holder of shares of Financial Common Stock at the Effective Time of the Merger (other than Mev, Subsidiary II or any affiliate of Mev or Subsidiary II) shall be entitled, upon surrender to the Exchange Agent, either directly or through the Paying Agent, of the certificate or certificates for such shares for cancellation, to receive in exchange therefor $55.00 in cash per share of Financial Common Stock. Until so surrendered to the Exchange Agent for cancellation, each certificate formerly representing shares of Financial Common Stock shall be deemed for all purposes, except as set forth below, to evidence only the right to receive the cash into which such shares shall be converted in the Merger and shall not evidence any right to exercise the rights of a holder of stock in the Surviving Corporation. In no event shall the holder of any such certificate have the right to receive any interest on any cash to be received.

(d) On or promptly after the Closing Date, Financial or the Surviving Corporation, as the case may be, shall furnish to all stockholders of Financial instructions as to the manner in which such stockholder's certificate or certificates formerly representing shares of Financial Common Stock shall be transmitted to the Exchange Agent or Paying Agent, including the form of transmittal letter or other documents to be used for that purpose, and in any event such instructions shall be furnished to all stockholders of Financial no later than five days following the Closing Date.

This attempts to deal with the "lost shareholder" problem.

(e) Upon the expiration of one year after the Effective Time of the Merger, any unpaid cash held by the Exchange Agent for the benefit of the holders of certificates formerly representing shares of Financial Common Stock shall be delivered to the Surviving Corporation, or its successor, if any, by the Exchange Agent and thereafter the Exchange Agent shall not be liable to any person claiming the same and the Surviving Corporation shall hold cash for such holders in accordance with applicable law.

2.3 *Certificate of Incorporation; By-Laws Officers.* (a) The Certificate of Incorporation of Subsidiary II in effect immediately prior to the Effective Time of the Merger shall be the Certificate of Incorporation of the Surviving Corporation after the Effective Time of the Merger until otherwise amended.

(b) The By-Laws of Subsidiary II in effect immediately prior to the Effective Time of the Merger shall be the By-Laws of the Surviving Corporation after the Effective Time of the Merger until otherwise amended.

(c) The directors of Subsidiary II in office at the Effective Time of the Merger shall be the directors of the Surviving Corporation until their successors are elected or appointed in accordance with the Articles of Incorporation and By-Laws of the Surviving Corporation.

(d) The officers of Financial in office at the Effective Time of the Merger shall be the officers of the Surviving Corporation, holding the respective offices in the Surviving Corporation which they hold in Financial, until their successors are elected or appointed in accordance with the Articles of Incorporation or By-Laws of the Surviving Corporation.

Article III

Certain Effects of Merger

The merger route allows the "dummy" to disappear at the Effective Time.

3.1. *Effect of Merger*. At and after the Effective Time of the Merger, the Surviving Corporation shall thereupon and thereafter possess all rights, privileges, immunities and franchises, as well of a public as of a private nature, of each of Subsidiary II and Financial; and all property, real, personal and mixed, and all debts due on whatever account, and all other choses in action, and all and every other interest of or belonging to or due to each of Subsidiary II and Financial shall be taken and deemed to be transferred to and vested in the Surviving Corporation without further act or deed; and the title to any real estate, or any interest therein, vested in Subsidiary II and Financial shall not revert or be in any way impaired by reason of the Merger; the Surviving Corporation shall thenceforth be responsible and liable for all the liabilities and obligations of each of Subsidiary II and Financial; and any claim existing or action or proceeding pending by or against either of Subsidiary II and Financial may be prosecuted as if the Merger had not taken place, or the Surviving Corporation may be substituted in its place. Neither the rights of creditors nor any liens upon the property of Subsidiary II or Financial shall be impaired by the Merger.

3.2. *Further Assurances*. Financial, Mev and Subsidiary II, respectively, shall take all such lawful action as may be necessary or appropriate in order to effectuate the transaction contemplated hereby. In case at any time after the Effective Time of the Merger any further action is necessary or desirable to carry out the purposes of this Agreement and to vest the Surviving Corporation with full title to all assets, rights, approvals, immunities and franchises of either of the Constituent Corporations, the officers and directors of each such corporation shall take all such lawful and necessary action.

Article IV

Representations and Warrantes

Note that the warranties track the usual pattern.

4.1. *Representations and Warranties by Financial.* Financial represents and warrants as follows:

(a) *Organization and Qualification, etc.* Financial is a validly existing corporation in good standing under the laws of the State of Georgia, and has full power and authority (corporate and other) to own or lease and operate all its properties and assets and to conduct its business as such business is presently being conducted. Financial is a holding company which conducts all of its operations through subsidiaries and a division which operates within the State of Georgia and is not required to be licensed or qualified to do business as a foreign corporation in any jurisdiction.

(b) *Subsidiaries.* Schedule 4.1(b) heretofore delivered to Mev by Financial sets forth with respect to each subsidiary of Financial (the "Financial Subsidiaries") its name, its jurisdiction of incorporation, the number of shares of its capital stock of each class which are authorized and outstanding and the jurisdictions in which it is licensed or qualified to do business. Except as set forth in Schedule 4.1(b), Financial directly or indirectly owns all the issued and outstanding shares of capital stock of each of the Financial Subsidiaries, all such stock is free and clear of any liens, changes, pledges, security interests or other encumbrances and all such capital stock (including director's qualifying shares) has been duly authorized and validly issued and is fully paid and nonassessable. No Financial Subsidiary has any commitment to issue or sell any shares of its capital stock, or has outstanding any securities or obligations which are convertible into or exchangeable for any shares of its capital stock, or is subject to any commitment to give any person any right to acquire from such Financial Subsidiary any shares of its capital stock. Each Financial Subsidiary is a validly existing corporation in good standing under the laws of the jurisdiction in which it is incorporated and has full power and authority (corporate and other) to own or lease and to operate its properties and to conduct its business as such business is presently being conducted. Each Financial Subsidiary is duly licensed, authorized or qualified to transact business and is in good standing as a foreign corporation in each jurisdiction in which the ownership of its property or the conduct of its business requires such license, authorization or qualification. No Financial Subsidiary is required to be licensed, authorized or qualified to transact business as a foreign corporation in any other jurisdiction, and, within the five-year period preceding the date hereof, except for routine inquiries from regulatory authorities, no jurisdiction in which it is not so licensed, authorized or qualified has demanded, requested or indicated that any Financial Subsidiary is required to be so licensed, authorized or qualified.

(c) *Authority*. Financial has full corporate power and authority to enter into this Agreement and, subject to appropriate approval of stockholders of Financial and compliance with applicable regulatory requirements, to perform its obligations hereunder and to consummate the transactions contemplated hereby. The Board of Directors of Financial has taken all action required by law, by its Articles of Incorporation, its By-Laws and otherwise, to authorize the execution and delivery of this Agreement and to perform its other obligations hereunder and this Agreement is a legal, valid and binding agreement of Financial in accordance with its terms. The copies of Financial's and each Financial Subsidiary's respective Articles of Incorporation and By-Laws which have been delivered to Mev are complete and correct and in full force and effect at the date hereof.

(d) *Non-Contravention*. The execution and delivery of this Agreement do not and the consummation of the transactions contemplated hereby (subject to the approval of the transactions contemplated hereby by the holders of Financial Common Stock, pre-merger notification and related filings with the Federal Trade Commission (the "FTC") and the Antitrust Division of the Department of Justice (the "Department of Justice") pursuant to the Hart-Scott-Rodino Antitrust Improvements Act of 1976 (the "Hart-Scott Act") and compliance with regulatory requirements of the Georgia Insurance Commissioner) will not violate any provision of the Articles of Incorporation or By-Laws of Financial or of any Financial Subsidiary, or violate, or result with the passage of time in violation of any provision of, or result in the acceleration of or entitle any party to accelerate (whether after the giving of notice or lapse of time or both) any obligation under, or result in the creation of imposition of any lien, charge, pledge, security interest or other encumbrance upon any property of Financial or any Financial Subsidiary pursuant to any provision of, any mortgage, lien, lease, agreement, license or instrument to which Financial or any Financial Subsidiary is a party or by which any of them is bound and will not violate or conflict with any law, order, arbitration award, judgment or decree or other restriction of any kind or character to which Financial or any Financial Subsidiary is subject, or by which any of their assets may be bound, nor will the same constitute an event permitting termination of any agreement to which Financial or any Financial Subsidiary is subject.

(e) *Capital Stock*. The authorized capital stock of Financial consists of 10,000,000 shares of Financial Common Stock, of which 2,439,344 shares are validly issued and outstanding, fully paid and nonassessable and 1,000,000 shares of Preferred Stock, no par value, none of which is issued or outstanding. There are no shares of Financial Common Stock held in the treasury of Financial. Financial has no commitment to issue or sell any shares of its capital stock or has outstanding any securities or obligations which are convertible into or exchangeable for any shares of its capital stock, nor is Financial subject to any commitment to give any person any right to acquire from Financial any shares of its capital stock or any other security of Financial.

(f) *Financial Statements.* The consolidated statements of financial condition of Financial and the Financial Subsidiaries as of December 31 of each of the years 1975 through 1979, and the related consolidated statements of income, shareholders' equity and changes in financial condition (including the notes thereto) for each of the five years ended December 31, 1979, certified by [national accounting firm] heretofore furnished by Financial to Mev, present fairly the consolidated financial condition of Financial as of such dates and the consolidated results of Financial's operations, consolidated shareholders' equity and consolidated changes in financial condition for each of such years, and each such statement has been prepared in accordance with generally accepted accounting principles applied on a consistent basis.

(g) *Changes.* Since December 31, 1979, there has not been:

(i) any material adverse change in the financial condition or results of operations of Financial and the Financial Subsidiaries considered as a whole from that reflected in the consolidated financial statements of Financial as of and for the year ended December 31, 1979 or any material change in the nature of the business of Financial or any Financial Subsidiary;

(ii) any damage, destruction or other casualty loss with respect to property owned or leased by Financial or any Financial Subsidiary (whether or not covered by insurance) materially and adversely affecting the business or financial condition or results of operations of Financial and the Financial Subsidiaries considered as a whole;

(iii) except for the repurchase of 803 shares of Financial Common Stock, any direct or indirect redemption, purchase or other acquisition of any shares of Financial Common Stock, or any declaration, setting aside or payment of any dividend or other distribution in respect of shares of Financial Common Stock, except for regular quarterly dividends of $.35 per share;

(iv) any purchase or sale of assets of Financial or any Financial Subsidiary, other than portfolio securities, and purchases and sales of assets in the ordinary course of business;

(v) except for entering into the premium finance business, any material change in the insurance agency arrangements of Financial or any Financial Subsidiary; or

(vi) any material transaction entered into by Financial or any Financial Subsidiary other than in the ordinary course of business.

(h) *Tax Returns and Payments.* Financial and the Financial Subsidiaries have filed all United States income tax returns and all state tax returns which are required to be filed by them and with respect to which extensions of the time for filing have not been granted, and in accordance with their customary practice have filed all local tax returns, and have paid or made provision for the payment of, all United States, state and local taxes which have or may have become due pursuant to said returns or pursuant to any assessment received by Financial and the Financial Subsidiaries, except such taxes, if any, as are being contested in good faith and as to which adequate reserves have been provided in the consolidated financial statements of Financial as of December 31, 1979. None of the returns or filings referred to in the preceding sentence when filed, and as of their respective dates, contained any materially false statements or omitted to state any material facts necessary to make the statements set forth therein not materially misleading. The United States income tax liability of Financial and the Financial Subsidiaries has been examined by the Internal Revenue Service for the respective years set forth in Schedule 4.1(h) heretofore delivered to Mev by Financial. Except as set forth in Schedule 4.1(h), Financial knows of no basis for a material deficiency assessment against it or any financial Subsidiary with respect to any of its tax returns which have not been examined.

(i) *Compliance with ERISA.* Financial and each Financial Subsidiary are in compliance in all material respects with the presently applicable provisions of the Employee Retirement Income Security Act of 1974, as amended ("ERISA"), and (i) no event which constitutes a Reportable Event as defined in Section 4043 of ERISA has occurred and is continuing with respect to any of their respective plans which is or was covered by ERISA, (ii) no such plan which is subject to Part 3 of Subtitle B of Title 1 of ERISA has incurred any "accumulated funding deficiency" (within the meaning of Section 302 or Section 412 of the Internal Revenue Code of 1954, as amended (the "Code")) whether or not waived, and (iii) no liability has been asserted against Financial or any Financial Subsidiary for any such plans within the meaning of Section 4975 of the Code, nor, to be best of Financial's knowledge, has any such prohibited transaction occurred. As of December 31, 1979, the last annual valuation date for such plans, the market value of the assets of such plans exceeded the present value of the vested benefits under such plans, and the total unfunded past service liability for such plans was not more than $50,000.

(j) *No Undisclosed Liabilities or Agreements.* Except as disclosed in this Agreement or in any Schedule hereto, neither Financial nor any Financial Subsidiary has any material liabilities or obligations, whether accrued, absolute, contingent or otherwise and whether due or to become due, which would be required to be reflected or provided for on the consolidated statement of financial condition of Financial and the Financial Subsidiaries as of December 31, 1979 (including the notes thereto) and were not so reflected or provided for, other than liabilities and obligations incurred in the ordinary course of business since December 31, 1979.

(k) *Reserves.* The reserves carried on the books of Financial and each Financial Subsidiary, including reserves for future insurance policy benefits, losses, claims and expenses, are adequate to cover the total amount of all reasonably anticipated liabilities of Financial and each Financial Subsidiary.

(l) *Litigation.* Except for the litigation described in Schedule 4.1(l) heretofore delivered to Mev by Financial, and except for routine defenses of actions based on insurance claims in the ordinary course of business as to which maximum liability in any one case is not in excess of $100,000, there is no action, suit or proceeding pending or, to the knowledge of Financial, threatened against Financial or any Financial Subsidiary before any court or arbitration tribunal or before or by any government department, agency or instrumentality.

(m) *Contracts*. Except as described in Schedule 4.1(m) heretofore delivered to Mev by Financial, neither Financial nor any Financial Subsidiary is a party or subject to:

(i) any written employment contract or arrangement (including any arrangements or obligations with respect to severance or termination pay liabilities or fringe benefits) with any officer, consultant, director or employee;

(ii) any written plan, contract or arrangement providing for bonuses, pensions, options, deferred compensation, retirement payments, profit sharing or similar arrangements;

(iii) any contract or agreement with any labor union;

(iv) any lease or form of lease used in a series of transactions involving payment as lessee or lessor of annual rentals in excess of $25,000;

(v) any mortgage, note, indenture or other document or instrument relating to the borrowing of money involving an amount (in any single case) in excess of $1,000,000;

(vi) any guarantee, or direct or indirect agreement or arrangement which is in effect a guarantee, of the indebtedness of any Financial Subsidiary;

(vii) any material contract not entered into in the ordinary course of business; or

(viii) any contract containing covenants limiting the freedom of Financial or any Financial Subsidiary to compete in any line of business or with any person.

All contracts, agreements, plans, leases and licenses of Financial and the Financial Subsidiaries which are material to the conduct of the business of Financial or any Financial Subsidiary as presently conducted are in effect and neither financial nor any Financial Subsidiary (nor, to the knowledge of Financial, any other party to any such contract, agreement, plan, lease or license) has breached any material provision of, or is in default in any material respect under the terms of, any such contract, agreement, plan, lease or license. No party to any such contract, agreement, plan, lease or license will have the right to terminate any or all of the provisions of any such contract, agreement, plan, lease or license as a result of the transactions contemplated by this Agreement. There are no contracts, arrangements, treaties or understandings with any party with respect to reinsurance, excess insurance, ceding of insurance or indemnification with respect to the insurance currently being provided by any Financial Subsidiary engaged in the insurance business that have been entered into outside the ordinary course of business.

(n) *Dividends*. Other than as restricted or limited by law or by the covenants contained in the agreements listed in Schedule 4.1(n) heretofore delivered to Mev by Financial, there are no restrictions or limitations on the payment of dividends by Financial or any of the Financial Subsidiaries.

(o) *Regulatory Filings*. Financial has heretofore made available for inspection by Mev with respect to Financial and each Financial Subsidiary each registration, filing or submission with any Federal regulatory commission, agency or authority and each annual statement filed with or submitted to any state insurance regulatory commission, agency or authority and any reports of examination issued by any such state insurance regulatory commission, agency or authority since December 31, 1975. Such filings or submissions were in material compliance with applicable law when filed, and no material deficiencies have been asserted by any such regulatory commission, agency or authority with respect to such filings or submissions.

(p) *Casualties*. Since December 31, 1979, neither the business or financial condition of Financial or any Financial Subsidiary nor any of the properties or assets of any thereof have been materially adversely affected in any way as a result of fire, explosion, earthquake, accident, strike or labor trouble, requisition or taking of property by any governmental agency, flood, rainstorm, drought, riot, act of God or the public enemy or any other casualty, whether or not covered by insurance.

(q) *Government Consent*. No consent, approval or authorization of, or designation, declaration or filing with, any governmental or regulatory authority, federal, state, local, foreign or other, is required in connection with the execution, delivery, or performance by Financial or any Financial Subsidiary of this Agreement or of any transactions contemplated hereby except for pre-merger notification and related filings pursuant to the Hart-Scott Act, approval of the Merger by the Georgia Insurance Commissioner, filing with any authorities required by applicable law of Financial's proxy statement (the "Financial Proxy Statement") under the Securities Exchange Act of 1934 relating to the Merger and filing of the Articles of Merger with the Secretary of State of Georgia.

(r) *Statutory Statements*. Financial has delivered to Mev copies of the unaudited statutory Annual Statements (the "Statutory Statements") of Security Insurance Company, Guaranty Insurance Company, Security Life Insurance Company, Family Life Insurance Company and Universe Life Insurance Company in the forms filed with the Georgia Insurance Department for the years 1975 through 1979. The statutory financial statements contained in each Statutory Statement fairly present the statutory financial condition of each of the respective corporations at December 31 of each of the years 1975 through 1979, respectively, and the statutory results of its operations and other data contained therein for each of the five years then ended, and have been prepared in accordance with required or permitted statutory insurance accounting requirements and practices, which have been applied on a consistent basis except as expressly set forth or disclosed in the notes, exhibits or schedules thereto. The exhibits and schedules included in each Statutory

Statement fairly present the data purported to be shown thereby. Neither Financial nor any Financial Subsidiary has, since the respective dates of filing the most recent of such Statutory Statements, received any notification or indication from the Georgia Insurance Department that it regards any of such Statutory Statements as deficient or inadequate in any material respect.

(s) *Labor Controversies*. There are no material controversies pending between Financial or any Financial Subsidiary and any of their employees and there are no known organizational efforts presently being made involving any of such employees.

(t) *Proxy Statement*. At the time the Financial Proxy Statement is mailed to the stockholders of Financial such statement, insofar as it relates to Financial and the Financial Subsidiaries (i) will comply in all material respects with the provisions of applicable law and (ii) will not contain an untrue statement of a material fact or omit to state a material fact required to be stated therein or necessary to make the statements therein, in the light of the circumstances under which they were made, not misleading; and at the time of the meeting of stockholders of Financial in connection with the Merger, the Financial Proxy Statement, as amended or supplemented, insofar as it relates to Financial and the Financial Subsidiaries, will not contain an untrue statement of a material fact or omit to state a material fact necessary to make the statements therein, in the light of the circumstances under which they were made, not misleading.

(u) *Compliance with Applicable Law*. Financial and each Financial Subsidiary are each, in the conduct of their businesses, in compliance in all material respects with all Federal, state or local laws, statutes, ordinances and regulations, the failure to comply with which would have a material adverse effect on the business of Financial or any Financial Subsidiary.

(v) *Accuracy of Information Furnished*. No representation or warranty by Financial contained in this Agreement, and no statement contained in any certificate or other instrument furnished to Mev or Subsidiary II by Financial pursuant hereto contains or will contain any untrue statement of a material fact, or omits or will omit to state any material fact which is necessary to make the statements contained therein, in the light of the circumstances under which they are made, not misleading.

4.2. *Representations and Warranties by Mev and Subsidiary II*. Mev and Subsidiary II represent and warrant as follows:

(a) *Organization and Qualification, etc*. Mev and Subsidiary II are each validly existing corporations in good standing under the laws of the State of Delaware (in the case of Mev) and Georgia (in the case of Subsidiary II). Each has power and authority (corporate and other) to own or lease and operate all of its properties and assets and to carry on its business as it is now being conducted. Mev is duly licensed, authorized or qualified to transact business and is in good standing in each jurisidiction in which the ownership of its property or the conduct of its business requires such license, authorization or qualification. Mev indirectly owns all of the outstanding shares of capital stock of Subsidiary II.

(b) *Authority*. Mev and Subsidiary II each has the corporate power and authority to enter into this Agreement, to perform its obligations hereunder and to consummate the transactions contemplated hereby. The respective Boards of Directors of Mev and Subsidiary II have taken all action required by law, by their respective Certificates or Articles of Incorporation, their By-Laws and otherwise, to authorize the execution and delivery of this Agreement and to perform their other obligations hereunder, and this Agreement is a legal, valid and binding agreement of Mev and Subsidiary II in accordance with its terms. The copies of Mev's and Subsidiary II's respective Certificates or Articles of Incorporation and By-Laws which have been delivered to Financial are complete and correct and in full force and effect at the date hereof.

(c) *Non-Contravention*. The execution and delivery of this Agreement do not and the consummation of the transactions contemplated hereby (subject to pre-merger notification and related filings with the FTC and the Antitrust Division pursuant to the Hart-Scott Act and compliance with regulatory requirements of the Georgia Insurance Commissioner) will not violate any provision of the respective Certificate or Articles of Incorporation or By-Laws of Mev or Subsidiary II or violate, or result with the passage of time in a violation of any provision of, or result in the acceleration of or entitle any part to accelerate (whether after the giving of notice or lapse of time or both) any obligation under, or result in the creation or imposition of any lien, charge, pledge, security interest or other encumbrance upon any of the property of Mev or Subsidiary II pursuant to any provision of, any mortgage, lien, lease, agreement, license or instrument, to which Mev or Subsidiary II is a party or by which any of them is bound and will not violate or conflict with any law, order, arbitration award, judgment or decree or other restriction of any kind or character to which Mev or Subsidiary II is subject or by which any of their assets may be bound, nor will the same constitute an event permitting termination of any agreement to which Mev or Subsidiary II is subject.

(d) *Disclosure*. In connection with the Financial Proxy Statement, Mev shall cooperate with Financial and, will furnish to Financial the information relating to Mev required by applicable law to be set forth in the Financial Proxy Statement. At the time the Financial Proxy Statement is mailed to the stockholders of Financial, the Financial Proxy Statement, insofar as it relates to Mev and is based on written information furnished by Mev (i) will comply in all material respects with the provisions of applicable law and (ii) will not contain an untrue statement of a material fact or omit to state a material fact required to be stated therein or necessary to make the statements therein, in the light of the circumstances under which they are made, not misleading; and at the time of the meeting of stockholders of Financial the Financial Proxy Statement, as amended and supplemented, insofar as it relates to Mev and is based on written material supplied by Mev, will not contain an untrue statement of a material fact or omit to state a material fact necessary to make the statements therein, in the light of the circumstances under which they were made, not misleading.

Article V

Additional Covenants and Agreements

5.1. Financial covenants as follows:

(a) *Conduct of Financial*. Except as otherwise consented to by Mev in writing, during the period from the date hereof to the Effective Date of the Merger, Financial shall, and shall cause each Financial Subsidiary to, conduct its operations and keep its books and records according to its ordinary and usual course of business consistent with past practice and use its best efforts to maintain and preserve its business organization, employees and relationships with agents and others and its insurance agency force and, except for this Agreement, neither Financial nor any Financial Subsidiary shall enter into any material transaction, contract or commitment or amend, modify or restructure any material transaction, contract or commitment other than contracts or commitments entered into or amended or modified in the usual and ordinary course of its business and required to be so amended or modified to conduct its business in the usual and ordinary course.

(b) *Limitations upon Dividends and Issurance of Securities*. Financial shall not, except as contemplated by this Agreement, make, declare or pay any dividend (provided, however, that Financial may pay to the holders of Financial Common Stock regular quarterly cash dividends at the rate of $.35 per share, it being understood that Financial will not declare any such dividend prior to the customary declaration date for such dividend) or make any distribution on, or directly or indirectly redeem, purchase or otherwise acquire, any shares of its outstanding capital stock, authorize the creation or issuance of or issue or sell any additional shares of its capital stock or any securities or obligations convertible or exchangeable for, or giving any person any right to acquire from Financial or any Financial Subsidiary, any shares of its capital stock or agree to take any such action.

(c) *Interim Financial Statements*. Financial shall deliver or make available to Mev as soon as available (i) its Form 10-Q for each quarterly period subsequent to December 31, 1979 through the Closing Date, (ii) any consolidating financial statements used in preparation of each such Form 10-Q, (iii) the Statutory Statements filed by Financial and by each Financial Subsidiary that is an insurance company for the year ending December 31, 1979 and (iv) all other material reports and financial statements filed by Financial or by any Financial Subsidiary with a state insurance regulatory body from December 31, 1979 through the Closing Date (all documents referred to in clauses (i) through (iv) hereof are hereinafter collectively referred to as the "Interim Statements"). At the time of their respective delivery to Mev each Interim Statement shall be complete and each Interim Statement that is a financial statement shall present fairly the financial position or results of operations of Financial or of the respective Financial Subsidiary, as the case may be, and except for Statutory Statements (which shall have been prepared in accordance with statutory standards consistently applied), shall have been prepared in accordance with generally accepted accounting principles applied on a consistent basis.

(d) *Stockholders' Meetings.* Financial shall (subject to the requirements of applicable law), in cooperation with Mev and its counsel, prepare and distribute the Financial Proxy Statement and give notice of and duly call a meeting of its stockholders to be held at the earliest practicable date for the purpose of voting on and approving this Agreement in accordance with the Georgia Business Corporation Code and, in connection therewith, Financial shall use its best efforts to obtain such approval of Financial's stockholders (including, but not limited to, the recommendation of the Financial Board of Directors of the adoption of this Agreement).

(e) *Pre-Merger Purchase of Financial Stock.* Prior to the Effective Time of the Merger, Mev and/or Subsidiary II may, subject to any required regulatory approval, purchase shares of Financial Common Stock in the open market or in privately negotiated transactions without the prior consent of any of the parties hereto, and Financial and its representatives shall take any and all actions necessary, including any actions with any regulatory authorities, to facilitate such purchases.

(f) *Investigation.* Mev and Subsidiary II may, prior to the Effective Time of the Merger, make or cause to be made such investigation of the business and properties of Financial and the Financial Subsidiaries and their financial and legal condition as Mev deems necessary or advisable to familiarize itself with such properties and other matters, provided that such investigation shall not interfere with normal operations. Financial agrees to permit Mev and Subsidiary II and their authorized representatives to have, after the date of execution hereof until the Effective Time of the Merger, full access to the premises, books and records of Financial and each Financial Subsidiary at reasonable hours, and it and each Financial Subsidiary and their respective officers will furnish Mev and Subsidiary II with such financial and operating data and other information with respect to the business and properties of Financial and each Financial Subsidiary as Mev and Subsidiary II shall from time to time reasonably request. No investigation by Mev or Subsidiary II heretofore or hereafter made shall affect the representations and warranties of Financial contained herein and each such representation and warranty shall survive any such investigation up to the Effective Time of the Merger. Financial shall not, without the prior consent of Mev, disclose any confidential information about Financial or any Financial Subsidiary (except as required by law) to any third party or solicit offers from or negotiate with any third party for the sale of Financial or its shares of capital stock or a substantial portion of its assets or the assets of any Financial Subsidiary.

(g) *Investigation by Accountants.* Financial agrees to give such assistance as the independent accountants for Mev, may reasonably request in connection with its review of the financial statements of Financial, including permission to use for such purpose the notes and workpapers prepared by [national accounting firm] (who are also the independent accountants for Financial) in connection with its examination of the accounts of Financial and the Financial Subsidiaries.

(h) *No Amendments to Articles of Incorporation or By-Laws*. From the date hereof to the Effective Time of the Merger, Financial will not, and will not permit any Financial Subsidiary to, amend its Certificate or Articles of Incorporation or By-Laws.

5.2. Mev and Subsidiary II covenant to Financial as follows:

(a) *Confidentiality*. Mev shall, and shall cause its affiliates and representatives to, use all information relating to Financial and the Financial Subsidiaries acquired by any of them pursuant to the provisions of this Agreement only in connection with the transactions contemplated hereby and shall cause all information obtained by them pursuant to this Agreement which is not publicly available to be treated as confidential prior to the Effective Time of the Merger (subject to the right of Mev to communicate with any of its representatives or affiliates with respect thereto), except as may otherwise be required by law or as may be necessary or appropriate in connection with the enforcement of this Agreement or any instrument or document referred to herein or contemplated hereby. Except as provided above, if the Merger is not consummated for any reason, Mev shall return any such information and/or documents acquired by it or its affiliates or representatives pursuant hereto and shall not, unless such information or documents have otherwise become publicly available, use or disclose the same to any party for any purpose without the prior written consent of Financial.

(b) *Consent of Sole Stockholder*. Prior to the Closing Mev will cause the stockholder of Subsidiary II to approve this Agreement.

5.3. Mev, Subsidiary II and Financial each convenant as follows:

(a) *Supplement to Schedules*. From time to time prior to the Effective Time of the Merger, Financial will deliver to Mev, and Mev will deliver to Financial, information concerning events subsequent to the date hereof necessary to supplement the schedules or other written information called for pursuant to Sections 4.1 and 4.2, respectively, or necessary to reflect changes from the representations stated in such Sections in order to keep such information therein current, complete and accurate.

(b) *Regulatory Filings*. Each party hereto will promptly prepare, file and prosecute diligently the applications and related documents required to be filed by such party with the applicable regulatory authorities in order to effect the transactions contemplated hereby. Each party hereto will use its best efforts to assist in such filings and the diligent prosecution thereof.

(c) *Compliance with Conditions Precedent*. Financial and Mev will each use its best efforts to cause the precedents to their respective obligations described in Article VII hereof over which they have control to be fulfilled.

Article VI

Closing Date

The closing for the consummation of the transactions contemplated by this Agreement shall be held at the offices of [law firm], Atlanta, Georga 30303, on a date (the ''Closing Date'') agreed to by the parties hereto, which date shall be as promptly as practicable after the last of the conditions to closing described in Sections 7.1(a), (b) and (c) and Section 7.3(f) shall have occurred or been waived by the parties hereto, it being the present intention of the parties to fix the Closing Date at July 31, 1980.

Article VII

Conditions To Closing

7.1. *Conditions to Obligations of Financial, Mev and Subsidiary II.* The obligations of Financial, Mev and Subsidiary II to consummate the Merger are subject to the fulfillment, prior to or on the Closing Date of the Merger of each of the following conditions:

(a) *Stockholder Approval.* This Agreement shall have been approved by the stockholders of Financial and the stockholder of Subsidiary II in accordance with applicable law and the other party shall have been furnished with certified copies of the resolutions adopted by such holders.

(b) *Consents.* All consents, authorizations, orders or approvals (or filing or registration with) any governmental commission, board or other regulatory body, including the approval of the Georgia Insurance Commissioner, required in connection with the execution, delivery and performance of this Agreement and for the Surviving Corporation to conduct the business of Financial in substantially the same manner as now conducted by Financial, shall have been obtained.

(c) *Hart-Scott Act.* The applicable waiting periods under the Hart-Scott Act shall have expired.

(d) *Litigation.* There shall not be instituted or pending any action or proceeding before any court or governmental agency or other regulatory or administrative agency or commission, by any governmental agency or other regulatory or administrative agency or commission, or by any other person, challenging the Merger or the transactions related thereto, which seeks to restrain, prevent or change the transactions contemplated hereby or questions the validity of any such transactions or seeks damages in connection with any such transactions or which, in the opinion of Mev, might affect the right of Mev to own, operate in their entirety or control the Surviving Corporation or any Financial Subsidiary.

7.2. *Conditions to the Obligations of Financial.* The obligations of Financial to consummate the Merger are subject to the fulfillment, prior to or on the Closing Date, of each of the following conditions:

(a) *Copies of Resolutions; Opinion of Mev Counsel.* Mev shall have furnished Financial with (i) certified copies of resolutions duly adopted by the respective Boards of Directors of Mev and Subsidiary II and the stockholder of Subsidiary II, approving the execution and delivery of this Agreement and all other necessary or proper corporate action to enable Mev and Subsidiary II, respectively to comply with the terms of this Agreement; and (ii) an opinion, dated the Closing Date, of [law firm] counsel for Mev and Subsidiary II, in form and substance satisfactory to Financial and its counsel, to the effect that:

(i) Mev and Subsidiary II are validly existing corporations in good standing under the laws of their respective jurisdictions of incorporation and have the corporate power to enter into and carry out this Agreement;

(ii) this Agreement has been duly authorized, executed and delivered by Mev and Subsidiary II, has been duly adopted by the stockholder of Subsidiary II and is the legal, valid and binding agreement of each of Mev and Subsidiary II in accordance with its terms;

(iii) no consent of any Federal, state or local authority (other than with respect to applicable insurance regulations, all of which have been duly complied with by Mev and Subsidiary II) is required in connection with the execution, delivery and performance of this Agreement by Mev and Subsidiary II;

(iv) the execution and delivery of this Agreement and the consummation of the transactions contemplated hereby do not and will not violate any provision of the respective Certificates or Articles of Incorporation or By-Laws of Mev and Subsidiary II or violate any provision of any material obligation under any mortgage, lien, lease, agreement, instrument, order, arbitration award, judgment or decree of which such counsel has knowledge and to which Mev and Subsidiary II is a party or by which it is bound, and, to the knowledge of such counsel, do not and will not violate or conflict with any other material restriction of any kind or character to which Mev and Subsidiary II is subject.

In rendering such opinion such counsel may rely to the extent specified therein (x) upon certificates as to matters of fact of officers of Mev and Subsidiary II and (y) upon the opinion of other counsel satisfactory to [Financial's law firm] as to all matters of the laws of states other than [state of Mev's counsel].

(b) *Representations.* The representations and warranties of Mev and Subsidiary II contained in this Agreement shall be true and correct in all material respects at the Closing Date, except for the representations and warranties specifically relating to a time or times other than the date hereof (which shall be true and correct in all material respects at such time or times) and except for changes contemplated and permitted by this Agreement, with the same force and effect as if made at and as of the Closing Date; and Mev and Subsidiary II each shall have performed or complied in all material respects with all agreements and covenants required by this Agreement to be performed by it at or prior to the Closing Date.

(c) *Certificate.* Mev shall have delivered to Financial a certificate, dated the Closing Date, of the President of Mev to the effect that the conditions specified in paragraph (b) of this Section 7.2 have been satisfied.

7.3 *Conditions to Obligations of Mev and Subsidiary II.* The obligations of Mev and Subsidiary II to consummate the Merger are subject to the fulfillment, prior to or on the Closing Date, of each of the following conditions:

(a) *Copies of Resolutions: Opinion of Financial Counsel.* Financial shall have furnished Mev with (i) certified copies of resolutions duly adopted by the Board of Directors and stockholders of Financial approving the execution and delivery of this Agreement and all other necessary or proper corporate action to enable Financial to comply with the terms of this Agreement; and (ii) an opinion, dated the Closing Date, of [law firm], counsel for Financial, in form and substance satisfactory to Mev and its counsel, to the effect that:

(i) Financial is a validly existing corporation in good standing under the laws of the State of Georgia, has the corporate power to enter into and carry out this Agreement, own all of its properties and assets and carry on its business as it is now being conducted;

(ii) each Financial Subsidiary is a validly existing corporation in good standing under the laws of the jurisdiction in which it is incorporated and has the corporate power to own all of its properties and assets and to carry on its business as it is now being conducted;

(iii) this Agreement has been duly authorized, executed and delivered by Financial, has been duly adopted by the stockholders of Financial and is a legal, valid and binding agreement of Financial in accordance with its terms;

(iv) the execution and delivery of this Agreement and the consummation of the transactions contemplated hereby do not and will not violate any provision of the respective Articles of Incorporation or By-Laws of Financial or any Financial Subsidiary, or violate any provision of any material obligation under any mortgage, lien, lease, agreement, instrument, order, arbitration award, judgment or decree of which such counsel has knowledge and to which Financial or any Financial Subsidiary is a party or by which any of them is bound and, to the knowledge of such counsel, do not and will not violate or conflict with any other material restriction of any kind or character to which Financial or any Financial Subsidiary is subject;

(v) the authorized capital stock of Financial consists of 10,000,000 shares of Financial Common Stock, and 1,000,000 shares of Preferred Stock, no par value, of which as of the date of such opinion not more than 2,439,344 shares of Common Stock are validly issued and outstanding, fully paid and nonassessable, and Financial does not have outstanding any options to purchase any shares of its capital stock or securities or obligations which are convertible into or exchangeable for any shares of its capital stock;

(vi) no consent, approval or authorization of or filing with any Federal, state or local authority (other than compliance with applicable insurance regulations, all of which have been duly complied with by Financial) is required in connection with the execution, delivery and performance of this Agreement by Financial;

(vii) except as described in Section 4.1(l), to the best knowedge of such counsel after due inquiry, there are no actions, suits or proceedings pending or threatened against Financial or any Financial Subsidiary before any court or arbitration tribunal or before or by any governmental department, agency or instrumentality, an adverse decision in which might materially and adversely affect the financial condition, results of operations or prospects of Financial and the Financial Subsidiaries considered as a whole or seeking to prevent or enjoin the Merger; and

(viii) at the time the Financial Proxy Statement was mailed to the stockholders of Financial and, at the time of the meeting of stockholders of Financial in connection with the Merger, the Financial Proxy Statement, as amended or supplemented, insofar as it related to Financial and the Financial Subsidiaries, complied in all material respects with the provisions of applicable law, and nothing had come to the attention of such counsel to cause such counsel to believe that such proxy statement contained any untrue statement of a material fact or omitted to state a material fact required to be stated therein or necessary to make the statements therein, in the light of the circumstances under which they were made, not misleading.

In rendering such opinion such counsel may rely to the extent specified therein (x) upon certificates as to matters of fact of officers of Financial or an Financial Subsidiary and (y) upon the opinion of other counsel satisfactory to [Mev's counsel] as to all matters of the laws of states other than Georgia.

(b) *Representations*. The representations and warranties of Financial contained in this Agreement shall be true and correct in all material respects at the Closing Date, except for the representations and warranties specifically relating to a time or times other than the date hereof (which shall be true and correct in all material respects at such time or times) and except for changes contemplated and permitted by this Agreement with the same force and effect as if made at and as of the Effective Time of the Merger; and Financial shall have performed or complied in all material respects with all agreements and convenants required by this Agreement to be performed by it at or prior to the Closing Date.

(c) *Certificate*. Financial shall have delivered to Mev a certificate, dated the Closing Date, of the President and Chief Executive Officer of Financial to the effect that the conditions specified in paragraph (b) of this Section 7.3 have been satisfied.

(d) *No Material Adverse Change*. There shall have been no material adverse change in the financial condition or results of operations of Financial and the Financial Subsidiaries considered as a whole since December 31, 1979 or any material adverse change in the nature of the business or the assets of Financial and the Financial Subsidiaries considered as a whole, and Mev shall have received a certificate, dated the Closing Date, of the President and Chief Executive Officer of Financial to such effect.

(e) *Letters from Accountants.* Mev shall have received from [national accounting firm] in their capacity as independent accountants for Financial, a letter dated as of a date not more than five days prior to the Closing Date to the effect that, (i) with respect to Financial and the Financial Subsidiaries they are independent public accountants within the meaning of the Exchange Act and the applicable rules and regulations thereunder; (ii) it is their opinion that the financial statements included in the Financial Proxy Statement comply as to form in all material respects with the applicable accounting requirements of the Exchange Act and the applicable rules and regulations thereunder, (iii) the tabular and statistical information set forth in the Financial Proxy Statement with respect to Financial and the Financial Subsidiaries which was derived from the accounting records of Financial and the Financial Subsidiaries is in agreement with the accounting records of Financial and each Financial Subsidiary or computations made therefrom; and (iv) on the basis of such procedures as are set forth therein but without performing an audit to enable them to express an opinion with respect to such matters, nothing has come to their attention which would lead them to believe that since December 31, 1979 to the date of such letter there has been any increase in the outstanding capital stock or rights, securities, options or obligations exercisable in exchange for or convertible into shares of capital stock or in the consolidated indebtedness of Financial and the Financial Subsidiaries or any decrease in the net assets thereof or any decrease in the consolidated net income of Financial as compared with the corresponding period of the prior year, except in all instances for any such increases or decreases referred to in or contemplated by the Financial Proxy Statement or specified in such letter.

(f) *Organization of Insurance Subsidiary.* The Secretary of State of Georgia shall have issued a Certificate of Incorporation to a subsidiary of Mev granting it the corporate powers and privileges of an insurance company organized under the laws of Georgia to transact the business of life and accident and sickness insurance.

Article VIII

Termination or Abandonment

8.1. *Termination of Suspension.* This Agreement and the Merger may be terminated and abandoned at any time prior to the Effective Time of the Merger, whether before or after approval by the stockholders of Financial:

(a) By mutual action of the respective Boards of Directors of Financial and Mev.

(b) By Financial, if the conditions set forth in Sections 7.1 and 7.2 shall not have been complied with or performed in any material respect and such noncompliance or nonperformance shall not have been cured or eliminated (or by its nature cannot be cured or eliminated) by Mev at or before the Closing Date.

(c) By Mev, if the conditions set forth in Sections 7.1 and 7.3 shall not have been complied with or performed in any material respect and such noncompliance or nonperformance shall not have been cured or eliminated (or by its nature cannot be cured or eliminated) by Financial at or before the Closing Date.

(d) By Financial or Mev, in the event the Merger is not consummated pursuant to this Agreement on or before December 31, 1980, unless the Boards of Directors of Financial, Mev, and Subsidiary II shall have agreed upon an extension of time in which to consummate the Merger.

8.2. *Effect of Termination.* In the event of the termination of this Agreement and the Merger pursuant to the foregoing provisions of this Article VIII, this Agreement shall become void and have no effect, without any liability on the part of any party or its stockholders or directors or officers in respect thereof, except for the provisions of Sections 5.2(a) and 9.9.

Article IX

Miscellaneous

9.1. *Waiver of Conditions.* Any party may, at its option, waive any or all of the conditions herein contained to which its obligations hereunder are subject.

9.2. *Notices.* Any notices or other communications required or permitted hereunder shall be sufficiently given if sent by registered or certified mail, postage prepaid, addressed, in the case of Mev and Subsidiary II, to New York, New York 10048, Attention: Allen R. Jone's (copy to James H. Smith, Esq., [firm name] Park Avenue, New York, New York 10017) or, in the case of Financial, to Financial Inc., Atlanta, Georgia 30308, Attention: F. L. Brown (copy to Black, Atlanta, Georgia 30303) or such other address as shall be furnished in writing by any party to the others prior to the giving of applicable notice or communication, and such notice or communication shall be deemed to have been given when received.

9.3 *Brokers.* Financial represents and warrants that no broker or finder is entitled to any brokerage or finder's fee or other commission from Financial or Mev based on agreements, arrangements or undertakings made by Financial in connection with the transactions contemplated hereby. Mev represents and warrants that, except as previously disclosed to Financial, no broker or finder is entitled to any brokerage or finder's fee or other commission from Financial or Mev based on agreements, arrangements or undertakings made by Mev in connection with the transactions contemplated hereby.

9.4. *Counterparts.* This Agreement may be executed simultaneously in two or more counterparts, each of which shall be deemed an original, but all of which together shall constitute one and the same instrument.

9.5. *Headings*. The headings of articles herein are for convenience of reference only, do not constitute a part of this Agreement, and shall not be deemed to limit or affect any of the provisions hereof.

9.6. *Variation and Amendment*. This Agreement, including the Schedules hereto, contains the entire agreement between the parties hereto with respect to the transactions contemplated herein and supersedes the agreement in principle with respect to the Merger previously entered into by Mev and Financial. This Agreement may be varied or amended by action of the respective Boards of Directors of Financial and Mev without action of any of the stockholders thereof, provided, however, no such variation or amendment shall reduce the Merger price to which the stockholders of Financial shall become entitled at the Effective Time of the Merger.

9.7. *Governing Law*. This Agreement shall be governed by and construed in accordance with the laws of the State of Georgia.

9.8. *No Survival of Representations and Warranties*. None of the representations and warranties included or provided for herein or in any schedule or certificate or other document delivered pursuant to this Agreement shall survive the Effective Time of the Merger.

Since none of the warranties survive, buyer assumes almost all of the risk of later regulatory problems arising from past acts.

9.9. *Expenses*. Each of the parties hereto shall bear its respective expenses in connection with the transactions herein contemplated.

In WITNESS WHEREOF, the parties hereto have caused this Agreement to be duly executed as of the date first above written.

Financial Inc.
By
      President

Attest:
 /s/
   Secretary

Mev Corporation
By
      President

Attest:

   Secretary

Frederick Corporation
By
      President

Attest:
   Secretary

AGREEMENT FOR MERGER

This agreement for a bank holding company, can be brief, since no new parties are really involved.

THIS AGREEMENT FOR MERGER ("Agreement") between BANK AND TRUST COMPANY ("Bank" or "Surviving Bank"), a Georgia Banking corporation having its principal office in DeKalb

County, Georgia, and INTERIM COMPANY, INCORPORATED ("Interim Company"), a Georgia Business corporation having its principal office in DeKalb County.

WITNESSETH:

All of the outstanding capital stock of Interim Company is owned by Bancshares, Inc., a Georgia business corporation ("Bancshares"); and

Bank and Interim Company and their respective Boards of Directors deem it advisable for the general welfare and advantage of such Banks and their respective shareholders that Interim Company merge with Bank pursuant to the laws of the State of Georgia whereupon Bank shall become the wholly-owned subsidiary of Bancshares (such merger being hereinafter called the "Merger") and the present shareholders of Bank shall have their shares of capital stock of Bank, $2.50 par value per share, exchanged by virtue of the Merger on a share-for-share basis for an equivalent number of shares of capital stock of Bancshares, $2.50 par value per share, which Bancshares has agreed to provide.

NOW, THEREFORE, in consideration of the mutual covenants contained herein, Bank and Interim Company hereby enter into and make this Agreement for Merger on the following terms and conditions:

1. MERGER

Upon the Merger Date (as hereinafter defined), Interim Company shall be merged with Bank and the separate existence of Interim Company shall cease. Surviving Bank shall continue its existence under Georgia law under its existing Charter (as amended); and Surviving Bank shall have, without further act or deed, all the property, rights, powers, trusts, duties and obligations of Bank and Interim Company, and Surviving Bank shall hold, enjoy and be subject to the same in the same manner and to the same extent as Interim Company and Bank had, held, owned, enjoyed, and was subject to the same immediately prior to the Merger Without limiting the obligations and duties of Surviving Bank, Surviving Bank effective upon the Merger Date expressly assumes:

(a) the due and punctual payment of the principal and interest and premium, if any, on all of the notes issued pursuant to the Subordinated Capital Note Agreement dated June 1, 1974 between Bank and Teacher's Retirement and the due and punctual observance and performance of all of the covenants and conditions of said notes of agreement;

(b) the due and punctual payment of the principal of and the interest on the note issued pursuant to the Subordinated Capital Note Agreement, dated June 10, 1974, between Bank and Jones Company and the due and punctual performance of all the covenants and conditions of said note and agreement; and

(c) the due and punctual payment of the principal of and interest on all the notes issued pursuant to the Resolution of the Board of Directors of Bank dated October 10, 1979, authorizing the issuance of up to $1,500,000 of aggregate principal amount of subordinated capital notes and the performance of every covenant to be performed or observed by Bank under said notes and resolution.

2. NAME

Upon and after the Merger Date, the name of Surviving Bank shall be:

BANK AND TRUST COMPANY

3. BY-LAWS

The By-Laws of Surviving Bank in effect immediately prior to the Merger shall continue to be the By-laws of Surviving Bank following the Merger, until altered or amended in the manner provided by such By-laws and the Financial Institutions Code of Georgia.

4. DIRECTORS

The Board of Directors of Bank immediately prior to the Merger shall continue to be The Board of Directors of Surviving Bank following the Merger, and until a new Board of Directors shall be elected by the shareholders of Surviving Bank as provided in the By-laws of Surviving Bank.

Said Board of Directors shall have full power and authority to manage the affairs of Surviving Bank in accordance with its Charter and By-laws and to take any action permitted to be taken by the Board of Directors of a bank chartered under the Financial Institutions Code of Georgia.

5. OFFICERS

All officers of Bank holding office immediately prior to the Merger shall continue to be the officers of Surviving Bank following the merger until new officers shall be elected by the Board of Directors of Surviving Bank as provided in the By-laws of Surviving Bank.

6. MANNER AND BASIS OF CONVERTING SHARES

The manner and basis of converting and exchanging the shares of Bank and the shares of Interim Company shall be as follows:

(a) Upon the Merger Date, the 1,106,200 outstanding shares of capital stock, $2.50 par value per share, of Bank shall be exchanged for fully-paid and nonassessable shares of capital stock, $2.50 par value per share, of Bancshares at the rate of one share of capital stock of Bancshares for each such outstanding share of capital stock of Bank (except for stock held by dissenting shareholders who demand payment of the fair cash value thereof in the manner provided in Section 22-1202 of the Georgia Code); and the outstanding certificates formerly representing shares of capital stock of Bank so exchanged shall thenceforth, without any further action or physical exchange of certificates represent the shares of capital stock of Bancshares for which Bank shares were exchanged.

(b) Upon the Merger Date, the 200 outstanding shares of capital stock, $2.50 par value per share, of Interim Company held by Bancshares shall be cancelled and retired, and Bancshares shall hold one million one hundred six thousand two hundred (1,106,200) shares of $2.50 par value common stock of Surviving Bank.

(c) Upon the Merger Date, the 200 outstanding shares of capital stock, $2.50 par value per share of Bancshares issued to and held by Charles B. Smith, the initial shareholder, shall be cancelled.

(d) Any shareholder of Bank who objects to the Merger shall be entitled to the rights and remedies of a dissenting shareholder as determined under the provisions of Section 22-1202 of the Georgia Code, relating to the rights of dissenting shareholders.

7. MERGER PROCEDURE

(a) Bank and Interim Company shall each hold a special meeting of their respective shareholders at which this Agreement shall be submitted to such shareholders for approval. Notice of such special meeting shall include a copy of this Agreement, a full statement of the rights and remedies of dissenting shareholders, the method of exercising such rights and remedies, and the limitations on such rights and remedies. If this Agreement is approved by the affirmative vote of the shareholders of Bank owning at least two-thirds of its outstanding stock and if this Agreement is approved by the affirmative vote of the shareholders of Interim Company owning at least two-thirds of its outstanding stock, then this Agreement shall be the Agreement of Bank and Interim Company.

(b) If this Agreement shall be thus duly approved by the respective shareholders of Bank and Interim Company, Bank and Interim Company shall cause articles of merger to be filed in duplicate, together with the required fee, in the office of the Secretary of State of Georgia as specified in Section 41A-2403 of the Financial Institutions Code of Georgia.

(c) Bank and Interim Company shall also cause to be filed in the office of the Commissioner of the Georgia Department of

Banking and Finance the information and fees required by
Section 41A-2404 of the Financial Institutions Code of Georgia.

(d) Notice of the proposed Merger shall be published in the manner provided in Section 41A-2404 of the Financial Institutions
Code of Georgia.

(e) Thereafter, at such time as (i) Bancshares has received approval from the Board of Governors of the Federal Reserve
System to become a bank holding company and evidence of
such approval satisfactory to counsel for Bank has been received, (ii) the Merger has been approved by the Federal
Deposit Insurance Corporation and evidence of such approval
satisfactory to counsel for Bank has been received, (iii) Bank
has received a satisfactory ruling from the Internal Revenue
Service to the effect that the Merger constitutes a tax-free
reorganization under the Internal Revenue Code and that no
gain or loss shall be recognized by Bank shareholders upon the
exchange of their Bank shares for Bancshares shares pursuant
thereto, (iv) Bancshares shall have filed a registration statement under the Securities Act of 1933, as amended, relating to
the issuance of the Bancshares shares to be exchanged for the
outstanding shares of Bank pursuant hereto and such registration statement shall have become effective within the meaning
of that Act, and (v) the Commissioner of the Georgia Department of Banking and Finance has given written notice of his
approval of the articles of merger and the Merger to the
Secretary of State and to Bank and Interim Company, such
Merger shall become effective as set forth in Paragraph 10
hereof; said Board of Governors approval, said Federal Deposit Insurance Coporation approval, receipt of said tax ruling,
the effectiveness of said registration statement and said written
notice of approval of the Commissioner of the Georgia Department of Banking and Finance being conditions precedent
to the effectuation of the Merger.

(f) The officers of Bank and the officers of Interim Company,
both prior to and following the Merger Date shall execute all
such other instruments and shall take all such other actions as
may be necessary or advisable to consummate the Merger and
to cause this Agreement to be carried out in accordance with its
terms.

8. ABANDONMENT OF MERGER

Notwithstanding any other provisions hereof, this Agreement
and the Merger contemplated hereby may be terminated and abandoned pursuant to action taken by mutual agreement of the respective Boards of Directors of Bank and the Interim Company at any
time before the Merger becomes effective, whether before or after
approval of this Agreement by the shareholders of either Bank or
Interim Company.

9. SPECIAL CONDITION

This agreement shall be void, and shall be of no further force and effect if the holders of 110,620 or more shares of the $2.50 par value capital stock of Bank file a notice of election to dissent and a demand for payment of the fair value of their shares in lieu of the shares of Bancshares pursuant to the requirements of Section 22-1202 of the Georgia Code relating to dissenting shareholders. Upon the occurrence of such condition, if said condition occurs, the Merger shall be deemed to be abandoned without the further act of any party.

10. MERGER DATE

The Merger shall become effective and shall be consummated by operation of law without further act or deed upon the part of either Bank or Interim Company at the time of the issurance of the certificate of merger by the Secretary of State, and the term "Merger Date" as used herein shall mean the date and time the Merger thus becomes effective.

IN WITNESS WHEREOF, pursuant to resolutions duly adopted by affirmative vote of a majority of the members of the Board of Directors of Bank and the Board of Directors of Interim Company, this Agreement for Merger has been executed under the respective corporate seals of Bank and Interim Company by the President and the Secretary of Bank, for an on behalf of Bank and its Board of Directors, and by the President and the Secretary of Interim Company, for and on behalf of Interim Company and its Board of Directors, this 10th day of May, 1980.

BANK AND TRUST COMPANY and its Board of Directors	INTERIM COMPANY, INCORPORATED and its Board of Directors
BY: /s/ Charles B. Smith	BY: /s/ Charles B. Smith
President	President
ATTEST:	ATTEST:
/s/R.W. Jones	/s/R.W. Jones
Secretary	Secretary

Appendix E

"C" Reorganization Agreement and Plan of Reorganization

The following is a plan for an assets acquisition where there was fairly equal bargaining power between the parties. Note provisions dealing with bulk sales and Rule 146.

This agreement involves the acquisition by a subsidiary of a publicly-held corporation of substantially all of the assets of a corporation having some financial difficulty. (See page 17 of text for discussion of "C" Reorganizations.)

AGREEMENT AND PLAN OF REORGANIZATION

The precise parties should be specified by their legal names and state of incorporation and a brief designation given to be used throughout the agreement.

THIS AGREEMENT AND PLAN OF REORGANIZATION is entered into as of this 28th day of February, 19_____, among KEYES CORPORATION ("Keyes"), a Delaware corporation, KEYES CORPORATION OF GEORGIA ("Subsidiary"), and HOMES CORPORATION, a Georgia corporation ("Homes").

Recitals

Here the typical "Whereas" clause is modernized, but the word "Recitals" is used to show that these are not intended to be operative portions of the agreement, but merely show the intention of the parties.

This agreement is entered into with reference to the following facts:

1. Homes is engaged in the manufacturing and sale of mobile homes in the states of Georgia and Texas, and in such business owns and uses certain assets, including merchandise inventory, trade accounts receivable, other accounts receivable, deposits, prepaid items, furniture and fixtures, motor vehicles, office equipment and supplies, real property and improvements, leases, leasehold improvements, trademarks, deferred pre-operating costs, other intangible properties, and its business as a going concern.

2. All of the issued or outstanding capital stock of Subsidiary is owned by Keyes.

3. The boards of directors of Keyes, Subsidiary, and Homes, respectively, deem it advisable and in the best interest of Keyes, Subsidiary, and Homes and their respective stockholders that Subsidiary acquire substantially all of the assets of Homes pursuant to this agreement and applicable provisions of law, and as a plan or reorganization within the purview of Section 368(a) (1) (C) of the Internal Revenue Code of 1954, as amended.

4. Contemporaneously with the execution and delivery of this agreement, the parties hereto are effecting the reorganization, as hereinafter set forth, pursuant to which Subsidiary is acquiring substantially all of the assets of Homes, for (a) solely Keyes' voting stock, namely twenty-one thousand (21,000) shares of common stock, par value $2.50 per share of Keyes ("Keyes Common Stock") and (b) the assumption by Subsidiary of certain liabilities and obligations of Homes. It is then contemplated that the twenty-one thousand (21,000) shares of Keyes common stock will then be distributed to the stockholders of Homes according to their respective interests (subject to the deposit thereof in an indemnity escrow) and that Homes will then be dissolved pursuant to applicable state laws.

Agreement

The operative portion of the agreement starts with a typical "Now, Therefore" clause.

NOW, THEREFORE, in consideration of the premises and the mutual agreements, provisions, and covenants hereinafter contained, Keyes, Subsidiary, and Homes hereby each agree as follows:

1. Sale of Assets and Business by Homes

On the basis of the representations and warranties herein contained, subject to the terms and conditions set forth herein, and for the consideration provided for herein, Homes is contemporaneously herewith conveying, transferring, assigning, and delivering to Subsidiary all those assets listed on Schedule "A" (which was true, correct, and complete excepting for the retention of Homes of the right to the refund of income taxes paid by Homes and certain corporate records of Homes hereinafter specified) as of January 31, 19_____, with the written consent of Keyes and Subsidiary and plus those assets acquired by Homes since January 31, 19_____.

2. Consideration

The consideration for the Homes assets consists of:

(a) Twenty-one thousand (21,000) shares of Keyes common stock, issued by Keyes to Homes, pursuant hereto.

(b) The assumption of Subsidiary of the liabilities and obligations of Homes as listed on Schedule "B" (which was true, correct, and complete as of January 31, 19_____), less those liabilities and obligations discharged by Homes since January 31, 19_____, with the written consent of Keyes and Subsidiary and plus those liabilities and obligations with the written consent of Keyes and Subsidiary incurred by Homes since January 31, 19_____ ("Homes Liabilities Assumed"). Any liabilities or obligations of Homes not within the Homes Liabilities Assumed shall continue to be the obligation of Homes, and Subsidiary shall not be liable with respect to such liabilities or obligations.

3. Representations and Warranties of Homes

Homes represents and warrants to Keys and Subsidiary as follows:

(a) Organization of Homes: Homes is a corporation duly organized, validly existing, and in good standing under the laws of the state of Georgia; it owns no capital stock, directly or indirectly, in any other corporation in excess of five percent (5%) of the issued and outstanding capital stock of each such corporation.

Homes has the corporate power to own and lease its properties and carry on its business the same as has been and is now being conducted, and it is duly qualified, licensed, and in good standing as a foreign corporation in the state of Texas, being the only jurisdiction where the facts are such as to require qualification as a foreign corporation under applicable laws.

Homes has the corporate power to execute and deliver this agreement; to perform hereunder; and to consummate the transaction described herein. The execution, delivery, and performance of this agreement have been duly and validly authorized and approved by the board of directors and stockholders of Homes, and Homes has taken all other actions required by law, its Articles of Incorporation, By-Laws, or otherwise to authorize such execution, delivery, *transaction. For instance, a restriction existing in articles of incorporation or by-laws could effect a transaction. Such a warranty should serve as a flag to the corporate secretary to carefully reread the articles and by-laws as well as all other relevant documents as to the basic corporate structure.*

A capital stock should be specified. The purpose here from the acquiring corporation's standpoint is to make sure that in fact all the shareholders approve of the transaction. From the acquired corporation's standpoint, it serves as a recitation and checklist for the corporate secretary.

The financial statements language must be prepared after consultation with the corporation's accountants. Warranties can range from "best of knowledge" to a very precise warranty as to the reliability of the financial statements.

Note the usual reference to not only "generally accepted accounting principles," but also the basis of consistent application throughout the period. The nature of generally accepted accounting principles gives certain broad range to accountants, and options available to them in preparing the financial statements. If consistency is required, this may resolve many of the possible elections as to which exact accounting principles are to be applied.

The assets list is discussed in detail and a precise warranty made indicating that the assets list is complete.

Leases must be carefully studied and must be in full force and effect.

or performance. The board of directors and stockholders of Homes have approved and authorized amending Homes' Articles of Incorporation to change its name to 1003 Corporation and the liquidation and dissolution of Homes, and Homes has taken all other actions required by law, its Articles of Incorporation, By-Laws, or otherwise to authorize such action.

True, correct, and complete copies of the Articles of Incorporation, as amended to date, and By-Laws, as amended to date, and the minute books of Homes have been heretofore delivered to Keyes or Subsidiary.

(b) Capital Stock: The authorized capital stock of Homes consist of six million (6,000,000) shares of common stock, par value $0.10 per share, of which one million eighty thousand (1,080,000) are issued and outstanding. The issued and outstanding shares are held by C.T. Carbone, as to 360,000 shares, R.J. Kroger, as to 360,000 shares, and L.S. Neugent, as to 360,000 shares, and are validly authorized and issued, fully paid, and non-assessable. There are no shares held in the treasury of Homes.

(c) Financial Information: True, correct, and complete copies of the financial information requested by Keyes and Subsidiary as listed in Schedule "B(1)" have been heretofore delivered to Keyes or Subsidiary. Where such statements were prepared by independent public accountants, all accompanying opinions of such accountants have been attached to the financial statements.

Each such financial statement delivered to Keyes or Subsidiary has been prepared in accordance with generally accepted accounting principles applied on a consistent basis throughout the periods covered by such statements, and present fairly the respective financial position, of Homes, covered by each such financial statement as of such dates and the results of its operation for such periods, except, in the case of unaudited statements for normal recurring accruals and audit adjustments.

(d) Assets: Schedule "A" contains as of January 31, 19_____, a true, complete, and correct listing of all of the assets (except the aforesaid refund claims, corporate records, and books of Homes), properties, leases, contracts, agreements, and rights of Homes of every type and description, real, personal, and mixed, tangible and intangible, including without limitation, all cash on hand and in banks, the right to the use of the name "HOMES CORPORATION" and all variants thereof, merchandise inventory, trade accounts receivable, other accounts receivable, deposits, prepaid items, furniture and fixtures, motor vehicles, office equipment and supplies, real property and improvements, leases and leasehold improvements, trademarks, deferred preoperating costs, other tangible properties, its business as a going concern, and dealer organizations. Since January 31, 19_____, Homes has not disposed of any assets, except with the written consent of Keyes and Subsidiary.

(i) Leases of Real Property: True, correct, and complete copies of all real property leases on which Homes is lessee have been heretofore delivered to Keyes and Subsidiary. Homes has not received

notice of violation of, or change in, any zoning regulation, ordinance, or other law, ordinance, or regulation relating to the real property leased by it. All such leases are in full force and effect, are valid and subsisting, and Homes is not in default thereunder except as specified in Schedule "C." There are no restrictions whatsoever prohibiting the present use of the real property covered by the leases. There are no leases on which Homes is a lessor.

This type of agreement, like any agreement contemplating the actual transfer of real property must be precise, both as to real property specified normally by a "metes and bounds" description tying in with the recent survey, and as to the encumbrances (e.g., mortgages) affecting the property.

(ii) Real Property Owned: Homes has good and marketable title to all of real property listed in Schedule "A" and identified therein as owned by Homes subject only to the encumbrances specified in Schedule "B." Homes has not received notice of violation of, or change in, any zoning regulation relating to the real property owned by it. There are no restrictions whatsoever prohibiting the present use of the real property owned by Homes.

In this day and age, there are normally many leases of office equipment and other equipment which should be transferred by the business.

(iii) Leases of Personal Property: True, correct, and complete copies of all personal property leases on which Homes is lessee have been heretofore delivered to Keyes or Subsidiary. All such leases are in full force and effect, are valid and subsisting, and Homes is not in default thereunder, except as specified in Schedule "C."

Trade Accounts Receivable are the subject for much discussion. Here the parties elected to have any deficiency in collection after 180 days owed in the reserve absolutely guaranteed by the acquiring corporation.

(iv) Trade Accounts Receivable: All of the trade accounts receivable included in the Homes Assets arose in the ordinary course of business, and except for the reserve established therefor as shown on Schedule "A" shall be fully paid within 180 days of the date hereof, and are not subject to any right of setoff.

Depending on the type of business, there may be patents, trade names, and other types of intangible property which must be transferred.

(v) Trade Names, Patents, Etc: True, correct, and complete copies of all documents relating to all patents, trade names, trademarks registration, copyrights or publication rights, and application for any of the foregoing, owned by Homes or owned or controlled by any of its respective officers, directors, or employees and related to the business of Homes have been heretofore delivered to Keyes or Subsidiary. The trademark, listed in Schedule "A," constitutes all of such rights used by Homes.

Each material agreement must be carefully studied by both parties and full warranties required by the acquiring corporation.

(vi) Agreements, Contracts, and Commitments: True, correct, and complete copies of all written agreements, contracts, and commitments (not delivered pursuant to any other provisions hereunder) have been heretofore delivered to Keyes and Subsidiary.

Except as specified in Schedule "D," Homes is not a party to (a) any agreement of guarantee or indemnification running from it to any person or entity, (b) any agreement, contract, or commitment containing any covenant limiting its freedom to engage in any line of business or compete with any person or entity, (c) any agreement, contract or commitment relating to the expenditure of sums in excess of $10,000 or having a duration of three months, or (d) any agreement, contract, or commitment relating to the acquisition or assets or capital stock of any business enterprise.

The lack of any default under the agreement and other provisions must be specified.

(vii) Agreements, in Full Force and Effect: Except as specified in Schedule "E": (a) all agreements, contracts, leases, commitments, insurance policies, plans, and licenses on which

Homes is named or to which it is a party, beneficiary, or obligee, are valid and in full force and effect, (b) Homes may immediately enjoy the rights to which it may be entitled thereunder, and (c) it has not breached any provision of, nor is it in default in any respect under the terms of any such agreement, contract, lease, commitment, insurance policy, plan, and license, nor after diligent inquiry and investigation, is Homes aware of the existence of any basis for any claim of default thereunder.

In a particular type of business, dealer organization may need special treatment.

(viii) Dealer Organization: Homes has heretofore delivered to Keyes or Subsidiary a true, correct, and complete list of all dealers with whom Homes is presently doing business. Homes does business with such dealers without any written agreements and on the terms described in Schedule "F."

(ix) Title: Homes has good and marketable title to the Homes Assets, free and clear of all mortgages, liens, pledges, restrictions, charges, or encumbrances of any nature whatsoever, except for Homes Liabilities Assumed.

It is advantageous to the acquiring corporation to specify that the operating assets are usable.

(x) Condition: Except as specified in Schedule "G": (a) all property owned or leased by Homes is in good repair, physical condition, working order, and condition, and in a state of good operating efficiency, ordinary wear and tear excepted; (b) all inventory is salable, usable, and in good condition; (c) all items of inventory and goods previously sold were of merchantable quality; (d) Homes has not breached any express or implied warranties in connection with previous sales of goods and items of inventory; and (e) no breaches or violations of any agreement relating to such sales have occurred, so as to require any action or payment by Homes.

The liabilities must be specified precisely.

(e) Liabilities: All the liabilities and obligations of Homes being assumed by Subsidiary consist of those (i) identified on Schedule "B," as of January 31, 19____; (ii) less those liabilities and obligations (or part thereof) discharged by Homes since January 31, 19____, with the written consent of Keyes and Subsidiary; and (iii) plus those liabilities and obligations incurred by Homes since January 31, 19____, with the written consent of Keyes and Subsidiary. Homes has no other liability or obligations either accrued, absolute, contingent, or otherwise, which is, or deemed to be assumed by Subsidiary, or which may be asserted against Subsidiary, other than listed in Schedule "B" or incurred after January 31, 19____, with the written consent of Keyes and Subsidiary.

Because of a questionable financial condition of the acquired corporation, claims were dealt with in some detail.

(i) Claims. There are no claims, nor after diligent inquiry and investigation, is Homes aware of any facts or circumstances which may give rise to any claims, against Homes: (a) not listed in Schedule "B" or (b) incurred since January 31, 19____, notice of which was given to Keyes and Subsidiary prior to the date hereof, which notice is acknowledged in writing.

The acquiring corporation should obtain a clear statement that all state, Federal,

(ii) Provision for Income Taxes: The provision for income taxes on Schedule "B" shall be adequate for the payment of all unpaid Federal, state, and local taxes payable by Homes, accrued

and local income taxes have either been paid or provided for.

This representation deals with the fact that trade accounts payable which are to be assumed by the acquiring corporation arose in the ordinary course of business.

In addition to getting representations as to the date of the latest financial statements, it is important, as is done here, to obtain assurance for the acquiring corporation that no adverse changes occurred since the date of such statements.

with respect to the period ending January 31, 19_____, and all periods prior thereto which Homes may have been liable at January 31, 19_____.

(iii) Trade Accounts Payable. The trade accounts payable listed in Schedule "B" and those incurred since January 31, 19_____, with the written consent of Keyes and Subsidiary, all arose in the ordinary course of business.

(f) Absence of Changes. Except as specified in Scheudle "B," between January 31, 19_____ and the date hereof: (a) Homes has not engaged in any transaction, whether or not in the ordinary course of business, representing a commitment for expenditure of sums in excess of $5,000, with respect to any one transaction or having a duration in excess of one month; and (b) there has not been, occurred, or arisen:

(i) Any material damage or destruction in the nature of a casualty loss, whether covered by insurance or not, on the properties or business of Homes.

(ii) Any increase, in the compensation paid or to become payable by Homes to any of its officers, directors, or employees, or in any bonus, insurance, pension, or other benefit plan, payment, or arrangement made to, for, or with any of such officer, director, or employee; or

(iii) Any extraordinary loss of Homes (as defined in Opinion No. 9 of the Accounting Principles Board of the American Institute of Certified Public Accounts) or any waiver by Homes of any rights of substantial value; or

(iv) Any declaration or setting aside or payment of any dividend of other distribution in respect to the capital stock of Homes; or

(v) Any direct or indirect redemption or purchase of the capital stock of Homes; or

(vi) Any issuance of shares of the capital stock of Homes; or

(vii) Any mortgage or pledge of any of the properties or assets of Homes.

The assurance given in this section deals with the fact that the business will continue to be productive in the ordinary course of business, since the acquiring corporation wants to obtain an ongoing business and its goodwill.

(g) Conduct of Business: Since January 31, 19_____, Homes has used its best efforts to conduct its business in such a manner as to preserve its assets, maintain and develop its dealer organization, and maintain and promote consumer goodwill, and by way of amplification and not limitation, Homes has:

(i) Retained the services of its officers and employees;

(iii) Maintained the production of mobile homes in such quantity as shall be sufficient to meet demand;

(iv) Continued to exercise a high level of quality control in the manufacturing of mobil homes:

(v) Operated each of its plants in accordance with sound industry standards and practices;

(vi) Done nothing detrimental to the existing dealer organization;

(vii) Continued such programs direct at dealers and intended to foster a relationship with such dealer's beneficiary to Homes;

(viii) Maintained a policy of servicing consumer complaints in such a manner as to foster, preserve, protect, and maintain the consumer goodwill associated with the mobil homes manufactured by Homes; and

(ix) Maintained its customary advertising expenditures.

Since February 18, 19_____, the appropriate officers and employees of Homes have conferred on matters of importance with and reported on the operations of Homes to Johnson Davis, the representative of Keyes and Subsidiary. He has kept fully apprised of all developments and activities of Homes, including without limitations, the acquisition or disposal of assets and the incurring and discharging of liabilities and obligations, since February 18, 19_____. However, such apprisal does not in any way affect any representations and warranties hereunder, nor Keyes' right to rely thereon.

It is the intention and understanding of the parties hereto that the arrangement involving Homes, Keyes, and Subsidiary, or the representative of Keyes and Subsidiary, in the period between February 18, 19_____, and the date hereof was solely to effect a smooth transition, and that Keyes and Subsidiary, by participating therein, are not to be deemed to have been exercising any proprietary or managerial rights in Homes or its operations, not assuming any of the risks attendant thereto.

See the comments at page 46 of the text concerning the bulk transfer laws. This provision is intended to assure compliance with those laws. Normally this means notice is given to the creditors of the acquired corporation of the impending transfer.

This provision deals with a myriad of reports required of most businesses now operated in the United States.

(h) Compliance with Bulk Transfer. Homes has complied with the bulk transfer provisions of the Uniform Commercial Code of Georgia and Texas in all respects.

(i) Taxes, Returns, Reserves, and Other Returns and Reports: All Federal, state, local, and foreign tax returns and tax reports required to be filed by Homes on or before February 28, 19_____, have been timely filed with the appropriate government agencies in all jurisdictions in which such returns and reports are to be filed; all Federal, state, local, and foreign income, profits, franchise, sales, use, occupation, property, excise, and other taxes (including interest and penalties) due from Homes have been fully paid or adequately listed as a liability on Schedule "B." The Federal income tax returns of Homes have not been audited by the Internal Revenue Service. No waiver of statutes of limitations have been given or requested; and there are no actual or potential deficiencies for any Federal, sate, local, and foreign income, profits, franchise, sales, use, occupation, property, excise, and other taxes (including interest and penalties). True, correct, and complete copies of all income tax returns, requests, and filings, together with all pertinent governmental audit reports, and notices, made by Homes, in compliance with, and pursuant to the Internal Revenue Code of 1954, as amended, applicable state statutes or ordinances, have been heretofore delivered to Keyes or Subsidiary. True, correct, and complete copies of all reports, returns, requests, and filings made by Homes, in compliance with and pursuant to state franchise tax, state sales tax law, and regulations have been heretofore delivered to Keyes or Subsidiary.

Homes is not subject to any penalty by reason of a violation of

The acquiring corporation obviously wants to know whether or not the employees of the acquired corporation have designated a collective bargaining representative.

The acquiring corporation should also determine, even if there does not now exist a collective bargaining agreement, whether or not there is a unionization attempt underway. In addition, the acquiring corporation should be very careful to obtain a specific representation to the effect that the acquired corporation has not committed any unfair labor practices.

All too often the agreements overlook the employee benefit plans which most businesses now have. These could indicate a substantial liability for the acquiring corporation.

It is very important that some specific provision be made as to insurance coverage, especially during the interim period between the contract and the closing.

The acquiring corporation should attempt to obtain a warranty as to specific compliance with specific laws. For instance, this agreement was entered into during the period of the Economic Stabilization Act and has specific reference to it as well as OSHA.

The acquiring corporation must be very careful to learn of any litigation pending or

any statute, order, rule, or regulation of, or default (including failure to file) with any Federal, state, local, foreign, or other governmental agency, department, commission, board, bureau, or instrumentality to which it is subject.

(j) Employment-Related Matters.

(i) Collective Bargaining Agreements: Homes is not a party to any collective bargaining agreements or any written employment-related agreements that contain any severance pay, liabilities, or obligations.

(ii) Absence of Union Activities: Homes has not been the subject of any union activity nor do the officers of Homes have any reason to suspect that it may be the subject of any union activity. Homes has not violated any applicable Federal or state law relating to labor, nor has Homes committed any unfair labor practices under applicable state and Federal statutes.

(iii) Compensation and Other Plans: Except as specified in Schedule "I," Homes does not have any (a) bonus, deferred compensation, pension, profit-sharing, or retirement plans, stock options, or other arrangements, and (b) any employment agreement, contract, or commitment with any employee of Homes. A true, correct, and complete list of all employees receiving compensation in excess of $15,000, officers and directors, together with their respective salaries, as well as the rates at which Homes is taxed under the Unemployment Compensation Law of each state in which it has employees, has been heretofore delivered to Keyes or Subsidiary.

(k) Insurance: True, correct, and complete copies of all insurance policies on which Homes is insured against any loss has been heretofore delivered to Keyes or Subsidiary. Except as specified in Schedule "J," Homes is not self-insured in any area.

All insurance policies held by Homes are in full force and effect and such policies or similar policies have been continuously in effect since inception of business, and such policies provide adequate coverage for any claim or loss that has or may arise out of the business conducted by Homes (including without limitation product liability claims).

(l) No Litigation or Adverse Events: Except as specified in Schedule "B," there is no suit action or legal, administrative arbitration, or other proceeding or governmental investigation, pending or threatened against Homes, nor after diligent inquiry and investigation is Homes aware of the existence of any facts upon which such may be initiated.

(m) No Violations or Breaches

(i) No Governmental Violation: To the best of its knowledge after diligent inquiry and investigation, including consultation of counsel, Homes is not in violation of any law, statute, rule, gov-

threatened, and to have its counsel examine in some detail the record in any pending case.

ernmental regulation, or order, nor after such inquiry and investigation is Homes aware of any facts upon which a violation thereunder could be asserted. Without limiting the generality of the foregoing, to the best of its knowledge, after diligent inquiry and investigation, including consultation with counsel, Homes has complied with and is not in violation of the Economic Stabilization Act of 1970 (and the rules and regulations promulgated thereunder) and the Occupational Safety and Health Act. Homes has implemented Federal and state regulations thereunder and state counterpart legislation, and Federal, state, and local environmental controls standards, statutes, rules, or regulations.

Homes holds every license, permit, or approval required of it to engage in its business in each of the jurisdictions where facts are such so as to require the obtaining of such licenses, permits, or approvals under applicable statutes. True, correct, and complete copies of all such license, permit, or approval so held by Homes have been heretofore delivered to Keyes or Subsidiary.

This provision deals specifically with assurances that the carrying out of the agreement will not breach any rule or agreement.

(ii) No Breaches: Except as specified in Schedule "C," neither the execution of this agreement, nor consummation of the transaction described herein, nor compliance by Homes with the terms and provisions hereof, will (a) breach any statute or regulation of any governmental authority, domestic or foreign, (b) conflict with or result in a breach of any of the terms, conditions, or provisions of any judgment, order, injunction, decree, or ruling of any court or governmental authority, domestic or foreign, to which Homes is subject or of any agreement or instrument to which Homes is a party or by which it is bound, (c) constitute or provide the basis upon which a default could mature or a right of termination, cancellation or acceleration could arise under any of the foregoing, or (d) give to others any interest in or right to any property, asset, or business of Homes.

This provisions deals specifically with necessary consents, such as those which might be required by the lenders of the acquired corporation.

(iii) Consents: Except as specified in Schedule "C," all consents or approval of each person or entity whose consent or approval is required, under any contractual authorization, in order to permit Homes to consummate the transaction described herein, have been obtained.

This specifically deals with statutes which might limit the transaction or consents which might need to be obtained prior to the closing.

(iv) Statutory Requirements: All statutory requirements for the valid consummation by Homes of the transaction described herein have been fulfilled; all authorizations, consents, and approvals of all Federal, state, and local governmental agencies and authorities required to be obtained in order to permit consummation by Homes of the transaction described herein and to permit the business presently carried on by Homes to be continued by Subsidiary unimpaired immediately following the date hereof, have been obtained.

(n) Banking Relations: A true, correct, and complete list of the names of each bank in which Homes has an account and the names of all persons authorized to draw thereon have been heretofore delivered to Keyes or Subsidiary; Homes has no safe deposit box.

(o) Power of Attorney: Homes has given no person or entity a Power of Attorney.

(p) Other Reports: True, correct, and complete copies of all material reports, returns, requests, and filings (not delivered pursuant to any other provision hereof) made by or of Homes, in compliance with and pursuant to any applicable statutes, rules, or regulations of any governmental agency, whether Federal, state, or local have been heretofore delivered to Keyes or Subsidiary.

(q) Broker's or Finder's Fees: No agent, broker, person, or firm acting on behalf of Homes or under the authority of it is or will be entitled to any commission or broker's or finder's fee from any of the parties hereto in connection with the transaction contemplated herein.

This provision is meant to indicate a compliance with Rule 146.

(r) Investment Representative: Thompson, Swaine & Davis has acted as investment representative to Homes and its stockholders in connection with the transaction described herein. Homes, its stockholders, and Thompson, Swaine & Davis have been given access by Keyes to: (a) the same kind of information, financial or otherwise, which would have been available had the shares of Keyes Common Stock issuable hereunder been registered pursuant to the Securities Act of 1933, as amended on Registration Statement Form S-14; (b) such other information as Homes, its stockholders, and Thompson, Swaine & Davis have requested; and (c) such other financial and operating data and other information with respect to Keyes' business and properties, as Homes, its stockholders, and Thompson, Swaine & Davis have requested in order to verify the information received under (a) and (b).

(s) Disclosure: No representation or warranty by Homes contained herein and no statement contained in any certificate, list, exhibit, or other instruments specified herein, whether heretofore delivered by Homes, contains or will contain any untrue statement, or omits or will omit to state any fact necessary to make the statements contained therein not misleading.

These representations and warranties parallel to a certain extent those given by the acquired corporation, but are somewhat narrower since much more information is available publicly as to the acquiring corporation.

4. Representations and Warranties of Keyes and Subsidiary

(a) Organization: Keyes and Subsidiary are corporations duly organized, validly existing, and in good standing under the laws of the states of Delaware and Georgia, respectively; and Subsidiary is duly qualified, licensed, and in good standing as a foreign corporation in the state of Texas, being the only jurisdiction where facts are such as to require qualification as a foreign corporation under applicable laws under the laws of the states of Delaware and Georgia, respectively. Each has the corporate power to own its property and carry on its business as now being conducted; and each has the corporate power to execute and deliver this agreement and consummate the transaction described herein.

(b) Capital Stock of Keyes: The authorized capital stock of

Keyes consists of twenty-five million (25,000,000) shares of Keyes common stock, par value $2.50 per share, of which 9,692,484 shares are issued and outstanding as of the date hereof, and one million (1,000,000) preferred shares, $2.50 par value per share, of which none are issued and outstanding. A true, correct, and complete copy of the charter documents, as amended to date, and by-laws, as amended to date, of Keyes and Subsidiary have been delivered to counsel for Homes; and since the delivery of such copies, no amendment of such charter documents or by-laws has been made or is presently contemplated. All shares of Keyes common stock to be issued pursuant hereto, when so issued, will be duly and validly authorized and issued, fully paid, and nonassessable, and will have been listed on the New York Stock Exchange and Pacific Stock Exchange, subject to official notice of issuance.

(c) Capital Stock of Subsidiary: The authorized capital stock of Subsidiary consists of 1,000 shares of common stock, par value $1.00 per share, all of which shares are issued and outstanding, fully paid and non-assessable, and owned of record and beneficially by Keyes.

(d) Financial: Keyes has heretofore delivered to Homes, its stockholders, and Thompson, Swaine & Davis, the investment representative of Homes, and its stockholders, its 19_____ Annual Report to stockholders containing financial statements certified by Swift, Dillon, McKee & Barrett, Inc. (since April 1, 19_____, Crawford and Jackson) for its fiscal years ended January 29, 19_____ and January 29, 19_____.

The financial statements set forth in the 19_____ Annual Report to stockholders have been prepared in accordance with generally accepted accounting principles applied on a consistent basis throughout the periods covered by such statements and present fairly the financial condition of Keyes and its consolidated subsidiaries as of such dates and the results of their operations for such periods.

Since January 27, 19_____, there has been no material adverse change in the business or condition, financial or otherwise, of Keyes.

Keyes has given to Homes, its stockholders, and Thompson, Swaine & Davis access to: (i) the same kind of information, financial or otherwise, to the extent such information is available, which would have been available if the shares of Keyes common stock issuable thereunder were registered pursuant to the Securities Act of 1933, as amended, on Registration Form S-14; and (ii) such other information as Homes, its stockholders, and Thompson, Swaine & Davis may have reasonably requested; and (iii) such other financial and operating data and other information with respect to the business and properties of Keyes, and Homes, its stockholders, and Thompson, Swaine & Davis may have reasonably requested to verify the information received under (i) and (ii).

Compliance of Bulk Transfer: Subsidiary has complied with the

Bulk Transfer provisions of the Uniform Commercial Code of Texas and Georgia in all respects.

(f) No Litigation and Adverse Events: Except as specified in Schedule "K" to the best knowledge of Keyes' officers, there are no suits, actions, or legal, administrative, arbitration, or other proceedings or governmental investigations pending or threatened against Keyes, its officers, or directors (whether or not purportedly on behalf of Keyes or otherwise or any of its subsidiaries) which have merit, and, which if concluded unfavorably to Keyes, would have a materially adverse effect on the business or financial condition of Keyes.

(g) Authorization of Agreement: The execution, delivery, and performance by Keyes and Subsidiary of this agreement have been duly and validly authorized and approved by the board of directors of Keyes, and the board of directors and sole stockholder of Subsidiary, respectively, and Keyes and Subsidiary have taken all other action required by law, their Certificate of Articles of Incorporation and By-Laws or otherwise to authorize such execution, delivery, and performance.

(h) No Breach of Statute or Contract; Govermental Authorizations.

(i) No Governmental Violation: Neither the execution and delivery of this agreement by Keyes of Subsidiary, nor the consummation of the transaction described herein, nor compliance by Keyes or Subsidiary, with the terms and provisions hereof will (a) breach any statute or regulation of any governmental authority, domestic or foreign; (b) will conflict with or result in a breach of any of the terms, conditions, or provisions of any judgment, order, injunction, decree, or ruling of any court or governmental authority, domestic or foreign, to which Keyes or Subsidiary is subject, or of any material agreement or material instrument to which Keyes or Subsidiary is a party or by which it is bound; (c) constitute or provide the basis upon which a material default could mature or a right of termination, cancellation, or acceleration could arise under any of the foregoing; or (d) give to others any material interest in or material right to any property, asset, or business of Keyes or Subsidiary.

(ii) Consents: All consents or approvals of each person or entity whose consent or approval is required, under any contractual authorization, in order to permit Keyes and Subsidiary to consummate the transaction described herein, have been obtained.

(iii) Statutory Requirements: All statutory requirements for the valid consummation of Keyes and Subsidiary to the transaction described herein have been fulfilled; and all authorizations, consents, and approvals of all Federal, state, and local governmental agencies and authorizations required to be obtained in order to permit consummation by Keyes and Subsidiary of the transaction described herein have been obtained.

(i) Authorized Representative: Johnson Davis is the duly authorized representative of Keyes and Subsidiary and is empowered and authorized to give written consent, acknowledgments, and other approvals on behalf of Keyes and Subsidiary as may be required pursuant to the terms of this agreement.

(j) Taxes: All Federal, state, local, and foreign income, profits, franchise, sales, use, occupation, property, excise, and other taxes, including interest and penalty reasonably believed to be due from Keyes for the period ending January 27, 19_____ (and all periods prior hereto) have been fully paid or adequately reflected as a liability on the balance sheet at January 27, 19_____.

(k) Disclosure: No representation or warranty by Keyes or Subsidiary contained herein and no statement contained in any certificate, list, exhibit, or other instruments specified herein, whether heretofore delivered by Keyes or Subsidiary, contains or will contain any untrue statement, or omits to state any fact necessary to make the statements contained therein not misleading.

5. Closing

It is important to set a date and time for the closing even if some modification is later required by mutual consent. Experience has shown that it is much easier to work towards a particular closing at a particular place and time than to try and arrange it at the last minute. The provision in the contract itself is a simple way to put all parties on notice of the time and place.

Since the agreement and the closing took place simultaneously in this transaction, the actual items delivered at the closing are specified in the agreement.

On March 7, 19_____, the date hereof, a closing was held at the First National Bank, South Bend, Indiana, at 12:00 p.m., South Bend time, for the purpose of consummating the transaction described herein contemporaneously with the execution and delivery of this agreement, and to exchange certificate, opinion letters, consideration, and any other document not heretofore delivered.

At such closing the following delivery occurred simultaneously:

(a) Items Delivered by Homes.

Homes delivered:

(i) Such good and sufficient warranty deeds, bills of sale with covenants of warranty, endorsements, assignments, and other good and sufficient instruments of sale, conveyance, transfer, and assignment, in form and substance satisfactory to Keyes' counsel and with all requisite documentary stamps, if any, affixed, as shall be required or as may be appropriate in order effectively to vest in Subsidiary good, indefeasible, and marketable title to the Homes Assets free and clear of all leases, liens, mortgages, conditional sales, and other title retention agreements, pledges, assessments, covenants, restrictions, reservations, easements, and all other encumbrances of every nature, except the Homes Liabilities Assumed.

(ii) All of the files, documents, papers, agreements, formulas, books of account, and records pertaining to the business conducted by Homes, other than its minute books and stock records.

(iii) Commitments to insure title relating to all of the real property owned and leased by Homes and listed in Schedule "A".

(iv) Evidence of compliance with the Bulk Transfer Provisions of the Uniform Commercial Codes of Georgia and Texas (including such affidavits and certificates as may be required and requested by Keyes and Subsidiary).

(v) A certified copy of the resolution or resolutions of the board of directors of Homes, approving and authorizing (a) the transfer of Homes of the Homes assets to Subsidiary upon the terms and conditions herein set out, (b) an amendment to Homes' Articles of Incorporation to its stockholders of the Keyes common stock in complete liquidation of Homes.

(vi) A certified copy of the resolution or resolutions of the stockholders of Homes approving and authorizing (a) the transfer by Homes of its assets to Subsidiary upon the terms and conditions herein set out, (b) an amendment to Homes' Articles of Incorporation changing its name to 1003 Corporation, and (c) the voluntary dissolution of Homes following the distribution to its stockholders of the Keyes common stock in complete liquidation of Homes.

(vii) A proposed amendment to the Articles of Incorporation of Homes, changing its name to 1003 Corporation, and an undertaking on behalf of Homes to promptly obtain such amendment and file such amendment with the Clerk of the Superior Court, Fulton County, Georgia and the Secretary of State of Georgia.

(viii) Evidence that all consents and approvals (including copies thereof) necessary to the consummation of the transaction described herein have been obtained.

(ix) A letter executed by Homes and each of its stockholders, in form and substance, acceptable to Keyes and Subsidiary, in which each of Homes and its stockholders makes certain commitments, covenants, representations, and warranties relating to the shares of Keyes and Subsidiary, in which each of Homes and its stockholders makes certain commitments, covenants, representations, and warranties relating to the shares of Keyes common stock to be received; attached to such letter is a copy of a letter from Johnson, Swaine & Davis which has acted as investment representative for Homes and its stockholders in this transaction.

(x) An agreement, in form and substance acceptable to Keyes and Subsidiary, executed by Homes and its stockholders, by which Keyes and Subsidiary are held harmless from and indemnified against loss, damage, or expense, in excess of fifteen thousand ($15,000) dollars, resulting from the falsity or breach of any of the representations, warranties, or agreements of Homes contained herein under which the twenty-one thousand (21,000) shares of Keyes common stock deliverable hereunder are deposited by Homes and all of its stockholders.

Often the agreement will specify the provisions in counsel's letter. Here, because of the simultaneous closing, the letter itself was attached as an exhibit.

(xi) An opinion of Brown, Jones & Smith, Homes' counsel, dated the date hereof in substantially the form of Exhibit "I" attached hereto.

(b) Items Delivered by Subsidiary. Subsidiary delivered:

(i) An undertaking by Keyes, in form and substance to Homes, regarding the 21,000 shares of Keyes common stock issuable to Homes hereunder.

(ii) An instrument, in form and substance acceptable to Homes, under which Subsidiary assumes and agrees to observe, fulfill, perform, pay, and discharge, in due course, the Homes Liabilities Assumed.

(iii) A certified copy of the resolution by Keyes as the sole stockholder of Subsidiary, authorizing and approving this agreement and the transaction described herein.

(iv) A certified copy of the resolution or resolutions of the board of directors (of the executive committee thereof) of Keyes and Subsidiary authorizing and approving this agreement and the transaction described herein.

(v) A certificate of the secretary or assistant secretary of Keyes, certifying to the authority of the officers of Keyes executing this agreement and the acknowledgment referred to in subparagraph (i) above.

(vi) An opinion of R.A. Benson, General Counsel, Keyes, dated the date hereof in substantially the form of Exhibit "2" attached hereto.

6. Survival of Representations and Warranties

All representations and warranties made by Homes, Keyes, and Subsidiary shall survive until February 28, 19_____, and shall not be limited by any investigation at any time made by or on behalf of Homes, Keyes, or Subsidiary. Without limiting Keyes' other remedies for breach of any warranty or falsity of any representation, any and all monetary damages resulting from such breach or falsity will be limited to the 21,000 shares of Keyes common stock held pursuant to the Indemnity and Deposit Agreement. Knowing that Keyes and Subsidiary will rely on the same, the representations and warranties contained herein were made by Homes with the express intent to induce Keyes and Subsidiary to enter into this agreement and consummate the transaction described herein.

7. Further Undertakings

Homes shall:

(i) Distribute the shares of Keyes common stock received by it pro rata among its stockholders as a part of a complete winding up, liquidation, and dissolution of Homes; such distribution, however, is subject to the Indemnity and Deposit Agreement provided for herein. Homes shall use its best efforts to complete such complete winding up, liquidation, and dissolution within one year of the date hereof; and

(ii) Promptly file all tax returns (Federal, state, and local) required to be filed by it. Such tax returns shall be prepared by their accountants and shall be subject to review by Keyes and Subsidiary prior to filing. Homes shall pay any and all taxes shown to be due on such tax returns.

Keyes shall apply to the New York Stock Exchange and the Pacific Stock Exchange for approval for listing, upon official notice of issuance, of the 21,000 shares of Keyes common stock issuable hereunder. Keyes agrees to use its best efforts to obtain such approval as soon as practicable from the date hereof.

All parties hereto agree that:

(i) Each of them shall treat the transaction described herein as a reorganization under Section 368(a)(1)(C) of the Internal Revenue Code of 1954, as amended; and

---

It is very important, especially from the standpoint of the acquired corporation, that there be a specific provision as to the duration of the warranties. From the standpoint of the acquiring corporation, it is very important that the acquiring corporation have the right of "set off" as to breaches of warranty against shares held in escrow for future payments to be made on notes, along with general rights to bring a lawsuit.

In this transaction, the acquiring corporation wanted to make sure that the acquired corporation promptly liquidated and filed all necessary tax returns.

The shareholders of the acquired corporation wanted to make sure that the shares of stock which they received were promptly listed on the stock exchange

It is a good idea to have a provision to the effect that each of the parties will treat the transaction as a tax-free reorganization since it may be to the acquired corporation's best interest to treat the transaction as a taxable transaction in order to obtain a stepped-up basis for the assets. An express provision in the contract can avoid future misunderstanding.

This type of provision often is omitted, but the author feels it is very important. If both parties do not agree as to the nature of the public announcements, an unseemly battle of the press releases sometimes results, to the detriment of all parties.

Note that the parties agreed to make the transaction effective as of the end of the prior month, to simplify accounting procedures.

A specific provision dealing with the form of giving notices can avoid certain tricky legal questions in the event notice is not received, although mailed, or the notices are sent to the wrong address or the wrong corporate officer.

This provision simply clarifies the intention of the parties that such rights as set off against escrowed stock are not the exclusive remedy and do not prevent the bringing of a lawsuit if required.

It is important, where various states' laws could be applicable, that the parties designate the law which they wish to apply, as the laws of several states, and certainly the various countries which could be involved, vary considerably as to their provisions. Generally speaking, in a commercial transaction, the parties may designate any law to control if it has some substantial relationship to the transaction.

This express provision is intended to make it clear that the parties intend the four corners of this agreement to set forth their entire deal and to supersede any prior negotiations or understandings.

(ii) No public announcement of the consummation of the transaction described herein shall be issued by any party hereto until after the text of such public announcement has been approved in writing by the other parties hereto.

(iii) The transfer of the Homes Assets shall, as among the parties hereto, be effective, and deemed to have been made as of the close of business on February 28, 19_____.

8. General

(a) Amendments: Subject to applicable law, this agreement may be amended upon authorization by the boards of directors (or the executive committeess thereof) of the parties hereto.

(b) Notices: All notices, requests, demands, and other communications hereunder shall be in writing and shall be deemed to have been duly given if delivered or if mailed by United States Certified or Registered Mail, postage prepaid, to the parties of their assignees at the following addresses (or at such other address as shall be received in writing by either party from the other):

HOMES: _____
                          _____
                          _____

KEYES and
SUBSIDIARY: _____
                          _____
                          _____

(c) Remedies not Exclusive: No remedy conferred by any of the specific provisions of this agreement is intended to be exclusive to any other remedy except to the extent specifically stated, and each and every remedy shall be cumulative and shall be in addition to every other remedy given hereunder or now or hereafter existing at law or in equity or by statute or otherwise. The election of any one or more remedies by any party hereto shall not constitute a waiver of the right to pursue other available remedies.

(d) Construction: This agreement shall be construed and enforced in accordance with the laws of the state of Georgia.

(e) Entire and Sole Agreement: This agreement constitutes the entire agreement between the parties and supersedes all prior agreements, representations, warranties, and understandings, whether oral or written, expressed or implied, with respect to the subject matter hereof.

(f) No Assignment: This agreement may not be assigned by operation of law, or otherwise, but shall be binding upon and inure to the benefit of the legal successors of the parties.

(g) Captions and Paragraph Headings: Captions and paragraph headings used herein are for convenience only and are not a part of this agreement and shall not be used in construing it.

It is likely that after closing, certain assets such as automobiles will require further action in order to transfer title of record. This express provision deals with such eventualities.

(h) Further Assurances: Homes shall execute and deliver such further instruments of sale, conveyance, transfer, and assignment and take such other action as Keyes and Subsidiary may request, in order more effectively to sell, convey, transfer, assign to, and vest in Subsidiary any of the Homes assets to confirm Subsidiary's title hereto.

Keyes shall execute and deliver such further instruments as may be required by Homes and its stockholders from time to time, in order to evidence and carry out the terms of this agreement, the liquidation of Homes, and transfer of the aforesaid 21,000 shares of Keyes common stock.

Any part of the cash resulting from the income tax refunds not required by Homes for the payment of fees and expenses of counsel, advisors, accountants, and taxes, including transfer taxes, if any, shall be delivered to Subsidiary upon Homes' final liquidation and winding up.

IN WITNESS WHEREOF, the parties hereto have duly executed this agreement on the day and year first above written.

Signatures should be provided in the proper corporate names of the parties, also naming their short designation in the agreement again. Normally, a president should execute an agreement on behalf of the corporation, the corporate seal should be affixed, and the secretary should sign attesting to both the president's signature and the seal, as well as the authority of the president to execute the agreement on behalf of the corporation. In addition, the parties will normally require certified copies of resolutions of the board of directors of shareholders or both

[signatures]

Appendix F

Selected Revenue Proceedings Dealing with IRS Rulings

See discussion beginning page 21.

Appendix F-1

26 CRF 601.201: Rulings and determination letters.

REV. PROC. 80-22

Section 1. Purpose and Nature of Changes

.01 The purpose of this revenue procedure is to supersede Rev. Proc. 79-14, 1979-1 C.B. 496, Rev. Proc. 79-52, 1979-2 C.B. 538, and Rev. Proc. 79-68, 1979-2 C.B. 600, by providing a revised list of those areas of the Internal Revenue Code under the jurisdiction of the Assistant Commissioner (Technical) in which the Internal Revenue Service will not issue advance rulings or determination letters.

.02 Changes.

1 New section 3.011 refers to section 79 of the Code.

2 New section 3.012 refers to section 83 of the Code.

3 New section 3.013 refers to section 105(h) of the Code.

4 New section 3.014 refers to sections 121 and 1034 of the Code.

5 New section 3.0113 refers to section 302 of the Code.

6 New Section 3.0119 refers to section 451 of the Code.

7 New section 3.0120 refers to sections 451 and 457 of the Code.

8 New section 3.027 refers to section 2031 of the Code.

9 New section 3.028 refers to section 2512 of the Code.

10 New sections 3.0129 through 3.0131 refer to section 7701 of the Code.

11 New section 3.026 refers to the tax consequences of proposed legislation.

12 New section 3.027 refers to determination of reasonable cause under Subtitle F (Procedure and Administration) of the code.

13 New section 3.028 refers to the applicability of criminal penalties to proposed transactions.

14 New sections 4.10 and 4.11 refer to section 7701 of the Code.

15 Section 4.011 now refers to sections 61 and 163 of the Code.

16 New section 4.013 refers to section 170(c) of the Code.

17 New section 5 lists temporary "no ruling" areas.

18 New section 5.01 refers to sections 61, 72, 79, 83, 101, 162, 264, and 641 of the Code.

19 New section 5.02 refers to section 117 of the Code.

20 New section 5.04 refers to section 1001 of the Code.

21 New section 5.05 refers to section 1372 of the Code.

22 New section 6 lists areas for which the Service cannot rule because of statutory prohibition against doing so.

23 New section 6.01 refers to section 61 of the Code.

24 New section 6.02 refers to section 162 of the Code.

25 New section 6.03 refers to section 170 of the Code.

Section 2. Background and Scope of Application

.01 Background

Whenever appropriate in the interest of sound tax administration, it is the policy of the Service to answer inquiries of individuals and organizations regarding their status for tax purposes and the tax effects of their acts or transactions, prior to the filing of returns or reports that are required by the revenue laws.

There are, however, certain areas in which, because of the inherently factual nature of the problems involved, or for other reasons, the Service will not issue advance rulings or determination letters. These areas are set forth in four sections of this revenue procedure. Section 3 reflects those areas in which advance rulings and determinations will not be issued. Section 4 sets forth those areas in which they will not ordinarily be issued. "Not ordinarily" connotes that unique and compelling reasons must be demonstrated to justify a ruling or determination letter. Those sections reflect a number of specific questions and problems as well as general areas. Section 5 lists specific areas for which the Service is temporarily not issuing advance rulings and determinations because those matters are under extensive study. Section 6 lists areas for which the Service is prohibited by statute from issuing rulings or determination letters.

With respect to the items listed, revenue rulings or revenue procedures may be published in the Internal Revenue Bulletin from time to time to provide general guidelines regarding the position of the Service.

Additions or deletions to this revenue procedure as well as restatement of items listed will be made by modification of this revenue procedure. A new revenue procedure will be published annually in the first quarter of the calendar year and changes made thereafter will be published quarterly. These lists should not be considered all inclusive. Decisions not to rule on individual cases, as contrasted with those that present significant pattern issues, are not reported in this revenue procedure and will not be added to subsequent revisions.

The authority and general procedures of the Technical Function of the National Office of the Internal Revenue Service of the Offices of the District Directors of the Internal Revenue with respect to the issuance of advance rulings and determination letters with respect to the Code sections under the jurisdiction of the Assistant Commissioner (Technical) are outlined in Rev. Proc. 80-20, page 7, this Bulletin.

.02 Scope of Application.

This revenue procedure is not to be considered as precluding the submission of requests for technical advice to the National Office from the Office of a District Director of Internal Revenue or a Chief, Appeals Office.

Section 3. Areas in Which Rulings or Determination Letters Will Not Be Issued

.01 Specific questions and problems.

1 Section 79.—Group Term Life Insurance Purchased for Employees.—Whether a group insurance plan for 10 or more employees qualifies as group term insurance if the amount of insurance is not computed under a formula that would meet the requirements of section 1.79-1(c)(2)(ii) if the group consisted of fewer than 10 employees.

2 Section 83.—Property Transferred in Connection with Performance of Services.—Whether a restriction constitutes a substantial risk of forfeiture if the employee is a controlling shareholder.

3 Section 105(h).—Amount Paid to Highly Compensated Individuals under a Discriminatory Self-Insured Medical Expense Reimbursement Plan.—Whether, following a determination that a self-insured medical expense reimbursement plan is discriminatory, that plan had previously made reasonable efforts to comply with tax discrimination rules.

4 Sections 121 and 1034.—One-Time Exclusion of Gain from Sale of Principal Residence by Individual Who Has Attained Age 55; Rollover of Gain on Sale of Principal Residence.— Whether at the time of its sale property qualifies as the taxpayer's principal residence.

5 Section 162.—Trade or Business Expenses.—Whether compensation is reasonable in amount.

6 Section 170.—Charitable Contributions and Gifts.—Whether a taxpayer who advances funds to a charitable organization and receives therefor a promissory note may deduct as contributions, in one taxable year or in each of several years, amounts forgiven by the taxpayer is each of several years by endorsements on the note.

7 Section 264(b).—Certain Amounts Paid in Connection with Insurance Contracts.— Whether "substantially all" the premiums of a contract of insurance are paid within a period of four years from the date on which the contract is purchased. Also, whether an amount deposited is in payment of a "substantial number" of future premiums on such a contract.

8 Section 264(c)(1).—Certain Indebtedness Incurred or Continued as Part of a Plan in Connection with Insurance Contracts.—Whether section 264(c)(1) of the Code applies.

9 Section 269.—Acquisition Made to Evade or Avoid Income Tax.—Whether an acquisition is within the meaning of section 269 of the Code.

10 Section 302.—Redemption of Stock.—Whether section 302(b) of the Code applies when the consideration given in redemption by a corporation consists entirely or partly of its notes payable, and the shareholder's stock is held in escrow or as security for payment of the notes with the possibility that the stock may or will be returned to the shareholder in the future, upon the happening of specified defaults by the corporation.

11 Section 302.—Redemption of Stock.—Whether section 302(b) of the Code applies when the consideration given in redemption by a corporation in exchange for a shareholder's stock consists entirely or partly of the corporation's promise to pay an amount that is based on, or contingent on, future earnings of the corporation, or when the promise to pay is contingent on working capital being maintained at a certain level, or any other similar contingency.

12 Section 302.—Redemption of Stock.—Whether section 302(b) of the Code applies to a redemption of stock if after the redemption the distributing corporation used property that is owned by the shareholder from whom the stock is redeemed and the payments by the corporation for the use of the property are dependent upon the corporation's future earnings or are subordinate to the claims of the corporation's general creditors. Payments for the use of property will not be considered to be dependent upon future earnings merely because they are based on a fixed percentage of receipts or sales.

13 Section 302.—Distributions in Redemption of Stock.—Whether the acquisition or disposition of stock described in section 302(c)(2)(B) of the Code has, or did not have, as one of its principal purposes the avoidance of federal income taxes within the meaning of that section, unless the facts and circumstances are materially identical to those set forth in Rev. Rul. 56-556, 1956-2 C.B. 177, Rev. Rul. 56-584, 1956-2 C.B. 179, Rev. Rul. 57-387, 1957-2 C.B. 225, Rev. Rul. 77-293, 1977-2 C.B. 91, or Rev. Rul. 79-67, 1979-1 C.B. 128.

14 Sections 311 and 336.—Taxability of Corporation on Distribution; General Rule.—Upon distribution of property in kind by a corporation to its shareholders, in complete liquidation under section 331 of the Code (when under the facts a sale of the property by the corporation would not qualify under section 337), in partical liquidation under section 346, or in redemption under section 302(a), followed by a sale of the property, whether the sale can be deemed to have been made by the corporation under the doctrine of *Commissioner v. Court Holding Company,* 324 U.S. 331 (1945), Ct. D. 1636, 1945 C.B. 58.

15 Section 312.—Earnings and Profits.—The determination of the amount of earnings and profits of a corporation.

16 Sections 331, 332, and 333.—Effects on Recipients of Distributions in Corporate Liquidations.—The tax effect of the liquidation of a corporation preceded or followed by the reincorporation of all or a part of the business and assets when more than a nominal amount of the stock (that is, more than 20 percent in value) of both the liquidating corporation and the transferee

corporation is owned by the same shareholders; or when a liquidation is followed by the sale of the corporate assets by the shareholders to another corporation in which such shareholders own more than a nominal amount of the stock (that is, more than 20 percent in value).

17 Section 337.—Gain or Loss; Certain Liquidations.—The application of this section to a corporation upon the sale of property, in connection with its liquidation, to another corporation, when more than a nominal amount of the stock (that is, more than 20 percent in value) of both the selling corporation and the purchasing corporation is owned by the same persons.

18 Section 346.—Partial Liquidation.—The amount of working capital attributable to a business or portion of a business terminated that may be distributed in partial liquidation.

19 Section 451.—General Rule for Taxable Year of Inclusion.—The tax consequences of a nonqualified unfunded deferred compensation arrangement with respect to a controlling shareholder employee eligible to participate in the arrangement.

20 Sections 451 and 457.—General Rule for Taxable Year of Inclusion; Deferred Compensation Plans With Respect to Service for State and Local Governments.—The tax consequences to unidentified independent contractors in nonqualified unfunded deferred compensation plans. This applies to plans established under section 451 of the Code by employers in the private sector and to eligible state plans under section 457. However, a ruling with respect to a specific independent contractor's participation in such a plan may be issued.

21 Section 453.—Revolving Credit Sales as Installment Sales.—Whether a proposed sampling procedure will be acceptable by the Service for the purpose of determining the portion of revolving credit balances to be treated as installment account balances. See Rev. Proc. 64-4, 1964-1 (Part 1) C.B. 644, and Rev. Proc. 65-5, 1965-1 C.B. 720.

22 Section 642(c).—Deduction for Amounts Paid or Permanently Set Aside for a Charitable Purpose.—Allowance of an unlimited deduction for amounts set aside by a trust or estate for charitable purposes when there is a possibility that the corpus of the trust or estate may be invaded.

23 Section 704(b)(2).—Partner's Distributive Share Determined.—Whether the allocation to a partner under the partnership agreement of income, gain, loss, deduction, or credit (or an item thereof) has substantial economic effect.

24 Section 704(e).—Family Partnerships.—Matters relating to the validity of a family partnership when capital is not a material income producing factor.

25 Section 1221.—Capital Asset Defined.—Whether specialty stock allocated to an investment account by a registered specialist on a national securities exchange is a capital asset.

26 Section 1551.—Disallowance of Surtax Exemption and Accumulated Earnings Credit.—Whether a transfer is within section 1551 of the Code.

27 Section 2031.—Definition of Gross Estate.—Actuarial factors for valuing interests in the prospective gross estate of a living person.

28 Section 2512.—Vaulation of Gifts.—Actuarial factors for valuing prospective or hypothetical gifts of a donor.

29 Section 7701.—Definitions.—Whether a foreign arrangement that is a participant in a domestic arrangement classified as a partnership for U.S. tax purposes will itself be classified as a partnership.

30 Section 7701.—Definitions.—Whether a foreign limited liability company will be classified as a partnership if the taxpayer requests classification as a partnership and (1) the taxpayer is a corporation and less than 20 percent of the interests in the limited liability company are held by independent parties or (2) the taxpayer is not a corporation and independent parties hold only a nominal interest in the company.

31 Section 7701.—Definitions.—The classification of arrangements formed as partnerships under local law where the members of such partnerships are professional corporations.

.02 General Areas.

1 The results of transactions that lack bona fide business purpose or have as their principal purpose the reduction of federal taxes.

2 A matter upon which a court decision adverse to the government has been handed down and the question of following the decision or litigating further has not yet been resolved.

3 A matter involving the prospective application of the estate tax to the property or the estate of a living person.

4 A matter involving alternate plans of proposed transactions or involving hypothetical situations.

5 A matter involving the federal tax consequences of any proposed federal, state, local, or municipal legislation. The Service may provide general information in response to an inquiry.

6 Whether reasonable cause exists under Subtitle F (Procedure and Administration) of the Code.

7 Whether a proposed transaction would subject the taxpayer to a criminal penalty.

8 A request that does not comply with the provisions of Rev. Proc. 80-20.

Section 4. Areas in Which Rulings or Determination Letters Will Not Ordinarily be Issued

.01 Specific questions and problems.

1 Sections 61 and 163.—Gross Income Defined; Interest.—Determinations as to who is the true owner of property or the true borrower of money in cases in which the formal ownership of the property or liability for the indebtedness is in another party.

2 Section 167.—Depreciation.

(a) Useful lives of assets.

(b) Depreciation rates.

(c) Salvage value assets.

3 Section 170(c).—Charitable, etc., Contributions and Gifts.—Whether a taxpayer who transfers property to a charitable organization and thereafter leases back all or a portion of the transferred property, may deduct the fair market value of the property transferred and leased back as a charitable contribution.

4 Section 302.—Redemption of Stock.—The tax effect of the redemption of stock for notes, when the payments on the notes are to be made over a period in excess of 15 years from the date of issuance of such notes.

5 Section 306.—Disposition of Certain Stock.—Whether the distribution or disposition or redemption of "section 306 stock" in a closely held corporation is a pursuance of a plan having as one of its principal purposes the avoidance of federal income taxes within the meaning of section 306(b)(4) of the Code.

6 Section 331.—Gain or Loss to Shareholders in Corporate Liquidations.—The tax effect of the liquidation of a corporation by a series of distributions, when the distributions in liquidation are to be made over a period in excess of three years from the adoption of the plan of liquidation.

7 Section 341.—Collapsible Corporations.—Whether a corporation will be considered to be a "collapsible corporation," that is, whether it was "formed or availed of" with the view of certain tax consequences. However, ruling requests will be considered on this matter when the enterprise (1) has been in existence for at least 20 years, (2) has had substantially the same owners during that period, and (3) has conducted substantially the same trade or business during that period.

8 Section 351.—Transfers to Controlled Corporation.—The tax effect of the transfer when part of the consideration received by the transferors consist of bonds, debentures, or any other evidences of indebtedness of the transferee.

9 Section 992.—Requirements of a Domestic International Sales Corporation.—The tax effects of a Domestic International Sales Corporation's stock being held by individuals who are also shareholders in a related supplier corporation.

10 Section 7701.—Definitions.—Whether what is generally known as a foreign corporation will be classified as a partnership for U.S. tax purposes if the taxpayer requests classification as a partnership.

11 Section 7701.—Definitions.—Whether a foreign partnership will be classified as an association for U.S. tax purposes if the taxpayer requests classification as an association.

.02 General areas.

1 Any matter in which the determination requested is primarily one of fact, e.g., market value of property, or whether an interest in a corporation is to be treated as stock or indebtedness.

2 The tax effect of any transaction to be consummated at some indefinite future time.

3 Any matter dealing with the question of whether property is held primarily for sale to customers in the ordinary course of trade or business.

Section 5. Areas Under Extensive Study in Which Rulings or Determination Letters Will Not Be Issued Until the Service Resolves the Issue Through Publication of a Revenue Ruling, Revenue Procedure, Regulations or Otherwise

.01 Section 79.—Group Term Life Insurance Purchased for Employees.—Whether life insurance provided for employees under a "retired lives reserve" plan will be considered group term insurance (also sections 61, 72, 83, 101, 162, 264, and 641).

.02 Section 117.—Scholarships and Fellowships Grants.—Whether an employer-related scholarship or fellowship grant is excludable from the employee's gross income if there is no intermediary private foundation distributing the grants, as there was in Rev. Proc. 76-47, 1976-2 C.B. 670.

.03 Section 368.—Definitions Relating to Corporate Reorganizations.—Whether the continuity of business enterprise requirement of section 1.368-1(b) of the regulations is satisfied if the transferee corporation does not continue the historic business (the business conducted most recently) of the transferor corporation or, when such business is not continued, the transferee does not use a significant portion of the assets of the transferor's historic business in the transferee's business.

.04 Section 1001.—Determination of Amount of and Recognition of Gain or Loss.—Determination of amount of, and recognition of, gain or loss in divorce property settlements.

.05 Section 1372.—Election by Small Business Corporation.—Whether trailer or mobile home parks or aircraft rental businesses qualify as electing small business corporations.

Section 6. Areas for Which the Service is Prohibited by Statute from Issuing Rulings or Determination Letters

.01 Section 61.—Gross Income Defined.—Employee fringe benefits. Pub. L. 96-167, 1980-5 I.R.B. 12.

.02 Section 152.—Trade or Business Expenses.—Expenses of commuting. Pub. L. 96-167.

.03 Section 170.—Charitable, etc., Contributions and Gifts.—Application of revenue ruling (Rev. Rul. 79-99, 1979-1 C.B. 108) to deny a charitable contribution deduction. Pub. L. 96-74, 1979-2 C.B. 473.

Section 7. Effect on Other Documents

Rev. Procs. 79-14, 79-52, and 79-68 are superseded.

Appendix F-2.1

Rev. Proc. 73-35

Section 1. Purpose

The purpose of this Revenue Procedure is to set forth in a convenient checklist questionnaire the information necessary to be included in a request for a ruling under sections 302 and 311 of the Internal Revenue Code of 1954 which relate to distributions in redemption of stock.

Section 2. Background

The Internal Revenue Service receives many requests for rulings in which the information furnished as to the proposed transaction is not complete enough to permit a determination to be made. In such cases it is necessary to secure additional facts from the taxpayer before the ruling request can be considered. This procedure is time consuming for both Service personnel and taxpayers and delays issuance of the final ruling letter. This checklist will facilitate the filing of requests for rulings under sections 302 and 311 of the Code by showing specific information which should be included so that the application will be as complete as possible when originally filed. However, since the information necessary to rule on a particular transaction depends upon all the facts and circumstances of that case, information in addition to that suggested in this Revenue Procedure may be required. Nevertheless, careful use of the checklist should avoid much needless delay and permit the issuance of rulings in the most expeditious fashion possible.

The authority and general procedures of the National Office of the Service and of the Office of the District Directors of Internal Revenue with respect to the issuance of advance rulings and determination letters are outlined in Rev. Proc. 72-3, 1972-1 C.B. 698. See also Rev. Proc. 72-9. 1972-1 C.B. 718. Careful attention to all the requirements of those Revenue Procedures will also serve to minimize needless delays in processing requests for rulings.

Section 3. Information to Be Included in Requests for Rulings Under Sections 302 and 311 of the Code

Each of the items included in this section should be specifically dealt with in the application even though apparent nonapplicability exists. Presentation of the information required should follow the format of this Revenue Procedure as closely as possible with the appropriate descriptive headings. If an item is not applicable, the letters "N.A." may be inserted after that section or subsection to so indicate.

01. Information regarding the corporation that is redeeming its stock.

1. Identification.—Name, taxpayer identification number, and place and date of incorporation of the corporation that is redeeming its stock (the Corporation).

2. Business.—Brief description of the business of the Corporation.

3. Jurisdiction.—The location of the District Office that will have audit jurisdiction over the return of the Corporation and a statement whether, to the best of knowledge of the taxpayer or his representative, the identical issue is being considered by any field office of the Service in connection with an active examination or audit of a tax return already filed or being considered by a branch office of the Appellate Division. See Rev. Proc. 72-3.

4. Financial Statement.—Submit the most recent balance sheet of the Corporation.

02. Description and ownership of stock.

1. Description of outstanding stock.—Furnish a complete description of each class of the Corporation's stock outstanding, setting forth the rights and privileges of each class.

2. Ownership of stock before the redemption.

(a) Shares actually owned.—The total actual number of shares of each class of stock outstanding immediately before the redemption, and the actual number of shares of each class owned by each shareholder immediately before the redemption. However, if the stock is widely held, the number of shares owned by each shareholder may be limited to those shareholders whose stock is being redeemed ("Redeemed Shareholder") and those shareholders whose stock is attributed, under section 318(a) of the Code, to a Redeemed Shareholder.

(b) Shares constructively owned.—State the number of shares constructively owned by each Redeemed Shareholder and the relationship within section 318(a) of the Code of the person or entity whose stock is attributed to the Redeemed Shareholder. In determining stock constructively owned by each redeemed Shareholder under section 318(a), ownership may be attributed any number of times from one individual or entity to another as provided in section 318(a)(5)(A). However, observe the exception in section 318(a)(5)(B) with respect to double attribution among members of the family under section 318(a)(1) and the exception in section 318(a)(5)(C) with respect to so-called sidewise attribution to (undersection 318(a)(3)) and from (undersection 318(a)(2)) a partnership, estate, trust, or corporation.

Also observe the exceptions to constructive ownership to (under section 318(a)(3) of the Code) and from (under section 318(a)(2)) an employees' trust described in section 401(a) which is exempt from tax under section 501(a) and to a trust (under section 318(a)(3)) when the beneficiary's interest is a remote contingent interest. If it is contended a trust is such an employees' trust or a beneficiary's interest is a remote contingent interest, submit information to support such contention.

(1) Section 318(a)(1) of the Code: family attribution.—When the Redeemed Shareholder is an individual, indicate the number of shares of stock of the Corporation owned actually and constructively under section 318(a) by members of the family of the Redeemed Shareholder described in section 318(a)(1).

(2) Section 318(a)(2) of the Code: attribution from a partnership, estate, trust, or corporation.—Indicate the number of shares of stock of the Corporation owned actually and constructively under section 318(a) by any partnership, estate, trust, or corporation in which the Redeemed Shareholder has an interest and the interest of the Redeemed Shareholder in each of these entities including constructive ownership under section 318(a) when the entity is a corporation.

(3) Section 318(a)(3) of the Code: attribution to a partnership, estate, trust, or corporation.—Indicate the number of shares of stock of the Corporation owned actually and constructively under section 318(a) by any of the partners if the Redeemed Shareholder is a partnership, or by any of the beneficiaries if the Redeemed Shareholder is a trust or estate, or by any of the shareholders, who owns actually or constructively, under section 318(a), 50 percent or more of the stock of the Redeemed Shareholder, if the Redeemed Shareholder is a corporation.

(4) Section 318(a)(4) of the Code: options to acquire stock of the Corporation.—Identify the holder of any options (including those in the form of convertible debentures and stock rights or warrants) to acquire stock of the Corporation and the relationship, direct or indirect, under section 318(a) of the holder of such options to each of the Redeemed Shareholders.

(c) Percent of stock owned.—Indicate the percent of each class of stock of the Corporation owned actually and constructively, as determined in 3.02-2(a) and (b) above, by each shareholder of the Corporation immediately before the redemption.

3. Stock to be redeemed.—State the number of shares of each class of stock to be redeemed from each shareholder of the Corporation listed in 3.02-2(a) above.

4. Ownership of stock after the redemption.—Indicate the number of shares of each class of stock of the Corporation owned actually and constructively by each shareholder and the total number of shares and the percentage of each class of stock owned actually and constructively by each Redeemed Shareholder immediately after the redemption determined in the same manner including the same information as required in 3.02-2(a) and (b).

03. Information to determine whether the redemption is an exchange or a dividend.

1. Substantially disproportionate redemption.—If it is contended the redemption is substantially disproportionate to one or more of the Redeemed Shareholders, furnish the information required in section 302(b)(2) of the Code with respect to each of those shareholders.

(a) Fifty-percent rule.—State the percent of the total combined voting power of all classes of stock entitled to vote owned actually and constructively by the Redeemed Shareholder as determined in 3.02-4 above.

(b) Eighty-percent rule.—Submit computations to show that the Redeemed Shareholder owns actually and constructively immediately after the redemption (as determined under 3.02-4 above) less than 80 percent of the percentage of the outstanding voting stock owned by him immediately before the redemption and less than 80 percent of the percentage of the outstanding common stock (voting and nonvoting) owned by him immediately before the redeption in accordance with the requirements in section 302(b)(2)(C) of the Code.

(c) Series of redemptions.—Give all facts relating to any prior redemptions of stock of the Corporation and state whether it is contemplated that any additional stock of the Corporation will be redeemed. This information is needed in order that a determination can be made whether the present redemption is part of a series of redemptions which (in the aggregate) would result in the present redemption not being substantially disproportionate. See section 302-(b)(2)(D) of the Code. In addition, if prior redemptions have occurred and/or future redemptions are contemplated, state whether these redemptions are pursuant to a plan of complete liquidation of the Corporation.

2. Termination of shareholder's interest.

(a) Complete termination of shareholder's stock interest.—Indicate those Redeemed Shareholders who will not own any stock of the Corporation either actually or constructively as determined in 3.02-2(a) and (b) above immeidately after the redemption.

(b) Termination of shareholder's interest except for constructive ownership under section 318(a)(1) of the Code.—If it is contended there has been a complete termination of an individual Redeemed Shareholder's interest except for constructive ownership from a family member under section 318(a)(1) and therefore section 302(b)(3) should apply by reason of the provisions of section 302(c)(2), furnish the following with respect to each of those Redeemed Shareholders:

(1) Redeemed Shareholders qualifying under sections 302(b)(3) and (c)(2) of the Code.— Identify those Redeemed Shareholders from the list and information contained in 3.02-4 above who own stock of the Corporation only by reason of attribution under section 318(a)(1).

(2) Acquisitions or dispositions of stock of the Corporation within the last 10 years.

(a) Acquisitions by Redeemed Shareholder within the last 10 years.—A statement that none of the stock to be redeemed was acquired by the Redeemed Shareholder, within 10 years preceding the date of redemption, from a person whose stock would be attributed under section 318(a) of the Code to the Redeemed Shareholder at the time of the redemption.

(B) Dispositions by Redeemed Shareholder within the last 10 years.—A statement that at the time of redemption no person whose stock would be attributed to the Redeemed Shareholder under section 318(a) of the Code owns stock of the Corporation which was acquired from the Redeemed Shareholder within 10 years preceding the redemption or if so acquiried such stock will be redeemed in the same transaction.

(C) Avoidance of Federal income tax.—If the statements in (A) and (B) immediately above cannot be furnished because of an acquisition or disposition described therein but it is contended that such acquisition or disposition as one of its principal purposes the avoidance of Federal income tax, furnish whatever facts are deemed relevant to support such a contention.

3. Stock issued by railroad corporation in certain reorganizations.—State whether the stock to be redeemed is the type described in section 302(b)(4) of the Code.

4. Distribution in redemption to pay death taxes.—If the redemption is from an estate, see section 303 of the Code which treats such redemption sunder certain circumstances as in full payment in exchange for the stock so redeeemed.

5. Redemption not essentially equivalent to a dividend.—If the redemption does not qualify as an exchange under 3.03-1 above (section 302(b)(2) of the Code) or 303-2 above (section 302(b)(3)) or 3.03-3 above (section 302(b)(4)) or 3.03-4 above (section 303), but it is contended "the redemption is not essentially equivalent to a dividend" within the meaning of section 302(b)(1), submit whatever facts are deemed relevant with respect to each Redeemed Shareholder which have not been furnished above to support such contention. See section 1.302-2 of the Income Tax Regulations and *United States v. Davis*, 397 U.S. 301 (1969), 1970-1 C.B. 62.

6. Interests in the Corporation after the redemption.

(a) Redemptions qualifying under sections 302(b)(3) and (c)(2) of the Code.

(1) No interests other than creditor and constructive owner under section 318(a)(1) of the Code.—Furnish a statement that the Redeemed Shareholder, after the redemption, will have no interest in the Corporation, including an interest as officer, director, or employee, other than an interest as a creditor as described in section 1.302-4(d) of the regulations (and constructive ownership under section 318(a)(1)).

(2) Agreement as to future interest.—Submit a statement that the Redeemed Shareholder will execute and file the agreement required in section 302(c)(2)(A)(iii) of the Code with respect to the acquisition of any interests in the Corporation within 10 years from the date of the redemption.

(b) In redemptions pursuant to section 302(b) of the Code, other than those qualifying under sections 302(b)(3) and (c)(2).—State the relationship, if any, of each Redeemed Shareholder to the Corporation, both before and after the redemption.

7. Other information to determine whether the redemption is an exchange, a dividend, or other ordinary income transaction to the Redeemed Shareholder or any other person.

(a) Transaction in which stock to be redeemed was acquired if acquired within the last 10 years.

(1) When acquired.—Give the date on which the stock was acquired.

(2) From whom acquired.—Identify the person or entity from whom the stock was acquired and the relationship of the person within the meaning of section 318(a) of the Code to the Redeemed Shareholder.

(3) Consideration.—Describe the amount and kind of consideration paid or transferred for the stock.

(b) "Section 306 stock."—If it is contended none of the stock be redeemed is section 306 stock within the meaning of section 306(c) of the Code, submit a statement to that effect. If the stock to be redeemed is preferred stock, furnish the following information:

(1) Issued for cash.—If issued for cash, furnish a statement to that effect and state whether the stock was paid for in full.

(2) Issued upon incorporation.—If the stock was issued upon incorporation in exchange for property, furnish a statement to that effect.

(3) Issued under other circumstances.

(A) When issued.—Give date or dates on which such stock was issued.

(B) Transaction.—Describe the transaction in which the stock was issued (whether a stock dividend, a reorganization, or other transaction).

(C) Consideration to the Corporation.—Describe the kind of property, if any, the Corporation received in exchange for such stock.

(c) Declared but unpaid dividends.—State whether there are any declared but unpaid dividends on any of the stock to be redeemed.

(d) Transactions.—In addition to the redemption.

(1) Multiple transaction.—Describe any property the Redeemed Shareholder will transfer or surrender in the transaction other than stock of the Corporation and the consideration to be received in exchange therefor.

(2) Redeemed Shareholder and Corporation in dual capacity.—State whether all or any part of the consideration from the Corporation will be received by a Redeemed Shareholder of a debtor, creditor, employee or in some capacity other than the shareholder of the Corporation whose stock is being redeemed pursuant to sections 317(b) and 302 of the Code.

(e) Distribution a partial liquidation in whole or in part.—If it is contended any part of the distribution will qualify as a partial liquidation under section 346 of the Code, state the amount and reasons why it qualifies under section 346.

(f) Sales of stock.—If any stock of the Corporation will be sold or otherwise disposed of other than in the redemption by any shareholder of the Corporation simultaneously with or shortly before or after the redemption, state the number of shares of each class, identify the parties to the transaction, the relationship of such parties and their relationship to any Redeemed Shareholder within the meaning of the section 318(a) of the Code, and the consideration to be received in exchange therefor. State whether the sale or disposition of such stock has been considered consummated in computing the ownership of stock before and after the redemption in 3.02-2 and 3.02-4 above. State whether the Corporation will be liable, directly or indirectly, for a part or all of the buyer's obligation in any such purchase of stock.

(g) Additional issuance of stock.—State whether the Corporation proposes to issue additional shares of stock in the near future. If so, describe the transaction, the number of shares, the relationship of the acquiring party to any Redeemed Shareholder within the meaning of section 318(a) of the Code, and the consideration to be received in exchange for the stock.

(h) Agreements between shareholders and the Corporation with respect to the stock to be redeemed.

(1) Buy-sell agreements.—If there are any existing, or recently terminated, agreements between a Redeemed Shareholder and other shareholders as to the acquisition or disposition of the stock to be redeemed, such as buy-sell agreements, options, etc., give full particulars.

(2) Financing of redemption.—State the source of the cash or other property to be distributed in the redemption. If cash has been or will be obtained for the redemption by loans, give full particulars as to the parties to, and terms of, the loan agreement.

(3) Stock not to be cancelled, retired, or held as treasury stock.—If a party other than the Corporation will hold the stock to be redeemed, give all facts concerning such an arrangement and the conditions, if any, under which the stock may be returned to the Redeemed Shareholder or any person other than the Corporation, and the relationship under section 318(a) of the Code of that person to the Redeemed Shareholder.

(4) Other agreements between Redeemed Shareholder and the Corporation.—Give details of any other agreements between the Redeemed Shareholder and the Corporation such as an employment contract, covenant not to compete, etc., and state whether such agreements had an effect upon the amount of property to be distributed in the redemption.

(i) Related steps or transactions.—Describe any distributions, redemptions of stock of any related corporation sales of stock by the Redeemed Stockholder, or other transactions, other than those occurring at arm's length in the normal course of business, that will occur or are contemplated, whether or not considered as related to or in connection with the redemption. State whether the redemption is one step in a two or more step transaction. If so, explain all steps in the transaction or plan. See Rev. Rul. 57-114, 1957-1 C.B. 122; Rev. Rul. 70-296, 1970-1 C.B. 62; and Rev. Rul. 71-336, 1971-2 C.B. 299.

(j) Indebtedness of the Corporation and Redeemed Shareholder.

(1) Outstanding indebtedness of the Corporation.—Describe in detail the terms of any indebtedness outstanding, other than that incurred in the ordinary course of business, the circumstances under which incurred, and the relationship, within the meaning of section 318(a) of the Code, between such creditors and shareholders of the Corporation.

(2) Debt Owed by Redeemed Shareholder to the Corporation.—If a Redeemed Shareholder owes any amount to the Corporation, state the circumstances under which the debt arose, the terms of the debt, and when and how it will be discharged.

04. Property distributed in redemption of the stock.

1. Cash.—Indicate the amount of cash to be distributed to each Redeemed Shareholder in redemption of his stock.

2. Property other than cash.

(a) Description.—Describe fully all types and categories of property, tangible and intangible, other than cash, to be distributed by the Corporation to each Redeemed Shareholder.

(b) Recognition of gain or income to the Corporation.—If it is contended that neither gain nor income will be recognized to the Corporation upon the distribution of property, state the reasons and nonapplicability of the exceptions to section 311(a) of the Code including the following:

(1) Inventory.—A statement whether any inventory will be distributed, and if distributed, whether the Corporation is on the LIFO method of inventory.

(2) Liability in excess of basis.—The amount of liabilities, if any, to be assumed by the Redeemed Shareholder and the amount of liability, if any to which the property distributed is subject, and the adjusted basis of such property in the hands of the Corporation.

(3) Appreciated property.—If any appreciated property is distributed by the Corporation to a Redeemed Shareholder as part of the redemption, state any exceptions or limitations in section 311(d)(2) of the Code which may be applicable to prevent recognition of gain to the Corporation and give reasons for their application.

(4) Unreported and anticipatory assignment of income.—State whether the Corporation will distribute any assets which represent unearned income to the Redeemed Shareholder such as receivables being reported on a cash basis, unfinished construction contracts, commissions due, or other assets resulting in an anticipatory assignment of income.

(5) Other property.—State whether the Corporation will distribute to a Redeemed Shareholder in the redemption any installment obligations (section 453(d) of the Code), or property described in sections 48, 341(f), 617(d), 1239(b), 1245(a), 1250(c), 1251(e), or 1252(a) (see section 1.311-1(a) of the regulations) or other assets the cost of which has been deducted for Federal income tax purposes.

(6) Reserve for bad debts.—If the Corporation will distribute to a Redeemed Shareholder any receivables, state the amount of any reserve for bad debts related to the receivables.

(7) Sale, lease, or other disposition of property.—State whether the Redeemed Shareholder will sell, lease, or otherwise dispose of any property received in redemption of his stock and give full particulars as to the circumstances and agreement with respect to such sale, lease, or other disposition. If property will be leased back to the Corporation, submit a copy of the lease and indicate whether the rental will be at prevailing rates for the geographical location.

(8) Cross-redemption.—If the Redeemed Shareholder is a corporation and the property to be distributed by the Corporation is stock of the Redeemed Shareholder, submit a statement concerning treatment of such cross-redemption upon each of the corporations together with a statement of relevant authorities to support such treatment.

3. Notes or other obligations of the Corporation.—If notes or other obligations of the Corporation will be distributed to a Redeemed Shareholder, furnish the following:

(a) Copy.—Provide a copy or prototype of the instrument which sets forth its terms.

(b) Period of payments.—Give the beginning and ending payment dates. See Sec. 4.01-3 of Rev. Proc. 72-9.

(c) Financial statements.—Submit profit-and-loss statements and balance sheets for the latest three years.

(d) Subordination.—Submit a statement as to whether the note or instrument is subordinate to the claims of general creditors.

(e) Default.—Indicate whether, in event of default of the note or other instrument, the stock of the Corporation will revert to the Redeemed Shareholder. See Sec. 3.01-5 of Rev. Proc. 72-9.

(f) Installment method.—If a Redeemed Shareholder intends to report gain from the redemption on the installment method under section 453 of the Code, furnish information to support the contention that the requirements in section 453(b)(2) will be met with respect to the Redeemed Shareholder.

05. Redemption Price.

1. Loss to Redeemed Shareholder.—If it is contended that any Redeemed Shareholder will realize a loss on the redemption of his stock, state reasons to establish why section 267 of the Code will not apply.

2. Redemption price and fair market value of the stock.—State whether the redemption price will equal the fair market value of the stock. If it will not, give a complete explanation.

3. Contingent payout.—If all or part of the consideration from the Corporation to the Redeemed Shareholder is contingent upon the future earnings of the Corporation over a period of years or some other presently indeterminate factor, furnish all the terms of the contingent payments and reasons why they should not be considered an equity interest in the Corporation.

06. Assumptions or representations, if applicable.

Section 4. Inquiries.

Inquiries in regard to this Revenue Procedure should refer to its number and should be addressed to Assistant Commissioner (Technical), Attention: T:I:R, Internal Revenue Service, Washington, D.C. 20224.

Appendix F-2.2

REV. PROC. 77-41

Rev. Proc. 77-37, 1977-41 I.R.B. 17, contains operating rules for the issuance of advance rulings as to matters within the jurisdiction of the Reorganization Branch of the Internal Revenue Service. Rev. Proc. 77-37 is amplified to include the following:

A ruling will usually be issued under section 302(a) of the Code that cash to be distributed to shareholders in lieu of fractional share interests arising in corporate reorganizations, stock splits, stock dividends, conversion of convertible stocks, and other similar transactions will be treated as having been received in part or full payment in exchange for the stock redeemed if the cash distribution is undertaken solely for the purpose of saving the corporation the expense and inconvenience of issuing and transferring fractional shares, and is not separately bargained-for consideration. The purpose of the transaction giving rise to the fractional share interests, the maximum amount of cash that may be received by any one shareholder, and the percentage of the total consideration that will be cash are among the factors that will be considered in determining whether a ruling is to be issued.

Rev. Proc. 73-35, 1973-2 C.B. 490, calls for the submission of certain information with requests for rulings under section 302 of the Code. This information need not be supplied with requests for rulings with respect to redemptions of fractional share interests. However, Rev. Proc. 72-3, 1972-1 C.B. 698, and section 601.201 of the Statement of Procedural Rules (26 CFR 601.201 (1977)), which contain the procedures to be followed for the issuance of ruling letters, should be complied with.

Rev. Proc. 77-37 is amplified and Rev. Proc. 73-35 is modified.

Appendix F-3

Part III. Administrative, Procedural, and Miscellaneous

26 CFR 601.201: Rulings and determination letters.

REV. PROC. 80-20

Section 1. Purposes

The purpose of this revenue procedure is to supersede Rev. Proc. 79-45, 1979-2 C.B. 508, by providing revised procedures for issuing rulings and determination and information letters, and for entering into closing agreements on specific issues involving the interpretation or application of the federal tax laws. It also tells taxpayers and their representatives where to send requests for rulings and determination and information letters. It gives the steps to follow so that requests may be handled more efficiently.

Section 2. Scope

This revenue procedure applies only to ruling requests, information letters, and closing agreements under the jurisdiction of the Assistant Commissioner (Technical), and to requests for determination letters under the jurisdiction of field offices that relate to Code sections under the jurisdiction of the Assistant Commissioner (Technical). The Assistant Commissioner (Technical) acts as the principal assistant to the Commissioner in providing basic principles and rules for the uniform interpretation and application of the federal tax laws under the jurisdiction of the Assistant Commissioner (Technical). The procedures for obtaining rulings, etc., that apply specifically to federal firearms taxes under subtitle E of the Internal Revenue Code are under the jurisdiction of the Bureau of Alcohol, Tobacco and Firearms. The procedures for obtaining rulings, determination letters, etc., on employee plans and exempt organizations are under the jurisdiction of the Assistant Commissioner (Employee Plans and Exempt Organizations). However, the jurisdiction of the Assistant Commissioner (Technical) includes section 521 of the Code, on exemption of farmers' cooperatives from tax; section 526, on shipowners' protection and indemnity associations; section 527(a), (b), (c), (d), (e), and (g), on political organizations, and section 528, on certain homeowners' associations.

Section 3. Changes

.01 Section 5.01 has been expanded to (1) incorporate the present practice that the National Office does not rule on the classification of an organization for which a return has been filed, and (2) to cross reference Rev. Proc. 79-63, 1979-2 C.B. 578, which concerns applications for extension of the time for making an election or application for relief pursuant to section 1.9100-1 of the regulations. In this connection section 5.01 now provides that if a request for an extension of time under section 1.9100-1 is submitted after the return is filed but before the return is examined, the procedures under Rev. Proc. 80-20 are applicable. However, if an examination of the return in such situation has begun, or is being considered by an Appeals office, the procedures of Rev. Proc. 80-21, page 19, this Bulletin, are applicable.

.02 Section 5.02 has been modified to permit issuance of rulings in estate tax matters after the estate tax return has been filed if the request for ruling is submitted before the return is filed.

.03 Section 5.02(c) has been clarified to state that the National Office will issue rulings regarding the application of the generation-skipping transfer tax effective date rules to wills, trusts, and trust equivalents in existence on June 11, 1976.

.04 Section 9.02 has been revised to cover specifically signatures on ruling requests from partnerships and trusts.

.05 Section 9.05 has been expanded to (1) explain additional procedures for extending the 21-day period for confirming additional material submitted, and (2) cite additional revenue procedures relating to specific Code or regulatory provisions.

.06 Section 9.06 has been expanded to (1) clarify by limiting the reference to issue pending in litigation to litigation involving an issue in a return of the taxpayer or a related taxpayer that is the same issue in the request for ruling, and (2) state the purpose of requiring the ruling request to be attached to a return filed before the ruling is received.

.07 Section 9.08 has been revised to encourage, rather than require, material on contrary authorities to be submitted.

.08 Section 9.09 has been expanded to make it clear that the disclosure procedures in section 9.09 are applicable to information submitted after the initial request.

.09 Section 11.1 has been clarified to point out that a conference must be held within 21 calendar days after the initial notification as to the time and place of the conference.

.10 Section 20 now provides the procedures for requesting application of 7805(b) of the Code to ruling letters and determination letters.

Section 4. General Practice and Definitions

.01 The Service answers inquiries of individuals and organizations, when appropriate in the interest of sound tax administration, about their status for tax purposes and the tax effects of their acts or transactions. The National Office issues rulings in such matters.

.02 District Directors of Internal Revenue apply the statutes and tax treaties, regulations, revenue rulings, and other precedents published in the Internal Revenue Bulletin in determining tax liability, collecting taxes, and issuing information letters and determination letters in answer to taxpayers' inquiries or requests. For purposes of this revenue procedure, any reference to District Director or district office includes, when appropriate, the director of an Internal Revenue Service Center and the Director of International Operations, or their respective offices.

.03 The word "taxpayer" includes all persons subject to any provision of the Internal Revenue Code and, when appropriate, their representatives. Any reference to National Office means only the Office of the Assistant Commissioner (Technical).

.04 A "ruling" is a written statement issued to a taxpayer by the National Office that interprets and applies the tax laws to the taxpayer's specific set of facts. Rulings are issued only by the National Office, under the general supervision of the Assistant Commissioner (Technical).

Issuing rulings has been largely delegated to the Directors of the Corporation Tax Division and the Individual Tax Division.

.05 A "determination letter" is a written statement issued by a District Director in response to a written inquiry by a taxpayer which applies the principles and precedents previously announced by the National Office to a specific set of facts. A determination letter is issued only when a determination can be made on the basis of clearly established rules in the statute or regulations, or by a position in a ruling, opinion, or court decision published in the Internal Revenue Bulletin that specifically answers the question presented. A determination letter will not be issued if a determination cannot be made, for example, when the question presents a novel issue, or if the matter is excluded from the jurisdiction of a District Director under section 7 of this revenue procedure.

.06 An "information letter" is a statement issued either by the National Office or by a District Director that calls attention to a well-established interpretation or principle of tax law, without applying it to a specific set of facts. It may be issued if the request indicates that the taxpayer is seeking general information. If the request does not meet the requirements of section 9 of this revenue procedure, but the Service thinks that the general information may help the individual or organization it may issue an information letter.

.07 A "revenue ruling" is an interpretation by the Service that has been published in the Internal Revenue Bulletin. It is the conclusion of the Service on how the law is applied to an entire set of facts. Revenue rulings are issued only by the National Office and are published for the information and guidance of taxpayers, Internal Revenue Service officials, and other interested parties.

.08 A "closing agreement" is an agreement between the Commissioner of Internal Revenue or the Commissioner's delegate and a taxpayer on a specific issue or issues or liability that is entered into under the authority in section 7121 of the Code. A closing agreement prepared in an office under the responsibility of the Assistant Commissioner (Technical) is based on a ruling that has been signed by the Commissioner, or the Commissioner's delegate, which says that a closing agreement will be entered into on the basis of the holding of the ruling letter. Closing agreements are final, unless fraud, malfeasance, or misrepresentation of a material fact can be shown. Closing agreements may be entered into when it is advantageous to have the matter permanently and conclusively closed, or when a taxpayer can show good and sufficient reasons for an agreement and the government will sustain no disadvantage by its consummation. In appropriate cases, taxpayers may be asked to enter into a closing agreement as a condition to the issuing of a ruling. If, in a single case, closing agreements are requested for each of a number of taxpayers, such agreements are entered into only if the number of taxpayers is 25 or less. However, if the issue and holding are identical for all the taxpayers and they number more than 25, a "mass closing agreement" will be entered into with the taxpayer who is authorized by the others to represent the entire group.

Section 5. Rulings Issued By the National Office

.01 *In income and gift tax matters*, the National Office issues rulings on prospective transactions and on completed transactions before the return is filed for them. However, the National Office will issue rulings after the return is filed if a ruling is required by section 367 of the Code and the ruling request is filed on time under that section. Further, see Rev. Proc. 79-63, 1979-2 C.B. 578, which concerns applications for extension of the time for making an election or application for relief pursuant to section 1.9100-1 of the regulations. If a request for an extension of time under section 1.9100-1 is submitted after the return is filed but before the return is examined the procedures under Rev. Proc. 80-20 are applicable. If an examination of the return has begun, or is being considered by an Appeals office, the procedures of Rev. Proc. 80-21 are applicable. The National Office issues rulings on the exempt status of organizations under section 521. See Rev. Proc. 80-25, page 39, this Bulletin. The National Office ordinarily does not issue rulings if at the time the ruling is requested, the identical issue is involved in the taxpayer's return for an earlier period, and (1) that issue is being examined by a District Director or is being considered by an Appeals office, or (2) that issue has been examined by a District Director or considered by an Appeals office and the statutory period of limitation on assessment or refund of tax has not expired, or (3) a closing agreement covering the issue or liability has not been entered into by a District Director or by an Appeals office. If a return dealing with an issue for a particular year is filed while a request for ruling on that issue is pending, the National Office will issue the ruling unless it is notified by the taxpayer that an examination of that issue or the identical issue on an earlier year's return has been started by a District Director. See section 9.06. However, even if an examination has begun, the National Office ordinarily will issue the ruling if the District Director agrees, by memorandum, to permit the ruling to be issued. The National Office does not issue rulings for the replacement of involuntarily converted property, even though replacement has not been made, if the taxpayer has filed a return for the tax year in which the property was converted. See section 7.05 on the District Directors' authority to issue determination letters in this connection. In addition, the National Office does not issue rulings on the classification of an organization if a return has been filed for the organization for an earlier period. The National Office also does not issue rulings on only part of an integrated transaction.

.02 *In estate tax matters*, the National Office issues rulings with respect to transactions affecting the estate tax of a decedent before the estate tax return is filed. If the estate tax return is due to be filed before the ruling is issued, the taxpayer should secure an extension of time for filing the return for the maximum period of six months, and notify the National Office Branch considering the request for ruling that an extension has been secured. If the return is filed before the ruling is issued, the taxpayer must disclose on the return that a ruling has been requested, attach a copy of the pending ruling request to the return, and notify the National Office that the return has been filed. The National Office will make every effort to issue the ruling within three months of the day on which the return was filed. If the ruling cannot be issued within that three-month period, the National Office will notify the District Director having jurisdiction of the return who may, by memorandum to the National Office, grant an additional period for the issuance of the ruling. The National Office will not rule on matters relating to the application of the estate tax to property or the estate of a living person.

1 *In generation-skipping transfer tax matter*, the National Office issues rulings on transactions that affect the generation-skipping transfer tax before the return is filed. Rulings are not issued until after the generation-skipping trust, or trust equivalent, has been established. Rulings are not issued on a generation-skipping transfer tax matter before the distribution or termination takes place. Notwithstanding the foregoing, the National Office will issue rulings regarding the application of the generation-skipping transfer tax effective date rules (section 2006(c) of the Tax Reform Act of 1976, Pub. L. 94-455, 1976-3 C.B. (Vol. 1) 1, 365, as amended by section 702(n)(1) of the Revenue Act of 1978, Pub. L. 95-600, 1978-3 C.B. (Vol.1) 1, 169) to wills, trusts, and trust equivalents in existence on June 11, 1976.

2 *In matters involving additional tax under section 2032A(c)*, the National Office issues rulings on prospective transactions and on completed transactions before the return is filed for those transactions.

.03 *In employment and excise tax matters*, the National Office issues rulings on prospective transactions and on completed transactions either before or after the return is filed for those transactions. In employment tax matters, generally the taxpayer is the person who employs the worker. However, if the worker asks for the ruling, both the worker and the person who employs the worker are considered to be the taxpayer and both are entitled to the ruling. The National Office usually will not issue rulings if at the time the ruling is requested, the identical issue is involved in the taxpayer's return for an earlier period and (1) that issue is under examination by a District Director or under consideration by an Appeals office, or (2) that issue has been examined by a District Director or considered by an Appeals office and the statutory period of limitation on assessment or refund of tax has not expired or (3) a closing agreement covering the issue or liability has not been entered into by a District Director or by an Appeals office. However, if a District Director began an examination of the issue involved in the ruling request, the National Office usually will issue the ruling if the District Director agrees, by memorandum, to permit the ruling to be issued.

.04 *In administrative provisions matters,* the National Office issues rulings on issues arising under the Internal Revenue Code and related statutes, and the regulations thereunder, that relate primarily to the time, place, manner, and procedures, for reporting and paying taxes; assessing and collecting taxes (including interest and penalties); abating, crediting, or refunding overassessments or overpayments of tax; and filing information returns. Rulings ordinarily are not issued, if at the time the ruling is requested, the identical issue is involved in the taxpayer's return for an earlier period and (1) that issue is being considered by a District Director or the Director of a Service Center, or (2) that issue has been considered and the statutory period of limitation on assessment or refund of tax has not expired, or (3) a closing agreement covering the issue or liability has not been entered into. If a return involving an issue for a particular year is filed while a request for a ruling on that issue is pending, the National Office will issue the ruling unless an examination of that issue or an examination of the identical issue on an earlier year's return has been started by a District Director or a Director of a Service Center. But, even if consideration has begun, the National Office ordinarily will issue the ruling if the District Director or the Director of a Service Center agrees, by memorandum, to permit the ruling to be issued. Rulings ordinarily are not issued if at the time the ruling is requested, the identical issue is involved in the taxpayer's return for an earlier period and (1) that issue is being considered by an Appeals office, or (2) that issue has been considered by an Appeals office and the statutory period of limitation on assessment or refund of tax has not expired, or (3) a closing agreement covering the issue or liabilitiy has not been entered into.

.05 The National Office does not issue rulings to business, trade, or industrial associations, or to similar groups concerning the application of the tax laws to members of the group. It may, however, issue rulings to these groups or associations on their own tax status or liability, if the tax status or liability is not an issue that is being examined by any field office (including consideration by any Appeals office) for the same taxpayer for the same or an earlier period under the conditions stated in section 5.

.06 Pending the adoption of regulations (either temporary or final) that interpret the provisions of any act, the issuing of rulings will be considered under the following conditions:

1 If the ruling request presents an issue on which the answer seems clear by applying the statute to the facts, a ruling will be issued under the usual procedures.

2 If the ruling request presents an issue on which the answers seems reasonably certain but not entirely free from doubt, a ruling will be issued only if it is established that a business emergency requires a ruling or that unusual hardship will result from failure to obtain a ruling. If the taxpayer believes that a business emergency exists or that an unusual hardship will result from failure to obtain a ruling, the taxpayer should submit with the request a separate letter stating the facts necessary for the Service to make a determination. In this connection, the Service will not consider a "business emergency" to result from circumstances under the taxpayer's control, such as, scheduling within an inordinately short time the closing date for a transaction or a meeting of the board of directors or the shareholders of a corporation. However, if the ruling request presents an issue that cannot be reasonably resolved before regulations are issued, a ruling will not be issued.

Section 6. Determinations Under Section 999(d) of the Code

Under Rev. Proc. 77-9, 1977-1 C.B. 542, procedures, the National Office issues determinations under section 999(d) of the Code that may deny certain benefits of the foreign tax credit, deferral of earnings of foreign subsidiaries, and domestic international sales corporation (DISC) to a person, if that person, or a member of a controlled group (within the meaning of section

993(a)(3)) that includes that person, or a foreign corporation of which a member of the controlled group is a United States shareholder, agrees to participate in or cooperate with an international boycott.

Section 7. Determination Letters Issued by District Directors

.01 *In income and gift tax matters,* District Directors issue determination letters in response to taxpayers' written requests on completed transactions that affect returns over which they have examination jurisdiction. This applies only if the question presented is specifically answered by statute or regulation, or by the position stated in a ruling, opinion, or court decision published in the Internal Revenue Bulletin. A determination letter usually is not issued for a question concerning a return to be filed by the taxpayer if the same question is involved in a return already filed. District Directors do not issue determination letters on the tax consequences of prospective or proposed transactions, except as provided in section 7.05.

.02 *In estate tax matters,* District Directors issue determination letters in response to written requests affecting the estate tax returns of decedents that they will examine, but only if the question presented is specifically answered by statute or regulation, or by the position stated in a ruling, opinion, or court decision published in the Internal Revenue Bulletin. District Directors do not issue determination letters on matters concerning the application of the estate tax to property or the estate of a living person.

1 *In generation-skipping transfer tax matters,* District Directors issue determination letters in response to written requests affecting the generation-skipping transfer tax returns that they will examine, but only if the questions presented are specifically answered by statute or regulation, or by a position stated in a ruling, opinion, or court decision published in the Internal Revenue Bulletin. District Directors do not issue determination letters or matters concerning the application of the generation-skipping transfer tax before the distribution or termination takes place.

.03 *In employment and excise tax matters,* District Directors issue determination letters on completed transactions in response to written requests from taxpayers over which they have examination jurisdiction, but only if the question presented is specifically answered by statute or regulation, or by the position stated in a ruling, opinion, or court decision published in the Internal Revenue Bulletin.

.04 Notwithstanding the provisions of sections 7.01, 7.02, and 7.03, a District Director will not issue a determination letter in response to a request that presents a question specifically answered by statute or regulation, or by the position stated in rulings, etc., published in the Internal Revenue Bulletin, if (1) it appears that the taxpayer has directed a similar inquiry to the National Office, (2) the same issue involving the same taxpayer is pending in a case before an Appeals office, (3) the determination letter is requested by an industry, trade association, or similar group, or (4) the request involves an industry-wide problem. Under no circumstances will a District Director issue a determination letter unless it is clearly shown that the request concerns a return that has been filed or is required to be filed over which the District Director has or will have examination jurisdiction. Notwithstanding the provisions of section 7.03, a District Director will not issue a determination letter on an employment tax question if the specific question for the same taxpayer has been or is being considered by the Central Office of the Social Security Administration or the Railroad Retirement Board. Nor will District Directors issue determination letters for determination of a constructive sales price under section 4216(b) or 4218(e) of the Code. The National Office, however, will issue rulings in this area. See section 8.03.

.05 District Directors issue determination letters on the replacement of involuntarily converted property under section 1033 even though the replacement has not been made, if the taxpayer has filed an income tax return for the year in which the property was involuntarily converted.

.06 A request received by a District Director on a question concerning an income, estate, or gift tax return already filed will, in general, be considered in connection with the examination of the return. If a response is made to such a request before the return is examined, it will be considered a tentative finding in any later examination of that return.

Section 8. Discretionary Authority to Issue Rulings and Determination Letters

.01 The Service ordinarily will not issue rulings or determination letters in certain areas because of the factual nature of the problem involved, or for other reasons. Rev. Proc. 80-22, page 26, this Bulletin, provides a list of these areas. This list is not all inclusive, since the Service may decline to issue a ruling or a determination letter on other questions, whenever warranted by the facts or circumstances of a particular case. The National Office and District Directors may, when it is considered appropriate and in the best interest of the Service, issue information letters calling attention to well-established principles of tax law.

.02 A ruling or a determination letter is not issued on alternative plans of proposed transactions or on hypothetical situations.

.03 The National Office will issue rulings in all cases on prospective or future transactions if the law or regulations require a determination of the effect of a proposed transaction for tax purposes, as in a transfer under sections 1491 and 1492 of the Code. The National Office will issue rulings on all transfers described in section 367(a)(1) if the request is filed within 183 days after the beginning of the transfer. The National Office also will issue rulings in all cases on the determination of a constructive sales price under section 4216(b) or 4218(e).

Section 9. Instructions to Taxpayer

.01 The taxpayer should submit a request for a ruling or a determination letter in duplicate if (1) more than one issue is presented in the request, or if (2) a closing agreement is requested on the issue presented. It is not necessary to submit requests in duplicate under other circumstances.

.02 A request for a ruling or determination letter and any factual information submitted at a later time must be accompanied by a declaration in the following form. "Under penalties of perjury, I declare that I have examined this request, including accompanying documents, and to the best of my knowledge and belief, the facts presented in support of the requested ruling or determination letter are true, correct, and complete." The declaration may not be made by the taxpayer's representative. It must be signed by the person or persons on whose behalf the request is made. The person who must sign for a corporate taxpayer must be an officer of the corporate taxpayer who has personal knowledge of the facts. The officer must be one whose duties are not limited to obtaining a ruling or determination letter from the Service. The person signing for a trust or partnership must be a trustee or partner who has personal knowledge of the facts.

.03 If more than one issue is presented in a request for a ruling, the Service generally will issue a single ruling letter. However, the taxpayer may request a separate ruling letter on any of the issues. Unless the Service determines that it is not feasible or not in the best interest of the Service to comply with such a request, it will issue separate ruling letters.

.04 When multiple issues are involved in a single factual situation and separate letters requesting rulings are submitted, a statement to this effect must be included in each ruling letter request. The Service in issuing each ruling will state that separate rulings have been issued or requests for rulings are pending.

.05 Each request for a ruling or a determination letter must contain a complete statement of all of the facts relating to the transaction. Such facts include: names, addresses, and taxpayer identification numbers of all interested parties; the location of the District Office that has or will have jurisdiction over the return; a full and precise statement of the business reasons for the transaction; and a carefully detailed description of the transaction. (The term "all interested parties" does not mean that a list is required of all shareholders of a widely-held corporation requesting a ruling relating to a reorganization, or a list of employees where a large number may be involved.) In addition, true copies of all contracts, wills, deeds, agreements, instruments, and other documents in the transaction must be submitted with the request. Original documents, such as contracts, wills, etc., should not be submitted because they become part of the Service's file and will not be returned. All material facts in documents must be included in the taxpayer's letter requesting a ruling or in supplemental letters, and not merely incorporated by reference, and must be accompanied by an analysis of their bearing on the issue or issues, specifying the provisions that apply. Material facts furnished to the Service by telephone or orally at a conference must be promptly confirmed by letter to the Service with a declaration in the form described in section 9.02. This confirmation must be furnished within 21 calendar days to be considered part of the request. An extension of the 21-day period will be granted only if justified in writing by the taxpayer and approved by the Chief or Assistant Chief of the Technical Branch to which the case is assigned. A request for extension should be submitted before the end of the 21-day period. If unusual circumstances close to the end of the 21-day period make a written request impractical, within the 21-day period the National Office should be told of the problem and that the written request for extension will be coming soon. Such a request must be sent promptly. The taxpayer or taxpayer's representative will be told promptly and later in writing of the approval or denial of the requested extension. There is no right of appeal to a denial of an extension request. Because the purpose of these procedures is to speed up the ruling process, the taxpayer is encouraged to submit the required relevant material promptly. Therefore, requests for extensions should be justified by compelling facts and circumstances. If the Service is not made aware, as provided above, of problems in meeting the 21-day period, or if the request is not sent promptly after the National Office is notified of problems in meeting the 21-day period, the Service will process the case on the assumption that no further submission will be received.

Specific guidelines for requesting rulings under certain code sections follow: Rev. Proc. 79-4, 1979-1 C.B. 483 (guidelines for submitting requests for rulings under sections 103 and 7478 on whether interest on certain governmental obligations can be excluded from the gross income of those who own them); Rev. Proc. 68-11, 1968-1 C.B. 761 (guidelines for a ruling request under section 117); Rev. Proc. 73-35, 1973-2 C.B. 490 (guidelines concerning a request for a ruling under section 302 or 311); Rev. Proc. 73-17, 1973-2 C.B. 465 (guidelines concerning a request for a ruling under section 332, 334(b)(1) or 334(b)(2)); Rev. Proc. 75-32, 1975-2 C.B. 555 (guidelines concerning a request for a ruling under section 337); Rev. Proc. 73-36, 1973-2 C.B. 496 (guidelines concerning a request for a ruling under section 331 or 346); Rev. Proc. 73-10, 1973-1 C.B. 760 (guidelines concering a request for a ruling under section 351); Rev. Proc. 75-35, 1975-2 C.B. 561 (guidelines concerning a request for a ruling under section 355); Rev. Proc. 68-23, 1968-1 C.B. 821, Rev. Proc. 69-19, 1969-2 C.B. 301, Rev. Proc. 74-36, 1974-2 C.B. 491, Rev. Proc. 76-20, 1976-1 C.B. 560, Rev. Proc. 77-5, 1977-1 C.B. 536, and Rev. Proc. 77-17, 1977-1 C.B. 577 (guidelines concerning a request for a ruling under section 367). However, see section 7.367 of the Temporary Income Tax Regulations under the Tax Reform Act of 1976, which superseded the previously mentioned revenue procedures relating to section 367, to the extent of overlapping rules. Rev. Proc. 75-29, 1975-1 C.B. 754, Rev. Proc. 76-4, 1976-1 C.B. 543, Rev. Proc. 76-24, 1976-1 C.B. 563, Rev. Proc. 76-44, 1976-2 C.B. 668, and Rev. Proc. 77-4, 1977-1 C.B. 536 (guidelines for changes to closing agreements as a condition to issuing rulings under section 367); Rev. Proc. 78-33, 1978-2 C.B. 532 (guidelines concerning a request for a ruling under section 368(a)(1)(E)); Rev. Proc. 77-30, 1977-2 C.B. 539, and Rev. Proc. 77-37, 1977-2 C.B. 568 as amplified by Rev. Proc. 77-41, 1977-2 C.B. 574 (guidelines concering requests for rulings handled by the Reorganization Branch of the Corporation Tax Division); Rev. Proc. 72-13, 1972-1 C.B. 735, Rev. Proc. 74-17, 1974-1 C.B. 438, and Rev. Proc. 75-16, 1975-1 C.B. 676 (guidelines on classification of limited partnerships); Rev. Proc. 79-1, 1979-1 C.B. 481 (guidelines on classification of organizations as liquidating trusts); Rev. Proc. 79-63, 1979-2 C.B. 578 (factors considered and information needed for granting extensions under section 1.9100-1 of the Income Tax Regulations). If the request concerns a corporate distribution, reorganization, or similar transaction, the corporate balance sheet and profit and loss statement closest to the date of the transaction should be submitted. (If the request relates to a prospective transaction, the most recent balance sheet and profit and loss statement should be submitted.)

.06 The request must contain a statement of whether, to the best of the knowledge of the taxpayer and the taxpayer's representative(s), if any, the identical issue is in a return of the taxpayer (or of a related taxpayer within the meaning of section 267 of the Code, or a member of an affiliated group of which the taxpayer is also a member within the meaning of section 1504) and, if so, whether the issue (1) is being examined by a District Director, (2) has been examined and the statutory period of limitation on assessment or refund of tax has not expired or a closing agreement covering the issue or liability has not been entered into by a District Director, (3) is being considered by an Appeals office in connection with the taxpayer's return for an earlier period, or that issue has been considered by an Appeals office and the statutory period of limitation on assessment or refund of tax has not expired or a closing agreement covering the issue or liability has not been entered into by an Appeals office, or (4) is pending in litigation in a case involving the taxpayer or a related taxpayer. The request must contain a statement whether, to the best of the knowledge of the taxpayer and the taxpayer's representative(s), the identical or similar issue has been ruled on by the Service to the taxpayer or to the taxpayer's predecessor and, if so, when and with what results. If after the request is filed but before a ruling is issued, the taxpayer knows that an examination of the issue by a District Director has been started, the taxpayer must notify the National Office of such action. If a return is filed before a ruling is received from the National Office concerning the return, a copy of the request must be attached to the return. This alerts the District Office and avoids premature District action on the issue.

If the request deals with only one step of a larger integrated transaction, the facts, circumstances, etc., relating to the entire transaction must be submitted.

.07 As an alternative procedure for the issuing of rulings on prospective transactions, the taxpayer may submit a summary of the facts considered to be controlling the issue, in addition to the complete statement required for ruling requests by section 9.05. If the National Office agrees with the summary, the National Office will use it as the basis for the ruling. To use this procedure, the taxpayer should submit the following with the request for a ruling:

1 A complete statement of facts about the transaction, together with related documents, as required by section 9.05; and

2 A summary statement of the facts believed to be controlling in reaching the requested conclusion. When the taxpayer's statement of controlling facts is accepted, the Service will base its ruling on these facts and only this statement will ordinarily be incorporated in the ruling letter. It is emphasized, however, that:

(a) The taxpayer may elect this procedure for a "two-part" ruling request. It is not to be considered a required substitute for the regular procedures provided by this revenue procedure;

(b) The taxpayer's rights and responsibilities are the same under the "two-part" ruling request procedure as those provided in this revenue procedure;

(c) The Service reserves the right to rule on the basis of a more complete statement of facts it considers controlling and to seek more information in developing facts and restating them; and

(d) The "two-part" ruling request procedure will not apply if it is inconsistent with other procedures, such as those dealing with: requests for permission to change accounting methods or periods; applications for recognition of exempt status under section 521 of the Code; or rulings on employment tax status.

.08 If the taxpayer asserts a particular determination, an explanation of the grounds for the assertion must be furnished, together with a statement of relevant authorities in support of the taxpayer's views. Even though the taxpayer is urging no particular determination of a proposed or prospective transaction, the taxpayer's views on the tax results of the proposed action and a statement of relevant authorities to support those views must be furnished. In addition, the taxpayer is encouraged to inform the Service of, and discuss the implications of, any legislation, or tax treaties, court decisions, regulations, revenue rulings or revenue procedures that the taxpayer determines to be contrary to the position advanced. If the taxpayer determines that there are no contrary authorities, a statement to this effect would be helpful in the ruling request. Identification and discussion of contrary authorities will generally enable Service personnel to arrive more quickly at a full understanding of the issue and the relevant authorities. There is a further advantage to the taxpayer. When Service personnel receive the request, they will have before them the taxpayer's thinking on the effect and applicability of contrary authorities. Such information should, therefore, make research easier and lead to earlier action by the Service. Conversely, failure to disclose and distinguish significant contrary authorities may result in requests for additional information memoranda which will delay action on the ruling request.

.09 To assist the National Office in making the deletions, required by section 6110(c) of the Code, from the text of rulings and determination letters, to be made open to public inspection under section 6110(a), a deletions statement must accompany requests. The statement must either state that no information other than names, addresses, and identifying numbers need be deleted, or if more information is proposed to be deleted, the statement must indicate the deletions proposed by the person requesting the ruling or determination letter. If the latter alternative is chosen, the statement must be made in a separate document, and it must be accompanied by a copy of the request for a ruling or determination letter and supporting documents, on which must be shown by the use of brackets, the material that the person making the request believes should be deleted pursuant to section 6110(c). The statement of proposed deletions must indicate the statutory basis, under section 6110(c), for each proposed deletion. The statement of proposed deletions must not appear or be referred to anywhere in the request for a ruling or determination letter. If the person making the request decides to ask for additional deletions before the ruling or determination letter is issued, additional statements may be submitted. The procedures in this paragraph also apply to additional information that is submitted after the initial request.

.10 A request by or for a taxpayer must be signed by the taxpayer or the taxpayer's authorized representative. If the request is signed by a representative, or if the representative is to appear before the Service in connection with the request, the representativie must be:

1 an attorney who is a member in good standing of the bar of the highest court of any state, possession, territory, commonwealth, or the District of Columbia, and who files with the Service a written declaration that he or she is currently qualified as an attorney and is authorized to represent the taxpayer;

2 a certified public accountant who is qualified to practice in any state, possession, territory, commonwealth, or the District of Columbia, and who files with the Service a written declaration that he or she is currently qualified as a certified public accountant and is authorized to represent the taxpayer; or

3 a person, other than an attorney or certified public accountant who is currently enrolled to practice before the Service, and who files with the Service a written declaration that he or she is currently enrolled (including in the declaration either the enrollment number or the expiration date of the enrollment card) and is authorized to represent the taxpayer. (See Treasury Department Circular No. 230 (31 CFR Part 10), revised, 1966-2 C.B. 1171, amended 1967-1 C.B. 433, and 1970-2 C.B. 644, for the rules on who may practice before the Service.) These requirements do not apply to an individual representing his or her full-time employer, or to a bona fide officer, administrator, administratrix, trustee, etc., representing a corporation, trust, estate, association, or organized group. An unenrolled preparer of a return (other than an attorney or certified public accountant referred to in (1) and (2) above) who is not a full-time employee or a bona fide officer, administrator, administratrix, trustee, etc., may not represent a taxpayer in connection with a ruling or a determination letter. Any authorized representative, whether or not enrolled to practice, must also comply with the conference and practice requirements of the Statement of Procedural Rules (26 CRF 601). Form 2848, Power of Attorney, and Form 2848-D, Authorization and Declaration, may be used with regard to rulings, closing agreements, and determination letters requested under this revenue procedure.

.11 If a taxpayer has more than one representative, it is sufficient to send a copy of the ruling to any one of them. Copies of rulings will be sent to no more than two representatives, provided that they are located at different mailing addresses. If a taxpayer does not designate which representative is to receive a copy of the ruling, a copy of the ruling will be sent to the first representative named on the latest power of attorney. If the original of the ruling is to be sent to a representative, the power of attorney should contain a statement to that effect and designate the mailing address of the representative.

.12 A request for a ruling letter by the National Office should be sent to the Internal Revenue Service, Assistant Commissioner (Technical), Attention T:FP:T, 1111 Constitution Avenue, N.W., Washington, D.C. 21224. A request for a determination letter should be sent to the District Director of Internal Revenue whose office has or will have examination jurisdiction over the taxpayer's return.

.13 If a request for a ruling or determination letter does not comply with all the provisions of this revenue procedure, the request will be acknowledged, and the requirements that have not been met will be pointed out. If a request for a ruling lacks essential information, the taxpayer will be told that if the information is not received within 30 days, the request will be closed. If the information is received after the request is closed, it will be reopened and treated as a new request as of the date the essential information is received. A request for a ruling letter sent to the District Director that does not comply with the provisions of this revenue procedure will be returned by the District Director for corrections before it is sent directly to the National Office.

.14 A taxpayer who wants to have a conference on the issue or issues involved should indicate this in writing when, or soon after, filing the request.

.15 The Service processes requests for ruling and determination letters in regular order and as expeditiously as possible. Consideration of a request for processing ahead of its regular order, or by a specified time, delays the processing of other matters. Requests for processing ahead of the regular order must be made in writing, preferably in a separate letter sent with, or soon after, the request. If the request is not made in a separate letter, then the letter in which the request is made should say, at the top of the first page: "Expeditious Handling Is Requested. See page of this letter." The request should give a compelling need for such treatment. The Service cannot give assurance that any letter will be processed by the time requested. For example, the scheduling of a closing date for a transaction or a meeting of the board of directors or shareholders of a corporation, without regard for the time it may take to obtain a ruling or determination letter, will not be considered sufficient reason for handling a request ahead of its regular order. Nor will the possible effect of fluctuation in the market price of stocks on a transaction be considered sufficient reason for handling a request out of order. Requests by telegram will be treated in the same manner as requests by letter. Ruling and determination letters ordinarily are not issued by telegram. A request for expeditious handling will not cause the Communications Branch to route the case to the Ruling Branch ahead of normal processing; and a request for expeditious handling will not be considered until the underlying ruling request has been found to satisfy the section 6110 requirements.

.16 The Director, Individual Tax Division, has primary responsibility for providing basic principles for uniform interpretation and application of the federal tax laws in those areas involving: income taxes of noncorporate taxpayers (including individuals, partnerships, estates, and trusts); political organizations under section 527 (except subsection (f)); employment taxes and taxes on self-employment income; estate, gift, generation-skipping transfer, and certain excise taxes; and procedure and administration provisions of the Internal Revenue Code, except those that apply specifically to employee plans, exempt organizations, and actuarial determinations.

.17 The Director, Corporation Tax Division, has primary responsibility for providing basic principles of and rules for uniform interpretation and application of the federal tax laws in those areas involving: income taxes and earnings and profits of corporate taxpayers; changes in methods and periods of accounting, depreciation, depletion, valuation and other engineering issues; the taxable status of exchanges and distributions in connection with corporate organizations, reorganizations, and liquidations; and the exemption of farmers' cooperatives (under section 521), shipowners' protection and indemnity associations (under section 526), and certain homeowners associations (under section 528).

.18 A taxpayer may obtain information regarding the status of a request by calling the person whose name and telephone number is shown on the acknowledgement of receipt of the request.

.19 If after receiving the notice under section 6110(f)(1) of the Code of intention to disclose the ruling or determination letter (including a copy of the version proposed to be open to public inspection and notations of third-party communications under section 6110(d)), the person requesting the ruling or determination letter wants to protest the disclosure of certain information in the ruling or determination letter, that person must within 20 days send a written statement to the Internal Revenue Service, Chief, Rulings Disclosure Section, Attention T:FP:T:D, 1111 Constitution Avenue, N.W., Washington, D.C. 20224, identifying those deletions that the Service has not made and that the person requesting the ruling or determination letter believes should have been made. That person must also submit a copy of the version of the ruling or determination letter proposed to be open to public inspection on which the person indicates, by use of brackets, the deletions proposed by the taxpayer that have not been made by the National Office. Generally, the Service will not consider the deletion under this subparagraph or any material that the taxpayer did not propose to be deleted before the ruling or determination letter was issued. Within 20 days after it receives the response to the notice under section 6110(f)(1), the National Office will mail to that person its final administrative conclusion regarding the deletions to be made. The taxpayer does not have the right to a conference to resolve any disagreements concerning material to be deleted from the text of the ruling. However, these matters may be taken up at any conference that is otherwise scheduled regarding the request.

.20 After receiving the notice under section 6110(f)(1) of the Code of intention to disclose (but no later than 60 days after the notice is mailed), the person requesting a ruling or determination letter may send a request for delay of public inspection under either section 6110(g)(3) or section 6110(g)(3) and (4). The request for delay must be sent to the Internal Revenue Service, Chief, Rulings Disclosure Section, Attention T:FP:T:D, 1111 Constitution Avenue, N.W., Washington, D.C. 20224. A request for delay must contain the date on which it is expected that the underlying transaction will be completed. The request for delay under section 6110(g)(4) must contain a statement from which the Commissioner may determine that there are good reasons for the delay.

.21 A taxpayer who receives a ruling or determination letter before filing a return about any transaction that has been consummated and that is relevant to the return being filed should attach a copy of the ruling or determination letter to the return when it is filed.

.22 Protests to adverse rulings under section 367 will be processed as follows:

Under Rev. Proc. 77-5, 1977-1 C.B. 536, a taxpayer may protest an adverse, or terms and conditions, ruling letter issued on or after January 31, 1977, under section 367(a)(1) of the Code. This includes a ruling on an exchange described in section 367(b) that began before January 1, 1978, or section 1042(e) of the Tax Reform Act of 1976 (Pub. L. 94-455, 1976-3 C.B. (Vol. 1) 1, 115). The protest may not be made later than the close of the 45th day after the date of the ruling letter. A protest is considered made on the date of the postmark of a letter of protest sent to the Assistant Commissioner (Technical), or the date that the letter is hand delivered to the Service. The letter must include: (1) a copy of the ruling letter; (2) the reasons for the protest including, if applicable, (a) the grounds for asserting that none of the principal purposes for the exchange is the avoidance of federal income tax, (b) the grounds for asserting that the terms and conditions in the ruling letter pursuant to which an exchange to which section 367 applies will be considered not to be in pursuance of tax avoidance are not reasonable, and (c) the arguments supporting a protest of the validity of a ruling position published by the Service, such as a position in the guidelines announced in Rev. Proc. 68-23, 1968-1 C.B 831 (factual material not previously submitted and considered by the Service should not be included in the protest); (3) a statement of whether a conference is desired; and (4) names of persons (including authorized representatives) expected to attend the conference, if a conference is granted. The Assistant Commissioner (Technical) will establish an ad hoc advisory board to consider each protest, whether or not a conference is requested. The taxpayer will be granted one conference upon request. Whether or not such a request is made the board may ask for one of more conferences or for written submissions. The taxpayer will be notified of the time, date, and place of the conference, and of the names of the members of the board. The board will consider all materials submitted in writing by the taxpayer and oral arguments presented at the conference. The board will make its recommendation to the Assistant Commissioner (Technical) who will make a decision in the matter. Any oral arguments made at a conference by the taxpayer, which have not previously been submitted to the Service in writing, may, if desired, be submitted to the Service in writing if postmarked no later than the end of the 7th day after the day of the conference. The taxpayer will be informed of the decision of the Assistant Commissioner by certified or registered mail.

.23 For appeal procedures with regard to adverse determination letters under section 521 of the Code and revocation or modification of exemption rulings and determination letters under section 521, see Rev. Proc. 80-25.

Section 10. Handling of Ruling Requests

.01 Within 15 work days after a ruling request is received in the branch, Service personnel will contact the taxpayer to discuss informally the procedural and substantive issues in the ruling request.

.02 The following subject matters are included in the 15-day procedure:

1 Individual Income Tax Branch

(a) Partnerships and trust

(b) Code section 103 (issues under its jurisdiction)

(c) Real estate investment trusts

(d) Stock options

(e) Charitable remainder trusts

(f) Pooled income funds

2 All matters within the jurisdiction of the Corporation Tax Branch, except cases

(a) involving a request for change in accounting methods or periods,

(b) relating to the last-in, first-out method of computing inventory,

(c) concerning insurance issues on contracts with reserves based on segregated asset accounts,

(d) concerning insurance issues requiring actuarial computations.

3 All matters within the jurisdiction of the Wage, Excise, and Administrative Provisions Branch, except ruling requests from individuals for employment status submitted on Forms SS-8.

4 All matters within the jurisdiction of the Engineering and Valuation Branch (except cases involving a request for a change in accounting methods), Reorganization Branch, and Estate and Gift Tax Branch.

.03 Procedures to be followed regarding ruling requests are:

1 Within 15 days after a ruling request has been received in the branch having jurisdiction, a representative of the branch will contact the taxpayer to discuss the procedural and substantive issues in the ruling requests covered by this procedure. As to each issue coming within the jurisdiction of the branch, the branch representative will tell the taxpayer:

(a) whether the branch representative will recommend the Service rule as the taxpayer requested, rule adversely on the matter, or not rule;

(b) whether the taxpayer should submit additional information or representations to enable the Service to rule on the matter; or

(c) whether because of the nature of the transaction, or the issue presented, a tentative conclusion on the issue cannot be reached.

2 When the rulings requested involve matters within the jurisdiction of more than one branch

or more than one office in the same branch, a representative of the branch that received the original ruling request will tell the taxpayer within the initial 15 work day contract period: (1) that the rulings requested involving matters within the jurisdiction of another branch or another office in the same branch have been referred to the other branch or office for consideration; and (2) that a representative of the other branch or office will contact the taxpayer within 15 work days after receiving the referral to informally discuss the procedural and substantive issues if covered by this procedure.

3 If something less than a fully favorable ruling is indicated, the branch representative will tell the taxpayer if minor modifications of the transaction or adherence to certain published positions will warrant the issuing of a favorable ruling. In addition, the branch representative may tell the taxpayer what representations must be furnished in a document to comply with the requirements of the Service. See Rev. Proc. 75-21, 1975-1 C.B. 715, and Rev. Proc. 75-28, 1975-1 C.B. 752. However, the branch representative will not suggest precise changes that would materially alter the form of the proposed transaction. If, at the conclusion of the discussion, the branch representative determines that a meeting in the National Office would better serve the purpose of developing or exchanging information, a meeting will be offered and an early meeting date arranged. This meeting will not be the taxpayer's conference of right, as described in this revenue procedure.

4 The Service will not be bound by the informal opinion expressed by the branch representative or any other authorized Service representative under this procedure, and such an opinion cannot be relied upon as a basis for granting retroactive relief under the provisions of section 7805(b) of the Code.

5 The ruling request will then be processed under present procedures.

Section 11. Conferences in the National Office

.01 A taxpayer may request a conference only in connection with a ruling request. Normally, a conference is scheduled only when the National Office considers it to be helpful in deciding the case or when an adverse decision is indicated. If conferences are being arranged for more than one request for a ruling involving the same taxpayer, they will be scheduled so as to cause the least inconvenience to the taxpayer. If a conference has been requested, the taxpayer will be notified by telephone, if possible, of the time and place of the conference. The conference must be held within 21 calendar days after such contact has been made. Procedures for requesting an extension of the 21-day period and notifying the taxpayer or the taxpayer's representative of the Service's decision are the same as those stated in section 9.05.

.02 A taxpayer is entitled, as a matter of right, to only one conference in the National Office unless one of the circumstances discussed in section 11.06 develops. This conference normally will be held at the branch level of the appropriate division in the office of the Assistant Commissioner (Technical) and will be attended by a person who, at the time of the conference, has authority to sign the ruling letter for the branch chief in the case being discussed. If more than one subject is to be discussed at the conference, the discussion will constitute a conference on each subject. In order to promote a free and open discussion of the issues, the conference usually will be held after the branch has had an opportunity to study the case. However, at the request of the taxpayer or representative, the conference of right may be held at an earlier stage in the consideration of the case than the Service ordinarily would designate. No taxpayer has a "right" to appeal the action of a branch to a division director or to any other offiical of the Service, nor is a taxpayer entitled, as a matter of right, to a separate conference in the Chief Counsel's office on a request for a ruling.

.03 In employment tax matters, only the party entitled to the ruling is entitled to a conference.

.04 Since conference procedures are informal, no tape, stenographic, or other verbatim recording of a conference will be made.

.05 The senior Service representative present at the conference insures that the taxpayer has full opportunity to present views on all of the issues that are in question. The Service representative explains the Service's tentative decision on the substantive issues and the reasons for that decision. If the taxpayer advances prospective application under section 7805(b) of the Code, the Service representative will discuss the tentative recommendation concerning the request for relief and the reasons for the tentative recommendation. No commitment will be made as to the conclusion that the Service will finally adopt.

.06 An invitation to an additional conference will be extended if after the conference of right an adverse holding is proposed but on a new issue or on the same issue but on different grounds from those discussed at the first conference. There is no right to another conference when a proposed holding is reversed at a higher level with a result less favorable to the taxpayer if the grounds or arguments on which the reversal is based were discussed at the conference of right. The provisions of this revenue procedure limiting the number of conferences a taxpayer is entitled to will not prevent a taxpayer from attending further conferences when, in the opinion of National Office personnel, such conferences are necessary. All additional conferences of the type discussed in this paragraph are held only at the invitation of the Service.

.07 It is the responsibility of the taxpayer to furnish in writing to the National Office any additional data, lines of reasoning, precedents, etc., that are proposed by the taxpayer and discussed at the conference but that were not previously or adequately presented in writing. The taxpayer must furnish the additional information within 21 calendar days. If the additional information is not received within that time, a ruling will be issued on the basis of the information on hand or, if appropriate, no ruling will be issued. Procedures for requesting an extension of the 21-day period and notifying the taxpayer or the taxpayer's representative of the Service's decision are the same as those stated in section 9.05.

Section 12. Referral of Matters to the National Office

.01 Requests for determination letters received by District Directors that, under the provisions of this revenue procedure, may not be acted upon by a district office, will be forwarded to the National Office for reply. The district office will let the taxpayer know that this action has been taken. District Directors also refer to the National Office any request for a determination letter that in their judgment should have the attention of the National Office.

.02 If the request involves an issue on which the Service will not issue a ruling or a determination letter, the request will not be forwarded to the National Office. The district office will let the taxpayer know that the Service will not issue a ruling or a determination letter on the issue. See section 8.01 of this revenue procedure.

Section 13. Referral of Matters to District Offices

Requests for rulings received by the National Office that, under section 5 of this revenue procedure, may not be acted upon by the National Office will be forwarded to the district office that has examination jurisdiction over the taxpayer's return. The taxpayer will be notified of this action. If the request is on an issue or in an area of the type discussed in section 8.01 and it is decided not to issue a ruling, the National Office will let the taxpayer know and the request will then be forwarded to the appropriate district office for association with the related return.

Section 14. Review of Determination Letters

Determination letters issued under sections 7.01, 7.02, and 7.03 are not reviewed by the National Office before they are issued. If a taxpayer believes that a determination letter of this type is in error, the taxpayer may ask the District Director to reconsider the matter. The taxpayer may also ask the District Director to request technical advice from the National Office. In such an event the procedure in Rev. Proc. 80-21 must be followed.

Section 15. Withdrawal of Requests

A request for a ruling or determination letter may be withdrawn at any time before the signing of the letter of reply. If a request for a ruling is withdrawn, the National Office may give its views on the subject matter of the request to the District Director whose office will have examination jurisdiction over the taxpayer's return for consideration in connection with any later examination of the taxpayer's return. Even though a request is withdrawn, all correspondence and exhibits will be kept by the Service and will not be returned to the taxpayer. In appropriate cases, the Service may publish its findings in a revenue ruling or revenue procedure.

Section 16. Oral Advice to Taxpayers

.01 The Service does not issue rulings or determination letters on oral requests. National Office officials and employees ordinarily do not discuss a substantive tax issue with a taxpayer before a written request for a ruling is received, since oral opinions or advice are not binding on the Service. This does not prevent a taxpayer from asking whether the Service will rule on a particular issue. In such cases, however, the name of the taxpayer and identifying number must be disclosed. The Service also will discuss questions relating to procedural matters about submitting a request for a ruling, including the application of the provisions of section 9 to a particular case.

.02 A taxpayer may seek oral technical assistance from a Taxpayer Service Representative in a district office or service center when preparing a return or report, under other established procedures. Oral advice is advisory only and the Service is not bound to recognize it in the examination of the taxpayer's return.

Section 17. Effect of Rulings

.01 A taxpayer may not rely on a ruling issued to another taxpayer. A ruling, except to the extent incorporated in a closing agreement, may be revoked or modified at any time under appropriate circumstances. See section 4.08 for the effect of a closing agreement. If a ruling is revoked or modified, the revocation or modification applies to all years open under the statutes, unless the Commissioner or the Commissioner's delegate exercises the discretionary authority under section 7805(b) of the Code to limit the retroactive effect of the revocation or modification. The manner in which this authority generally is exercised is given later in this section. For information on rulings relating to the sale or lease of articles subject to the manufacturer's excise tax and the retailer's excise tax, see section 17.08.

.02 When determining a taxpayer's liability, the District Director must ascertain whether (1) any ruling previously issued to the taxpayer has been properly applied, (2) the representations upon which the ruling was based reflected an accurate statement of the material facts, and (3) the transaction actually was carried out substantially as proposed. If, in the course of determining the tax liability, the District Director finds that a ruling should be modified or revoked, the findings and recommendations of the District Director will be forwarded to the National Office for consideration before further action. Such a referral to the National Office will be treated as a request for technical advice and the procedures of Rev. Proc. 80-21 will be followed. Otherwise the ruling is to be applied by the district office in its determination of the taxpayer's liability.

.03 Appropriate coordination with the National Office will be undertaken if any field official having jurisdiction over a return or other matter proposes to reach a conclusion contrary to a ruling previously issued to the taxpayer.

.04 A ruling found to be in error or not in accord with the current views of the Service may be modified or revoked. Modification or revocation of a ruling may be made by (1) a notice to the taxpayer to whom the ruling was issued, (2) an enactment of legislation or ratification of a tax treaty, (3) a decision of the United States Supreme Court, (4) the issuing of temporary or final regulations, or (5) the issuing of a revenue ruling, a revenue procedure, or other statement published in the Internal Revenue Bulletin. Consistent with these provisions, if a ruling relates to a continuing action or a series of actions, the ruling will ordinarily be applied until any one of the actions described above has taken place, or until specifically withdrawn.

.05 Except in rare or unusual circumstances, the revocation or modification of a ruling will not be applied retroactively to the taxpayer for whom the ruling was issued or to a taxpayer whose tax liability was directly involved in the ruling if (1) there has been no misstatement or omission of material facts, (2) the facts developed later are not materially different from the facts on which the ruling was based, (3) there has been no change in the applicable law, (4) the ruling was originally issued with respect to a prospective or proposed transaction, and (5) the taxpayer directly involved in the ruling acted in good faith in reliance upon the ruling and the retroactive revocation would be to the taxpayer's detriment. For example, the tax liability of each shareholder is directly involved in a ruling on the reorganization of a corporation. However, the tax liability of members of an industry is not directly involved in a ruling issued to one of the members, and the holding in a revocation or modification of a ruling to one member of a industry may be retroactively applied to other members of that industry. By the same reasoning, a tax practitioner may not obtain the nonretroactive application to one client of a modification or revocation of a ruling previously issued to another client. If a ruling is revoked by letter with retroactive effect, the letter will, except in fraud cases, state the grounds upon which the revocation is being made and the reasons why the revocation is being applied retroactively.

.06 A ruling issued on a particular transaction represents a holding of the Service on that transaction only. However, the application of that ruling to the transaction will not be affected by the later issuing of regulations (either temporary or final), if the conditions specified in section 17.05 are met. If the ruling is later found to be in error or no longer in accord with the position of the Service, it will not give the taxpayer protection for a like transaction in the same or later year.

.07 However, if a ruling is issued covering a continuing action or a series of actions and it is determined that the ruling was in error, or no longer in accord with the position of the Service, the Assistant Commissioner (Technical) ordinarily will limit the retroactivity of the revocation or modification to a date that is not earlier than that on which the ruling is modified or revoked. To illustrate, if a taxpayer receives a ruling that certain payments are excludable from gross income for federal income tax purposes and it is later determined that the ruling is in error or no longer in accord with the position of the Service, the Assistant Commissioner (Technical) ordinarily will restrict the retroactive application of the revocation or modification of the ruling. If a taxpayer rendered service or provided a facility that is subject to the excise tax on services or faciliites, and in reliance on a ruling issued to the same taxpayer did not pass the tax on to the user of the service or the facility, the Assistant Commissioner (Technical) ordinarily will restrict the retroactive application of the revocation or modification of the ruling. If an employer incurred liability under the Federal Insurance Contributions Act, but in reliance on a ruling made to the same employer, neither collected the employee tax nor paid the employee and employer taxes under the Act, the Assistant Commisioner (Technical) ordinarily will restrict the retroactive application of the revocation or modification of the ruling for both the employer tax and the employee tax. In the last situation, however, the restriction of retroactive application ordinarily will be conditioned on the furnishing by the employer of wage data, as may be required by section 31.601(a)-1 of the Employment Tax Regulations. Publication of a notice of proposed rulemaking will not affect the application of any ruling issued under the procedures stated in this revenue procedure.

.08 A ruling holding that the sale or lease of a particular article is subject to the manufacturer's excise tax or the retailer's excise tax may not retroactively revoke or modify an earlier ruling holding that the sale or lease of such an article was not taxable, if the taxpayer to whom the ruling was issued, in reliance upon the earlier ruling, parted with possession or ownership of the article without passing the tax on to the customer. Section 1108(b), Revenue Act of 1926.

.09 For rulings involving completed transactions, other than those described in sections 17.07 and 17.08, taxpayers will not be given the protection against retroactive revocation provided in section 17.05, since they will not have entered into the transactions in reliance on the ruling.

Section 18. Effect of Determination Letters

A determination letter issued by a District Director has the same effect as a ruling issued to a taxpayer under section 17 of this revenue procedure. However, if the District Director is of the opinion that a conclusion contrary to that expressed in the determination letter is indicated, the matter need not be referred to the National Office. A District Director may not limit the modification or revocation of a determination letter but may refer the matter to the National Office for the possible exercise by the Commissioner or the Commissioner's delegate of the authority to limit the modification or revocation.

Section 19. Effect of Information Letters

An information letter issued by the National Office or by a District Director is advisory only and the provisions of section 17 do not apply.

Section 20. Procedure for Requesting Application of Section 7805(b) in the Case of Rulings and Determination Letters

.01 Pursuant to section 7805(b) of the Code, it is within the discretion of the Commissioner or the Commissioner's delegate to prescribe the extent, if any, to which any ruling (including determination letters) will be applied without retroactive effect.

A taxpayer to whom a ruling or determination letter has been issued may request that the Assistant Commissioner (Technical), the Commissioner's delegate, exercise the discretionary authority under section 7805(b) of the Code to limit the retroactive effect of any subsequent revocation or modification of the ruling or determination letter.

.02 In the case of a ruling, a request to limit the retroactive effect of the revocation or modification of a ruling must be in the form of, and meet the requirements for a ruling request generally. These requirements are set forth in section 9 of this revenue procedure. Specifically, the request must state that it is being made pursuant to section 7805(b), contain a statement of the relief sought and an explanation of the reasons and arguments in support of the relief requested, and also be accompanied by any documents bearing on the request. The explanation in support of the application of section 7805(b) should include a discussion of the five items enumerated in section 17.05 of this revenue procedure as they relate to the taxpayer's particular situation.

A request for the application of section 7805(b) of the Code may take the form of a separate request for ruling when, for example, a revenue ruling has the effect of modifying or revoking a ruling previously issued to the taxpayer or when the Service notifies the taxpayer of a change in position that will have the effect of revoking or modifying such a ruling. However, when such notice is given by the District Director during the course of an examination of the taxpayer's return, or during consideration by the Chief, Appeals Office, a request to limit the retroactive effect of the modification or revocation of a ruling must be made in the form of a request for technical advice. See section 12.03 of Rev. Proc. 80-21. When germane to a pending ruling request, a request for the application of section 7805(b) may be made as part of the request, either initially or at any time before the ruling is issued. When a ruling that concerns a continuing transaction is modified or revoked by, for example, a subsequent revenue ruling, a request to limit the retroactive effect of the modification or revocation of the ruling must be made before a return is examined that contains the transaction that is the subject of the request for ruling.

.03 When a request for the application of section 7805(b) of the Code is made in a separate ruling request, the taxpayer has the right to a conference in the National Office in accordance with the provisions of section 11 of this revenue procedure. If the request is made initially as part of a pending ruling request or is made before the conference of right is held on the substantive issues, the section 7805(b) issue will be discussed at the taxpayer's one conference of right. (See section 11.05 of this revenue procedure.) If the request for the application of 7805(b) is made as part of a pending ruling request after a conference has been held on the substantive issue, and the Service determines that there is justification for having delayed the request, then the taxpayer will have the right to one conference of right concerning the application of section 7805(b) with the conference limited to discussion of this issue.

.04 In the case of a determination letter that the District Director proposes to modify or revoke, a request to limit the modification or revocation of the determination letter must be made by requesting the District Director who issued the determination letter to seek technical advice from the National Office, since a District Director has not been delegated authority under section 7805(b) of the Code to limit the modification or revocation of a determination letter. See section 12.03 of Rev. Proc. 80-21. The taxpayer's request must state that it is being made pursuant to section 7805(b), contain a statement of the relief sought and an explanation of the reasons and arguments in support of the relief requested, and also be accompanied by any documents bearing on the request. The explanation in support of the application of section 7805(b) should include a discussion of the five items enumerated in section 17.05 of this revenue procedure as they relate to the taxpayer's particular situation.

.05 When technical advice is requested with respect to the application of section 7805(b) of the Code under the circumstances set forth in .04 above, the taxpayer has a right to a conference in the National Office to the same extent as does any taxpayer who is the subject of a technical advice request. See section 8 of Rev. Proc. 80-21.

Section 21. Effect on Other Documents

Rev. Proc. 79-45 is superseded.

Appendix G

RULING REQUEST AND RULING

See discussion of ruling requests beginning at page 21, and of private annuities beginning *at page 111.*

261

Appendix G-1 Sample Request for IRS Ruling

May 2, 19____

Commissioner of Internal Revenue
Internal Revenue Building
Washington, D.C. 20004

Attention: Assistant Commissioner (Technical)
              —Income Tax Division

Re: Jones Corporation—Stock Redemption

Dear Sir:

Your ruling is respectfully requested as to the Federal income tax consequences of the proposed redemption of the stock of Mr. and Mrs. M.A. Jones, Sr. in Jones Corporation pursuant to the provisions of the Internal Revenue Code of 1954. This request is made on behalf of Jones Corporation and Mr. and Mrs. M.A. Jones, Sr. The identical issues involved in this Request for Ruling are not pending before any field office of the Internal Revenue Service.

See discussion in text at page 111, dealing with the use of private annuities.

BACKGROUND FACTS CONCERNING PARTIES

A. Business:

Jones Corporation ("Corporation") is a Maryland Corporation licensed as a motor common carrier by the Interstate Commerce Commission and by various other regulatory authorities. The Corporation's employer identification number is 58-1111111, and its Federal income tax return is filed with the District Director of Internal Revenue, Baltimore, Maryland. The Corporation has its principal office in the state of Maryland and serves the states of Maryland, Delaware, Pennsylvania, and New Jersey. Mr. M.A. Jones, Sr. is chairman of the board of directors of the Corporation,

It is important to conform any ruling request with the precise requirements then in effect by the Internal Revenue Service. Here the precise name of the corporation and its business is designated as well as its Federal tax number.

263

was the founder of the Corporation, and has been active in managing the affairs of the Corporation since its incorporation in 1938. True copies of the Articles of Incorporation and By-Laws of the Corporation are attached as Exhibit A hereto.

B. Capital Structure:

The present capital structure and its history has been specified.

The total authorized and outstanding capital stock of the Corporation consists of 18,000 shares of common stock at no par value and 152 shares of preferred stock at $250 par value, which is owned as follows:

Common Stock	Shares
M.A. Jones, Sr.	11,080
Mrs. M.A. Jones, Sr.	1,860
M.A. Jones, Jr.	1,265
Sam Jones	1,265
Bill Jones	1,265
Susan Jones Smith	1,265
	18,000

Preferred Stock	Shares
Ownership per Exhibit B	152

Mr. M.A. Jones, Sr. (SS#235-45-4476, filing Federal income tax returns with District Director, Baltimore, Maryland) acquired his shares in the Corporation by original issue from the Corporation in the year 1938. Mr. Jones' age is 66 and his life expectancy is 14.4 years in accordance with Table I, Regulation § 1.72-9. Mrs. Jones' age is 67 years and her life expectancy is 16.9 years. Mrs. M.A. Jones, Sr. (SS#432-55-1281, filing Federal income tax returns with District Director, Baltimore, Maryland) acquired her shares by gifts over the years from Mr. Jones, Sr. as follows:

1500 shares	1971
100 shares	1970
110 shares	1969
150 shares	1965

The other common stock shareholders in the Corporation acquired their shares as follows:

Name and Age	Dates Acquired	# of Shares	Manner of Acquisition	Relationship to Mr. and Mrs. Jones, Sr.
M.A. Jones, Jr. (32)	1955	400	gift	son
Jim Jones (31)	1962	255	gift	son
Bill Jones (29	1963	250	gift	son
Susan Jones Smith (27)	1965	150	gift	daughter
	1969	110	gift	
	1970	100	gift	
		1,265		

As it will be seen by the preceding tables, holders of common stock in the Corporation have acquired their shares through gifts from M.A. Jones, Sr. as part of a regular giving program of M.A. Jones, Sr. based upon the love and affection of M.A. Jones, Sr. for his wife and children. At the time of the gifts, M.A. Jones, Sr. had no principal purpose of avoiding Federal income taxes. In addition to the gifts indicated by the foregoing table, Mr. Jones contemplates a gift between the date of this request and the date of the consummation of the transaction as to which request for ruling is made in the amount of 562 shares to his son, the president of the Corporation, M.A. Jones, Jr. The reasons for the contemplated gift to Mr. Jones, Jr. is to assure the Corporation that the principal manager of the Corporation, its president, M.A. Jones, Jr., shall have the ownership of a greater portion of the relative equity of the Corporation than that owned by Mr. Jones, Jr.'s brothers and sister. Mr. Jones, Jr. has for many years been a principal executive officer of the Corporation.

Certain real property and personal property leased to the corporation which will continue after the annuity was designated so that an express ruling could be obtained to the effect that such payments on the lease after the time of the annuity closing would not jeopardize the annuity transaction.

Mr. Jones, Sr., commencing at his 65th birthday, at the present time, and until August 31, 19____, receives a monthly benefit from the Jones Corporation, Retirement Plan (and the Trust thereunder) in the amount of $963,000. After August 31, 19____, and for the remainder of his life, he shall receive a benefit of $120.00 per month. A copy of the most recent Determination Letter regarding the Plan and Trust is attached as Exhibit C. Mr. Jones, Sr., is chairman of the Retirement Committee of the Plan. He will resign all posts under the Plan or Trust upon consummation of the transaction. Mr. Jones, Sr.'s rights under such Plan and Trust will continue. Mr. Jones, Sr. also is a party to a deferred compensation agreement and beneficiary of insurance benefits, a copy of which Plan and description of insurance benefits is attached as Exhibit D. Because Mr. Jones, Sr. will not be able to render consulting services to the Corporation after the proposed redemption date, said Deferred Compensation Agreement shall terminate at the time of the proposed redemption. Normal retired employee rights to insurance coverage as shown in Exhibit D (life insurance of $13,000 and $2,500 lifetime medical benefits) shall continue after the time of the proposed redemption.

Mr. Jones, Sr. and Mrs. Jones presently lease certain real or personal property to the Corporation under lease agreements. Mr. and Mrs. M.A. Jones, Sr. also own 171 shares (3.6 percent) each of the common stock of Maryland Realty and Transportation Company, a Maryland corporation ("MRTC"). The Corporation owns 1,200 shares or approximately 25.5 percent. Unrelated parties (some of whom are employees of the Corporation) own approximately 63.6 percent of the shares of MRTC. MRTC leases terminal facilities to the Corporation. Copies of all the leases between the Corporation and Mr. or Mrs. M.A. Jones, Sr. or MRTC are attached as Exhibit E. The Corporation may exercise options stated in the contracts to renew any or all of such leases, but no new leases will be entered into involving the Corporation and Mr. or Mrs. Jones, Sr. At the time of the proposed transaction, Mr. and Mrs. M.A. Jones, Sr. will resign any and all offices and directorships in MRTC, and the Corporation will purchase all shares of MRTC

Similarly, minority interests were to be retained in corporations which in turn leased to Jones Corporation.

owned by Mr. or Mrs. M.A. Jones, Sr. at the book value of such shares ($34.75 per share) or a total of approximately $6,000 each.

Mr. and Mrs. M.A. Jones, Sr. own and plan to continue to own 20 shares (16⅔ percent) each of the common stock of Road Leasing Corp., a Maryland corporation, which leases personal property to the Corporation. Mr. M.A. Jones, Sr. owns and plans to continue to own 60 shares (22.2 percent) of the common stock of High Lift, Inc., a Maryland corporation which leases personal property to the Corporation. Most of the remaining shares of said two corporations are held by children of Mr. and Mrs. M.A. Jones, Sr.

The Corporation is on a calendar year fiscal year, and attached hereto as Exhibit F are true copies of the balance sheets and a statement of income and retained earnings for the years 1969 through 1974.

The entire proposed transaction is set out in some detail. It is very important to set out all aspects of the transactions since the facts given control the validity and usefulness of the ruling obtained. It is possible to use a so-called "two-part" ruling request in which the facts which will actually be picked up in the ruling itself are specified. This is a matter of choice involving a judgment tax counsel requesting the ruling.

PROPOSED TRANSACTION

Mr. M.A. Jones, Sr. presently is chairman of the board of directors of the Corporation and participates actively in the management of the Corporation. Mr. Jones, Sr. has indicated for some time that he would like to retire from the active management of the Corporation, and because of the increasingly competitive situation and growth of the Corporation, the board of directors of the Corporation has determined that it would be in the best interest of the Corporation to redeem 100 percent of the common stock of both Mr. and Mrs. M.A. Jones, Sr. as follows:

1. 2,437 shares of the common stock of M.A. Jones, Sr. would be redeemed at the closing for $400,000 in cash; and
2. The balance of the common stock of M.A. Jones, Sr., 8,081 shares, would be redeemed for an annuity payable during the lifetime of M.A. Jones, Sr. as hereinafter described; and
3. All of the shares of Mrs. M.A. Jones, Sr., 1,860 shares of common stock, would be redeemed for the annuity payable to Mrs. Jones hereinafter described.

It has been agreed by the Corporation and the redeeming shareholders that, contingent upon the receipt of a favorable ruling from the Commissioner of Internal Revenue upon the questions herein raised, and contingent upon the receipt of a favorable determination or other indication from the Interstate Commerce Commission and the Maryland Public Service Commission, the Corporation will effectuate proposed redemption from the redeeming shareholders for the consideration above set forth. A copy of the agreements relating to the annuity redemption are attached hereto as Exhibits G and H. No contractual obligation of any kind relating to the purchase of the shares of common stock in the Corporation held by either Mr. and Mrs. M.A. Jones, Sr. exists between Mr. or Mrs. M.A. Jones, Sr. and any of the parties who will remain as shareholders of the Corporation after the redemption. Neither Mr. nor

Mrs. M.A. Jones, Sr., nor the surviving shareholders are, or will immediately subsequent to the proposed redemptions be, beneficiaries together of any income or estate trusts owning any shares of the Corporation.

Immediately upon such redemptions, both Mr. and Mrs. Jones, Sr. will resign all offices and directorships in the Corporation and will thereafter cease to be employees, officers, or directors of the Corporation, and will have no further interest in the Corporation, (although the lease agreements shown in Exhibit E will continue).

It is presently contemplated that the Corporation will borrow any part of the amount payable under the annuity in order to effectuate the annuity proposed. However, in the event borrowing will become necessary, no part of the Corporation's obligation being assumed will be personally endorsed, guaranteed, or secured in any way by any of the shareholders of the Corporation.

All annuity payments will be in no way related to the earnings of either the redeemed shares or earnings of the Corporation, and will be in no way chargeable to the property transferred. The obligations to be paid under the annuity and other redemption agreement are and will be fixed and certain.

The corporation has never issued any annuity or similar contract at any time, and at the present time, the Corporation contemplates no issuance in the future of any annuity agreement other than the two which are the subject of this Request for Ruling.

As shown more particularly in Exhibits G and H, annuities to be issued to Mr. and Mrs. M.A. Jones, Sr. and the additional amount to be paid to Mr. Jones, Sr., will be given in return for the absolute redemption of the stock in the Corporation owned by either Mr. or Mrs. M.A. Jones, Sr., and the Corporation shall have an absolute obligation to make the payments in an amount certain without regard to the income from the property transferred, and without regard to any reserved or set aside property whatsoever.

The officers and directors of the Corporation are as follows:

M.A. Jones, Sr.	Chairman of the Board, Director
M.A. Jones, Jr.	President, Director Secretary-Treasurer, Director
Bill Jones	Vice President-Customer Service, Director
Tom Davis	Vice President-Traffic, Director
Harry Brown	Vice President
Susan Jones Smith	Director
Sam Jones	Director

As it will be seen, the burden of management of the Corporation after Mr. Jones, Sr.'s retirement will fall upon the president, M.A. Jones, Jr. and others.

BUSINESS REASONS

Just as there must be a business purpose in a corporate reorganization (see page 6), *there must always be a corporate as well as tax purpose behind any transaction as to which a tax ruling is to obtain. A mere transaction to save taxes will not be recognized.*

The business reasons for the proposed redemptions are to allow a majority of the common equity ownership of the Corporation to be held by the persons who will be the active managers of the Corporation upon Mr. M.A. Jones, Sr.'s retirement. The board of directors of the Corporation and the officers of the Corporation believe that it is definitely in the best interest of the Corporation to have a substantial identity between the voting common stock majority ownership and the active key executive employees of the Corporation. Since its formation, this has been the case with the Corporation, and the board of directors and officers of the Corporation believe that a great deal of the success of the Corporation can be attributed to this fact. Mr. M.A. Jones, Sr. has definitely decided to retire in the near future from an active management role in the Corporation. The proposed completion redemption of Mr. and Mrs. Jones' shares will enable the Corporation to maintain a majority common equity ownership in its active managers and provide an inducement to the redeeming shareholders to surrender their shares of stock in the Corporation.

The motor common carrier or trucking business is a highly competitive and high risk business which is tied to such variable factors as the general economy, the local economies in the states of Maryland, Delaware, Pennsylvania, and New Jersey, the cost of equipment, the degree of competition from other common carriers and from competing forms of transportation, the costs of borrowed funds, labor, and other overhead costs. The Corporation hopes in the future to enter into a period of expansion which could involve additional risks which might be acceptable to the retired holder of a majority of the voting shares of stock in the Corporation.

REQUEST FOR RULING

The precise rulings of tax law requested must be specified.

Based on the foregoing, it is respectfully requested that the Commissioner rule as follows:

1. Provided both Mr. and Mrs. M.A. Jones, Sr. file the agreement described in § 302(c)(2)(A)(iii) of the Internal Revenue Code in accordance with § 1.302-4(a) of the Income Tax Regulations, the redemption by Corporation of all of the shares of stock incorporation, owned by either M.A. Jones, Sr. of Mrs. M.A. Jones, Sr. will be a complete termination of both of their interests, in each instance, within the meaning of § 302(b)(3) of the Internal Revenue Code of 1954.
2. For Federal income tax purposes, the private annuity transaction that both Mr. M.A. Jones, Sr. (with respect to 8,081 shares) and Mrs. M.A. Jones, Sr. (with respect to 1,860 shares) will enter into will be taxes in the manner prescribed in Revenue Ruling 69-74 (69-1 C.B. 43).
3. No income or loss will be recognized to the remaining share-

holders of Corporation as a result of the proposed transactions described above.

PROCEDURAL STATEMENTS

These statements are required by the previous procedures issued by the Internal Revenue Service. The attorney or accountant or both requesting the ruling should sign the ruling request.

In accordance with the provisions of Revenue Procedure 80-20, there is attached hereto a memorandum in support of a favorable determination with respect to each of the aforesaid questions.

If there is any further information which you require, we shall be pleased to comply. If information is desired, please telephone George C. Johnson at (404) 233-8000, collect. In the event you contemplate issuance of a ruling contrary to our request, an oral hearing at the National Office prior to such issuance is respectfully requested.

Enclosed is a requisite Authorization designating George C. Johnson as attorney and William E. Harkness as C.P.A. to represent each of the representing parties before the Internal Revenue Service in connection with this Request for Ruling. Please send the original of the Ruling letter to George C. Johnson, Esq.

Respectfully submitted,

[Attorney and C.P.A. signatures]

[EXCERPT FROM IRS RULING]

This is an excerpt from the actual ruling obtained in response to the preceding ruling request. The facts were first recited by the National Office of the Internal Revenue Service in substantially the same form as set forth in the request.

[Facts First Recited]

Upon surrender of their stock, the redeeming shareholders will immediately resign as directors, officers, and employees of Corporation, and will file the agreements required by section 302(c)(2)(A)(iii). There is no obligation of any kind on the part of any shareholder to purchase the redeeming shareholders' stock, and no shareholder will be personally liable, directly or as a guarantor, indemnitor, or otherwise, for the obligations of Corporation to the redeeming shareholders.

This provision is necessary in order to assure that the redeemed shareholders will not have a prohibited interest in the corporation after the annuity redemption. See page 21 of the text.

It is represented that husband and wife have no options to acquire any shares of Corporation's stock. It is not presently contemplated that Corporation will borrow any money specifically to effectuate the proposed redemption, but in the event such borrowing becomes necessary, no part of Corporation's obligation thereby assumed will be personally endorsed, guaranteed, or secured by the redeeming shareholders or any other shareholder of Corporation.

Corporation presently provides husband with a pension for life and other normal retired employee's benefits, which commenced upon his 65th birthday. Husband and wife are currently parties to agreements which lease real and personal property to Corporation, but no new lease agreements will be entered into and some existing leases will be prematurely terminated by arm's length negotiation at fair market value. The pension, other benefits, and the leases are entirely separate from and unrelated to the proposed stock redemption and are not calculated in any manner with respect to future earnings and profits of Corporation.

Based solely on the facts presented, it is held as follows:

This paragraph deals with the express disclosed pensions and leases which will continue after the redemption.

1. Provided that husband and wife each files the agreement described in section 302(c)(2)(A)(iii) of the Internal Revenue Code of 1954 in accordance with section 1.302-4 (a) of the Income Tax Regulations, the redemption by Corporation of all its stock held by husband and wife, as described above, will, in each instance, constitute a complete termination of interest within the meaning of section 302(b)(3). The redemption will be treated as a distribution in full payment in exchange for the stock redeemed as provided in section 302(a). However, this ruling is subject to the conditions stated in sections 302(c)(2)(A)(i) and 302(c)(2)(A)(ii).

Note how carefully circumscribed is the ruling obtained. In substance, this paragraph will assure the taxpayers that they will not receive dividend treatment on redemptions.

2. For Federal income tax purposes, the redemption of each redeeming shareholder's shares of stock, which will be exchanged for a private annuity contract, as described above, will, in each instance, be considered a sale of his stock for an annuity contract, the proceeds of which will be taxed in accordance with the rules prescribed in section 72 of the Code and Revenue Ruling 69-74, Cumulative Bulletin 1969-1, 43.

This paragraph confirms the tax treatment of the annuity payments.

3. As provided by section 1001, gain or loss will be realized by husband measured by the difference between the cash received and the adjusted basis of the 2,437 shares of stock surrendered as determined under section 1011. Provided section 341 (relating to collapsible corporations) is not applicable and the stock is a capital asset in the hands of husband, the gain, if any, will be recognized and will constitute capital gain subject to the provisions and limitations of Subchapter P of Chapter 1. Pursuant to the provisions of section 267, no loss will be allowable to husband.

This paragraph, with many provisos assures capital gain treatment.

4. The remaining shareholders of Corporation will not receive a constructive dividend upon the redemption of the redeeming shareholder's stock, as described above. (See Revenue Ruling 58-614, Cumulative Bulletin 1958-2, 920.)

This paragraph provides that the remaining shareholders will not be treated as having received a dividend. Such a paragraph is very important where there is a kinship between the remaining shareholders and redeemed shareholders.

The above rulings are effective to the extent that the amounts distributed by Corporation in redemption of its stock represent the fair market value of the stock surrendered. No opinion is expressed as to the tax treatment of the amount, if any, by which the distribution in redemption of the stock exceeds, or is less than, the fair market value of the stock redeemed. A determination of the fair market value of the stock is specifically reserved until the Federal income tax returns of the taxpayers involved have been filed for the taxable year in which the transaction occurs.

Note that no comfort is obtained as to the valuation used for the stock itself. This is the reason that careful practitioners like to have an independent appraisal of the shares in hand.

No opinion is expressed as to the tax treatment of the transaction under the provisions of any of the other sections of the Code and Regulations which may also be applicable thereto or to the tax

The ruling leaves open the possibility that the Internal Revenue Service could contest the transaction on the basis of some gift tax, depending upon

the fair market value of the shares redeemed.

It is important to attach a copy of the letter to the taxpayer's return, and is required by the Internal Revenue Service to alert the agent reviewing the return as to the opinion of the National Office on the transaction.

treatment of any conditions existing at the time of, or effects resulting from the transactions which are not specifically covered by the above rulings.

A copy of this letter should be attached to the Federal income tax returns of the taxpayers involved for the taxable year in which the transaction covered by this ruling is consummated.

Sincerely yours,

Chief, Reorganization Branch

Appendix G-2

Excerpt from IRS Letter Ruling allowing proposed merger; an "A" reorganization
[IRS Letter Ruling 8006060, November 16, 1979]

This is in reply to a letter dated July 19, 1979, in which a ruling was requested about the Federal income tax consequences of a proposed transaction. Additional information was received in a letter dated August 28, 1979. The information submitted for consideration is substantially as summarized below.

Corp. X is a corporation engaged in business activities in the areas of transportation and natural resources. As of December 31, 1978, Corp. X had outstanding 12,506,971 shares of no par value common stock, 2,535,306 shares of $10 par value preferred stock, and 2,344,850 shares of no par value convertible preferred stock, all of which were widely held by approximately 59,000 shareholders and actively traded.

Corp. Y is a corporation engaged primarily in the operation of an integrated rail transportation system. As if December 31, 1978. Corp. Y had outstanding 2,635,465 shares of no par value common stock which were held by approximately 8,000 shareholders and actively traded. A, the largest shareholder of Corp. Y, beneficially owned approximately 10 percent of the outstanding Corp. Y stock and B beneficially owned approximately 7 percent.

The managements of Corp. X and Corp. Y have concluded that the best interests of both corporations and their respective shareholders would be served by the merger of Corp. X and Corp. Y, since the proposed merger would unite geographically complementary systems and achieve substantial operating efficiencies and economies.

Accordingly, Corp. X and Corp. Y have entered into an agreement of merger and plan of reorganization (the "Plan") which has been approved by the shareholders of both corporations. Pursuant to the Plan, Corp. Y will be merged with and into Corp. X in accordance with the laws of their respective states of incorporation and the Act. On the effective date of the proposed merger, the separate existence of Corp. Y will cease and all its assets and liabilities will become assets and liabilities of Corp. X by operation of law.

Each share of Corp. Y common stock outstanding on the effective date of the proposed merger will be automatically converted into (i) 95/100 of a share of Corp. X common stock and (ii) ½ of a share of newly created no par value nonvoting Corp. X preferred stock. The number of shares of Corp. X common and preferred stock to be issued in the proposed merger is subject to adjustment prior to the effective date of the merger to prevent dilution. Dissenting shareholders of Corp. Y will not have any appraisal rights.

The new Corp. X preferred stock will bear cumulative dividends at the rate of $2.125 per share per year payable quarterly. It will not be redeemable for five years after issuance. Thereafter it will be redeemable in whole or in part only at the option of Corp. X at a price beginning at $26.40 per share and declining at specific annual amounts to $25 per share 15 years after issuance, plus accrued and unpaid dividends. The new Corp. X preferred stock will be subject to a mandatory sinking fund designed to retire all of such stock between the fifth and twentieth year after issuance at a price of $25 per share plus accrued and unpaid dividends. In the event of an involuntary liquidation of Corp. X, the holders of the new preferred stock will be entitled to receive $25 per share plus accrued and unpaid dividends. In the event of a voluntary liquidation, the holders of the new preferred stock will be entitled to receive a sum per share beginning at $27.125 in the first year and declining by specified

(1) Provided that the proposed merger of Corp. Y with and into Corp. X qualifies as a statutory merger under applicable state law, the merger will constitute a reorganization within the meaning of section 368(a)(1)(A) of the Internal Revenue Code of 1954. Corp. X and Corp. Y will each be "a party to a reorganization" within the meaning of section 368(b).

(2) No gain or loss will be recognized to Corp. Y on the transfer of its assets to Corp. X in exchange for shares of Corp. X common and preferred stock and the assumption by Corp. X of the liabilities of Corp. Y (sections 357(a) and 361(a)).

(3) No gain or loss will be recognized to Corp. X on the receipt of the assets of Corp. Y in exchange for Corp. X common and preferred stock (section 1032(a)).

(4) The basis of the assets of Corp. Y to be received by Corp. X will be the same as the basis of those assets in the hands of Corp. Y immediately prior to the exchange (section 362(b)).

(5) The holding period of the assets of Corp. Y to be received by Corp. X will include the holding period of those assets in the hands of Corp. Y immediately prior to the exchange (section 1223(2)).

(6) No gain or loss will be recognized to the Corp. Y shareholders on the receipt of Corp. X common and preferred stock (including fractional share interests to which they may be entitled) in exchange for their Corp. Y stock (section 354(a)(1)).

(7) The basis of the Corp. X common and preferred stock (including fractional share interests to which they may be entitled) to be received by the Corp. Y shareholders will be the same as the basis of the Corp. Y common stock surrendered in exchange therefor (section 358(a)), allocated between the shares of Corp. X common and preferred received according to their respective fair market values on the date of the exchange (section 1.358-2(a)(2) of the Income Tax Regulations).

(8) The holding period of the Corp. X common and preferred stock (including fractional share interests to which they may be entitled) to be received by the Corp. Y shareholders will include the holding period of the Corp. Y common stock surrendered in exchange therefor, provided the Corp. Y common stock was held as a capital asset on the date of the exchange (section 1223(1)).

(9) The payments of cash in lieu of fractional share interests in Corp. X will be treated for Federal income tax purposes as if the fractional shares were distributed as part of the exchange and then were redeemed by Corp X. These cash payments will be treated as having been received as distributions in full payment in exchange for the stock redeemed as provided in section 302(a) (See Rev. Proc. 77-41, 1977-2 C. B. 574).

(10) To the extent the Corp. X preferred stock to be received in exchange for Corp. Y common stock constitutes "section 306 stock" within the meaning of section 306(c), the provisions of section 306(a)(1) and (2) will not apply to a disposition or redemption of such "section 306 stock" since the distribution and disposition or redemption will not be in pursuance of a plan having as one of its principal purposes the avoidance of Federal income tax within the meaning of section 306(b)(4).

(11) As provided by section 381(c)(2) of the Code and section 1.381(c)(2)-1 of the regulations, Corp. X will succeed to and take into account the earnings and profits, or deficit in earnings and profits, of Corp. Y as of the date or dates of transfer. Any deficit in earnings and profits of either Corp. X or Corp. Y will be used only to offset earnings and profits accumulated after the date or dates of transfer.

No opinion was requested and none is expressed about the application of section 305(b) and (c) to the difference, if any, between the issue price and the redemption price of the Corp. X preferred stock.

No opinion is expressed about the tax treatment of the transaction under other provisions of the Code and regulations or about the tax treatment of any conditions existing at the time of, or effects resulting from, the transaction that are not specifically covered by the above rulings.

It is important that a copy of this letter be attached to the Federal income tax returns of the taxpayers involved for the taxable year in which the transaction covered by this ruling letter is consummated.

Pursuant to the power of attorney on file in this office, a copy of this letter has been sent to your authorized representative.

annual amounts to $25 in the fifteenth year after issuance, plus accrued and unpaid dividends. With respect to Corp. X stock outstanding on December 31, 1978, as to dividends and distributions in liquidation, the new preferred stock will rank prior to Corp. X common stock and equally with the $10 par value preferred stock and the no par value convertible preferred stock. The holders of the new preferred stock will not have voting rights, except with respect to certain class votes and the right to elect two directors of Corp. X in the event of default in payment of the equivalent of six quarterly dividends. The new preferred stock will not be convertible into Corp. X common stock.

Fractional shares of Corp. X common and preferred stock will not be issued. In lieu thereof, Corp. X will pay cash to the shareholders of Corp. Y. The amount of cash that may be paid to any one Corp. Y shareholder cannot exceed the sum of (i) the fraction of a share of Corp. X common stock which the shareholder would otherwise be entitled to receive multiplied by the closing market price of the Corp. X common stock on the trading day immediately preceding the effective date of the merger, and (ii) $25 multiplied by the fraction of a share of Corp. X preferred stock to which such shareholder would otherwise be entitled.

Under the Plan, the terms and provisions of Corp. Y's nonqualified stock option plan will continue in full force and effect and govern all options granted thereunder, except that any options outstanding as of the effective date of the proposed merger will become options to purchase Corp. X common and preferred stock. Each optionee will be entitled to purchase at the same option price the same number of full shares of Corp. X common and preferred stock as such optionee would have been entitled to receive had he exercised his option in full immediately prior to the effective date of the proposed merger.

The following representations have been made in connection with the proposed transaction described above:

(a) The managements of Corp. X and Corp. Y believe that the fair market value of the Corp. Y common stock to be surrendered in exchange for Corp. X common and preferred stock will, at the effective date of the proposed merger, be approximately equal to the fair market value of such Corp. X common and preferred stock.

(b) Following the proposed merger, Corp. X will continue the existing business of Corp. Y and has no intention of selling or otherwise disposing of any of Corp. Y's properties which it will receive in the merger, except in the ordinary course of business.

(c) The liabilities of Corp. Y that Corp. X will assume in the proposed merger (other than liabilities arising out of the merger) will have arisen in the normal operation of Corp. Y's business and will have been associated with the assets to be acquired by Corp. X.

(d) The adjusted basis and fair market value of the assets of Corp. Y immediately prior to the proposed merger will exceed the sum of the amount of the liabilities assumed by Corp. X as a result of the merger plus the amount of any other liabilities to which such assets may be subject.

(e) To the best of the knowledge of the managements of Corp. X and Corp. Y, there is no prearranged plan or intention on the part of the Corp. Y shareholders to dispose in the foreseeable future of more than fifty percent in value of the Corp. X common and preferred stock to be received by them, in the aggregate, in the proposed merger.

(f) There will be no redemption of the Corp. X preferred stock, by tender or otherwise, within five years after the effective date of the proposed merger.

(g) There is no intercorporate debt existing between Corp. Y and Corp. X which was acquired or will be settled at a discount as a result of the proposed merger.

(h) After the merger, one or more employees of Corp. Y (some of whom are shareholders of Corp. Y) will become employees of Corp. X. The total salary or other compensation payable by Corp. X to each such individual will be commensurate with the duties which he will agree to perform. In the case of any such individual who is a shareholder of Corp. Y, no part of such salary or other compensation will represent consideration for his Corp. Y common stock.

(i) No two corporate parties to the Plan are investment companies within the meaning of section 368(a)(2)(F) of the Internal Revenue Code of 1954.

(j) Corp. X and Corp. Y and their respective shareholders will each pay their own expenses incurred in connection with the proposed merger, whether or not it is consummated.

(k) The cash payment by Corp. X in lieu of fractional shares of Corp. X common and preferred stock is not separately bargained for consideration and represents merely a mechanical rounding off of fractions.

(l) The percentage of the total consideration to be received by the Corp. Y shareholders in the proposed merger that will be represented by cash paid for fractional shares of Corp. X common and preferred stock is expected to be less than one percent.

Appendix H

The Installment Sales Revision Act of 1980

Due to the sweeping beneficial effect of the October 1980 enactment of the first major overhaul of the installment sales rules, this appendix provides a concise explanation of the law, reproduces the text of the Installment Sales Revision Act of 1980 in its entirety, and the text of the Congressional Committee Reports explaining it in detail.

For reader convenience, this appendix has its own Table of Contents, Index and List of 1954 Code sections affected by the Act.

This material is reproduced with the permission of Prentice-Hall, Inc., Englewood Cliffs, N.J. 07632.

Note: Specific applications of the law as it relates to acquisitions and exchanges, are discussed in Chapter 2.

TABLE OF CONTENTS
INSTALLMENT SALES
REVISION ACT OF 1980

INSTALLMENT SALES REVISION ACT OF 1980

[¶ 101]   New Law Restructures Installment Sale Rules

To make things easier for taxpayers seeking installment sale treatment, the new law breaks down the installment sale rules, all of which were previously contained in Sec. 453, into three separate Code sections:

Rules for sales of real property and casual sales of personal property are now found in Sec. 453.

Rules for personal property dealer transactions are in Sec. 453A.

Rules for dispositions of installment obligations are in Sec. 453B.

≫**BIG CHANGES FOR NONDEALERS→** Except for one change relating to election of the installment method by accrual method dealers (¶ 112), the new law doesn't substantively change the rules for installment sales by dealers of personal property. The substantive changes made by the new law relate to sales of realty and nondealer sales of personal property.

Basic concepts the same. In addition to the structural modifications described above, the new law makes a number of significant changes in the installment sale rules. However, most of the basic concepts remain the same:

Gain from an installment sale is reported ratably over the period the payments are received. Each payment has two elements: (1) return of capital and (2) income in the same proportion the gross profit (selling price less seller's adjusted basis) bears to the total contract price (amount to be received by seller).

> **Example.** Jones, a nondealer, sells a building to Smith for $100,000. Jones' basis is $50,000. Jones receives $10,000 each year for 10 years. The ratio of gross profit to contract price is 50%, so $5000 of each payment is income.

Losses are still reported without regard to the installment sale rules.

Sec. 2 repeals Code Sec. 453 and adds new Code Secs. 453, 453A and 453B, generally effective for dispositions after the date of enactment.

More Nondealer Sales Now Qualify For Installment Reporting

To get some idea of how the new law eases the installment sales rules for nondealers, let's look at how some typical sales stack up under prior law and under the new law.

Sale Terms	Prior Law	New Law
Sale for $100,000. $50,000 in year of sale, $50,000 over the next 5 years.	Sale disqualified. Year-of-sale payment exceeds 30% of selling price.	Sale qualifies. ¶ 103.
Sale for $100,000. $30,000 in year of sale, remainder over 10 years, no stated interest.	Sale disqualified. Sec. 483 imputes interest. Selling price reduced by amount treated as interest, making initial payment more than 30% of selling price.	Sale qualifies. ¶ 103. WARNING: Imputed interest rules still apply.
Sale for $100,000. $100 payable in year of sale, remainder payable in 5 years.	Sale qualifies.	Sale qualifies.
Sale for $100,000. Entire purchase price payable in 5 years.	Sale disqualified. Rules require two payments in two different tax years.	Sale qualifies. ¶ 104.
Sale of personal property for $900. $100 in year of sale, remainder in next year.	Sale disqualified. Selling price for personal property must exceed $1000.	Sale qualifies. ¶ 105.
Sale of personal property for $900. Entire price payable in year following year of sale.	Sale disqualified. Sale violates both minimum price and two-payment rules.	Sale qualifies. ¶ 104 and ¶ 105.
Sale for $100,000, payable over 10 years. Seller takes no steps to elect the installment method.	Sale disqualified. Installment method must be elected.	Sale qualifies. ¶ 106.
Corp. sells assets on installment basis and distributes obligation to shareholder in Sec. 337 liquidation.	Sale disqualified. Shareholder cannot report gain on the installment method.	Sale qualifies. ¶ 110.
Sale for a contingent selling price.	Sale disqualified. Price must be fixed and determinable.	Sale qualifies. ¶ 111.

[¶ 103]   Year-of-Sale Payment Limit Dropped

Taxpayers planning installment sales of real estate or nondealer personal property will no longer have to worry about how much of the purchase price they receive in the year of sale. The new law eliminates the rule that denied installment sale treatment for gain from such sales if payments received in the year of sale exceeded 30% of the selling price.

Retroactive effect. The 30% limit won't be applied to any disposition made in a tax year ending after the date of enactment of the new law, even if the actual disposition took place before that date.

Sec. 2 repeals Code Sec. 453(b)(2)(B) and adds new Code Sec. 453(b)(1), effective for dispositions after the date of enactment. However, in the case of dispositions before that date in taxable years ending after that date, old Code Sec. 453 will be applied without regard to the 30% limit of Sec. 453(b)(2)(B).

[¶ 104]　One-Payment Rule Adopted

Under prior law, IRS and the courts took the position that installment reporting was available only if the purchase price was payable in two or more installments in two or more taxable years. If the entire purchase price was payable in a lump sum in a year subsequent to the year of sale, installment treatment was denied. Under the new law, a sale will qualify for installment reporting so long as at least one payment is to be received after the close of the tax year in which the sale occurs, regardless of the total number of payments.

Retroactive effect. The new one-payment rule is effective for dispositions occuring in tax years ending after the date of enactment, even if the disposition occurred before that date.

⫸**TAX PLANNING STRATEGY**→　The new one-payment rule makes it easier than ever to qualify for installment treatment. What's more it opens the way for year-end income shifting using the installment sale rules. If you want to nail down a sale of property this year but don't want the income taxed on this year's return, you can make an installment sale. Simply provide for the entire purchase price to be paid next year.

Sec. 2 adds new Code Sec. 453(b)(1), effective for dispositions after the date of enactment. However, in the case of dispositions before that date in taxable years ending after that date, old Code Sec. 453 will be applied without regard to any requirement that more than one payment be received.

[¶ 105]　Minimum Sale Price Rule Repealed

The new law eliminates the requirement that a casual sale of personal property be for a price of more than $1000 to qualify for the installment method. Now, any sale, no matter how small, may qualify if it meets the other installment reporting requirements.

⫸**WARNING**→　Think carefully about how you want to treat even the smallest deferred payment sale. Installment reporting is automatic under the new rules (¶ 106), but if you inadvertently report the entire gain in the year of sale it will probably be treated as an election out of the installment sale rules. And an election out is irrevocable.

Sec. 2 repeals Code Sec. 453(b)(1)(B) and adds new Code Sec. 453, effective for dispositions after the date of enactment.

[¶ 106]　Installment Reporting Becomes Automatic

The new law does away with the requirement that a taxpayer must elect the installment method to report gains from sales of real property or non-

¶ 106

dealer personal property. Instead, installment treatment will *automatically* apply to a qualified sale unless the taxpayer *elects out* of the installment sales rules.

Electing out. The new law leaves it up to IRS to make regulations detailing the election process. However, unless the regulations provide otherwise, the election must be made by the due date (including extensions) for filing the return for the year of the disposition. Furthermore, it's likely that reporting the entire gain as income for the year of the sale will qualify as an election out of the installment method. The election, once made, is irrevocable without IRS' consent.

≫≫**WHEN TO ELECT OUT**→ A taxpayer should consider reporting the entire gain from an installment sale if losses in or loss carryovers to the year of the sale could be used to offset the gain. A taxpayer might also think about electing out if it's anticipated that income will rise in later years so that the deferred payments would be taxed in higher brackets. Similarly, in some cases, reporting the entire gain and taking advantage of the income averaging rules (Sec. 1301 et seq.) might be a greater tax-saver than installment reporting. Installment reporting could be undesirable if the sale is for such a small amount that reporting the gain over an extended period will be cumbersome.

≫≫**YEAR-END TAX TIP**→ If you made a deferred payment sale earlier in 1980, be sure to review the sale provisions before you file your 1980 return. Sales that wouldn't have qualified for the installment method when they were made may now qualify since elimination of the year-of-sale payment limit (¶ 103) and the two-payment rule (¶ 104) is effective for *all* of calendar year 1980. But remember, the new rule making installment reporting automatic technically applies only to sales after the date of enactment of the new law. For sales before that date, installment reporting is elective.

Special rules. Under prior law, gain from a deferred payment sale by a nonresident alien did not become taxable as payments were received after the seller became a resident or citizen subject to U.S. tax. It's expected that IRS' regulations will continue that treatment in appropriate cases under the new law. It's also expected that similar treatment will be given to deferred payment sales by tax-exempt organizations that later receive payments after losing their tax-exempt status.

Sec. 2 repeals Code Sec. 453(b)(1) and adds new Code Sec. 453(d), effective for dispositions after the date of enactment.

[¶ 107] New Law Cracks Down on Intra-Family Installment Sales

The new law sets out strict new rules for installment sales between related parties when there is a second disposition of the property. There are also new rules for sales of depreciable property between certain closely related parties.

Related party disposition rule. The aim of the new rules is to prevent related taxpayers from using the installment sale rules to cash in on an asset's appreciation without paying current tax. In the past, a taxpayer could make an installment sale of the appreciated property to a related party, like a spouse or child, who could then obtain cash proceeds by reselling the property. The courts approved these transactions, so long as the seller didn't directly or indirectly have "control over the proceeds or possess the economic benefit therefrom."

How it works. Under the new law, a resale by a related purchaser will trigger recognition of gain by the initial seller, based on his gross profit ratio, to the extent the amount realized on the resale exceeds actual payments made under the installment sale. If the second disposition isn't a sale or exchange, the fair market value of the property is the amount realized. In either case, any portion of the amount realized that's attributable to improvements made by the installment purchaser won't be taken into account. In calculating the gain, all payments received on the installment sale before the end of the tax year are taken into account—even if the payments are received after the second disposition. Subsequent payments received by the initial seller will be recovered tax-free until they equal the amount realized on the resale.

Related persons include spouses, children, grandchildren, and parents, but *not* brothers and sisters. A corporation is related if its stock would be attributed to the other party under the general attribution rules of Sec. 318. Those rules also apply in determining whether a partnership, trust or estate is related.

Time limits. In the case of marketable securities, the new rule applies without time limit to resales made before the installment obligation is fully paid. For other property, the rule only applies to resales within two years after the initial sale. The two year period is suspended for any period that the installment buyer's risk of loss is substantially diminished by such things as holding a put or option or a short sale.

Exceptions. There are a number of exceptions to the new rule:

(1) It doesn't apply to a nonliquidating installment sale of stock to the issuing corporation.

(2) It doesn't apply to an involuntary conversion *if* the initial sale occurred before the threat or imminence of conversion.

(3) It doesn't apply to a second disposition after the death of the installment seller or buyer.

(4) It doesn't apply to any transaction that does not have a tax-avoidance purpose. This exception is intended to apply to involuntary dispositions, such as foreclosures, or to subsequent installment sales with terms that are equivalent to or longer than those of the first sale.

≫**WARNING→** The new rule applies to installment sales (first dispositions) after May 14, 1980.

Accrual rule for sales of depreciable property between closely-related parties. Under the new law, accrual accounting is in effect required for deferred payment sales of depreciable property between (1) a taxpayer and spouse, (2) a taxpayer and a partnership or corporation that's 80% owned by the taxpayer and/or spouse, or (3) partnerships and corporations that are 80% owned by the taxpayer and/or spouse. The deferred payments are to be treated as if they were received in the year of sale. This rule is intended to deter transactions that allow the related buyer the benefits of depreciation deductions based on a stepped-up basis before the seller is required to include gain on the sale in income.

Exception. The special rule doesn't apply to sales without a tax avoidance purpose, including sales between spouses who are legally separated or sales pursuant to a settlement proceeding that culminates in legal separa-

¶ **107**

tion. The nontax-avoidance exception also encompasses sales that don't achieve significant tax deferral.

≫≫NO IMPACT ON PENDING CASES→ No inference should be drawn from the new law as to the proper tax treatment of related party installment sales made before the effective dates of the new rules.

Capital gains exception for related party sales. The new law also changes the definition of related persons for purposes of Sec. 1239(a), which denies capital gains treatment to gain on the sale of depreciable property between related persons, to conform to the new installment sale rule.

Sec. 2 adds Code Sec. 453(e), effective for first dispositions after May 14, 1980. It adds Code Secs. 453(f) and (g), effective for dispositions after the date of enactment. Sec. 5 amends Sec. 1239(b) and (c), effective for dispositions after the date of enactment.

[¶ 108] Third Party Guarantees Aren't Payments

The new law makes it clear that a third party guarantee (including a standby letter of credit) that's used as security for a deferred payment sale won't be treated as a payment received on the installment obligation. Thus, a taxpayer who gets such a guarantee won't be denied installment reporting on the grounds of having received full payment in the year of sale nor will the taxpayer be taxed on guaranteed amounts until payment is due.

Third party notes and other third party obligations that are transferable or marketable prior to default by the installment buyer *will* be treated as payments, however.

Sec. 2 adds Code Sec. 453(f)(3), effective for dispositions after the date of enactment.

[¶ 109] New Rule for Like-Kind Exchanges Coupled With Installment Sales

Transfers of certain types of property for like-kind property plus cash payments can qualify for both installment reporting and nonrecognition treatment for the gain attributable to the like-kind exchange. Gain to be recognized on the installment method is the total gain on the transaction less the gain eligible for nonrecognition.

Under prior law, the value of the like kind property was taken into account in determining the amount of the selling price, the contract price and payments received for installment reporting purposes. While this treatment did not affect the amount of gain to be realized, it did accelerate recognition of gain.

How it works. Under the new law, the gross profit will be the amount of gain recognized on the exchange if the installment obligation were satisfied in full at its face amount. The total contract price will consist solely of money or nonlike-kind property received plus the face amount of the installment obligation. The basis of the like-kind property will be determined as if the installment obligation were satisfied at its face amount. The seller's basis in the property transferred is allocated first to the like-kind property up to its fair market value and then ratably among the installment obligation, cash and nonlike-kind property.

Example. Jones exchanges property with a basis of $400,000 for like-kind property worth $200,000 plus an installment obligation worth $800,000, with $100,000 payable in the year of sale and the rest payable the next year. Let's compare the treatment under prior law and under the new law:

Prior law. Under prior law, the contract price is $1,000,000, since the like-kind property is taken into account. Gross profit is $600,000. Gross profit ratio is 60%. Since the like-kind property is treated as a payment in the year of sale, Jones reports $180,000 gain (60% of $300,000) that year. The next year, he reports $420,000 (60% of $700,000). Total gain: $600,000.

New law. The contract price is $800,000, since the like-kind property isn't included. Gross profit is $600,000. Gross profit ratio is 75%. The like-kind property isn't counted as a payment in the year of sale, so Jones reports gain of $75,000 (75% of $100,000) that year. He reports $525,000 (75% of $700,000) the next year. Total gain: $600,000.

What exchanges qualify? Like-kind exchanges qualifying for this treatment are those described in Sec. 1031(b). Similar treatment is also available for an exchange under a plan of corporate reorganization that's not treated as a dividend.

Sec. 2 adds Code Sec. 453(f)(6), effective for dispositions after the date of enactment.

[¶ 110] New Break for Installment Obligations Distributed in Sec. 337 Liquidations

A shareholder who owns stock in a corporation may sell the stock to an unrelated buyer and report the gain on the installment method. Thanks to the new law, the shareholder will also be allowed installment treatment if the corporation's assets are sold instead of its stock.

>>>**GOOD NEWS**→ The new tax break applies to all distributions after March 31, 1980.

How it works. If a corporation sells its assets on an installment basis during a 12-month liquidation under Sec. 337 and then distributes the installment obligation to a shareholder as a liquidating distribution, the installment obligation won't be treated as a payment received by the shareholder in exchange for his stock. Instead, the shareholder can report on the installment method, taking gain into account as payments are received on the installment obligation. Installment obligations received by a subsidiary during a Sec. 337 liquidation of the parent-sub group will qualify for installment reporting by the parent corporation's shareholders.

Exceptions: There are a few exceptions to the new rule:

(1) Obligations received by the corporation from sales of inventory, other than bulk sales, don't qualify for installment treatment by the shareholder.

(2) If the installment obligation is attributable to a sale of depreciable property to either the shareholder's spouse or a corporation or partnership that's 80% owned by the shareholder and/or spouse, gain will be recognized by the shareholder when the obligation is distributed.

(3) If a related party, other than those above, purchases the corporation's assets and then disposes of them, the new related party disposition rules (¶ 107) will apply to the shareholder who received the installment obligation.

Sec. 2 adds Code Sec. 453(h), effective for distributions of installment obligations after March 31, 1980.

[¶ 111] Contingent Sales Qualify for Installment Reporting

The new law allows installment reporting for sales with a contingent selling price. Under prior case law, installment reporting generally was

¶ 111

not available unless the selling price was fixed and determinable. The new law doesn't spell out specific rules for contingent sales. Rather, it requires IRS to adopt regulations "providing for ratable basis recovery in transactions where the gross profit or the total contract price (or both) cannot be readily ascertained." Congress does, however, intend the following rules to apply:

Stated maximum selling price. If there is a stated maximum selling price, income will be reported pro rata with respect to each payment using the maximum selling price to determine the total contract price and gross profit ratio. The maximum selling price is the largest price that could be paid under the contract assuming all contingencies work in the seller's favor. The maximum selling price will be determined from the "four corners" of the contract and incidental or remote contingencies won't be taken into account.

If it later turns out that a contingency won't be satisfied, so that the maximum selling price is reduced, the seller's income from the sale will be recomputed. The seller will report reduced income, as adjusted, for the adjustment year and all subsequent years. If the seller has already reported more income from the installment payments received in prior years than the total amount of recomputed income, the excess is deductible as a loss in the adjustment year.

Example (1). Jones owns a retail store with a basis of $1,500,000. In 1980, Jones agrees to sell the store to Smith. Smith will pay $1,000,000 in 1981. In 1982 and 1983, he'll pay Jones a stated percentage of his gross receipts, but not more than $1,000,000 each year. Since the most Jones can get under the contract is $3,000,000, his income is computed using that figure. The ratio of gross profit ($1,500,000) to contract price ($3,000,000) is 50%, so half of each payment is treated as income.

Payable over a fixed period. If the selling price is so indefinite that no maximum selling price can be determined, but the obligation is payable over a fixed period of time, basis will be recovered ratably over the period.

Example (2). Jones agrees to sell Smith the store on the same terms as in Example (1), but there's no cap on the 1982 and 1983 payments. Since no maximum selling price is stated, Jones will recover his $1,500,000 basis ratably over the three year payment period. $500,000 of each payment will be treated as return of capital.

Selling price and payment period both indefinite. In cases where the selling price and payment period are both indefinite, basis will be recovered over a reasonable period of time. In appropriate cases, basis recovery would be allowed under an income forecast type method.

≫≫COST RECOVERY METHOD LIMITED→ Under prior law, cash method taxpayers receiving a promise of future payments whose fair market value was not readily ascertainable could treat the transaction as "open" and use the cost-recovery method to report their gain. Under that method, no gain is realized until the entire basis is recovered. Now that Congress has expanded installment reporting to cover many "open" transactions, it intends to limit the use of the cost-recovery method to "rare and extraordinary" cases.

≫≫WHAT TO DO→ Until IRS issues final Regs on contingent sales, it may be difficult to decide whether or not to take advantage of installment reporting for such sales. Generally, an election not to use installment reporting is irrevocable. But in the case of contingent sales, Congress expects IRS to consent to revocation of elections made before adoption of final Regs if the request for revocation is made within a reasonable time after Regs are adopted. So, it looks like you can safely play it either way—and still have a chance to change your mind.

Sec. 2 adds Code Sec. 453(i)(2), effective for dispositions after the date of enactment.

[¶ 112]   Rules Eased for Dealers Who Elect Installment Reporting

Under the new law, an accrual method dealer who elects to change to the installment method will report gain as payments are received only for sales made *after* the effective date of the election. Under prior law, a dealer who made such a switch had to report gain from *all* payments received after the election, even if the gain from those payments had been included in income for tax years before the election. There was an off-setting— although not entirely effective—adjustment to tax to mitigate the double inclusion in income.

Sec. 2 repeals Code Sec. 453(c) and adds Code Sec. 453A, effective for taxable years ending after the date of enactment.

[¶ 113]   New Nonrecognition Rule for Transfers To Life Insurance Companies

Transfers of installment obligations to life insurance companies are now eligible for the same nonrecognition treatment provided for transfers to other taxpayers. However, the life insurance company must elect to report any remaining gain on the obligation as taxable investment income as payments are received. Under prior law, any transfer of an installment obligation to a life insurance company was treated as a taxable transaction.

Sec. 2 repeals Code Sec. 453(d)(5) and adds Code Sec. 453B(e), effective for dispositions after the date of enactment.

[¶ 114]   Cancellation of Obligation is a Disposition

The new law makes it clear that if a seller cancels a buyer's installment obligation, the cancellation will be treated as a disposition of the obligation. The seller will recognize gain or loss to the extent of the difference between the fair market value of the obligation at the time of disposition and its basis.

Related persons.   If the seller and buyer are related persons (see ¶ 107) the fair market value of the obligation will be treated as not less than face value.

> **Example.** Dad transfers family home to Son in an installment sale. Dad's basis is $10,000. Son agrees to pay $50,000 in five equal annual installments. Dad immediately cancels Son's obligation. On cancellation, Dad will recognize gain to the extent of the difference between the FMV (face) value of the obligation ($50,000) and his basis ($10,000). Under prior law, it was argued that on cancellation Dad was liable for gift tax but no income tax, even though Son got a stepped-up basis in the house.
>
> *Sec. 2 adds Code Sec. 453B(f), effective for installment obligations becoming unenforceable after the date of enactment.*

[¶ 115]   Bequest of Installment Obligation to Obligor Won't Avoid Tax

Generally, when an installment seller dies holding an installment obligation, any unreported gains are treated as income in respect of a dece-

¶ 115

dent. The seller's estate or the recipient of the obligation is taxed on receipt of the installment payments in the same way the deceased seller would have been taxed had he or she lived to receive the payments. Thus, taxpayers argued that if an installment obligation was bequeathed to the buyer (obligor) there could be no tax because there would be no collection of the unpaid balance once the interests of the obligor and obligee merged. The new law makes it clear, however, that the regular installment obligation disposition rules will apply in such cases.

How it works. Gain or loss will be recognized to the extent of the difference between the obligation's basis and its fair market value at the time of disposition. Absent an act that amounts to cancellation under local law, the disposition will be treated as having taken place no later than the time administration of the estate is concluded. If cancellation occurs at the death of the holder of the obligation, the cancellation is treated as a transfer by the decedent's estate. But, if the obligation is held by someone other than the decedent, such as a trust, the cancellation will be treated as a transfer by that person immediately after the decedent's death.

Related persons. If the decedent and the obligor were related persons (see ¶ 107) the fair market value of the obligation will be treated as not less than face value.

Sec. 3 adds Code Sec. 691(a)(5), effective for decedents dying after the date of enactment.

[¶ 116] Deceased Seller's Estate Gets Break For Foreclosure Gain

A deceased seller's estate or beneficiary will now be entitled to the same nonrecognition treatment on foreclosure of real property sold on the installment method as the deceased seller would have gotten. IRS has ruled that under prior law a deceased seller's estate couldn't succeed to the nonrecognition treatment that would have been available to the seller because the estate is a separate taxable entity.

Limited recognition. When real property is reacquired by a deceased seller's estate in partial or full satisfaction of a purchase money debt, gain will be recognized only to the extent of cash or property received less the gain on the original sale already included in income. Gain is further limited to the gain on the original sale less gain already reported and less repossession costs.

Basis. The estate's basis in the property will be the same as if the property had been reacquired by the original seller increased by the amount of the Sec. 691(c) deduction for income in respect of a decedent that would have been allowed had the repossession been taxable.

Sec. 4 adds Code Sec 1038(g), effective for acquisitions of real property after the date of enactment.

NEW LAW

[¶ 131] This division reproduces new law enacted by the Installment Sales Revision Act of 1980:

● 1954 Code sections appear as amended, added or repealed starting at ¶ 135. They are in Code section order. New matter is shown in *italics*. Deleted matter and effective dates are shown in footnotes.

● Cross references at the end of each Code section refer you to the exact place in the Committee Reports division of the handbook where you will find the official explanation of the change.

● If you prefer, you can read the P-H explanation of the changes before consulting these amended Code sections. The Concise Explanation begins at ¶ 101. References in the explanation to the Code sections will lead you to the statutory language in this division.

1954 Code Sections as Amended By
The Installment Sales Revision Act of 1980

[¶ 135] CODE SEC. 311. TAXABILITY OF CORPORATION ON DISTRIBUTION.

(a) **General Rule.**—Except as provided in subsections (b), (c), and (d) of this section and section ¹*453B*, no gain or loss shall be recognized to a corporation on the distribution, with respect to its stock, of—

(1) its stock (or rights to acquire its stock), or

(2) property.

* * * * * * * * * *

[For official explanation, see Committee Reports, ¶ 152; 156]

[¶ 136] CODE SEC. 336 (as in effect on 4-1-80, the day before the date of the enactment of the Crude Oil Windfall Profit Tax Act of 1980) GENERAL RULE.

Except as provided in section ¹*453B* (relating to disposition of installment obligations), no gain or loss shall be recognized to a corporation on the distribution of property in partial or complete liquidation.

[For official explanation, see Committee Reports, ¶ 152; 156]

[¶ 137] CODE SEC. 336 (as amended by the Crude Oil Windfall Profits Tax Act of 1980). DISTRIBUTIONS OF PROPERTY IN LIQUIDATION.

(a) **General Rule.**—Except as provided in subsection (b) of this section and in section ¹*453B* (relating to disposition of installment obligations), no gain or loss

---

[Footnote ¶ 135] Matter in *italics* in Sec. 311(a) added by section 2(b)(1), Installment Sales Revision Act of 1980, which struck out:
(1) "453(d)"
Effective date (Sec. 6(a)(1), Installment Sales Revision Act of 1980).—Applies to dispositions made after date of enactment of this Act in taxable years ending after such date.
[Footnote ¶ 136] Matter in *italics* in Sec. 336 (as in effect on 4-1-80, the day before the date of the enactment of the Crude Oil Windfall Profit Tax Act of 1980) added by section 2(b)(1), Installment Sales Revision Act of 1980, which struck out:
(1) "453(d)"
Effective date (Sec. 6(a)(1), Installment Sales Revision Act of 1980).—Applies to dispositions made after date of enactment of this Act in taxable years ending after such date.

shall be recognized to a corporation on the distribution of property in partial or complete liquidation.

(b) LIFO Inventory.—

(1) **In general.—**If a corporation inventorying goods under the LIFO method distributes inventory assets in partial or complete liquidation, then the LIFO recapture amount with respect to such assets shall be treated as gain to the corporation recognized from the sale of such inventory assets.

(2) **Exception where basis determined under section 334(b)(1).—**Paragraph (1) shall not apply to any liquidation under section 332 for which the basis of property received is determined under section 334(b)(1).

(3) **LIFO recapture amount.—**For purposes of this subsection, the term "LIFO recapture amount" means the amount (if any) by which—
   (A) the inventory amount of the inventory assets under the first-in, first-out method authorized by section 471, exceeds
   (B) the inventory amount of such assets under the LIFO method.

(4) **Definitions.—**For purposes of this subsection—
   (A) **LIFO method.—**The term "LIFO method" means the method authorized by section 472 (relating to last-in, first-out inventories).
   (B) **Other definitions.—**The term "inventory assets" has the meaning given to such term by subparagraph (A) of section 311(b)(2), and the term "inventory amount" has the meaning given to such term by subparagraph (B) of section 311(b)(2) (as modified by paragraph (3) of section 311(b)).

[For official explanation, see Committee Reports, ¶ 152; 156]

[¶ 138] CODE SEC. 337. GAIN OR LOSS ON SALES OR EXCHANGES IN CONNECTION WITH CERTAIN LIQUIDATIONS.

* * * * * * * * * * *

(f) Special Rule for LIFO Inventories.—

(1) **In general.—**In the case of a corporation inventorying goods under the LIFO method, this section shall apply to gain from the sale or exchange of inventory assets (which under subsection (b)(2) constitute property) only to the extent that such gain exceeds the LIFO recapture amount with respect to such assets:

(2) **Definitions.—**The terms used in this subsection shall have the same meaning as when used in section 336(b).

(3) **Cross reference.—**

For treatment of gain from the sale or exchange of an installment obligation as gain resulting from the sale or exchange of the property in respect of which the obligation was received, see the last sentence of section ¹*453B(a)*.

[For official explanation, see Committee Reports, ¶ 152; 156]

[Footnote ¶ 137] Matter in *italics* in Sec. 336 (as amended by the Crude Oil Windfall Profit Tax Act of 1980) added by section 2(c)(1), Installment Sales Revision Act of 1980, which struck out:
   (1) "453(d)"

Effective date (Sec. 6(a)(6), Installment Sales Revision Act of 1980 and Sec. 403(b)(3), '80 Crude Oil Windfall Profit Tax Act).—Applies to distributions and dispositions pursuant to plans of liquidation adopted after 12-31-81.

[Footnote ¶ 138] Matter in *italics* in Sec. 337(f) added by section 2(c)(2), Installment Sales Revision Act of 1980, which struck out:
   (1) "453(d)(1)"

Effective date (Sec. 6(a)(6), Installment Sales Revision Act of 1980 and Sec. 403(b)(3), '80 Crude Oil Windfall Profit Tax Act).—Applies for distributions and dispositions pursuant to plans of liquidation adopted after 12-31-81.

[¶ 139] CODE SEC. 381. CARRYOVERS IN CERTAIN CORPORATE ACQUISITIONS.

(a) **General Rule.**—In the case of the acquisition of assets of a corporation by another corporation—

(1) in a distribution to such other corporation to which section 332 relating to liquidations of subsidiaries applies, except in a case in which the basis of the assets distributed is determined under section 334(b)(2); or

(2) in a transfer to which section 361 (relating to nonrecognition of gain or loss to corporation) applies, but only if the transfer is in connection with a reorganization described in subparagraph (A), (C), (D) (but only if the requirements of subparagraphs (A) and (B) of section 354(b)(1) are met), or (F) of section 368(a)(1),

the acquiring corporation shall succeed to and take into account, as of the close of the day of distribution or transfer, the items described in subsection (c) of the distributor or transferor corporation, subject to the conditions and limitations specified in subsections (b) and (c).

*   *   *   *   *   *   *   *   *   *   *

(c) **Items of the Distributor or Transferor Corporation.**—The items referred to in subsection (a) are:

*   *   *   *   *   *   *   *   *   *   *

(8) **Installment method.**—If the acquiring corporation acquires installment obligations (the income from which the distributor or transferor corporation *¹reports on the installment basis under section 453 or 453A*) the acquiring corporation shall, for purposes of section 453 *or 453A*, be treated as if it were the distributor or transferor corporation.

*   *   *   *   *   *   *   *   *   *   *

[For official explanation, see Committee Reports, ¶ 152; 156]

[¶ 140] CODE SEC. 453. INSTALLMENT METHOD.

(a) **General Rule.**—Except as otherwise provided in this section, income from an installment sale shall be taken into account for purposes of this title under the installment method.

(b) **Installment Sale Defined.**—For purposes of this section—

(1) **In general.**—The term "installment sale" means a disposition of property

---

[Footnote ¶ 139] Matter in *italics* in Sec. 381(c)(8) added by section 2(b)(2), Installment Sales Revision Act of 1980, which struck out:
(1) "has elected, under section 453 to report on the installment basis"
Effective date (Sec. 6(a)(1), Installment Sales Revision Act of 1980).—Applies to dispositions made after date of enactment of this Act in taxable years ending after such date.

[Footnote ¶ 140] Sec. 453 added by section 2(a), Installment Sales Revision Act of 1980.
Effective date (Sec. 6(a)(1)—(3), Installment Sales Revision Act of 1980).—Generally applies to dispositions made after date of enactment of this Act in taxable years ending after such date.
Sec. 453(e), '54 Code applies to first disposition made after 5-14-80.
Sec. 453(h)(1) and (2), '54 Code applies in the case of distributions of installment obligations after 3-31-80.

Former Sec. 453 reads as follows:
CODE SEC. 453. INSTALLMENT METHOD.
(a) **Dealers in Personal Property.**—
(1) **In general.**—Under regulations prescribed by the Secretary, a person who regularly sells or otherwise disposes of personal property on the installment plan may

Code § 453(b)(1)   ¶ 140

where at least 1 payment is to be received after the close of the taxable year in which the disposition occurs.

(2) **Exceptions.**—The term "installment sale" does not include—

(A) **Dealer disposition of personal property.**—A disposition of personal property on the installment plan by a person who regularly sells or otherwise disposes of personal property on the installment plan.

(B) **Inventories of personal property.**—A disposition of personal property of a kind which is required to be included in the inventory of the taxpayer if on hand at the close of the taxable year.

(c) **Installment Method Defined.**—For purposes of this section, the term "installment method" means a method under which the income recognized for any taxable year from a disposition is that proportion of the payments received in that year which the gross profit (realized or to be realized when payment is completed) bears to the total contract price.

(d) **Election Out.**—

(1) **In general.**—Subsection (a) shall not apply to any disposition if the taxpayer elects to have subsection (a) not apply to such disposition.

(2) **Time and manner for making election.**—Except as otherwise provided by regulations, an election under paragraph (1) with respect to a disposition may be made only on or before the due date prescribed by law (including extensions) for filing the taxpayer's return of the tax imposed by this chapter for the taxable year in which the disposition occurs. Such an election shall be made in the manner prescribed by regulations.

(3) **Election revocable only with consent.**—An election under paragraph (1) with respect to any disposition may be revoked only with the consent of the Secretary.

[Footnote ¶ 140 continued]

return as income therefrom in any taxable year that proportion of the installment payments actually received in that year which the gross profit, realized or to be realized when payment is completed, bears to the total contract price.

(2) **Total contract price.**—For purposes of paragraph (1), the total contract price of all sales of personal property on the installment plan includes the amount of carrying charges or interest which is determined with respect to such sales and is added on the books of account of the seller to the established cash selling price of such property. This paragraph shall not apply with respect to sales or personal property under a revolving credit type plan or with respect to sales or other dispositions of property the income from which is, under subsection (b), returned on the basis and in the manner prescribed in paragraph (1).

(b) **Sales of Realty and Casual Sales of Personalty.**—

(1) **General rule.**—Income from—
(A) a sale or other disposition of real property, or
(B) a casual sale or other casual disposition of personal property (other than property of a kind which would properly be included in the inventory of the taxpayer if on hand at the close of the taxable year) for a price exceeding $1,000,
may (under regulations prescribed by the Secretary) be returned on the basis and in the manner prescribed in subsection (a).

(2) **Limitation.**—Paragraph (1) shall apply only if in the taxable year of the sale or other disposition—
there are no payments, or
the payments (exclusive of evidences of indebtedness of the purchaser) do not exceed 30 percent of the selling price.

(3) **Purchaser evidences of indebtedness payable on demand or readily tradable.**—In applying this subsection, a bond or other evidence of indebtedness which is payable on demand, or which is issued by a corporation or a government or political subdivision thereof (A) with interest coupons attached or in registered form (other than one in registered form which the taxpayer establishes will not be readily tradable in an established securities market), or (B) in any other form designed to render such bond or other evidence of indebtedness readily tradable in an established securities market, shall not be treated as an evidence of indebtedness of the purchaser.

(c) **Change From Accrual to Installment Basis.**—

(1) **General rule.**—If a taxpayer entitled to the benefits of subsection (a) elects

(e) Second Dispositions by Related Persons.—

(1) In general.—If—

(A) any person disposes of property to a related person (hereinafter in this subsection referred to as the "first disposition"), and

(B) before the person making the first disposition receives all payments with respect to such disposition, the related person disposes of the property (hereinafter in this subsection referred to as the "second disposition"),

then, for purposes of this section, the amount realized with respect to such second disposition shall be treated as received at the time of the second disposition by the person making the first disposition.

(2) 2-year cutoff for property other than marketable securities.—

(A) In general.—Except in the case of marketable securities, paragraph (1) shall apply only if the date of the second disposition is not more than 2 years after the date of the first disposition.

(B) Substantial diminishing of risk of ownership.—The running of the 2-year period set forth in subparagraph (A) shall be suspended with respect to any property for any period during which the related person's risk of loss with respect to the property is substantially diminished by—

(i) the holding of a put with respect to such property (or similar property),

(ii) the holding by another person of a right to acquire the property, or

(iii) a short sale or any other transaction.

[Footnote ¶ 140 continued]

for any taxable year to report his taxable income on the installment basis, then in computing his taxable income for such year (referred to in this subsection as "year of change") or for any subsequent year—

(A) installment payments actually received during any such year on account of sales or other dispositions of property made in any taxable year before the year of change shall not be excluded; but

(B) tax imposed by this chapter for any taxable year (referred to in this subsection as "adjustment year") beginning after December 31, 1953, shall be reduced by the adjustment computed under paragraph (2).

(2) **Adjustment in tax for amounts previously taxed.**—In determining the adjustment referred to in paragraph (1)(B), first determine, for each taxable year before the year of change, the amount which equals the lesser of—

(A) the portion of the tax for such prior taxable year which is attributable to the gross profit which was included in gross income for such prior taxable year, and which by reason of paragraph (1)(A) is includible in gross income for the taxable year, or

(B) the portion of the tax for the adjustment year which is attributable to the gross profit described in subparagraph (A).

The adjustment referred to in paragraph (1)(B) for the adjustment year is the sum of the amounts determined under the preceding sentence.

(3) **Rule for applying paragraph (2).**—For purposes of paragraph (2), the portion of the tax for a prior taxable year, or for the adjustment year, which is attributable to the gross profit described in such paragraph is that amount which bears the same ratio to the tax imposed by this chapter, other than by sections 55 and 56, for such taxable year (computed without regard to paragraph (2)) as the gross profit described in such paragraph bears to the gross income for such taxable year.

(4) **Revocation of election.**—An election under paragraph (1) to report taxable income on the installment basis may be revoked by filing a notice of revocation, in such manner as the Secretary prescribes by regulations, at any time before the expiration of 3 years following the date of the filing of the tax return for the year of change. If such notice of revocation is timely filed—

(A) the provisions of paragraph (1) and subsection (a) shall not apply to the year of change or for any subsequent year;

(B) the statutory period for the assessment of any deficiency for any taxable year ending before the filing of such notice, which is attributable to the revocation of the election to use the installment basis, shall not expire before the expiration of 2 years from the date of the filing of such notice, and such deficiency may be assessed before the expiration of such 2-year period notwithstanding the provisions of any law or rule of law which would otherwise prevent such assessment; and

(C) if refund or credit of any overpayment, resulting from the revocation of

(3) Limitation on amount treated as received.—The amount treated for any taxable year as received by the person making the first disposition by reason of paragraph (1) shall not exceed the excess of—

(A) the lesser of—

(i) the total amount realized with respect to any second disposition of the property occurring before the close of the taxable year, or

(ii) the total contract price for the first disposition, over

(B) the sum of—

(i) the aggregate amount of payments received with respect to the first disposition before the close of such year, plus

(ii) the aggregate amount treated as received with respect to the first disposition for prior taxable years by reason of this subsection.

(4) Fair market value where disposition is not sale or exchange.—For purposes of this subsection, if the second disposition is not a sale or exchange, an amount equal to the fair market value of the property disposed of shall be substituted for the amount realized.

(5) Later payments treated as receipt of tax paid amounts.—If paragraph (1) applies for any taxable year, payments received in subsequent taxable years by the person making the first disposition shall not be treated as the receipt of payments with respect to the first disposiiton to the extent that the aggregate of such payments does not exceed the amount treated as received by reason of paragraph (1).

(6) Exception for certain dispositions.—For purposes of this subsection—

(A) **Reacquisitions of stock by issuing corporation not treated as first dispositions.**—Any sale or exchange of stock to the issuing corporation shall not be treated as a first disposition.

(B) **Involuntary conversions not treated as second dispositions.**—A compulsory or involuntary conversion (within the meaning of section 1033) and any transfer thereafter shall not be treated as a second disposition if the first disposition occurred before the threat or imminence of the conversion.

(C) **Dispositions after death.**—Any transfer after the earlier of—

(i) the death of the person making the first disposition, or

(ii) the death of the person acquiring the property in the first disposition,

and any transfer thereafter shall not be treated as a second disposition.

[Footnote ¶ 140 continued]

the election to use the installment basis, for any taxable year ending before the date of the filing of the notice of revocation is prevented on the date of such filing, or within one year from such date, by the operation of any law or rule of law (other than section 7121 or 7122), refund or credit of such overpayment may nevertheless be made or allowed if claim therefor is filed within one year from such date. No interest shall be allowed on the refund or credit of such overpayment for any period prior to the date of the filing of the notice of revocation.

(5) **Election after revocation.**—If the taxpayer revokes under paragraph (4) an election under paragraph (1) to report taxable income on the installment basis, no election under paragraph (1) may be made, except with the consent of the Secretary, for any subsequent taxable year before the fifth taxable year following the year of change with respect to which such revocation is made.

(d) Gain or loss on Disposition of Installment Obliations.—

(1) **General rule.**—If an installment obligation is satisfied at other than it face value or distributed, transmitted, sold, or otherwise disposed of, gain or loss shall result to the extent of the difference between the basis of the obligation and—

(A) the amount realized, in the case of satisfaction at other than face value or a sale or exchange, or

(B) the fair market value of the obligation at the time of distribution, transmission, or diposition, in the case of the distribution, transmission, or disposition otherwise than by sale or exchange.

Any gain or loss so resulting shall be considered as resulting from the sale or exchange of the property in respect of which the installment obligation was received.

(7) **Exception where tax avoidance not a principal purpose.**—This subsection shall not apply to a second disposition (and any transfer thereafter) if it is established to the satisfaction of the Secretary that neither the first disposition nor the second disposition had as one of its principal purposes the avoidance of Federal income tax.

(8) **Extension of statute of limitations.**—The period for assessing a deficiency with respect to a first disposition (to the extent such deficiency is attributable to the application of this subsection) shall not expire before the day which is 2 years after the date on which the person making the first disposition furnishes (in such manner as the Secretary may by regulations prescribe) a notice that there was a second disposition of the property to which this subsection may have applied. Such deficiency may be assessed notwithstanding the provisions of any law or rule of law which would otherwise prevent such assessment.

(f) **Definitions and Special Rules.**—For purposes of this section—

(1) **Related person.**—Except for purposes of subsections (g) and (h), the term "related person" means a person whose stock would be attributed under section 318(a) (other than paragraph (4) thereof) to the person first disposing of the property.

(2) **Marketable securities.**—The term "marketable securities" means any security for which, as of the date of the disposition, there was a market on an established securities market or otherwise.

(3) **Payment.**—Except as provided in paragraph (4), the term "payment" does not include the receipt of evidences of indebtedness of the person acquiring the property (whether or not payment of such indebtedness is guaranteed by another person).

(4) **Purchaser evidences of indebtedness payable on demand or readily tradable.**—Receipt of a bond or other evidence of indebtedness which—

    (A) is payable on demand, or
    (B) is issued by a corporation or a government or political subdivision thereof and is readily tradable.

shall be treated as receipt of payment.

[Footnote ¶ 140 continued]

(2) **Basis of obligation.**—The basis of an installment obligation shall be the excess of the face value of the obligation over an amount equal to the income which would be returnable were the obligation satisfied in full.

(3) **Special rule for transmission at death.**—Except as provided in section 691 (relating to recipients of income in respect of decedents), this subsection shall not apply to the transmission of installment obligations at death.

(4) **Effect of distribution in certain liquidations.**—

    (A) Liquidations to which section 332 applies.—If—
      (i) an installment obligation is distributed in a liquidation to which section 332 (relating to complete liquidations of subsidiaries) applies, and
      (ii) the basis of such obligation in the hands of the distributee is determined under section 334(b)(1),
then no gain or loss with respect to the distribution of such obligation shall be recognized by the distributing corporation.

    (B) Liquidations to which section 337 applies.—If—
      (i) an installment obligation is distributed by a corporation in the course of a liquidation, and
      (ii) under section 337 (relating to gain or loss on sales or exchanges in connection with certain liquidations) no gain or loss would have been recognized to the corporation if the corporation had sold or exchanged such installment obligation on the day of such distribution,
then no gain or loss shall be recognized to such corporation by reason of such distribution. The preceding sentence shall not apply to the extent that under paragraph (1) gain to the distributing corporation would be considered as gain to which section 341 (f), 617(d)(1), 1245(a), 1250(a), 1251(c), "or" [2] 1252(a), or 1254(a) applied.

(5) Readily tradable defined.—For purposes of paragraph (4), the term "readily tradable" means a bond or other evidence of indebtedness which is issued—

(A) with interest coupons attached or in registered form (other than one is registered form which the taxpayer establishes will not be readily tradable in an established securities market), or

(B) in any other form designed to render such bond or other evidence of indebtedness readily tradable in an established securities market.

(6) Like-kind exchanges.—In the case of any exchange described in section 1031(b)—

(A) the total contract price shall be reduced to take into account the amount of any property permitted to be received in such exchange without recognition of gain,

(B) the gross profit from such exchange shall be reduced to take into account any amount not recognized by reason of section 1031(b), and

(C) the term "payment" shall not include any property permitted to be received in such exchange without recognition of gain.

Similar rules shall apply in the case of an exchange which is described in section 356(a) and is not treated as a dividend.

(7) Depreciable property.—The term "depreciable property" means property of a character which (in the hands of the transferee) is subject to the allowance for depreciation provided in section 167.

[Footnote ¶ 140 continued]

(5) **Life insurance companies.**—In the case of a disposition of an installment obligation by any person other than a life insurance company (as defined in section 801(a)) to such an insurance company or to a partnership of which such an insurance company is a partner, no provision of this subtitle providing for the nonrecognition of gain shall apply with respect to any gain resulting under paragraph (1). If a corporation which is a life insurance company for the taxable year was (for the preceding taxable year) a corporation which was not a life insurance company, such corporation shall, for purposes of this paragraph and paragraph (1), be treated as having transferred to a life insurance company, on the last day of the preceding taxable year, all installment obligations which it held on such last day. A partnership of which a life insurance company becomes a partner shall, for purposes of this paragraph and paragraph (1), be treated as having transferred to a life insurance company, on the last day of the preceding taxable year of such partnership, all installment obligations which it holds at the time such insurance company becomes a partner.

(e) **Carrying Charges Not Included in Total Contract Price.**—If the carrying charges or interest with respect to sales of personal property, the income from which is returned under subsection (a)(1), is not included in the total contract price, payments received with respect to such sales shall be treated as applying first against such carrying charges or interest. This subsection shall not apply with respect to sales or other dispositions of property the income from which is, under subsection (b), returned on the basis and in the manner prescribed in subsection (a)(1).

Special rule for application of former Sec. 453, above, to certain dispositions. Sec. 6 (a)(7), Installment Sales Revision Act of 1980, reads:

(7) **Special rule for application of former section 453 to certain dispositions.**—In the case of any disposition made on or before the date of the enactment of this Act in any taxable year ending after such date, the provisions of Sec. 453(b) '54 Code, as in effect before such date, shall be applied with respect to such disposition without regard to—
(A) paragraph (2) of such section 453(b), and
(B) any requirement that more than 1 payment be received.

Section 2(c)(4), Installment Sales Revision Act of 1980, repeals section 403(b)(2)(B) of the Crude Oil Windfall Profit Tax Act which amended former Sec. 453(d)(4)(B), effective for distributions and dispositions pursuant to plans of liquidation adopted after 12-31-81, by adding at the end thereof the following sentence:
In the case of any installment obligation which would have met the requirements of clauses (i) and (ii) of the first sentence of this subparagraph but for section 337(f), gain shall be recognized to such corporation by reason of such distribution only to the extent gain would have been recognized under section 337(f) if such corporation had sold or exchanged such installment obligation on the day of such distribution.

(g) Sale of Depreciable Property to Spouse or 80-Percent Owned Entity.—

(1) **In general.**—In the case of an installment sale of depreciable property between related persons within the meaning of section 1239(b), subsection (a) shall not apply, and, for purposes of this title, all payments to be received shall be deemed received in the year of the disposition.

(2) **Exception where tax avoidance not a principal purpose.**—Paragraph (1) shall not apply if it is established to the satisfaction of the Secretary that the disposition did not have as one of its principal purposes the avoidance of Federal income tax.

(h) Use of Installment Method by Shareholders in Section 337 Liquidations.—

(1) **Receipt of obligations not treated as receipt of payment.—**

(A) **In general.**—If, in connection with a liquidation to which section 337 applies, in a transaction to which section 331 applies the shareholder receives (in exchange for the shareholder's stock) an installment obligation acquired in respect of a sale or exchange by the corporation during the 12-month period set forth in section 337(a), then, for purposes of this section, the receipt of payments under such obligation (but not the receipt of such obligation) by the shareholder shall be treated as the receipt of payment for the stock.

(B) **Obligations attributable to sale of inventory must result from bulk sale.**—Subparagraph (A) shall not apply to an installment obligation described in section 337(b)(1)(B) unless such obligation is also described in section 337(b)(2)(B).

(C) **Special rule where obligor and shareholder are related persons.**—If the obligor of any installment obligation and the shareholder are related persons (within the meaning of section 1239(b)), to the extent such installment obligation is attributable to the disposition by the corporation of depreciable property—

(i) subparagraph (A) shall not apply to such obligation, and

(ii) for purposes of this title, all payments to be received by the shareholder shall be deemed received in the year the shareholder receives the obligation.

(D) **Coordination with subsection (e)(1)(A).**—For purposes of subsection (e)(1)(A), disposition of property by the corporation shall be treated also as disposition of such property by the shareholder.

(E) **Sales by liquidating subsidiary.**—For purposes of subparagraph (A), in any case to which section 337(c)(3) applies, an obligation acquired in respect of a sale or exchange by the selling corporation shall be treated as so acquired by the corporation distributing the obligation to the shareholder.

(2) **Distributions received in more than 1 taxable year of shareholder.**—If—

(A) paragraph (1) applies with respect to any installment obligation received by a shareholder from a corporation, and

(B) by reason of the liquidation such shareholder receives property in more than 1 taxable year,

then, on completion of the liquidation, basis previously allocated to property so received shall be reallocated for all such taxable years so that the shareholder's basis in the stock of the corporation is properly allocated among all property received by such shareholder in such liquidation.

(i) Regulations.—

(1) **In general.**—The Secretary shall prescribe such regulations as may be necessary or appropriate to carry out the provisions of this section.

Code § 453(i)1)   ¶ 140

(2) **Selling price not readily ascertainable.**—The regulations prescribed under paragraph (1) shall include regulations providing for ratable basis recovery in transactions where the gross profit or the total contract price (or both) cannot be readily ascertained.

[For official explanation, see Committee Reports, ¶ 152; 156]

[¶ 141] CODE SEC. 453A. INSTALLMENT METHOD FOR DEALERS IN PERSONAL PROPERTY.

(a) **General Rule.**—

(1) **In general.**—Under regulations prescribed by the Secretary, a person who regularly sells or otherwise disposes of personal property on the installment plan may return as income therefrom in any taxable year that proportion of the installment payments actually received in that year which the gross profit, realized or to be realized when payment is completed, bears to the total contract price.

(2) **Total contract price.**—For purposes of paragraph (1), the total contract price of all sales of personal property on the installment plan includes the amount of carrying charges or interest which is determined with respect to such sales and is added on the books of account of the seller to the established cash selling price of such property. This paragraph shall not apply with respect to sales of personal property under a revolving credit type plan.

(b) **Carrying Charges Not Included in Total Contract Price.**—If the carrying charges or interest with respect to sales of personal property, the income from which is returned under subsection (a)(1), is not included in the total contract price, payments received with respect to such sales shall be treated as applying first against such carrying charges or interest.

[For official explanation, see Committee Reports, ¶ 152; 156]

[¶ 142] CODE SEC. 453B. GAIN OR LOSS ON DISPOSITION OF INSTALLMENT OBLIGATIONS.

(a) **General Rule.**—If an installment obligation is satisfied at other than its face value or distributed, transmitted, sold, or otherwise disposed of, gain or loss shall result to the extent of the difference between the basis of the obligation and—

(1) the amount realized, in the case of satisfaction at other than face value or a sale or exchange, or

(2) the fair market value of the obligation at the time of distribution, transmission, or disposition, in the case of the distribution, transmission, or disposition otherwise than by sale or exchange.

Any gain or loss so resulting shall be considered as resulting from the sale or exchange of the property in respect of which the installment obligation was received.

(b) **Basis of Obligation.**—The basis of an installment obligation shall be the excess of the face value of the obligation over an amount equal to the income which would be returnable were the obligation satisfied in full.

[Footnote ¶ 141] Sec. 453A added by section 2(a), Installment Sales Revision Act of 1980.

Effective date (Sec. 6(a)(4), Installment Sales Revision Act of 1980).—Applies to taxable years ending after date of enactment of this Act.

[Footnote ¶ 142] Sec. 453B added by section 2(a), Installment Sales Revision Act of 1980.

Effective date (Sec. 6(a)(1), (5), (6), Installment Sales Revision Act of 1980 and 403(b)(3), '80 Crude Oil Windfall Profit Tax Act).—Generaly applies to dispositions made after date of enactment of this Act in taxable years ending after such date.

Sec. 453B(f), '54 Code applies to installment obligations becoming unenforceable after date of enactment of this Act.

The last sentence in Sec. 453B(d)(2), '54 Code, as added by section 2(c)(3), applies to distributions and dispositions pursuant to plans of liquidation adopted after 12-31-81.

(c) Special Rule for Transmission at Death.—Except as provided in section 691 (relating to recipients of income in respect of decedents), this section shall not apply to the transmission of installment obligations at death.

(d) Effect of Distribution in Certain Liquidations.—

(1) **Liquidations to which section 332 applies.**—If—

(A) an installment obligation is distributed in a liquidation to which section 332 (relating to complete liquidations of subsidiaries) applies, and

(B) the basis of such obligation in the hands of the distributee is determined under section 334(b)(1),

then no gain or loss with respect to the distribution of such obligation shall be recognized by the distributing corporation.

(2) **Liquidations to which section 337 applies.**—If—

(A) an installment obligation is distributed by a corporation in the course of a liquidation, and

(B) under section 337 (relating to gain or loss on sales or exchanges in connection with certain liquidations) no gain or loss would have been recognized to the corporation if the corporation had sold or exchanged such installment obligation on the day of such distribution,

then no gain or loss shall be recognized to such corporation by reason of such distribution. The preceding sentence shall not apply to the extent that under paragraph (1) gain to the distributing corporation would be considered as gain to which section 341(f), 617(d)(1), 1245(a), 1250(a), 1251(c), 1252(a), or 1254(a) applies. In the case of any installment obligation which would have met the requirements of subparagraphs (A) and (B) of the first sentence of this paragraph but for section 337(f), gain shall be recognized to such corporation by reason of such distribution only to the extent gain would have been recognized under section 337(f) if such corporation had sold or exchanged such installment obligation on the date of such distribution.

(e) Life Insurance Companies.—

(1) **In general.**—In the case of a disposition of an installment obligation by any person other than a life insurance company (as defined in section 801(a)) to such an insurance company or to a partnership of which such an insurance company is a partner, no provision of this subtitle providing for the nonrecognition of gain shall apply with respect to any gain resulting under subsection (a). If a corporation which is a life insurance company for the taxable year was (for the preceding taxable year) a corporation which was not a life insurance company, such corporation shall, for purposes of this subsection and subsection (a), be treated as having transferred to a life insurance company, on the last day of the preceding taxable year, all installment obligations which it held on such last day. A partnership of which a life insurance company becomes a partner shall, for purposes of this subsection and subsection (a), be treated as having transferred to a life insurance company, on the last day of the preceding taxable year of such partnership, all installment obligations which it holds at the time such insurance company becomes a partner.

(2) **Special rule where life insurance company elects to treat income as investment income.**—Paragraph (1) shall not apply to any transfer or deemed transfer of an installment obligation if the life insurance company elects (at such time and in such manner as the Secretary may by regulations prescribe) to determine its life insurance company taxable income—

(A) by returning the income on such installment obligation under the installment method prescribed in section 453, and

(B) if such income would not otherwise be returnable as an item referred to in section 804(b) or as long-term capital gain, as if the income on such obligations were income specified in section 804(b).

(f) **Obligation Becomes Unenforceable.**—For purposes of this section, if any installment obligation is canceled or otherwise becomes unenforceable—

(1) the obligation shall be treated as if it were disposed of in a transaction other than a sale or exchange, and

(2) if the obligor and obligee are related persons (within the meaning of section 453(f)(1)), the fair market value of the obligation shall be treated as not less than its face amount.

[For official explanation, see Committee Reports, ¶ 152; 156]

[¶ 143] CODE SEC. 481. ADJUSTMENTS REQUIRED BY CHANGES IN METHOD OF ACCOUNTING.

*   *   *   *   *   *   *   *   *   *   *

[(d) struck out][1]

[For official explanation, see Committee Reports, ¶ 152]

[¶ 144] CODE SEC. 644. SPECIAL RULE FOR GAIN ON PROPERTY TRANSFERRED TO TRUST AT LESS THAN FAIR MARKET VALUE.

*   *   *   *   *   *   *   *   *

(f) **Special Rule for Installment Sales.**—If the trust [1]*reports* income under section 453 on any sale or exchange to which subsection (a) applies, under regulations prescribed by the Secretary—

(1)· subsection (a) (other than the 2-year requirement of paragraph (1)(A) thereof) shall be applied as if each installment were a separate sale or exchange of property to which such subsection applies, and

(2) the term "includible gain" shall not include any portion of an installment received by the trust after the death of the transferor.

[For official explanation, see Committee Reports, ¶ 152; 156]

[¶ 145] CODE SEC. 691. RECIPIENTS OF INCOME IN RESPECT OF DECEDENTS.

(a) **Inclusion in Gross Income.—**

(1) **General rule.**—The amount of all items of gross income in respect of a decedent which are not properly includible in respect of the taxable period in which falls the date of his death or a prior period (including the amount of all items of gross income in respect of a prior decedent, if the right to receive such amount was acquired by reason of the death of the prior decedent or by bequests, devise, or inheritance from the prior decedent) shall be included in the gross income, for the taxable year when received, of:

[Footnote ¶ 143] Section 2(b)(3), Installment Sales Revision Act of 1980, struck out from Sec. 481.
(1) "(d) **Exception for change to Installment Basis.**—This section shall not apply to a change to which section 453 (relating to change to installment method) applies.
Effective date (Sec. 6(a)(1), Installment Sales Revision Act of 1980).—Applies to dispositions made after date of enactment of this Act in taxable years ending after such date.
[Footnote ¶ 144] Matter in *italics* in Sec. 644(f) added by section 2(b)(4), Installment Sales Revision Act of 1980, which struck out:
(1) "elects to report"
Effective date (Sec. 6(a)(1), Installment Sales Revision Act of 1980).—Applies to dispositions made after date of enactment of this Act in taxable years ending after such date.
[Footnote ¶ 145] Matter in *italics* in Sec. 691(a)(4) added by section 2(b)(5), Installment Sales Revision Act of 1980; which struck out:
(1) "received by a decedent on the sale or other disposition of property, the income from which was properly reportable by the decedent on the installment basis under section 453"
(2) "453(d)"
Effective date (Sec. 6(a)(1), Installment Sales Revision Act of 1980).—Applies to dispositions made after date of enactment of this Act in taxable years ending after such date.

Sec. 691(a)(5) added by section 3, Installment Sales Revision Act of 1980.

Effective date (Sec. 6(b), Installment Sales Revision Act of 1980).—Applies in the case of decedents dying after date of enactment of this Act.

(A) the estate of the decedent, if the right to receive the amount is acquired by the decedent's estate from the decedent;

(B) the person who, by reason of the death of the decedent acquires the right to receive the amount, if the right to receive the amount is not acquired by the decedent's estate from the decedent; or

(C) the person who acquires from the decedent the right to receive the amount by bequest, devise, or inheritance, if the amount is received after a distribution by the decedent's estate of such right.

(2) **Income in case of sale, etc.**—If a right, described in paragraph (1), to receive an amount is transferred by the estate of the decedent or a person who received such right by reason of the death of the decedent or by bequest, devise, or inheritance from the decedent, there shall be included in the gross income of the estate of such person, as the case may be, for the taxable period in which the transfer occurs, the fair market value of such right at the time of such transfer, plus the amount by which any consideration for the transfer exceeds such fair market value. For purposes of this paragraph, the term "transfer" includes sale, exchange, or other disposition, or the satisfaction of an installment obligation at other than face value, but does not include transmission at death to the estate of the decedent or a transfer to a person pursuant to the right of such person to receive such amount by reason of the death of the decedent or by bequest, devise, or inheritance from the decedent.

(3) **Character of income determined by reference to decedent.**—The right, described in paragraph (1), to receive an amount shall be treated, in the hands of the estate of the decedent or any person who acquired such right by reason of the death of the decedent, or by bequest, devise, or inheritance from the decedent, as if it had been acquired by the estate or such person in the transaction in which the right to receive the income was originally derived and the amount includible in gross income under paragraph (1) or (2) shall be considered in the hands of the estate or such person to have the character which it would have had in the hands of the decedent if the decedent had lived and received such amount.

(4) **Installment obligations acquired from decedent.**—In the case of an installment obligation [1]*reportable by the decedent on the installment method under section 453 or 453A*, if such obligation is acquired by the decedent's estate from the decedent or by any person by reason of the death of the decedent or by bequest, devise, or inheritance from the decedent—

(A) an amount equal to the excess of the face amount of such obligation over the basis of the obligation in the hands of the decedent (determined under section [2]453B) shall, for the purpose of paragraph (1), be considered as an item of gross income in respect of the decedent; and

(B) such obligation shall, for purposes of paragraphs (2) and (3), be considered a right to receive an item of gross income in respect of the decedent, but the amount includible in gross income under paragraph (2) shall be reduced by an amount equal to the basis of the obligation in the hands of the decedent (determined under section [2]453B).

(5) *Other rules relating to installment obligations.—*

(A) In general.—In the case of an installment obligation reportable by the decedent on the installment method under section 453 or 453A, for purposes of paragraph (2)—

(i) the second sentence of paragraph (2) shall be applied by inserting "(other than the obligor)" after "or a transfer to a person",

(ii) any cancellation of such an obligation shall be treated as a transfer, and

(iii) any cancellation of such an obligation occurring at the death of the decedent shall be treated as a transfer by the estate of the decedent

(or, if held by a person other than the decedent before the death of the decedent, by such person).

(B) Face amount treated as fair market value in certain cases.—In any case to which the first sentence of paragraph (2) applies by reason of subparagraph (A), if the decedent and the obligor were related persons (within the meaning of section 453(f)(1)), the fair market value of the installment obligation shall be treated as not less than its face amount.

(C) Cancellation includes becoming unenforceable.—For purposes of subparagraph (A), an installment obligation which becomes unenforceable shall be treated as if it were canceled.

*　*　*　*　*　*　*　*　*　*　*　*　*

[For official explanation, see Committee Reports, ¶ 152; 153; 156]

[¶ 146] CODE SEC. 1038. CERTAIN REACQUISITIONS OF REAL PROPERTY.

*　*　*　*　*　*　*　*　*　*　*

(g) Acquisition by Estate, Etc., of Seller.—Under regulations prescribed by the Secretary, if an installment obligation is indebtedness to the seller which is described in subsection (a), and if such obligation is, in the hands of the taxpayer, an obligation with respect to which section 691(a)(4)(B) applies, then—

(1) for purposes of subsection (a), acquisition of real property by the taxpayer shall be treated as reacquisition by the seller, and

(2) the basis of the real property acquired by the taxpayer shall be increased by an amount equal to the deduction under section 691(c) which would (but for this subsection) have been allowable to the taxpayer with respect to the gain on the exchange of the obligation for the real property.

[For official explanation, see Committee Reports, ¶ 154; 156]

[¶ 147] CODE SEC. 1239. GAIN FROM SALE OF DEPRECIABLE PROPERTY BETWEEN CERTAIN RELATED TAXPAYERS.

(a) **Treatment of Gain as Ordinary Income.**—In the case of a sale or exchange of property, directly or indirectly, between related persons, any gain recognized to the transferor shall be treated as ordinary income if such property is, in the hands of the transferee, of a character which is subject to the allowance for depreciation provided in section 167.

(b) **Related Persons.**—For purposes of subsection (a), the term "related persons means"—

[1]*(1) the taxpayer and the taxpayer's spouse,*

(2) the taxpayer and an 80-percent owned entity, or

(3) two 80-percent owned entities.

(c) 80-Percent Owned Entity Defined.—

(1) General rule.—For purposes of this section, the term "80-percent owned entity" means—

[Footnote ¶ 146] Sec. 1038(g) added by section 4, Installment Sales Revision Act of 1980.

Effective date (Sec. 6(c), Installment Sales Revision Act of 1980).—Applies to acquisitions of real property by the taxpayer after date of enactment of this Act.

[Footnote ¶ 147] Matter in *italics* in Sec. 1239(b) and (c) added by section 5, Installment Sales Revision Act of 1980, which struck out:

(1) "(1) a husband and wife,

(2) an individual and a corporation 80 percent or more in value of the outstanding stock of which is owned, directly or indirectly, by or for such individual, or

(3) two or more corporations 80 percent or more in value of the outstanding stock of each which is owned, directly or indirectly, by or for the same individual.

(c) **Constructive Ownership of Stock.**—Section 318 shall apply in determining the ownership of stock for purposes of this section, except that sections 318(a)(2)(C) and 318(a)(3)(C) shall be applied without regard to the 50-percent limitation contained therein."

Effective date (Sec. 6(a)(1), Installment Sales Revision Act of 1980).—Applies to dispositions made after date of enactment of this Act in taxable years ending after such date.

(A) *a corporation 80 percent or more in value of the outstanding stock of which is owned (directly or indirectly) by or for the taxpayer, and*

(B) *a partnership 80 percent or more of the capital interest or profits interest in which is owned (directly or indirectly) by or for the taxpayer.*

(2) *Constructive ownership.—For purposes of subparagraphs (A) and (B) of paragraph (1), the principles of section 318 shall apply, except that—*

(A) *the members of an individual's family shall consist only of such individual and such individual's spouse, and*

(B) *paragraphs (2)(C) and (3)(C) of section 318(a) shall be applied without regard to the 50-percent limitation contained therein.*

[For official explanation, see Committee Reports, ¶ 155; 156]

[¶ 148] CODE SEC. 1255. GAIN FROM DISPOSITION OF SECTION 126 PROPERTY.

(a) General Rule.—

(1) Ordinary income.—Except as otherwise provided in this section, if section 126 property is disposed of, the lower of—

(A) the applicable percentage of the aggregate payments, with respect to such property, excluded from gross income under section 126, or

(B) the excess of—

(i) the amount realized (in the case of a sale, exchange, or involuntary conversion), or the fair market value of such section 126 property (in the case of any other disposition), over

(ii) the adjusted basis of such property,

shall be treated as ordinary income. Such gain shall be recognized notwithstanding any other provision of this subtitle, except that this section shall not apply to the extent such gain is recognized as ordinary income under any other provision of this part.

(2) Section 126 property.—For purposes of this section "section 126 property" means any property acquired, improved, or otherwise modified by the application of payments excluded from gross income under section 126.

(3) Applicable percentage.—For purposes of this section, if section 126 property is disposed of less than 10 years after the date of receipt of payments excluded from gross income under section 126, the applicable percentage is 100 percent. If section 126 property is disposed of more than 10 years after such date, the applicable percentage is 100 percent reduced (but not below zero) by 10 percent for each year or part thereof in excess of 10 years such property was held after the date of receipt of the payments.

(b) Special Rules.—Under regulations prescribed by the Secretary—

(1) rules similar to the rules applicable under section 1245 shall be applied for purposes of this section, and

(2) for purposes of section 163(d), 170(e), 341(e)(12), [1] *453B(d)(2),* and 751(c), amounts treated as ordinary income under this section shall be treated in the same manner as amounts treated as ordinary income under section 1245.

[For official explanation, see Committee Reports, 152; 156]

[Footnote ¶ 148] Matter in *italics* in Sec. 1255(b)(2) added by section 2(b)(6), Installment Sales Revision Act of 1980, which struck out:

(1) "453(d)(4)(B)"

Effective date (Sec. 6(a)(1), Installment Sales Revision Act of 1980).—Applies to dispositions made after date of enactment of this Act in taxable years ending after such date.

[The page following this is 51]

Code § 1255(b)   ¶ 148

CONGRESSIONAL COMMITTEE REPORTS

Explaining Law Enacted by the Installment Sales Revision Act of 1980

[¶ 151] This subdivision of the booklet reproduces all important parts of the official explanations of the Installment Sales Revision Act of 1980. The material comes from the Senate Committee Report. It is arranged in the order of the Act section numbers. If a Committee Report is correct except for section numbers, other numbers, dates, etc., correct numbers and dates are supplied and enclosed in brackets.

You may prefer to read the P-H explanation of the changes before consulting this official material. The Concise Explanation begins at ¶ 101. References to Act section in the explanation will lead you to the official material on the changes.

Background:

Installment Sales Revision Act of 1980

● HR 6883 Reported by Ways and Means, 5-21-80; House Report No. 96-1042, dated 5-21-80.

● Passed by House as reported, 6-17-80.

● HR 6883 Reported by Senate Finance, 9-26-80; Senate Report No. 96-1000, dated 9-26-80.

● Passed by Senate with a technical amendment on the Floor 10-1-80.

● House agreed to Senate changes 10-2-80.

≫NOTE: LOOK AT THE LAW→ It is always necessary to consult the law itself to ascertain the exact law changes made.

[¶ 152] SECTION 2. INSTALLMENT SALES RULES

(Secs. 453, 453A, 453B, 481, 311, 336, 337, 381, 691, 1255 of the Code and Sec. 403 of the Crude Oil Windfall Profit Tax Act of 1980)

[Senate Explanation]

A. Installment Sales Generally (Sec. 2 of the bill and present Sec. 453 of the Code)

Present law.—Generally, under present law (Code sec. 453), income from a sale of property on the installment basis may be reported as the payments are received. If the installment method is elected for qualifying sales, the gain reported for any taxable year is the proportion of the installment payment received in that year which the gross profit, realized or to be realized when payment is completed, bears to the total contract price. In general, the contract price is the amount which will be paid to the seller.

The function of the installment method of reporting income is to permit the spreading of the income tax over the period during which payments of the sales price are received. Thus, the installment method alleviates possible liquidity problems which might arise from the bunching of gain in the year of sale when a portion of the selling price has not been actually received.

* * * * * * *

Explanation of provision.—In general. —Although the bill makes structural revisions of existing law and makes the specific changes described below, most of the basic concepts of existing law are continued. As under present law, the provisions relate to installment reporting of gains and do not affect the time for recognizing losses from the sale or exchange of property for deferred payments.

Except as otherwise provided for sales subject to a contingency or for sales to certain related persons, gain from an installment sale would continue to be recognized for any taxable year with respect to the payments received in the year in the same proportion as the gross profit from the sale bears to the total contract price. The payments taken into account as being received in a taxable year would

Act § 2, ¶ 152

not include the purchaser's obligation of future payment, whether dischargeable in money or other property (including foreign currency), unless that obligation is a bond or other evidence of indebtedness which is either payable on demand or has been issued by a corporation or government and is readily tradable.

Structural improvements.—U n d e r present law, a single provision (Code sec. 453) prescribes rules for installment method reporting for dealers in personal property, for sales of real property and nondealer personal property, and special disposition rules. Under the bill, the rules for nondealer transactions are contained in one Code section (sec. 453), the rules for personal property dealer transactions are contained in another section (sec. 453A), and generally applicable installment obligation disposition rules are contained in a third section (sec. 453B).

Generally, in making these structural changes and certain language changes, few substantive changes are intended to be made by the bill with respect to the provisions relating to installment sales by dealers in personal property. Except for an amendment relating to the election of the installment method by an accrual basis dealer, the substantive changes under the bill relate only to sales of realty and casual sales of personal property.

Under the bill, gain from the sale of property which is not required to be inventoried by a farmer under his method of accounting will be eligible for installment method of reporting as gain from a casual sale of personal property even though such property is held for sale by the farmer. The committee also intends that deferred payment sales to farmer cooperatives are to be eligible for installment reporting as under present law (Rev. Rul. 73-210, 1973-1 C.B. 211).

B. Initial Payment Limitation (Sec. 2 of the bill and present Sec. 453(b)(2) of the Code)

Present law.—Under present law, gain from the sale of realty or nondealer personal property may not be reported under the installment method if the payments received in the taxable year of sale exceed 30 percent of the selling price.

* * * * * * * *

Explanation of provision.—The bill

eliminates the 30-percent initial payment limitation for reporting gain on the installment method from the disposition of real property or nondealer personal property.

C. Two Payment Rule (Sec. 2 of the bill and present Sec. 453 of the Code)

Present law.—Under present law, it is the position of the Internal Revenue Service that a taxpayer may not elect to report income from the sale of real property on the installment method if the total purchase price is payable in a lump sum in a taxable year subsequent to the year of sale.[1] The same issue may arise with respect to casual sales of personal property. The rationale for the ruling is that the installment concept generally calls for two or more payments of the purchase price in two or more taxable years and that a single payment sale cannot be considered to be payable in installments. The courts have agreed with the Service's interpretation.[2]

* * * * * * * *

Explanation of provision.—The bill eliminates the requirement that a sale must be for two or more payments to qualify for installment method reporting. Thus, under the bill, income from the sale of qualifying property for a purchase price payable in a lump sum in a taxable year subsequent to the year of sale may be reported in the year in which payment is received. It is anticipated that the Treasury Department will prescribe regulations to extend a similar rule to deferred payment sales by dealers in personal property.

D. Selling Price Limitation for Casual Sales of Personal Property (Sec. 2 of the bill and present Sec. 453(b)(1)(B) of the Code)

Present law.—Under present law, a casual sale of personal property must be for a selling price in excess of $1,000 to qualify for installment reporting.

* * * * * * * *

Explanation of provision.—The bill eliminates the selling price requirement to qualify for installment reporting.

E. Election of Installment Reporting (Sec. 2 of the bill and new Sec. 453 (d) of the Code)

Present law.—Under present law, an election may be made to report gain from an installment sale on a timely

[Footnote ¶ 152] (1) Rev. Rul. 69-462, 1969-2 C.B. 107, amplified by Rev. Rul. 71-595, 1971-2 C.B. 223.

(2) *Baltimore Baseball Co., Inc.* v. *U.S.*, 481 F.2d 1283 (Ct. Cl. 1973); *10-42 Corp.*, 55 TC 593 (1971)

filed return, a delinquent return, or on an amended return for the year of sale not barred by the statute of limitations, if the facts indicate no position inconsistent with the installment election had been taken with respect to the sale (Rev. Rul. 65-297, 1965-2 C.B. 152). If a return is filed which includes in gross income the entire gain from an installment sale, an amended return or claim for refund cannot be used to elect installment sale reporting for the sale because the election to report the gain in full is treated as a binding election not to report on the installment method.[3]

* * * * * * *

Explanation of provision.—The bill eliminates the present law requirement that the installment method must be elected for reporting gains from sales of realty and nondealer personal property. Instead, installment reporting would automatically apply to a qualified sale unless the taxpayer elects not to have the provision apply with respect to a deferred payment sale. Generally, the election not to have installment method reporting apply to a deferred payment sale must be made in the manner prescribed by regulations on or before the due date (including extensions of time for filing) for filing the income tax return for the year in which the sale occurs. It is anticipated that reporting the entire gain in gross income for the taxable year in which the sale occurs will operate as an election not to have installment sale reporting apply. It is anticipated that, under regulations, late elections will be permitted in rare circumstances when the Internal Revenue Service finds that reasonable cause for failing to make a timely election exists under the particular circumstances of each case.

Generally, an election made under this provision is to be irrevocable. However, an election may be revoked with the consent of the Internal Revenue Service. Generally, it is anticipated that consent would be given by the Internal Revenue Service in circumstances when a revocation does not have as one of its purposes the avoidance of income taxes. Also it is anticipated that consent to revocation will generally be granted in cases involving a contingent selling price if the election is made prior to adoption of final regulations under the provisions of the bill relating to contingent selling price sales and the request for revocation is filed within a reasonable time after the regulations are adopted.

It is anticipated that the regulations will prescribe election rules relating to the treatment of gains from deferred payment sales of property by a nonresident alien. Under the installment method rules of present law, these gains do not become taxable as payments are received after the seller becomes a resident or citizen subject to U.S. income tax for a taxable year subsequent to the year in which the sale was made. It is intended that the election regulations will continue this treatment in appropriate cases. Further, it is intended that similar treatment will be provided for a deferred payment sale by a tax-exempt organization which later receives payments after losing its tax-exempt status.

F. Related Party Sales (Sec. 2 of the bill and new Sec. 453(e), (f) and (g) of the Code)

Present law.—Under present law, the installment sale statutory provision does not preclude installment sale reporting for sales between related parties. Further, the statutory provision does not preclude installment sale reporting for sales of marketable securities although the seller might readily obtain full cash proceeds by market sales.

Under the existing statutory framework, taxpayers have used the installment sale provision as a tax planning device for intra-family transfers of appreciated property, including marketable securities. There are several tax advantages in making intra-family installment sales of appreciated property. The seller would achieve deferral of recognition of gain until the related buyer actually pays the installments to the seller, even if cash proceeds from the property are received within the related party group from a subsequent resale by the installment buyer shortly after making the initial purchase. In addition to spreading out the gain recognized by the seller over the term of the installment sale, the seller may achieve some estate planning benefits since the value of the installment obligation generally will be frozen for estate tax purposes. Any

[Footnote ¶ 152 continued]
(3) *Robert F. Kock*, T.C. Memo 1978-271; *Pacific National Co.* v. *Welch*, 304 U.S. 191 (1938).

Act § 2, ¶ 152

subsequent appreciation in value of the property sold, or in property acquired by reinvestment of the proceeds from the property sold on the installment basis, would not affect the seller's gross estate since the value of the property is no longer included in his gross estate.

With respect to the related buyer, there is usually no tax to be paid if the appreciated property is resold shortly after the installment purchase. Since the buyer's adjusted basis is a cost basis which includes the portion of the purchase price payable in the future, the gain or loss from the buyer's resale would represent only the fluctuation in value occurring after the installment purchase. Thus, after the related party's resale, all appreciation has been realized within the related group but the recognition of the gain for tax purposes may be deferred for a long period of time.

In the leading case, *Rushing v. Commissioner*,[4] the test was held to be that, in order to receive the installment benefits, the "seller may not directly or indirectly have control over the proceeds or possess the economic benefit therefrom." In this case, a sale of corporate stock was made to the trustee of trusts for the benefit of the seller's children. Since the sales were made to trusts created after the corporations had adopted plans of liquidation, the Government made an assignment of income argument. The Court upheld installment sale treatment for the stock sold to the trustee under the "control or enjoyment" test because the trustee was independent of the taxpayer and owed a fiduciary duty to the children. The Court rejected the assignment of income argument because it found that no income was being assigned.

The *Rushing* case has been followed in another case where the stock sold to a family trust was that of a cor-poration which was to be liquidated after the sale.[5] The liquidation was formally authorized after the sale to the trust. In other cases, the Tax Court has rejected the Service's substance over form and constructive receipt arguments and held that sales to a family trust qualified for installment method reporting.[6] In the *Pityo* case, the taxpayer's wife was the beneficiary of one of the trusts to which the installment sale was made. In the *Roberts* case, the trustees were the seller's brother and personal accountant. In both cases, installment sale reporting was allowed because the Tax Court held that the trustees were independent of the seller and satisfied the *Rushing* control or enjoyment test.

In another case, installment method reporting was allowed for a sale of marketable stock by a wife to her husband although a resale by the husband was contemplated.[7] In this case, the Court held that the husband could not be considered a mere conduit for the wife's sale of the stock since both were "very healthy economic entities" and the husband had an independent purpose for obtaining needed funds for an investment at a low rate of interest.

In the few cases in which the Service has prevailed, installment method reporting has been denied with respect to transactions involving a controlled corporation,[8] a sale to a son where the son was forced to resell the stock and invest the proceeds in other securities held in escrow,[9] and, in the case of a sale by a husband to his wife where the Court found there was no bona fide purpose for the transaction other than tax avoidance.[10]

* * * * * * *

Explanation of provision.—The bill prescribes special rules for situations involving installment sales to certain re-

[Footnote ¶ 152 continued]

(4) 441 F.2d 593 (5th Cir. 1971), *aff'g*, 52 T.C. 888 (1969).

(5) *Carl E. Weaver*, 71 T.C. 443 (1978).

(6) *William D. Pityo*, 70 T.C. 225 (1978); *Clair E. Roberts*, 71 T.C. 311 (1978). Also, in *William J. Goodman*, 74 T.C. No. 53 (July 16, 1980), a prearranged resale was made by the trustees of a family trust one day after the installment sales were made to the trusts of which the installment sellers were the trustees. The two-step installment sales were used because the taxpayers believed that "a cash sale was not attractive because of the income tax liability on such a sale."

(7) *Nye v. U.S.*, 407 F. Supp. 1345, 75-1 USTC ¶ 9150 (M.D.N.C. 1975).

(8) *Griffiths v. Helvering*, 308 U.S. 355 (1939). This case involved the creation of a corporation to receive the assignment of a settlement owed to the taxpayer with the corporation agreeing to pay the money received from the settlement to the taxpayer over a 40-year term. The Court held that there had been an anticipatory assignment of income and therefore the income was taxable to the shareholder rather than the corporation.

(9) *Paul G. Lustgarten*, 71 T.C. 303 (1978). The Court held that the taxpayer had constructively received the proceeds from the "resale."

(10) *Phillip W. Wrenn*, 67 T.C. 576 (1976).

lated parties who also dispose of the property and for situations involving installment sales of depreciable property between a taxpayer and his spouse or certain trusts, and 80-percent owned corporations or partnerships.

Sales other than sales of depreciable property between certain closely-related parties.—Under the bill, the amount realized upon certain resales by the related party installment purchaser will trigger recognition of gain by the initial seller, based on his gross profit ratio, only to the extent the amount realized from the second disposition exceeds actual payments made under the installment sale. Thus, acceleration of recognition of the installment gain from the first sale will generally result only to the extent additional cash and other property flows into the related group as a result of a second disposition of the property. In the case of a second disposition which is not a sale or exchange, the fair market value of the property disposed of is treated as the amount realized for this purpose. For these purposes, the portion of the amount realized from a second disposition will not be taken into account to the extent attributable to any improvements which had been made by the related installment purchaser.

The excess of any amount realized from resales over payments received on the first sale as of the end of a taxable year will be taken into account. Thus, the tax treatment would not turn on the strict chronological order in which resales or payments are made. If, under these rules, a resale results in the recognition of gain to the initial seller, subsequent payments actually received by that seller would be recovered tax-free until they have equaled the amount realized from the resale which resulted in the acceleration of recognition of gain.

In the case of property other than marketable securities, the resale rule will apply only with respect to second dispositions occurring within 2 years of the initial installment sale. For this purpose, the running of the 2-year period would be suspended for any period during which the related purchaser's risk of loss with respect to the property is substantially diminished. This rule will apply with respect to the holding of a put, the holding of an option by another person, a short sale, or any other transaction which has the effect of substantially diminishing the risk of loss. However, for this purpose, a typical close corporation shareholders' agreement is not intended to be taken into account. Further, the holding of an option is not to be considered to have the effect of substantially diminishing risk of loss if the option purchase price is to be determined by reference to the fair market value of the property at the time the option is exercised.

In the case of marketable securities, the resale rule would apply without a time limit for resales occurring before the installment obligation is satisfied. For this purpose, the term "marketable security" means any security for which, as of the date of disposition, there was a market on an established securities market, or otherwise.[11]

The bill also contains several exceptions to the application of these rules. Since gain from the sale of a corporation's treasury stock is nontaxable and therefore its basis is in the stock is irrelevant, this related party rule will not apply to any nonliquidating installment sale of stock to the issuing corporation. In addition, there would be no acceleration of recognition of gain as a result of a second disposition which is an involuntary conversion of the property if the first sale occurred before the threat or imminence of the conversion. Further there would be no acceleration of recognition of gain from a second disposition which occurs after the death of the installment seller or purchaser. Generally, it is intended that this exception will apply after the death of either spouse when the spouses hold their interests in the installment obligation or the purchased property as community property or as equal undivided joint interests. Finally the resale rules will not apply in any

[Footnote ¶ 152 continued]
(11) The term "marketable securities" includes securities which are listed on the New York Stock Exchange, the American Stock Exchange, or any city or regional exchange in which quotations appear on a daily basis, including foreign securities listed on a recognized foreign national or regional exchange; securities regularly traded in the national or regional over-the-counter market, for which published quotations are available; securities locally traded for which quotations can readily be obtained from established brokerage firms; and units in a common trust fund. Mutual fund shares for which redemption prices are published would also be considered marketable securities.

Act § 2, ¶ 152

case where it is established to the satisfaction of the Internal Revenue Service that none of the dispositions had as one of its principal purposes the avoidance of Federal income taxes.

In the exceptional cases to which the nonavoidance exception may apply, it is anticipated that regulations would provide definitive rules so that complicated legislation is not necessary to prescribe substituted property or taxpayer rules which would not be of general application. In appropriate cases, it is anticipated that the regulations and rulings under the nontax avoidance exception will deal with certain tax-free transfers which normally would not be treated as a second disposition of the property, e.g., charitable transfers, like-kind exchanges, gift transfers, and transfers to a controlled corporation or a partnership. Generally it is intended that a second disposition will qualify under the nontax avoidance exception when it is of an involuntary nature, e.g., foreclosure upon the property by a judgment lien creditor of the related purchaser or bankruptcy of the related purchaser. In addition it is intended that the exception will apply in the case of a second disposition which is also an installment sale if the terms of payment under the installment resale are substantially equivalent to, or longer than, those for the first installment sale, However, the exception would not apply if the resale terms would permit significant deferral of recognition of gain from the initial sale when proceeds from the resale are being collected sooner.

Under the bill, the period for assessing a deficiency in tax attributable to a second disposition by the related purchaser will not expire before the day which is 2 years after the date the initial installment seller furnishes a notice that there was a second disposition of the property. The notice is to be furnished in the manner prescribed by regulations. Under the bill, a protective notification may be filed to prevent the tolling of the period of limitations for assessing a deficiency in cases where there are questions as to whether a second disposition has occurred (e.g., a lease which might be characterized as a sale or exchange for tax purposes) or whether there is a principal purpose of Federal income tax avoidance.

For purposes of the related party rules, the bill adopts a definition of related parties which will include spouses, children, grandchildren, and parents but will exclude brothers and sisters.

In the case of a corporation, it will be considered to be related to another taxpayer if stock which is or might be owned by it is or would be treated as owned by the other taxpayer under the general corporate attribution rules (Code sec. 318). Generally, a related corporation will be one in which a person directly or indirectly owns 50 percent or more in value of the stock in the corporation. Also for this purpose, the principles of the general corporate stock ownership attribution rules (Code sec. 318) will apply in determining the related party status of partnerships, trusts, and estates.

It is to be understood that the provisions governing the use of the installment method to report sales between related parties, and the definition of such relationships, are not intended to preclude the Internal Revenue Service from asserting the proper tax treatment of transactions that are shams.

Sales of depreciable property between certain closely-related parties.—Under the bill, the accrual method of accounting in effect is required for deferred payment sales of depreciable property between certain closely-related parties.[12] In general, this rule is intended to deter transactions which are structured in such a way as to give the related purchaser the benefit of depreciation deductions (measured from a stepped-up basis) prior to the time the seller is required to include in income the corresponding gain on the sale. For transactions to which the special rule will apply, the deferred payments will be deemed to be received in the taxable year in which the sale occurs. In the case of sales for contingent future payments, it is intended that, in general, the amount realized in the year of sale will be equal to the value of the property sold.

[Footnote ¶ 152 continued]

(12) In the case of transfers which are treated as tax-free transfers to a controlled corporation or to a partnership. (Code secs. 351, 362, 721, and 723), the provisions of present law would continue to apply and would not be affected by the provision. Also, in the case of transactions which are governed by the doctrine of liquidation-reincorporation under present law, the tax treatment for those transactions would continue to be governed by present law and would not be effected by the provision.

This special rule will apply only to deferred payment sales between a taxpayer and the taxpayer's spouse; the taxpayer and a partnership or corporation which is 80-percent owned by the taxpayer and/or the taxpayer's spouse; and between partnerships and corporations which are 80-percent owned by the taxpayer and/or the taxpayer's spouse. The rule will not apply if it is established to the satisfaction of the Internal Revenue Service that the sale did not have as one of its principal purposes the avoidance of Federal income taxes.

Thus, the special rules will not apply if, at the time of the installment sale, the husband and wife are legally separated under a decree of divorce or separate maintenance. Also, they will not apply if the installment sale occurs pursuant to a settlement in a proceeding which culminates in a decree of divorce or separate maintenance. Further, the rule will not apply if no significant tax deferral benefits will be derived from the sale.

Statement of committee intention.— The committee intends that no inference be drawn from these provisions as to the proper treatment of any related party installment sale occurring prior to the effective date provided under the bill.

The Committee on Finance believes that, as a principle of tax policy, a taxpayer should be permitted to contest on an equal footing in the appropriate courts matters in dispute with the government. The Committee recognizes that two sections of the pending legislation (new Code secs. 453 (e)(7) and (g)) put a taxpayer at a disadvantage if he or she should seek a court ruling on the merits of the issue.

The Committee accepts the pending legislation only with the specific understanding that—

(1) The foregoing sections are designed to give an opportunity to taxpayers to qualify who might otherwise not be able to qualify under this legislation for the reporting of income on the installment method,

(2) Under the preceding sections in determining the question of tax avoidance, the Commissioner shall treat taxpayers fairly and equitably in light of all the facts and circumstances of each particular case in a manner consistent with the remedial intent of the preceding sections, and

(3) The preceding sections are not to be considered as a precedent for future legislation.

The Committee shall monitor closely the administration of the sections and the Commissioner shall report annually its actions to the appropriate Congressional committees. Further, the General Accounting Office shall not later than two years after the enactment of this legislation report to the Congress on the manner in which the preceding sections are being administered.

G. Treatment of Third Party Guarantee (Sec. 2 of the bill and new Sec. 453(f)(3) of the Code)

Present law.—Generally, under present law (Code sec. 453), income from a sale of property on the installment basis may be reported as the payments are received. If the installment method is elected for qualifying sales, the gain reported for any taxable year is the proportion of the installment payment received in that year which the gross profit, realized or to be realized when payment is completed, bears to the total contract price. In general, the contract price is the amount which will be paid to the seller. The payments taken into account as being received in a taxable year would not include the purchaser's obligation of future payment, whether dischargeable in money or other property (including foreign currency), unless that obligation is a bond or other evidence or indebtedness which is either payable on demand or has been issued by a corporation or government and is readily tradable.

In a recent case, the Tax Court held that, by reason of a standby letter of credit used to secure future payment for the sale of a cotton crop, the taxpayer had received full payment in the year of sale and could not report the transaction on the installment method.[13] However, the Tenth Circuit Court of Appeals has recently held that a letter of credit used to secure payment for the sale of stock did not constitute payment for purposes of the installment sale provisions.[14]

* * * * * * *

[Footnote ¶ 152 continued]

(13) *J. K. Griffith*, 73 T.C. No. 76 (Feb. 28, 1980).
(14) *Sprague* v. *U.S.*, — F.2d — (10th Cir., Aug. 14, 1980).

Act § 2, ¶ 152

Explanation of provision.—Under the bill, a third party guarantee (including a standby letter of credit) will not be taken into account in determining if the buyer's evidence of indebtedness constitutes payment to the seller. **For this** purpose, a guarantee which is not treated as payment would not include a third party note (or any other type of third party obligation which is transferable or marketable prior to default in payment by the installment purchaser).

H. Receipt of Like Kind Property (Sec. 2 of the bill and new Sec. 453(f)(6) of the Code)

Present law.—Under present law, the transfer of property for cash payments and like kind property may qualify both for installment method reporting and, with respect to the gain attributable to the like kind exchange, nonrecognition treatment (Code sec. 1031 and Rev. Rul. 65-155, 1965-1. C.B. 356). In this case, the gain to be recognized under installment method reporting is the total gain realized on the transaction less the gain eligible for nonrecognition under the like kind exchange provision. However, the value of the like kind property received by the seller is taken into account in determining the amount of the selling price, the contract price, and payments received for purposes of the installment sale provision.[15] The value of the like kind property received in the taxable year in which the sale or exchange is made.

* * * * * * * *

Explanation of provision.—Under the bill, property permitted to be received without recognition of gain in an exchange described in Code section 1031 (b)[16] will not be treated as payment for purposes of reporting income under the installment method.

Thus, in reporting the gain on the exchange under the installment method where an installment obligation is received in addition to the like kind property, the gross profit will be the amount of gain which will be recognized on the exchange if the installment obligation were satisfied in full at its face amount. Also, the total contract price will not include the value of the like kind property but instead will consist solely of the sum of the money and fair market value of other property received plus the face amount of the installment obligation.

	Rev. Rul. 65-155— Like kind property taken into account	Like kind property not taken into account
Contract price	$1,000,000	$800,000
Gross profit	600,000	600,000
Gross profit ratio (percent)	(60)	(75)
Gain to be reported for:		
1. Taxable year of sale:		
(a) 60% of $300,000 (payments "received" of $100,000 cash and $200,000 value of like property)	180,000	
(b) 75% of $100,000 (cash payments)		75,000
2. Succeeding taxable year:		
(a) 60% of $700,000 (cash received)	420,000	
(b) 75% of $700,000 (cash received)		525,000
Total gain recognized	600,000	600,000
3. Basis of like kind property received	200,000	200,000

[Footnote ¶ 152 continued]

(15) Rev. Rul. 65-155, 1965-1 C.B. 356; *Clinton H. Mitchell,* 42 T.C. 953, 965 (1964); *Albert W. Turner,* TC Memo 1977-437. A similar case under present law involves the treatment of an installment obligation received as "boot" in exchange by a shareholder under a plan of corporate reorganization (sec. 356(a)(1)). Present law is unclear whether the exchange qualifies for installment sale reporting.

(16) This provision includes like kind exchanges (sec. 1031), exchanges of certain insurance policies (sec. 1035), certain exchanges of stock of the same corporation (sec. 1036), and certain exchanges of United States obligations (sec. 1037).

The basis of the like kind property received, (determined under section 1031 (d)) will be determined as if the obligation had been satisfied at its face amount.[17] Thus, the taxpayer's basis in the property transferred will first be allocated to the like kind property received (but not in excess of its fair market value) and any remaining basis will be used to determine the gross profit ratio.

The bill also provides that similar treatment applies in the case of an exchange under a plan of corporate reorganization described in section 356(a) which is not treated as a dividend.

These provisions may be illustrated by the following example [see end of preceding page]. Assume that the taxpayer exchanges property with a basis of $400,000 for like kind property worth $200,000, and an installment obligation for $800,000 with $100,000 payable in the taxable year of the sale and the balance payable in the succeeding taxable year. The example compares present law, which takes like kind property into account as payment, with the bill which reserves this rule.

I. Installment Obligations Distributed in a 12-Month Corporate Liquidation (Sec. 2 of the bill and new Sec. 453(h) of the Code)

Present law.—Under present law, gain or loss is not generally recognized at the corporate level for sales and exchanges occurring during the 12-month period after the corporation has elected a plan of complete liquidation (Code sec. 337). A special rule provides that in this situation gain or loss generally is not recognized to the liquidating corporation for distributions of installment obligations (Code sec. 453(d)(4)(B)). Gain or loss is recognized by the shareholders with respect to the liquidating distributions. No special exception applies for the distribution of installment obligations to shareholders so that the shareholders may defer reporting gain from the obligations.

* * * * * * *

Explanation of provision.—Under the bill, in the case of a corporate liquidation the receipt by a shareholder (under Code sec. 331) of an installment obligation which was received by the corporation during its 12-month liquidation period (under Code sec. 337) generally will not be treated as the receipt of payment by the shareholder.[18] Instead, the shareholder may report gain from the exchange of stock on the [installment] method, taking gain into account as payments are received on the installment obligation received as a liquidating distribution. Where a parent liquidating corporation had a subsidiary which received an obligation during the subsidiary's liquidation (to which sec. 337 (c)(3) applied) that obligation also will qualify for installment reporting by the shareholders of the parent corporation. However, in no event will obligations received by the liquidating corporation from the sale of inventory, other than from the bulk sale, qualify for installment treatment by the shareholder.

Where liquidating distributions are received by a shareholder in more than one taxable year, the shareholder will be required to recompute the gain reported from the liquidation by allocating basis in the stock pro rata over all payments received (or to be received). This may require amended returns if all of the liquidating distributions are not received during the same taxable year of the shareholder.

The following example will illustrate the operation of this rule. Assume that the taxpayer is the sole shareholder of a corporation with an adjusted basis of $200,000 in the stock (all of the stock having been acquired in the same transaction at the same cost), and is a calendar year taxpayer. Also, assume that the corporation adopts a plan of liquidation in July 1982, that the corporation sells all of its assets in August 1982 to an unrelated purchaser for $1 million, consisting of $250,000 in cash and an installment note for $750,000, that the entire gain qualifies for nonrecognition under section 337, that there is no imputed interest income or original issue discount, that the corporation distributes

[Footnote ¶ 152 continued]

(17) This is the same rule as presently set forth in Rev. Rul. 65-155.

(18) This treatment will apply to the target company in an acquisition if it is treated as having liquidated under Code section 337 (Rev. Rul. 69-6, 1969-1 C.B. 104). Further, in the case of a corporate acquisition involving the use of a "transitory" or "phantom" company, the obligations issued by the acquiring parent company would be considered issued by the "purchaser", although the assets of the acquired company are technically transferred to the transitory company set up to effect the acquisition, if that company is disregarded for Federal tax purposes under present law.

Act § 2, ¶ 152

the cash in November 1982 and that the note is distributed in complete liquidation in June 1983. The taxpayer would initially report a gain [of] $50,000 in 1982 ($250,000 cash received less $200,000 basis in the stock).

After the distribution of the note in 1983, under the installment method, the taxpayer would recompute the gain reported in 1982 by allocating basis according to the installment sales rules. Thus, 75 percent ($750,000 (face amount of installment obligation) divided by $1 million (total distribution)) of the taxpayer's basis in the stock, or $150,000 (75 percent times $200,000) would be allocated to the installment obligation. Further, 25 percent ($250,000 divided by $1 million) of the taxpayer's basis in the stock or $50,000 (25 percent times $200,000) is allocated to the distribution of the cash. The taxpayer thus is required to file an amended return for 1982 to reflect an additional $150,000 of gain (cash received of $250,000 less the sum of $50,000 basis and $50,000 gain initially reported). Eighty percent of each payment on the note (other than interest) must be reported as gain by the taxpayer (gain of $600,000 ($750,000 face amount of obligation less basis of $150,000) divided by $750,000 (contract price)).

Under the bill, nonrecognition treatment will not be available to the extent the obligation is attributed to a sale of depreciable property by the corporation if the installment purchaser is either the shareholder-distributee's spouse, or a corporation or a partnership which is 80-percent owned by the shareholder-distributee and/or his spouse. This provision applies if the property sold by the corporation is depreciable in the hands of the purchaser. Under the provision, gain will be recognized by the shareholder for his taxable year in which the installment obligation is distributed.

Finally, if another related party (a person who is not covered by the preceding special recognition rule but who is related within the meaning of new sec. 453(f)(1)) purchases the corporate assets and then disposes of them, the related party disposition rules (as previously described under part F of this report) will apply to the shareholder who received the related party's installment obligations as a liquidating distri-

bution. In other words, in these cases, the shareholder-distributee will be substituted for the liquidated corporation for purposes of applying the related party resale rules provided under the bill.

J. Sales Subject to a Contingency (Sec. 2 of the bill and new Sec. 453(i) of the Code)

Present law.—As a general rule, installment reporting of gain from deferred payments is not available where all or a portion of the selling price is subject to a contingency. The case law holds that the selling price must be fixed and determinable for section 453 (b) to apply.[19] An agreement, however, to indemnify the purchaser for breach of certain warranties and representations by offset against the purchase price will not disqualify an installment sale under section 453(b).[20] Exactly how broad such contingencies can be is unclear.

Where an installment sale is subject to a contingency with respect to the price and the installment method is not available, the taxpayer is required to recognize all of the gain in the year of the sale with respect to all of the payments to be made, even though such payments are payable in future taxable years. In the case of a cash-method taxpayer where the future payments have no readily ascertainable fair market value, the taxpayer may treat the transaction with respect to those payments as "open" and use the cost-recovery method under *Burnet* v. *Logan,* 2830 U.S. 404 (1931).

* * * * * * * *

Explanation of provision.—The bill permits installment sale reporting for sales for a contingent selling price. In extending eligibility, the bill does not prescribe specific rules for every conceivable transaction. Rather, the bill provides that specific rules will be prescribed under regulations.

However, it is intended that, for sales under which there is a stated maximum selling price, the regulations will permit basis recovery on the basis of a gross profit ratio determined by reference to the stated maximum selling price. For purposes of this provision, incidental or remote contingencies are not to be taken into account in determining if

[Footnote ¶ 152 continued]
(19) *Gralap v. United States,* 458 F.2d 1158 (10th Cir. 1972); *In re Steen,* 509 F.2d 1398 9th Cir. 1975).
(20) See Rev. Rul. 77-56, 1977-1 C.B. 135.

there is a stated maximum selling price. In general, the maximum selling price would be determined from the "four corners" of the contract agreement as the largest price which could be paid to the taxpayer assuming all contingencies, formulas, etc., operate in the taxpayer's favor. Income from the sale would be reported on a pro rata basis with respect to each installment payment using the maximum selling price to determine the total contract price and gross profit ratio. If, pursuant to standards prescribed by regulations, it is subsequently determined that the contingency will not be satisfied in whole or in part, thus reducing the maximum selling price, the taxpayer's income from the sale would be recomputed. The taxpayer would then report reduced income, as adjusted, with respect to each installment payment received in the taxable year of adjustment and subsequent taxable years. If the maximum price is reduced in more than one taxable year, e.g., because of successive changes in the status of the contingency, each such year of reduction would constitute an adjustment year.

Where the taxpayer has reported more income from installment payments received in previous taxable years than the total recomputed income, the taxpayer would be permitted to deduct the excesses in the adjustment year as a loss.

In cases where the sales price is indefinite and no maximum selling price can be determined but the obligation is payable over a fixed period of time, it is generally intended that basis of the property sold would be recovered ratably over that fixed period. In a case where the selling price and payment period are both indefinite but a sale has in fact occurred, it is intended that the regulations would permit ratable basis recovery over some reasonable period of time. Also, in appropriate

cases, it is intended that basis recovery would be permitted under an income forecast type method.[21]

The creation of a statutory deferred payment option for all forms of deferred payment sales significantly expands the availability of installment reporting to include situations where it has not previously been permitted. By providing an expanded statutory installment reporting option, the Committee believes that in the future there should be little incentive to devise convoluted forms of deferred payment obligations to attempt to obtain deferred reporting. In any event, the effect of the new rules is to reduce substantially the justification for treating transactions as "open" and permitting the use of the cost-recovery method sanctioned by *Burnet* v. *Logan*, 283 U.S. 404 (1931). Accordingly, it is the Committee's intent that the cost-recovery method not be available in the case of sales for a fixed price (whether the seller's obligation is evidenced by a note, contractual promise, or otherwise), and that its use be limited to those rare and extraordinary cases involving sales for a contingent price where the fair market value of the purchaser's obligation cannot reasonably be ascertained.

K. Election of Installment Method by Accrual Method Dealer (Sec. 2 of the bill and present Secs. 453(c) and 481(d) of the Code)

Present law.—Under present law (Code sec. 453(c)), an accrual basis dealer in personal property who elects to change to the installment method of accounting must include in income the gain attributable to payments received with respect to sales which had been included in income for taxable years prior to electing the installment method. In mitigation for double inclusion of income from the sales, an adjustment to tax is permitted. However, the amount

[Footnote ¶ 152 continued]

(21) In general, the income forecast method for basis recovery is considered appropriate for a transaction with respect to which it may be demonstrated that receipts will be greater for the earlier years of the payment period and then decline for the later years of the payment period. It is intended that the regulations will deal with the application of this method with respect to sales of property qualifying for depreciation under the income forecast method (e.g., movies), mineral rights when the selling price is based on production, a sale under which the amount payable to the seller is based on a declining percentage of the purchaser's revenues, and similar sales. In developing these regulations, the committee intends that the Treasury Department will prescribe rules for this method to avoid, whenever possible, leaving a seller with an unrecovered basis in the obligation, and thereby creating a capital loss, after the final payment is received. For qualifying transactions, a more rapid basis recovery under this method is to be allowed even if there is a fixed period over which payments are to be received.

Act § 2, ¶ 152

of the adjustment is limited to the lesser of the portion of income tax attributable to inclusion in income for the taxable year of sale or the portion of income tax attributable to inclusion of the gross profit for the taxable year in which installment payments are received. The formula for determining the tax "attributable to" the inclusion of the gain in income results in a higher total tax for both years taken together than if the gain had been reported only once.

* * * * * * * *

Explanation of provision.—Under the bill, an accrual method dealer who elects the installment method of reporting will report gain as payments are received only for sales made on or after the effective date of the installment method election (Code sec. 481(a)).

It is intended that, under Treasury regulations, a failure to report the full amount of gain from sales may be treated as an election of the installment method. For example, it is intended that a dealer, who treats a transaction as a lease of personal property and only reports the payments received as rental income, may be eligible for installment reporting under the regulations if the transaction is recharacterized as a sale rather than a lease in an audit by the Internal Revenue Service. However, it is intended that no taxpayer who has reported sales under the accrual method will be required to change from that method under the regulations.

L. Transfers of Installment Obligations to Life Insurance Companies (Sec. 2 of the bill and new Sec. 453B(e)(2) of the Code)

Present law.—Generally, under present law, any unreported gain must be recognized when a taxpayer disposes of an installment obligation. However, in the case of certain tax-free transfers, disposition of an installment obligation will not trigger the recognition of gain. In these cases, the transferee succeeds to the basis of the installment seller and reports the remaining gain as payments are received. Under a special rule (Code sec. 453(d)(5)), transfers of installment obligations to a life insurance company are not eligible for nonrecognition treatment for otherwise tax-free transfers.

* * * * * * * *

Explanation of provision.—Under the bill, the special disposition rules for transfers of obligations to a life insurance company will not apply if the life insurance company elects to report any remaining gain as investment income (under Code sec. 804(b)) as payments are received.

M. Cancellation of Installment Obligation (Sec. 2 of the bill and new Sec. 453B(f) of the Code)

Present law.—Under present law, some have argued that the installation obligation disposition rules can be avoided by making gift cancellations of the obligation or the installments as they come due. In other words, by making an installment sale and then cancelling the obligation or a number of installment payments, it is argued that the seller will incur no income tax liability, but possibly some gift taxes, and the buyer will have a cost basis in the property sold although no income tax cost will have been incurred on the transaction. If a direct gift is made, the donee's basis is generally the same as the donor's basis rather than a "cost" basis which reflects future payments which will never be made.

This cancellation technique is based on a District Court's decision in *Miller v. Usry.*[22] In that case, the court held that the disposition rules for obligations disposed of other than by sale or exchange were directed at corporate transfers and should not be applied to a cancellation of the obligation where there has been no actual, real, or material gain to the taxpayer. The court did not consider the possible benefit to the donee from acquiring a cost basis through the installment sale. Next, the court held that the disposition rules for satisfaction at other than face value did apply to a cancellation but no tax was incurred because no amount was realized by the taxpayer.

* * * * * * * *

Explanation of provision.—The bill makes it clear that the cancellation of an installment obligation is treated as a disposition of the obligation. In the case where the obligor is a related party, the amount taken into account as a disposition triggering recognition of unreported gain attributable to the obligation is not to be less than the face amount of the installment obligation.

Effective date.—[For effective dates of Act Sec. 2, see ¶ 156.—Ed.]

[Footnote ¶ 152 continued]
　(22)　160 F. Supp. 368, 58-1 USTC ¶ 9393 (W.D. La. 1958).

[¶ 153] SECTION 3. COORDINATION WITH SECTION 691
(Sec. 691 of the Code)

[Senate Explanation]

Present law.—Under present law, the installment obligation disposition rules do not apply to the transmission of installment obligations at death (Code secs. 453(d)(3) and 691(a)(4)). However, unreported gains attributable to installment obligations are treated as items of gross income in respect of a decedent so that the recipient is taxed upon receipt of the installment payments in the same manner as the deceased seller would have been had he lived to receive the payments. A special rule allows a deduction for the estate taxes attributable to the unreported gain on the installment obligation (Code sec. 691(c)).

Another provision (Code sec. 691 (a)(2)) provides that the transfer of an installment obligation to the estate of the deceased seller will not be treated as a transfer requiring the reporting of gain. In addition, this rule applies to a transfer to a person pursuant to the right of such person to receive the installment obligation by reason of the death of the seller or by bequest, devise, or inheritance from the seller.

* * * * * * * *

Explanation of provision.—The bill provides that any previously unreported gain from an installment sale will be recognized by a deceased seller's estate if the obligation is transferred or transmitted by bequest, devise, or inheritance to the obligor or is cancelled by the executor.

In the absence of some act of cancelling the obligation by distribution or notation which results in cancellation under the Uniform Commercial Code or other local law, the disposition will be considered to occur no later than the time the period of administration of the estate is concluded.

If the cancellation occurs at the death of the holder of the obligation, the cancellation is to be treated as a transfer by the estate of the decedent. However, if the obligation were held by a person other than the decedent, such as a trust, the cancellation will be treated as a transfer immediately after the decedent's death by that person.

If the decedent and the obligor were related persons (within the meaning of new Code section 453(f)(1)), the fair market value of the obligation for disposition purposes is not to be treated as less than its face amount.

For purposes of this provision, if an installment obligation becomes unenforceable, it will be treated as if it were cancelled.

Effective date.—[Applies in the case of decedents dying after the date of enactment.—Ed.]

[¶ 154] SECTION 4. AMENDMENT OF SECTION 1038
(Sec. 1038 of the Code)

[Senate Explanation]

Present law.—Under present law, the recognition of gain upon a reconveyance of real property to the seller in partial or full satisfaction of purchase money debt is limited (Code sec. 1038). Losses, including bad debt losses, are also not recognized upon a reconveyance of real property. With respect to gains, the amount of gain required to be recognized upon reconveyance of the real property sold generally is limited to the lesser of the amount of any remaining unreported portion of the original gain or the amount by which the sum of the money and fair market value of property received prior to the reacquisition exceeds the amount of gain previously reported. The Internal Revenue Service has ruled that this provision does not apply to a reconveyance to the estate of a deceased taxpayer who made the original sale (Rev. Rul. 69-83, 1969-1, C.B. 202). In other words, a decedent's estate is not permitted to succeed to the tax treatment which would have been available to the decedent had he lived to receive the reconveyance because the estate is considered to be a separate taxable entity.

* * * * * * * *

Explanation of provision.—Under the bill, the estate or beneficiary of a deceased seller will be entitled to the same nonrecognition treatment upon the acquisition of real property in partial or full satisfaction of secured purchase money debt as the deceased seller would have been entitled.

Act § 4, ¶ 154

The basis of the property acquired will be the same as if the property had been reacquired by the original seller, increased by an amount equal to the section 691(c) deduction for estate taxes which would have been allowable had the repossession been taxable.

The committee intends that no inference is to be drawn from this provision as to the application of present law.

Effective date.—[Applies to acquisitions of real property by the taxpayer after the date of enactment.—Ed.]

[¶ 155] SECTION 5. COORDINATION WITH SECTION 1239
(Sec. 1239 of the Code)

[Senate Explanation]

Present law.—Under present law, gain from the sale or exchange of depreciable property between certain related parties is denied capital gains treatment (and is taxed as ordinary income). Related parties include husband and wife, an individual and an 80-percent controlled corporation, and two 80-percent controlled corporations. The attribution rules of Code section 318 are generally applied to determine ownership in a corporation.

Reasons for change.—The committee believes that the same related party rules should apply with respect to the characterization of income from sales of depreciable property between a husband and wife or their controlled entity and to the special installment sale rules for sales of depreciable property between husband and wife or their controlled entity. For these purposes, the committee also believes that the attribution of ownership rules should be narrowed to exclude family members other than husband and wife.

Explanation of provision.—Under the bill, the provisions of section 1239(a) denying capital gain treatment on the sale or exchange of depreciable property will apply to sales between husband and wife, between the taxpayer and a partnership or corporation which is 80-percent owned by the taxpayer and/or the taxpayer's spouse; and between partnerships and corporations which are 80-percent owned by the taxpayer and/or the taxpayer's spouse. For these purposes, the person treated as the owner of a trust under the grantor trust rules is to be treated as the owner of the assets in the trust.

Under the provision, ownership is to be attributed in accordance with the principles under the general corporate ownership attribution rules (Code sec. 318) except that an individual's family will only include a spouse and the entity attribution rules will be applied without regard to the percentage of ownership limitations.

Effective date.—[For effective date of Act Sec. 5, see ¶ 156.—Ed.]

[¶ 156] SECTION 6. EFFECTIVE DATES

[Senate Explanation]

In general, the provisions of the bill are effective for dispositions of property, cancellations and reacquisitions of real property, as the case may be, occurring after the date of enactment. The provisions which eliminate the 30-percent initial payment and the two or more payments requirements are effective for transactions occurring in taxable years ending after the date of enactment.

However, the related party installment sale rules would apply to installment sales (first dispositions) after May 14, 1980. The provision relating to the distribution of installment obligations in connection with a 12-month corporate liquidation would apply with respect to installment obligations distributed after March 31, 1980. (A liquidating distribution made after March 31, 1980, will qualify for nonrecognition treatment to a shareholder even if the obligation is from a sale which is ineligible for installment reporting by the corporation because the sale occurred before the effective date of the other rules revised or eliminated under the bill.)

[List of '54 Code Sections Affected appears on following page]

¶ **199**

LIST OF 1954 CODE SECTIONS AFFECTED

[¶ 200] The table below contains a complete list of sections or subsections of the 1954 Code amended, added or repealed by the Installment Sales Revision Act of 1980. The Act section making the amendment is listed opposite each change.

1954 Code Sec.	1980 Act Sec.	1954 Code Sec.	1980 Act Sec.
311(a) amended	2(b)(1)	481(d) struck out	2(b)(3)
336 amended	2(b)(1)	644(f) amended	2(b)(4)
336(a) amended	2(c)(1)	691(a)(4) amended	2(b)(5)(A)
337(f)(3) amended	2(c)(2)	691(a)(4) amended	2(b)(5)(B)
381(c)(8) amended	2(b)(2)(A)	691(a)(5) added	3
381(c)(8) amended	2(b)(2)(B)	1038(g) added	4
453 amended	2(a)	1239(b) amended	5
453A added	2(a)	1239(c) amended	5
453B added	2(a)	1255(b)(2) amended	2(b)(6)
453B(d)(2) amended	2(c)(3)		

Appendix I

Pro-Buyer
Stock Purchase Agreement

The attached agreement is an actual agreement used in a proposed sale of stock for cash and notes in a situation in which the purchasers had strong bargaining power. Also included is a copy of a skeleton form of secured note in such a transaction and a covenant not to compete for such a transaction. *See discussion of the installment sale beginning at page 25.*

STOCK PURCHASE AGREEMENT

The legal names of the parties need to be specified. Here, because there were a large number of stockholders, their names were not specified at the beginning of the agreement.

These clauses are desirable to set the context of the legally effective portion of the agreement.

THIS AGREEMENT is made this _____ day of _____, 19_____, among the undersigned stockholders, hereinafter collectively referred to as "Sellers," and GOLIATH ENTERPRISES, INCORPORATED, a Delaware corporation, hereinafter referred to as "Buyer."

WHEREAS, Sellers are the owners and holders of all of the outstanding stock of DAVID CORPORATION, a California corporation, hereinafter referred to as "Company"; and

WHEREAS, Sellers are desirous of selling to Buyer, and Buyer is desirous of purchasing from Sellers all of the shares of stock of Company upon the terms and conditions and for the consideration hereinafter set forth;

NOW, THEREFORE, in consideration of the mutual covenants herein contained, the parties hereto agree as follows:

Article 1. Purchase

The precise stock transaction is specified.

For the purchase price, and on the terms and subject to the conditions set forth in this Agreement, Sellers hereby sell, assign, transfer, and deliver to Buyer, and Buyer hereby purchases from Sellers, all of the issued or outstanding capital stock of Company, consisting of 372,614 shares of the common stock of Company (the "stock"). Any requirements of any state regulatory authority for such transfer shall be met by the Sellers at their expense, prior to

The closing time and place should be specified to avoid later misunderstanding.

closing, and confirmation of such approval shall be furnished Buyer at closing in such form as Buyer shall reasonably require. The closing of the transaction (the "closing") shall be held at 10:00 a.m. on Thursday, September 30, 19 _____, in the offices of Buyer's counsel, Messrs. _____, First National Bank Tower, Atlanta, Georgia 30303.

Article 2. Purchase Price

Price

Section 2.01. The purchase price to be paid by Buyer to Sellers for the Stock is $2,800,000.00.

Payment

Section 2.02. At closing, Buyer shall pay to Sellers the purchase price as follows:

It is a good idea to agree as to the form of the note in the agreement itself.

(a) $600,000.00 by certified check or wired funds; and
(b) Buyer's Note in the amount of $2,200,000.00 in the form of Schedule A attached to this Agreement.

Article 3. Warranties of Sellers

Compare the strength of these warranties and their general absolute nature with the limited warranties given in the purchase agreement.

Section 3.01. Sellers hereby jointly and severally warrant, represent, and covenant to Buyer, and this Agreement is made in reliance on the following, each of which is deemed to be a separate covenant, representation, and warranty:

(a) The Sellers jointly own, beneficially and of record, free and clear of all liens, charges, claims, equities, restrictions, or encumbrances, all of the shares of stock and have the full right, power, and authority to sell, transfer, and deliver to the Buyer, in accordance with this Agreement, all of the stock free and clear of all liens, charges, claims, equities, restrictions, and encumbrances. The sale by the Sellers of the stock does not constitute a breach or violation of, or default under, any will, deed of trust, agreement, or other instrument.

(b) Company is a corporation duly organized, validly existing, and in good standing under the laws of the state of California. Company has full corporate power and authority to carry on the respective businesses of the Company and to own or lease properties related thereto as and in the places where such businesses are now conducted and such properties are now owned, leased, or operated, and is duly qualified to do business and is in good standing in the state of California which is the sole jurisdiction in which its ownership of real property or the nature of the businesses conducted by the Company makes such qualification necessary.

(c) All shares of the stock of Company and all rights to any shares of Company and to vote any shares of Company are owned of record and beneficially by Sellers in accordance with Schedule B. Sellers have previously furnished to Buyer full and complete copies of the Certificate of Incorporation and By-Laws of Company and such Certificate of Incorporation and By-Laws remain unmodified and of full force and effect. Sellers have also furnished to Buyer and for Buyer's inspection the minute books of Company, and no meetings or resolutions adopted by the shareholders, directors, or others on behalf of Company in any way restrict or adversely affect the obligation of Sellers under this Agreement, or the business of Company. Company has neither paid nor declared any dividend or other distribution with respect to any shares of stock of Company since December 31, 19_____.

(d) Sellers have furnished Buyer with audited financial statements of Company as of the fiscal years ending December 31, 19_____, 19_____, 19_____, 19_____, and 19_____. Such financial statements include all assets and liabilities related to Company as of each of those respective dates and statements of income and retained earnings for the period ending on each respective date. Such financial statements present fairly, in conformity with generally accepted accounting principles, consistently applied, the financial condition of Company as of the respective dates of each of said statements and the results of the operations for the respective periods indicated in said statements of income and retained earnings. All inventory shown on such financial statements and owned by Company at closing is usable and in good condition and has been written down to realizable market value and is kept on a first-in, first-out basis. None of the financial statements of Company furnished to Buyer reflect any non-recurring income or other special item nor any transactions made between Company and any Seller, or any entity or person in any way affiliated financially or by kinship to any Seller. Company has made no election and has filed no consent with respect to any subsection of Section 341 of the Internal Revenue Code of 1954. Company has not taken any investment credit or utilized any accelerated method of depreciation which could be subject to recapture under provision of the Internal Revenue Code.

(e) On the date of this Agreement, Company has no material liabilities, absolute or contingent, concerning it which are not shown or provided for in said financial statements at December 31, 19_____, except those arising in the ordinary course of the business of Company after December 31, 19_____.

(f) Schedule C contains a description of all real property owned by Company. Company owns outright the fee simple title in and to all of such real property, free and clear of all liens, mortgages, charges, or encumbrances of any nature whatsoever except as specified in Schedule C. All leases to which Company is a party, either as lessor or lessee, are specified in Schedule C. The present business activities conducted on any such real property comply with local zoning and use requirements in all cases. No claim of any zoning or use violation has been communicated to Company.

(g) Company owns outright, free of any liens or encumbrances of any type: (i) all equipment utilized by Company in the operation of its business, including but not limited to all equipment specified in Schedule D; and (ii) all other assets and property reflected in said financial statement of December 31, 19_____, or acquired after said date (other than assets sold or otherwise disposed of in the ordinary course of business since December 31, 19_____).

(h) Company is not a licensor or licensee in respect of any patents, trade secrets, inventions, trademarks, or trade names which are used by Company. Company owns all trade secrets, trademarks, trade names, and copyrights necessary to conduct the business of Company as now operated and has not received any notice of conflict with the asserted rights of others.

(i) The respective properties and business of Company are adequately insured under such policies to the extent usually insured by corporations engaged in the newspaper business against loss or damage of the kind customarily insured against by such corporations, all as shown on Schedule E.

(j) Company is not a party to any written or oral, express or implied: (i) contract or negotiation with any labor union; (ii) lease to it as lessee of personal property with an unexpired term (including any period covered by an option to renew exercisable without action by it) of one year or more; (iii) lease under which it is lessor; or (iv) other material contract or commitment not disclosed in writing to buyer. Company is not a party to any written or oral, express or implied: contract for the employment of any person, or bonus, pension, profit-sharing, retirement, stock purchase, vacation benefit, stock option, hospitalization, insurance, or similar plan or practice, formal or informal, in effect with respect to any employees or others.

(k) There are no actions, suits, or proceedings (whether or not purportedly on behalf of Company) pending or threatened against, affecting or related to Company, or the continued use of the names now used by any publication of Company, in equity or otherwise, or before or by any Federal, state, municipal, or other governmental department, commission, board, bureau, agency, or instrumentality; (ii) Company is not in default with respect to any order, writ, injunction, or decree of any court or any Federal, state, municipal, or other governmental department, commission, board, bureau, agency, or instrumentality which relates to its operation of Company; (iii) there are no disputes involving in the aggregate more than $300 concerning, or default (or any event which upon notice or lapse of time, or other would constitute a default) by Company under any contract; and (iv) no present or former employee of Company has any claim growing out of employment by Company for overtime pay, wages, or salaries other than for work done in the current payroll period, or any violation of any statute, ordinance, or regulation relating to minimum wages, hours, or conditions of work.

(l) All Federal, state, and local tax returns required to be filed by Company have been duly filed. No tax audit or investigation, local, state, or Federal, concerning or related to the respective business of Company has been conducted for any fiscal year. Company has timely paid any required taxes, fees, and assessments of any type with respect to the business of Company, and has adequately provided for all taxes, fees, and assessments of any type which shall become due with respect to Company to and including the closing date.

(m) Since December 31, 19_____, neither Sellers nor Company have: (i) incurred any indebtedness which is secured by any asset of Company, or any indebtedness which restricts either the Seller's or Company's right to fully perform or comply with all of Seller's obligations hereunder; (ii) incurred any obligation or liability relating to Company or its respective properties or assets, except current liabilities incurred in the ordinary course of business; (iii) mortgaged, pledged, or subjected to lien, charge, or other encumbrance any of the assets, tangible or intangible, used by Company; (iv) sold, assigned, or transferred any of the tangible assets used by Company except in the ordinary course of business; (v) sold, assigned, or transferred any patents, trademarks, trade names, copyrights, or other similar assets; (vi) waived any rights except in the ordinary course of business or suffered any extraordinary losses; or (vii) otherwise entered into any transaction other than in the ordinary course of business.

(n) Since December 31, 19_____, there has been no material adverse change in the business or property of Company, or its financial condition as a whole. Since December 31, 19_____, the business of Company has been operated only in the ordinary course, and in compliance with all applicable laws and regulations.

(o) The execution and carrying out of this Agreement in accordance with the terms hereof will not conflict with, or result in any breach of the terms, conditions, or provisions of, or constitute a default (or an event upon which notice or lapse of time, or both, would constitute a default) under any indenture, mortgage, or lease, or other material agreement or instrument affecting Company or any Seller, or result in the creation of any lien, charge, or encumbrance upon any of the properties or assets of Company. The execution and carrying out of this Agreement will not violate any provision of law.

(p) Company is not a party to any collective bargaining negotiations concerning any employee of Company; and Company has not been notified that any employees of Company wish or may wish to be represented by any labor organization.

This language parallels that of Rule 10b-5 of the Securities and Exchange Commission. It is catchall warranty as to disclosure which should be included where possible.

(q) No statement, warranty, or representation by Sellers contains any untrue statement of a material fact or omits to state a material fact necessary in order to make the statements made, in light of the circumstances under which such statements are made, not misleading.

The representations and warranties made in this Agreement shall be correct in all material respects on and as of the closing date with the same force and effect as though such representations and warranties had been made at the closing.

Compare the abbreviated warranties of Buyer with the lengthy warranties being required of the Seller.

Article 4. Warranties of Buyer

Buyer hereby warrants, represents, and covenants to Sellers, and this Agreement is made in reliance on the following, each of which is deemed to be a separate covenant, representation, and warranty:

(a) Buyer is a duly organized and existing corporation under the laws of the state of California and has all of the corporate powers and authority necessary to carry on the business it now conducts.

(b) Buyer has the power and authority to purchase all of the capital stock of Company from Sellers on the terms, conditions, and for the purchase price set forth herein.

Article 5. Survival of Warranties

Note that the warranties are not limited as to time. A Seller in a strong position would certainly want to limit the warranties to one or two years if possible.

The warranties, representations, and covenants of each of the parties hereto shall survive the execution of this Agreement and the closing hereunder. At closing each party shall execute a certificate in such reasonable form as the other party may require, certifying that each and every warranty, representation, and covenant made in this Agreement is true as of the closing.

Article 6. Books and Records: Resignations

At closing, Sellers shall deliver to Buyer all of the books and records of the Company, and the resignations of all officers and directors of Company, effective at Closing. Prior to closing, Buyer shall have full access to all books, records, and business premises of Company, including but not limited to, auditor's worksheets and inventory records and all tax and other returns filed with any governmental agency.

Remember that reasonable amounts paid for genuine covenants not to compete are usually deductible for Federal income tax purposes as ordinary and necessary business expenses.

Article 7. Covenant Not to Compete

Each Seller agrees that at closing he will enter into a Covenant Not to Compete in the form and on the terms specified in Schedule F.

Article 8. Conditions to Obligations of Sellers

The obligations of Sellers under this Agreement are, at the option of Sellers, subject to the conditions that, at the closing:

(a) All the terms, covenants, and conditions of this Agreement to be complied with and performed by Buyer on or before the closing shall have been fully complied with and performed in all material respects.

(b) The representations and warranties made by Buyer herein shall be correct in all material respects, on and as of the closing, with the same force and effect as though such representations and warranties had been made at the closing.

(c) Sellers shall have received an opinion of Messrs. _____ _____, General Counsel for Buyer, based with respect to matters of Delaware law upon the opinion of California counsel, and dated the closing date in form and substance satisfactory to Sellers and their counsel, to the effect that:

(i) Buyer is a corporation duly organized, validly existing, and in good standing under the laws of the State of Delaware; and

(ii) Buyer has full power and authority to purchase and acquire the stock from Sellers, and all corporate acts and other proceedings required to be taken by and on the part of Buyer to authorize it to carry out this Agreement and to deliver the cash and Note at the closing as provided herein, have been duly and properly taken, and this Agreement has been duly executed and delivered on behalf of Buyer and is a legal, valid, and binding obligation of Buyer in accordance with its terms.

Article 9. Conditions to Respective Obligations of Buyer

The obligations of Buyer under this Agreement, are at the option of Buyer, subject to the conditions that at the closing:

(a) All the terms, covenants, and conditions of this Agreement to be complied with and performed by Sellers on or before the closing shall have been fully complied with and performed in all material respects.

(b) Representations and warranties of Sellers contained herein shall be true, on and as of the closing, with the same effect as though all such representations and warranties have been made on and as of that date, and Sellers have caused to be delivered to Buyer a certificate dated at the closing signed by each Seller to such effect.

(c) Buyer shall have received an opinion of Messrs. _____ _____, counsel to Sellers, dated the closing, in form and substance satisfactory to Buyer and its counsel, to the effect that:

(i) Company is a corporation duly organized, validly existing, and in good standing under the laws of California, and has full corporate power and authority to carry on its business and own and lease its properties in the places where such business is being conducted and where such properties are now owned, leased, or operated, and is duly qualified as a foreign corporation in any jurisdiction in which such qualification is required;

(ii) Company has a duly authorized capital stock consisting of 500,000 shares of common stock, par value $1.00 per share, of which 372,614 shares have been validly issued and are outstanding, and all of such shares are fully paid and nonassessable. Company has no other authorized or issued capital stock or rights to obtain such capital stock;

(iii) No provision of the certificate of incorporation or by-laws of Company, or of any contract, instrument, or proceeding known to such counsel, prevents Sellers from delivering good title to the Stock in the manner contemplated in this Agreement;

(iv) Upon the consummation of the transaction contemplated hereby, Buyer will own 372,614 shares of the common stock of Company, which shall be all of the then issued or outstanding stock of Company in any type of class;

(v) This Agreement has been duly executed and delivered on behalf of each Seller and is a legal, valid, and binding obligation of each Seller in accordance with its terms.

Resignations of officers and directors should be routinely required although most modern corporate statutes allow them to be removed at will. Some few states still impose difficulties on the removal of the officers or directors without cause before the end of the fiscal year.

A clause such as (e) is important in order to minimize the risk that one party or the other would compel closing of the

(d) Buyer shall have received on or before the closing the signed resignations of such officers and directors of Company as Buyer shall designate.

(e) No action or proceeding shall be pending or threatened on the closing wherein a favorable judgment, decree, or order would prevent or make unlawful the carrying out of this Agreement or would cause the transactions contemplated by this Agreement to be rescinded or would require Buyer to divest itself of the shares to be acquired or any of the assets of Company. In the event of the receipt of any communication from any department or agency of government prior to the closing with regard to any transaction contemplated hereby, Buyer shall be the sole judge of whether such communication shall be interpreted as a threat of any such proceeding.

transaction in the face of a pending claim such as an anti-trust complaint being filed by the Department of Justice.

The right to liquidate the Company and substitute collateral can be a very important right, particularly if stock is being purchased with an intention to liquidate the corporation under § 334(b)(2) of the Internal Revenue Code, which generally allows the basis of the assets liquidated to be increased to the purchase price of the stock if the liquidation occurs within two years of the purchase of the stock.

Article 10. Right to Liquidate Company and Substitute Collateral

Sellers specifically agree that Buyer shall be entitled at any time after the closing to transfer any and all shares of the stock to any person, firm, or entity, including, but not limited to, a corporation controlled by or affiliated with Buyer, provided that no such transfer shall in any way relieve Buyer of its obligations under this Agreement or under the terms of the Note. In the event of any such transfer, the transferee shall be authorized to liquidate and dissolve Company, provided that the corporation or other entity into which the assets of Company are liquidated shall be a Delaware corporation and shall have no other material assets or liabilities other than such stock at the time of such liquidation, and that all of the shares of stock in such entity shall be substituted as collateral for the shares of stock of Company as to which a security interest is granted to Sellers under the terms of the Secured Note, a copy of which is attached as Schedule A. In the event of any such transfer and dissolution, the parties specifically agree to execute or cause to be executed as reasonably requested by any other party from time to time such instruments and documents as may be necessary in order to carry out and effectuate the purposes of this Agreement and particularly of this Article 10.

Article 11. Indemnification

Each party hereto shall indemnify and hold harmless all other parties hereto from any loss, damage, cost, or expense (including any attorneys' fees or court cost) incurred as a result of any warranty, representation, or covenant made herein by such party proving to be untrue.

Article 12. Miscellaneous

Notices

All notices required or permitted to be given hereunder shall be in writing and shall be deemed given three days after mailing via United States First-Class Certified Mail, postage prepaid, deposited in the United States mail in California, and if intended for the Sellers shall be given to each of the Sellers and shall be addressed:

[names and addresses]

and if intended for the Buyer, shall be addressed:

[name and address]

Any party hereto, by written notice to the other parties, may change the address for notices to be sent to him.

Governing Law

All questions with respect to the construction of this Agreement, and the rights and liabilities of the parties hereto, shall be governed by the laws of the state of Georgia.

Inurement

Subject to the restrictions against assignment as herein contained, this Agreement shall inure to the benefit of, and shall be binding upon, the assigns, successors in interest, personal representatives, estates, heirs, and legatees of each of the parties hereto.

Attorneys' Fees

In the event of any controversy, claim, or dispute between the parties hereto, arising out of or relating to this Agreement, or the breach thereof, the prevailing party shall be entitled to recover from the losing party reasonable expenses, attorneys' fees, and costs.

Entire Agreement

This Agreement contains the entire agreement of the parties hereto, and supersedes any prior written or oral agreements between them concerning the subject matter contained herein. There are no representations, agreements, arrangements, or understandings, oral or written, between and among the parties hereto, relating to the subject matter contained in this Agreement, which are not fully expressed herein.

Broker

It shall be the sole responsibility of the Sellers to pay any Broker's commission incident to this transaction, and Sellers shall indemnify and hold Buyer harmless from any and all claims for such commission.

IN WITNESS WHEREOF, the parties hereto have caused this Agreement to be executed and their seals affixed, the day first above written.

"SELLERS":

[Signature line for each Seller]

Witnessed as
to Sellers:

_____

_____

"BUYER"
GOLIATH ENTERPRISES,
INCORPORATED

By:_____

President

[Corporate Seal]
Attest:

_____

Secretary

SCHEDULE A

SECURED NOTE

$2,200,000.00   _____, 19_____

FOR VALUE RECEIVED, GOLIATH ENTERPRISES, IN-
CORPORATED promises to pay to the order of
_____, the principal sum of two million,
two hundred thousand and no/100 ($2,200,000) dollars, in legal
tender of the United States, with interest thereon from date at the
rate of seven per centum (7%) per annum, on the unpaid balance
until paid. Principal and interest shall be payable at
_____, or at such other place as the
holder hereof may designate in writing as follows:

1. On the 1st anniversary hereof, $100,000, plus all accrued
   interest.
2. On the 2nd anniversary hereof, $150,000, plus all accrued
   interest.
3. On the 3rd anniversary hereof, $175,000, plus all acrued
   interest.
4. On the 4th through the 7th anniversaries hereof, $200,000,
   plus all accrued interest.
5. On the 8th anniversary hereof, the entire unpaid balance plus
   all acrued interest.

*A purchaser should always at-
tempt to have the right of set-
off against a note (essentially
making it non-negotiable).
Otherwise, a purchaser may
find that it has full obligation
for the purchase price to some
third party, such as a bank to
whom the note is discounted,
while having nothing other*

Maker reserves the right at any time after January 1, 19_____, to
prepay this Note in which or in part.

This Note is given as a portion of the purchase price for
372,614 shares of the common stock of DAVID CORPORATION,
a California corporation, in accordance with a Stock Purchase
Agreement dated _____, 19_____, and all amounts due
hereunder are subject to rights of counterclaim and set-off in the
event of any breach of any portion of said Agreement by any Payee
hereunder.

than a court claim against the seller for a specific breach of warranty.

All sums due hereunder are secured by a security interest which is hereby granted to Payees in said 372,614 shares of the common stock of DAVID CORPORATION, which shares are held in pledge by holder. So long as no default exists hereunder, Maker shall have the right to vote such shares and receive dividends thereon. Payee shall have all other rights in such shares as a secured party under the Uniform Commercial Code of California.

The entire unpaid principal sum evidenced by this Note, with all accrued interest, shall, at the option of the holder, after 10 days' notice (such default not having been cured) become due and may be collected forthwith, time being of the essence of this contract and the undersigned hereby waives demand, protest, notice of demand, protest, and non-payment, except for such 10 days' notice. It is further agreed that failure of the holder to exercise this right of accelerating the maturity of the debt, or indulgence granted from time to time, shall in no event be considered as a waiver of such right of acceleration or estop the holder from exercising such right.

Installments not paid when due shall bear interest at the rate of eight (8%) percent per annum from maturity. Should this Note, or any part of the indebtedness evidenced hereby, be collected by law or through an attorney-at-law, the holder shall be entitled to collect reasonable attorneys' fees and all costs of collection.

IN WITNESS WHEREOF, GOLIATH ENTERPRISES, INCORPORATED has caused this Promissory Note to be executed and its seal affixed the date above written.

GOLIATH ENTERPRISES,
INCORPORATED

[Corporate Seal]   By:_____
                                                President

Attest:

_____
Secretary

SCHEDULE F

COVENANT NOT TO COMPETE

THIS AGREEMENT is made the _____ day of _____, 19_____, between GOLIATH ENTERPRISES, INCORPORATED ("Goliath"), a Delaware corporation, and each of the undersigned persons ("Officer"), each of whom is an employee, officer, or director of, or consultant to DAVID CORPORATION, a California corporation ("Company"). Company publishes newspapers of general circulation from offices in _____, Georgia. Each officer has had access to subscription lists, advertising information, and other proprietary information of Company which, if used in competition to the business of Company, could seriously and adversely affect the business of Company.

IN CONSIDERATION of the mutual benefits to each party and in order to induce Goliath to acquire all of the outstanding stock of Company, and in further consideration of the payments to be made by Goliath to each officer, it is agreed as follows:

1. No officer will, for a period of two years from the date hereof, within a 10-mile radius of the present city limits of _____, Georgia, directly or indirectly (except in connection with employment by Goliath or a corporation affiliated with Goliath or with Goliath's written consent):

(a) own, manage, operate, be employed, or participate in the ownership, management, operation, of, or be connected in any manner with, any incorporated or unincorporated newspaper, magazine, circular, folder, shopper, throw-away, or similar printed advertising, or other printed news media, or any incorporated or unincorporated job printing business; or

(b) solicit or cause to be solicited or written, any substantial business of any type described in (a) above, including, but not limited to soliciting any advertising for the same.

2. Goliath agrees to pay each officer separately the sum of thirty thousand and no/100 ($30,000) dollars payable in three equal annual installments in the amount of $10,000, each on the first through the third anniversary dates of the Agreement, without interest.

3. The provisions of this Covenant have been separately bargained for. Each officer shall report all sums received hereunder as ordinary income for income tax purposes.

4. The amount bargained for herein is a lump sum, and therefore the death or incapacity of any officer shall not affect Goliath's obligations hereunder, nor shall amounts due hereunder be otherwise forfeited or reduced except for breach of any officer's agreements as set forth herein or in a Stock Purchase Agreement among the parties dated _____, 19____. In the event of any officer's death, amounts due hereunder shall be paid as and when due to his executors, administrators, heirs, and assigns.

5. Each officer agrees that Goliath's remedy at law for any breach by any officer of his covenants and undertaking set forth herein will not be adequate, and that Goliath shall be entitled to injunctive relief with respect to any such breach, provided that nothing herein contained shall prevent Goliath from bringing an action at law for any damages which it might sustain from any such breach.

6. This Agreement shall be construed in accordance with, and governed by, the laws of the state of Georgia, and shall be binding upon and inure to the benefit of the parties hereto, and their respective successors and assigns.

IN WITNESS WHEREOF, the parties have caused this Covenant

Not to Compete to be executed and their seals affixed the day first above written.

_____ (SEAL)

_____ (SEAL)

("Officer")

[Corporate Seal]   GOLIATH ENTERPRISES, INCORPORATED

Attest:
Secretary   By: _____
                                         President

("Goliath")

CAVEAT: Covenants Not to Compete are not favored in the law. It is very important that the laws of all jurisdictions involved be carefully examined by counsel. As a general rule, separately bargained for covenants having reasonable consideration will be enforced if they are reasonable as to duration and as to territory as well as to the business activities restrained.

Appendix J

Pro-Seller
Stock Purchase Agreement

The attached agreement is an actual agreement used in a recent sale of stock for cash in a situation in which the seller had strong bargaining power. In a more typical situation, such an agreement would constitute the seller's first draft of what the seller would like to obtain in the contract. Compare these warranties with those in Appendix I in which the *buyer* had the bargaining power. *See discussion at page 32.*

STOCK PURCHASE AGREEMENT

The parties should be specified by their legal name as well as a shorter designation.

THIS STOCK PURCHASE AGREEMENT is made and entered into as of this _____ day of _____ April _____, 19_____, by and among those individuals listed on Schedule A attached hereto (individually "Stockholder" and collectively "Stockholders"), being the owners of all the issued and outstanding shares of capital stock of _____ (the "Company"), a _____ corporation with offices at _____ _____ ("DS") a _____ corporation having its principal office at _____ and _____ ("NA") a corporation having its principal office at _____ with reference to the following:

Recitals:

A "Recitals" provision was used in this agreement, which is a more modern way of dealing with the usual "Whereas" clauses.

A. The number of shares of the common stock, $100 par value, of the Company and number of shares of the preferred stock, $100 par value, of the Company, owned by each stockholder are listed on Schedule A hereof. The aggregate amount of the common and preferred stock is sometimes referred to herein as the "Company Stock."

B. The Company is engaged in the business of distributing a general line of _____ to customers in states which include Alabama, Florida, North Carolina, South Carolina, and Tennessee.

C. DS is a wholly owned subsidiary of NA.

D. The stockholders desire to sell all of the common and preferred stock of the Company owned by them to DS for the considerations as set forth in Paragraph 2 below, upon and subject to the terms and conditions hereinafter set forth.

NOW, THEREFORE, in consideration of the recitals and of the respective covenants, representations, and agreements herein contained, it is hereby covenanted and agreed by and among the parties that they shall carry out and consummate the following Stock Purchase Agreement (the "Agreement"):

The precise stock to be purchased must be specified.

1. *Purchase and Sale of Stock.* Each stockholder, in reliance on the representations, warranties, and covenants of DS contained herein and subject to the terms and conditions of this agreement, shall sell all of the shares of the Company stock which he owns for a percentage of the aggregate purchase price set forth in Paragraph 2 equal to his percentage ownership of Company stock, as shown on Schedule A hereto. DS, in reliance on the representations, warranties, and covenants of the stockholders contained herein and subject to the terms and conditions of this Agreement, shall purchase the Company stock for such aggregate purchase price.

2. *Purchase Price.* The aggregate purchase price to be paid by DS to the stockholders for all of the Company stock shall be a base

purchase price of $5,200,000, plus such additional considerations as are set forth in paragraphs 6.4, 9.8, and 13(b).

The closing time and place should be specified in the contract as well as the precise transactions which are to take place at closing.

3. *Closing.* The closing (herein the "Closing") of such purchase and sale of stock shall take place at the offices of _____ First National Bank Building, Macon, Georgia, April 16, 19____ at 9:30 a.m., or at such other time and place as shall be mutually agreed upon by DS and the stockholders (the date of closing being herein referred to as the "Closing Date").

At the closing, the stockholders shall deliver, free and clear of all liens, encumbrances, claims, and other charges thereon of every kind, the certificates for the shares of the Company stock in negotiable form, duly endorsed in blank or with separate stock transfer powers attached, with signatures guaranteed by a bank or trust company or by a firm having membership in the New York Stock Exchange, Inc., to DS upon delivery by DS to the stockholders of certified or bank cashiers checks drawn by The First National Bank of Atlanta in Atlanta Clearing House funds to the order of the stockholders in such amounts as hereinbefore provided in paragraph 1 hereof. Any transfer taxes due and payable on the delivery and transfer of the Company stock from the stockholders to DS shall be paid by the stockholders.

At the closing, the stockholders shall cause the Company to make available to DS the written resignations of all the directors and officers of the Company effective as of the closing, and to turn over or make available to DS all minute books, stock record books, books of account, corporate seals, leases, contracts, agreements, securities, customer and subscriber lists, files and other documents, instruments, and papers belonging to the Company, and shall cause full possession and control of all of the assets and property of every kind and nature, tangible and intangible, of the Company (it being understood that two desks and several chairs at the Atlanta office are not owned by the Company and may be taken and retained by the owners) and of all other things and matters pertaining to the operation of the business of the Company to be transferred and delivered to whatever directors and officers may be elected to succeed the resigned directors and officers of the Company.

For accounting purposes, the transfer of the Company stock to DS shall be deemed to be effective at 12:01 a.m., prevailing time on January 1, 19____, regardless of the actual date of the closing.

4. *Default at Closing.* Notwithstanding the provisions of paragraph 4.1 hereof, if any of the stockholders shall fail or refuse to deliver any of the Company stock as provided in paragraph 3 hereof, or if any of the stockholders shall fail or refuse to consummate the transactions described in this Agreement prior to the closing date, such failure or refusal shall not relieve the other stockholders of any obligations under this Agreement, and DS at its option and without prejudice to its rights against any such defaulting stockholder, may either (a) acquire the remaining Company stock which it is entitled to acquire hereunder, or (b) refuse to make such acquisition and thereby terminate all of its obligations hereunder with respect to the Company. The stockholders acknowledge that the Company stock is unique and otherwise not available and agree that in addition to

In this situation, the stockholders were in adverse positions among themselves, and the purchaser wanted to protect against a default by one stockholder although the other stockholders might be willing to close the transaction.

Stockholders were able to obtain several liability and not joint liability. Normally, a purchaser would want to insist on joint and several liabilities.

Compare very carefully the limited nature of the warranties given to those set forth in the more stringent warranty provisions of the stock purchase agreement found at Appendix I.

any other remedies, DS may invoke any equitable remedies to enforce performance hereunder, including, without limitation, an action or suit for specific performance.

4.1 *Damages and Limit of Liability of Stockholders.* Each stockholder shall be liable, severally but not jointly, to DS for his material breach of his representations, warranties, and covenants which results in a failure to perform his obligations under paragraph 1 and the second paragraph of paragraph 3, but only to the extent of the expenses incurred by DS in connection with the transactions contemplated by this Agreement.

5. *Representations and Warranties of the Stockholders, and Maximum Liability of Stockholders.* Each stockholder hereby severally and not jointly with the other stockholders represents and warrants to DS as follows [but no stockholder shall be liable under any circumstance under this Agreement for an amount of losses, claims, or liabilities (whether or not resulting from breach of representations, warranties, or any other agreements) in excess of the result of multiplying the amount of such losses, claims, or liabilities by his percentage of ownership of Company Stock as shown in Schedule A, nor for an aggregate amount of all such losses, claims, or liabilities (whether or not resulting from breach of representations, warranties, and any other agreements) in excess of the result of multiplying $550,000 by his percentage of ownership of Company stock as shown in Schedule A]:

5.1 *Organization, Standing, Qualification, and Capitalization.* The Company is a corporation duly organized, validly existing, and in good standing under the laws of the state of _____ and has the corporate power to perform its business as presently conducted and to own and lease the properties used in connection therewith. A complete and correct copy of the Charter and all amendments thereto of the Company certified by the Secretary of State of the state of _____ and a complete and correct copy of its By-Laws and all amendments thereto, certified by its secretary, have been delivered to D.S. The Company is duly qualified to do business and is in good standing in each jurisdiction wherein the stockholders believe that the conduct of its business or the ownership of its property requires such qualification.

The total authorized capital stock of the Company consists of $500,000 capital stock, of which 1,728 shares of common stock and 500 shares of preferred stock (both $100 par value) are validly issued and outstanding, fully paid and non-assessable, and 672 shares of common stock are issued and held as treasury stock.

Neither the Company nor any of the stockholders is, or at the closing will be, a party to or bound by any written or oral contract or agreement which grants to any person an option or right of first refusal or other right of any character to acquire at any time, or upon the happening of any stated events, shares of Company stock whether or not presently issued or outstanding.

5.2 *Stock of Ownership.* Each stockholder is the lawful owner of record and beneficially of the number of shares of Company stock set forth in Schedule A hereto, and at the closing such shares will be free and clear of all liens, encumbrances, claims, and other charges of every kind, and each stockholder has full legal power and all authorization required by law to transfer and deliver said shares in accordance with this Agreement.

5.3 *Subsidiaries of the Company*. The Company is not a member of any partnership or joint venture, and owns no stock in any corporation except fewer than 50 shares of common stock of _____.

5.4 *Financial Information*. The stockholders' equity of Company at December 31, 19_____ as determined in accordance with generally accepted accounting principles applied on a basis consistent with that of the preceding accounting period, was not less than $5,532,254, reduced, however, by an amount equal to the reduction of such stockholders' equity by reason of the Company's contribution of _____ accrued during the year 19_____ and paid in 19_____ into the _____ Contributory Pension Plan. Stockholders have delivered to DS the audited balance sheet of the Company at December 31, 19_____ as Schedule A-1 hereto (the 19_____ Balance Sheet of Company). Notwithstanding any language to the contrary in any other representation and warranty, the representations and warranties contained in the first sentence of this paragraph 5.4 and the first sentence of paragraph 5.13 are not limited to the best knowledge of the stockholders.

Stockholders have also delivered Company's audited financial statements for the years ended December 31, 19_____ through 19_____, examined and reported on by _____, and to the best of Stockholders' knowledge these statements present fairly the financial condition and operations of the Company for said years.

To the best knowledge of the stockholders:

(a) *Accounts Receivable*. The accounts receivable of the Company reflected on the 19_____ balance sheet of the Company, and all accounts receivable acquired by the Company subsequent to December 31, 19_____ have arisen only in the ordinary course of business.

(b) *Inventory*. All inventory of the Company reflected on the 19__ balance sheet of the Company consisted, and at the closing date will consist, of a quality and quantity usable or salable in the ordinary course of business of the Company, except for repair parts, damaged, obsolete, and slow-moving material, all of which are stated at net realizable market value (as defined below); the value at which inventories are carried is the lower of cost or market on a first-in, first-out (FIFO) basis, or net relizable market value (defined as estimated selling price less general, administrative, selling, and distribution expenses, estimated costs to complete, and normal profit, determined in accordance with the schedule previously delivered to DS and initialled for identification). Such valuation methods have been applied on a basis consistent with those of prior periods.

(c) *Fixed Assets*. The fixed assets of the Company on the 19 __ balance sheet of the Company are stated at cost, less aggregate allowances for depreciation and amortization, which have

Note that other than stock ownership and matters of corporate organization as set forth in 5.1, 5.2, and 5.3 above, the warranty of minimum equity is the only principal material warranty not limited by the "best knowledge of the stockholders of the corporation." As a practical matter, such language as "to the best knowledge of the stockholders" makes almost unenforceable the other warranties unless actual fraud is involved.

been provided based upon the estimated useful lives of the assets currently used in the operations and to reduce idle fixed assets to net realizable value; and Schedule B correctly identifies and locates these assets.

5.5 *Title to Properties.* To the best knowledge of the stockholders, the Company has good and marketable title to all its properties and assets reflected on the 19_____ balance sheet of the Company, free and clear of all mortgages, liens, pledges, charges, or other encumbrances of any nature whatsoever, except (i) mortgages, liens, pledges, charges, or other encumbrances disclosed on the books of the Company; (ii) liens for current taxes not yet due and payable or being contested in good faith by appropriate proceedings; or (iii) such imperfections of title and encumbrances, if any, as are not substantial and do not materially detract from the value, or interfere with the present use, of the properties subject thereto or affected thereby, or otherwise materially impair business operations as heretofore conducted by the Company (except that elevators at _____ are not in proper operating condition); but substantially all plants, structures, and equipment owned or used by the Company are, with minor exceptions, in operating condition. Schedule C hereto lists all real property of the Company.

5.6 *Tax Matters.* To the best knowledge of the stockholders, the Company has filed all required Federal income tax returns and paid all taxes shown to be due thereby; the Company has filed with all other appropriate governmental agencies all tax returns and tax reports which are required to be filed by it and has paid all taxes shown to be due thereby; the liabilities and reserves for taxes on the balance sheet of the Company as of December 31, 19_____ are sufficient for the payment of all taxes attributable to income earned prior to and including December 31, 19_____ and include adequate provision for deferred taxes in accordance with generally accepted accounting principles; the Federal income tax returns of the Company have been audited by the Internal Revenue Service for all years to and including the fiscal year ended December 31, 19_____ the results of such audits are properly reflected in the financial statements referred to in paragraph 5.4 hereof, all deficiencies proposed as a result of such audits having been paid or settled; and there are no agreements by the Company for the extension of the time for the assessment of any tax prior to those owed or to be owed for the calendar year 19_____, except, however, the Company has obtained an extension of time in which to file its 19_____ tax returns.

5.7 *Litigation.* To the best knowledge of stockholders, and except as provided for or disclosed in the balance sheet of the Company as of December 31, 19_____

(a) there is no litigation, proceeding, or governmental investigation pending or to the knowledge of the stockholders threatened, against or related to the Company, or its properties or business, other than those on which the Company's insurer has reported by separate letter dated March 22 19___, and

(b) the Company is not in default with respect to any order, writ, injunction, or decree against it of any court or Federal, state, municipal, or governmental department, commission, board, bureau, agency, or instrumentality,

which involves the possibility of any judgment or liability which may result in any material adverse change in the financial condition, assets, liabilities, properties, or businesses of the Company, except as shown in Schedule D hereof.

5.8 *Insurance.* To the best knowledge of stockholders, Schedule E contains a true and complete schedule of all policies or binders of fire, liability, product liability, vehicular and other insurance held by or on behalf of the Company or relating to its business or any of its assets or properties (specifying the insurer, the amount of the coverage, the type of insurance, the risks insured, the policy number, if any, and any pending claims thereunder); the Company shall seek to continue to carry all such policies or binders or similar policies or binders during the pendency of this Agreement; and no notice of cancellation or non-renewal for any such policy has been received.

5.9 *Patents and Trademarks.* To the best knowledge of stockholders, the Company has no patents or trademarks, except as listed and described in Schedule F hereto.

5.10 *Contracts and Commitments.* To the best knowledge of stockholders, except as listed and described in Schedule G hereto, the Company is not a party to any written or oral:

(a) contract or commitment with any present or former director or employee or consultant, except with _____ as listed and described in Schedule G hereto;

(b) contract or commitment with any labor union; or any contract or commitment for future purchase of, or payment for, raw materials, supplies, or products at fixed prices except such contracts or commitments as are issued for normal stock materials and which will be fully satisfied within six months after closing, and except certain other purchases for future delivery which are fully covered by firm sales commitments from the Company's customers at prices in excess of the Company's cost therefor (and except contract with _____ Incorporated), or contracts to sell or supply products at fixed prices, or to perform services, in excess of $50,000, except such sales commitments as are offset by firm commitments from the Company's vendors at cost prices prices below the Company's committed selling prices therefor;

(c) except such as have arisen in the normal course of business of the Company, (i) contracts or commitments continuing over a period of more than one year from the date of this Agreement, (ii) representative or sales agency contracts and commitments, (iii) leases under which it is either lessor or lessee (except said _____ Street property), (iv) pledges for any charitable contributions, or (v) contracts or commitments for capital expenditures in excess of $25,000;

(d) bonus, pension, profit sharing, retirement, stock purchase, stock option, hospitalization, insurance, vacation pay, or similar plan or practice, formal or informal, in effect with respect to any of its employees;

(e) contract or commitment for the borrowing of money or other agreement or arrangement for a line of credit; or

(f) material contract not made in the ordinary course of business.

Except as may be disclosed in Schedule G, no party to the contracts listed therein has been declared to be in default thereunder, and no notice has been received that an event has occurred which but for the passage of time or the giving of notice would constitute a default thereunder.

5.11. *Absence of Undisclosed Liabilities*. To the best knowledge of stockholders, there are no material liabilities or obligations of the Company, known or unknown, fixed or unfixed, liquidated or unliquidated, accrued, absolute, contingent, or otherwise, including, but not limited to, any tax liabilities due or to become due, and whether incurred in respect of or measured by the net income of the Company for any period prior the close of business on December 31, 19_____ or arising out of transactions entered into, or any state of facts existing, prior hereto, except:

(a) as disclosed, or adequately and specifically reserved for or against, in the balance sheet of the Company as of December 31, 19___ and not heretofore paid or discharged, and

(b) as incurred, consistent with past business practices, in or as a result of the normal and ordinary course of business since December 31, 19_____

5.12. *Absence of Default*. To the best knowledge of stockholders, the Company is not in default in the performance, observance, or fulfillment of any material obligation, covenant, or condition contained in any debenture or note, or contained in any conditional sale or equipment trust agreement, or loan or other borrowing agreement to which the Company is a party.

5.13. *Existing Condition*. Since December 31, 19_____ there has not been any adverse change in the stockholders' equity in the Company or any material and adverse change in its operations, business, or property, or in its financial condition, operations, business, or property. To the best knowledge of stockholders, except as disclosed in Schedule H, since December 31, 19_____ there has not been (i) any damage, destruction, or loss, whether covered by insurance or not, materially and adversely affecting the operations, business, or property of the Company; (ii) any declaration, setting aside, or payment of any dividend, or any distribution in respect of capital stock of the Company, except a dividend of $50 per share on the common stock of the Company paid on or about March 15, 19_____ or any redemption, purchase, or other acquisition of any of such shares of the Company; (iii) any increase in the compensation payable or to become payable by the Company to any of its officers or directors, except a raise to _____, other than contributions already made, or increases in accordance with existing plans, any increase in the amounts paid, payable, or to become payable under any bonus, insurance, pension, or other benefit plan, or any arrangement made for or with any such officers, directors, or employees; or (iv) any labor trouble other than routine grievance matters, none of which is material.

5.14. *Employment Agreements*. Except as disclosed by the company on Schedule G hereto, a company is not a party to any employment contract, although it will become so with reference to _____ as provided in Paragraph 9.8 hereto. The company has no pension and retirement agreements or programs, except those which have been disclosed on Schedule G hereto. Copies of all such agreements or programs, including their financial statements, have been delivered to DS, and the actuarially determined cost for 19____, which includes normal cost, 10 percent amortization of the past service cost base, and an expense loading factor, is fully accrued and reflected on the balance sheet of the Company at December 31, 19____. To the best knowledge of the shareholders, unfunded past service costs at December 31, 19____ approximated _____.

5.15. *Validity of Contemplated Transactions*. Neither the execution and delivery of this Agreement nor the consummation of the transaction provided for herein will violate any agreement to which the Company is a party or by which it is bound, or any law, order, or decree or any provision of the Charter or By-Laws of the Company.

5.16. *Restrictions*. The Company is not subject to any charter or other corporate restriction or any judgment, order, writ, injunction, decree, rule, or regulation which materially and adversely affects or, so far as the stockholders can now foresee, may in the future materially and adversely affect, the business, operations, prospects, properties, assets, or condition, financial or otherwise, of the Company, except as shown in Exhibit I hereof.

5.17. *Compliance with Laws*. To the best knowledge of shareholders, the operations of the Company are not in material violation of any existing statute or regulation of the United States of America or any country, province, state, municipality, or agency in respect of the conduct of its business and the maintenance and operations of its properties; and, in particular, not declared to be in material violation of any existing environmental, safety or health law, rule, or regulation or of any provision of the Economic Stabilization Act.

5.18. *Directors, Officers, and Authorized Persons*. Schedule J is a list of the names and addresses of all directors of the Company, all officers of the Company, all persons authorized to borrow funds on behalf of the Company, all persons authorized to make withdrawals from bank or checking accounts of the Company, and all persons having access to safes, vaults, or safety deposit boxes in any bank in the name of the Company. Schedule J also contains a list, including the address or location, of all such bank and checking accounts, safes, vaults, and safety deposit boxes.

5.19. *Disclosure*. To the best knowledge of the shareholders, no representation or warranty by the stockholders in this Agreement contains any untrue statement of material facts or omits to state any material fact necessary to make any statement herein not misleading.

5.20. *Transactions with Affiliates.* No director, officer, or stockholder of the Company owns or during the last one year has owned, directly or indirectly, or has, or during the last one year has had, an ownership interest in any business, corporate or otherwise, which is a party to, or in any property which is the subject of business arrangements or relationships of any kind with the Company.

5.21. *Knowledge of Stockholders.* For purposes of this Agreement, the actual knowledge of any stockholder shall be considered to be the knowledge of all the stockholders.

6. *Representations and Warranties of DS and NA represent and warrant to the stockholder that:*

6.1 *Organization, Good Standing, and Authority.* DS is a corporation duly organized, validly existing, and in good standing under the laws of the state of _____ and has full corporate power and authority to own its properties and assets and to carry on its business as it has been and is conducted. NA is a corporation duly organized, validly existing, and in good standing under the laws of the state of _____ and has full corporate power and authority to own its properties and assets and to carry on its business as it has been and is conducted. The execution and delivery of this Agreement and the consummation of the transaction contemplated hereby are within the corporate power of DS and NA and have been duly authorized by all necessary corporate and other action, and the undertakings and obligations of DS and NA hereunder are valid, binding, and enforceable in accordance with their terms.

6.2 *Validity of Contemplated Transactions.* Neither the execution and delivery of this Agreement nor the consummation of the transaction provided herein will violate any agreement to which DS or NA is a party or by which it is bound, or any law, order, or decree or any provision of the Certificate of Incorporation or By-Laws of DS or NA.

6.3. *Investment Representations—Securities Compliance.* The Company stock being delivered pursuant to the provisions of this Agreement will be held by DS for its own account and not with a view to, or for resale in connection with, the distribution thereof. DS will execute any consents, affidavits, or undertakings that may, in the opinion of counsel for the Company, be appropriate to indicate that this sale is not in violation of any state or Federal securities laws.

6.4. *Employee Benefits.* The Company shall keep in effect its present Pension Plan and Profit Sharing Plan, without curtailment of the benefits accured for any current participants in the Plans, and without taking any action which might cause disallowance of any contributions heretofore made to the Plans, and any disallowance thus caused, or any additional income taxes resulting therefrom, will not be considered in determining any loss, claim, or liability for which the stockholders might otherwise be accountable or liable.

7. *Conduct of Business Pending Closing.* Each stockholder

jointly with the other stockholders and severally represents, warrants, and agrees that, pending the closing and except as otherwise approved in advance in writing by DS, he will use his best efforts to see that:

7.1 *Business in the Ordinary Course.* The Company shall refrain from engaging in transactions other than in the ordinary course of business.

7.2. *Accounting and Credit Changes.* The Company shall not make any change in its accounting procedures and practices, except as otherwise disclosed in this Agreement.

7.3 *Capitalization, Options, and Dividends.* No change shall be made in the Charter of the Company, it shall not issue or reclassify or alter any shares of its issued, issued and outstanding, or unissued capital stock, it shall not grant options, warrants, or other rights of any kind to purchase, or agree to issue any shares of its capital stock, it shall not purchase, redeem, or otherwise acquire for a consideration any shares of its capital stock, and it shall not declare, pay, set aside, or make any dividends or other distributions or payment in respect of its capital stock other than the dividend described in paragraph 5.13.

7.4. *Encumbrance of Assets.* Except as may be required to comply with loan agreements, obligations, or indentures in force from time to time, and except in connection with the acquisition of equipment, no mortgage, pledge, or encumbrance of any of the Company's properties or assets shall be made.

7.5. *Employment Agreements. Etc.* The Company shall refrain from entering into any employment agreements other than collective bargaining agreements, except as provided in paragraph 9.8 hereof.

7.6 *Real Property Acquisitions, Dispositions, and Leases.* The Company shall refrain from acquiring or agreeing to acquire, or disposing, or agreeing to dispose of, real estate and from entering into or agreeing to enter into leases of real estate or equipment for a period in excess of one year.

7.7. *Litigation During Interim Period.* The Company will promptly advise DS in writing of the commencement or threat against the Company of any claim, litigation, proceeding, or tax audit not covered by insurance, when the amount claimed is in excess of $20,000.

7.8 *Access.* DS and its officers, attorneys, accountants, and representatives shall be permitted to examine the property, books, and records of the Company, and its title to real estate, and such officers, attorneys, accountants, and representatives shall be afforded free access to such property, books, records, and titles, and the Company will upon request furnish DS with any information reasonably required in respect to its property, assets, and business. However, no contact shall be made hereunder with any persons other than with officers, attorneys, or accountants of the Company.

7.9. *Best Efforts and Cooperation of the Company.* The Company will use its best efforts in promptly taking any and all action appropriate to the consummation of this Agreement.

7.10. *Goodwill.* The Company will use its best efforts to

preserve the goodwill of its customers and suppliers and others having business relations with it.

8. *Indemnification and Limitations.* (a) The stockholders, severally but not jointly, shall indemnify and hold harmless DS in the manner hereinafter set forth, but each such indemnity and all liabilities of any kind of the stockholders are limited as stated in paragraph 5. The matters thus indemnified against relate to:

(i) Any and all damage, loss of bargain under this Agreement, other loss, deficiency, costs, and expenses resulting from any misrepresentation, breach of warranty, or non-fulfillment of any agreement or covenant or from any misrepresentation in or omission from any schedule or list contained in this Agreement, certificate, or other instrument furnished by the stockholders in connection herewith; and

(ii) Any and all actions, suits, proceedings, audits, demands, assessments, judgements, costs, and legal and other expenses incident to any of the foregoing or the enforcement of this paragraph 8.

Provided, however, that the stockholders shall not be liable to DS under this paragraph 8 or otherwise for any matter which was not set forth in a claim presented in full detail in writing to the stockholders within two years from the closing date.

(b) Before DS may assert a claim for indemnity or loss, the prospective claimant must promptly give, or cause to be given, written notice of such claim to the stockholders. The stockholders shall have the right to contest and defend against any such claim by a third party at their own expense and through counsel of their own choosing in their own name or in the name of Company, provided that if the stockholders shall fail to notify the prospective claimant within 15 days of the giving of the foregoing notice of their election to contest and defend any such claim by a third party, then the prospective claimant shall have the right to take such action as it deems appropriate to defend, contest, settle, or compromise any such claim or liability.

(c) As a limitation on any and all representations, warranties, and various undertakings by stockholders, and on all claims or demands that may be made upon the stockholders, it is further provided that no deficiency or loss shall be deemed to have occurred, nor any claim or obligation or liability to have arisen with respect to the first sentences of paragraphs 5.4 and 5.13 unless the stockholders' equity of Company at December 31, 19_____ or at closing, shall be actually less than the amount specified in paragraph 5.4 hereof, and then only as to the amount of such deficiency. In addition, as to each and every obligation of the stockholders hereunder assumed or assumed at the closing (other than related to the transfer of the Company stock as required in paragraph 3) as to each of the Representations and Warranties of the Stockholders (including but not limited to those in paragraph 5), as to each and every Statement by the Stockholders Relative to Conduct of Business Pending Closing (including but not limited to those in paragraph 7), as to the Indemnification (by the stockholders) (including but not limited to those in paragraph 8), and as to each and every Condition Precedent to DS's Obligations (including but not limited to those in paragraph 9), as to the Survival of Representations and Warranties (including but not limited to those in paragraph 12), as to the Covenant not to Compete and Right of Set-Off (including but not limited to those in paragraph 13), it is agreed that if there is any deficiency (which must be based on a claim or obligation asserted hereunder) against the stockholders or any of them, there shall first be subtracted, as credits, from such deficiency, loss, claim, or obligation, a deductible amount of $100,000 of tax deductible items, or $50,000 of non-tax-deductible items, the purpose of this provision being to eliminate claims for relatively small amounts.

Note the "bucket" of $100,000 of tax deductible items granted by the purchaser before any warranty loss is triggered. From a seller's standpoint, it is very important to always seek to obtain a cut-off as to certain "minimal" liabilities which may not have been disclosed and which will simply be thrown in the "bucket" rather than charged against the sellers.

9. *Conditions Precedent to DS's Obligations.* All obligations of DS under this Agreement are subject to the fulfillment, prior to or at the closing, of each of the following conditions:

9.1 *Representations and Warranties.* The stockholders' representations and warranties contained in this Agreement or in any list, certificate, or document delivered pursuant to the provisions hereof shall be true at and as of the time of closing as though such representations and warranties were made at and as of such time and the stockholders shall have delivered to DS a certificate dated the closing date and signed by them to such effect.

9.2 *Compliance with Agreements.* The stockholders and the Company shall have performed and complied with all agreements and conditions required by this Agreement to be performed or complied with by them prior to or at the closing, and the stockholders shall have delivered to DS a certificate dated the closing date and signed by them to such effect.

9.3 *Opinion of Counsel.* The stockholders shall have delivered to DS an opinion of their counsel, _____ dated the closing date and in form and substance satisfactory to DS to the effect that:

(a) Each of the stockholders is the lawful owner of record of all the number of shares of the Company Stock set forth beside his name in Schedule A, free and clear of any liens, encumbrances, equities, and claims known to such counsel, and, if they are of legal age and competent (which need not be verified by such counsel), each has full legal power and all authorization required by law (including, but not limited to, all authorization required under any Georgia law) to transfer and deliver said shares in accordance with this Agreement, and, assuming the signatures are as indicated thereon, by delivery of a certificate or certificates therefor will transfer to DS valid and marketable title to said shares, free and clear of any liens, encumbrances, equities, and claims, known to such counsel. Further, under Georgia law, the unqualified guarantee of the signature of an endorser constitutes a warranty that at the time of signing, the signature was genuine and the signer was an appropriate person to endorse and the signer had legal capacity to sign.

(b) The Company is not known to them to be a party to, or bound by, nor do they have any reason to believe that the company is a party to or bound by, any written or oral contract or agreement which grants to any person an option or right of first refusal or other right to acquire at any time, or upon the happening of any stated events, shares of the capital stock of the Company.

(c) The Company's authorized capital stock consists of $580,000 capital stock, of which 1,728 shares of common stock and 500 shares of preferred stock (both $100 par value) have been validly issued, are presently outstanding, and are fully paid and nonassessable, and 672 shares of common stock have been issued and are held as treasury stock.

(d) The Company is a corporation duly organized, validly existing, and in good standing under the laws of the state of incorporation, that under present Georgia law, its Articles of Incorporation have perpetual duration, and it has the corporate power to conduct its business as said counsel understands it to be presently conducted and to own and hold the properties used in connection therewith.

(e) The Company has qualified to do business as a foreign corporation in all jurisdictions wherein it has stated to such counsel that the conduct of its business or ownership of property requires such qualification.

(f) The consummation of the transactions contemplated by this Agreement will not result in a breach of any term or provision of or constitute a default under the Charter or By-Laws of the Company, or any indenture, agreement, instrument, or understanding known to such counsel to which the Company is a party or by which it is bound.

(g) Such counsel knows of no litigation, proceeding, or investigation pending against the Company which would materially and adversely affect its assets or its operations or its right to consummate the transactions contemplated hereby.

In furnishing such opinion, counsel may rely upon certificates of officers of the Company, opinion of counsel in foreign jurisdictions, and such other documents and data as they deem appropriate as a basis for their opinion, and make their opinion subject to the accuracy thereof.

9.4 *Resignations*. The stockholders shall have delivered to DS copies of the resignations tendered by the officers and directors of the Company as provided in section 3 hereof.

9.5 *Anti-Trust Matters*. No suit, action, investigation, or legal or administrative proceedings shall have been brought or shall have been threatened by any governmental body which questions the validity or legality of, or in the opinion of DS (after consultation with counsel) would make imprudent under the anti-trust laws the transactions contemplated hereby.

9.6 *Material Damage*. The business or properties of the Company shall not have been and shall not be threatened to be materially and adversely affected in any way as a result of fire, explosion, earthquake, disaster, accident, labor dispute, flood, drought, embargo, riot, civil disturbance, uprising, activity of armed forces, or act of God or public enemy.

9.7 *Approval of Counsel.* All steps to be taken and all resolutions, papers, and documents to be executed, and all other legal matters in connection with the purchase and sale of Company Stock and related matters, including compliance with applicable Federal and state securities laws, shall be subject to the reasonable approval of DS's counsel, _____, Esq.

9.8 *Employment Agreements.* The Company shall have entered into employment agreements with _____ and _____ in the forms hitherto signed between the parties. Mandatory retirement at age 65 for _____ shall be waived and provided against by the Company's board of directors for the entire period of his employment contract, and such waivers shall be by such resolutions as will permit his continued employment despite the provisions of any pension or profit-sharing plan.

10. *Conditions Precedent to Stockholders' Obligations.* All obligations of the stockholders under this Agreement are subject to the fulfillment, prior to or at the closing, of each of the following conditions:

10.1 *Representations and Warranties.* DS's representations and warranties contained in this Agreement or in any certificate or document delivered pursuant to the provisions hereof or in connection with the transactions contemplated hereby shall be true at and as of the time of closing as though such representations and warranties were made at and as of such time, and DS shall have delivered to the stockholders a certificate dated the closing date and signed by its president or any vice president to such effect.

10.2 *Compliance with Agreements.* DS shall have performed and complied with all agreements and conditions required by this Agreement to be performed or complied with by it prior to or at the closing, and shall have delivered to the stockholders a certificate dated the closing date and signed by its president or any vice president to such effect.

10.3 *Opinion of Counsel.* DS shall have delivered to the stockholders an opinion of its counsel, _____ dated the closing date, and in form and substance satisfactory to the stockholders, with respect to the matters referred to in subsections 6.1, 6.2, and 6.3 hereof.

11. *Broker and Finder's Fees.* The stockholders represent and warrant to DS that they have not engaged or dealt with any broker or other person who may be entitled to any brokerage fee or commission in respect of the executions of this Agreement or the consummation of the transactions contemplated hereby. DS represents and warrants to the stockholders that neither it nor any corporate affiliate has engaged or dealt with any broker or other person who may be entitled to any brokerage fee or commission in respect of the execution of this Agreement or the consummation of the transactions contemplated hereby.

Each of the parties hereto shall indemnify and hold the others harmless against any and all claims, losses, liabilities, or expenses which may be asserted against such other parties as a result of such first-mentioned party's dealings, arrangements, or agreements with any such broker or person.

12. *Survival of Representations and Warranties.* All representations, indemnifications, warranties, and agreements made by DS and the stockholders in this Agreement or pursuant hereto shall survive the closing for a period not to exceed two years; except the agreements contained in paragraphs 6.4, 9.8, and 13 hereof shall survive the closing for a period of five years. Notwithstanding any investigation or audit conducted before or after the closing date, the parties shall be entitled to rely upon the representations and warranties set forth in this Agreement.

13. *Covenant not to Compete and Right of Set-Off.* (a) Each of the stockholders agrees that, for a period of five years from and after the date of the closing, he will not, unless acting with DS's prior written consent, directly or indirectly, own, manage, operate, join, control, or participate in the ownership, management, operation, or control of, or be connected as an officer, employee, partner, or otherwise with, any business engaged in the business of distributing plumbing and heating supplies and related products within _____, except any stockholder may own up to 1 percent of the common stock of any company whose stock is traded in any stock exchange or over the counter. The stockholders agree that the remedy at law for any breach of the foregoing will be inadequate and that the Company and DS shall be entitled, inter alia, to temporary and permanent injunctive relief without the necessity of proving actual damage to the Company or DS.

(b) In consideration of the stockholders' agreement not to compete set forth in subparagraph (a) above, but regardless of whether or not such agreement is legally enforceable (and regardless of whether or not any stockholder remains in life or remains as custodian), DS agrees to pay the stockholders (or to their successors or legal representatives) $110,000 each year for five years, the payment of which shall be allocated among the stockholders _____ as shown on Schedule _____. The first such payment shall be made 12 months after the closing date, and the remaining four payments annually thereafter.

(c) In the event that the stockholders incur any liability under this Agreement to DS over and above the limitations herein provided, DS shall allocate such liability among such stockholders pro rata in accordance with their respective stock ownership as shown on Schedule A, and shall then have the right to set off such proportionate liability against the payments required by subparagraph (b) above. The rights of DS to indemnification shall not be limited to the right of set-off, but shall not in any event exceed the amount of $550,000.

In the event of a controversy between the stockholders and DS with respect to the liability of the stockholders or DS hereunder, the matter shall be settled by arbitration to be held in the City of Atlanta, Georgia, before a panel of three arbitrators appointed in accordance with the rules of the American Arbitration Association. The decision of the arbitrators shall be final and binding upon the parties both as to law and to fact, shall be enforceable at law or equity, and shall not be appealable to any Court in any jurisdiction. The expenses of the arbitration shall be shared equally by DS and the stockholders.

14. *Expenses.* Except as otherwise provided in paragraph 4.1, the stockholders shall bear the expenses incurred by them in connection with the consummation of the transactions contemplated by this Agreement; Company shall bear its own expenses; and DS shall likewise bear its expenses. Such expenses of the Company under this paragraph 14 shall not be considered in determining whether there is any reduction in stockholders' equity or in the Company's earnings or in testing any representation, warranty, or agreement of the stockholders.

15. *Further Actions and Assurances.* DS and the stockholders will execute and deliver any and all documents, and will cause any and all other action to be taken, either before or after closing, which may be necessary or proper to effect or evidence the provisions of this Agreement and the transactions contemplated hereby.

16. *Counterparts.* This Agreement may be executed in several counterparts each of which is an original and any stockholder may become a party hereto by executing a counterpart hereof. This Agreement and any counterpart so executed shall be deemed to be one and the same instrument. It shall not be necessary in making proof of this Agreement or any counterpart hereof to produce or account for any of the other counterparts.

17. *Contents of Agreement; Parties in Interest.* This Agreement sets forth the entire understanding of the parties. Any previous agreements or understandings between the parties regarding the subject matter hereof are merged into and superseded by this Agreement. All representations, warranties, covenants, terms, conditions, and provisions of this Agreement shall be binding upon and inure to the benefit of and be enforceable by the respective heirs, legal representatives, successors, and assigns of the stockholders and DS.

18. *Georgia Law to Govern.* This Agreement is being delivered and is intended to be performed in the State of Georgia and shall be construed and enforced in accordance with the laws thereof.

19. *Section Headings and Gender.* The section headings herein have been inserted for convenience of reference only and shall in no way modify or restrict any of the terms or provisions hereof. The use of the masculine pronoun herein when referring to any party has been for convenience only and shall be deemed to refer to the particular party intended regardless of the actual gender of such party.

20. *Schedules.* All schedules referred to in this Agreement are intended in be and are hereby specifically made a part of this Agreement.

21. *Notices.* All notices which are required or permitted hereunder shall be sufficient if given in writing and delivered personally or by registered or certified mail, postage prepaid, as follows (or to such other addressee as shall be set forth in a notice given in the same manner):

If to DS:

If to Stockholders:

22. *Confidential Information*. Notwithstanding any termination of this Agreement, DS and its representatives agree to hold in confidence any information not generally available to the public or the trade received by them from the Company or the stockholders pursuant to the terms of this Agreement. If this Agreement is terminated for any reason, DS and its representatives will continue to hold such information in confidence and will, to the extent requested by the Company, promptly return to the Company all written material and all copies or abstracts thereof furnished to DS pursuant hereto. Notwithstanding any termination of this Agreement, stockholders and their representatives agree to hold in confidence any information not generally available to the public or to the business community received by them from the Company and DS pursuant to the terms of this Agreement. If this Agreement is terminated for any reason, stockholders and their representatives will continue to hold such information in confidence and will, to the extent requested by DS, promptly return to DS all written material and all copies or abstracts thereof given to the Company, or stockholders, or their representatives pursuant hereto.

23. *Guaranty by N.A.* As an additional inducement to the stockholders to consummate the transactions contemplated by this Agreement, NA hereby guarantees the performance by DS of its obligations under paragraphs 6.4, 9.8, and 13(b).

24. *Assent to Sale of Company Stock.* In the event the sale of the Company stock is actually consummated, then each of the individual stockholders agrees to such sale and waives, surrenders, and agrees not to exercise any right that such stockholder might have to purchase any Company stock.

[Signature Page]

Appendix K

Comparison Chart of
Sec Rules 242, 240, and 146

See discussion beginning at page 44.

Rules 146, 240 & 242
COMPARISON CHART

Comparison Item	Rule 242	Rule 240	Rule 146
Aggregate Sales Price	3(b) — $2,000,000/6 mos. (including all §3(b) sales)	$100,000/12 mos. (including all sales of exempt securities)	Unlimited
Commission Prohibition	No	Yes	No
Manner of Offering	No general solicitation or general advertising	No general solicitation or general advertising	No general solicitation or general advertising
Nature of Offerees	Not regulated	Not regulated	Must be capable of evaluating the merits and risks of prospective investment and/or be wealthy
Nature of Purchasers	Not regulated	Not regulated	Must be sophisticated and/or wealthy with offeree representative
Number of Purchasers	Reasonable basis to believe and believe, after reasonable inquiry, 35 or fewer, not counting accredited purchasers and purchasers of $100,000 of securities	Available only if 100 or fewer total beneficial owners of securities	Reasonable basis to believe and believe, after reasonable inquiry, 35 or fewer, not counting purchasers of $150,000 of securities
Applicability of Sec. 10b and Rule 10b-5	Applies	Applies	Applies
Information Requirement	(1) **Non-accredited purchasers:** (a) reporting companies — most recent annual report, definitive, proxy statement and recent periodic reports. (b) non-reporting companies — info required by Part I of Form S-18 to the extent material (2) **Accredited purchasers:** No specific requirement, unless both accredited and non-accredited purchasers involved and then all purchasers required to be furnished same info	None	Must furnish (unless offeree has access via economic bargaining power): (1) **$1,500,000 offerings** — info may be limited to Schedule I (Reg A) info; (2) **Other offerings** — (a) reporting companies — recent Form S-1 or From 10, definitive proxy statement and recent periodic reports (b) Non-reporting companies — Info that would be required to be included in registration statement on form which issuer would be entitled to use
Opportunity for Questions	Yes	No	Yes
Resales Restricted	Yes	Yes	Yes
Report of Sales	Yes, condition of Rule	Yes, but not condition of Rule	Yes, condition of Rule

359

Appendix L

SEC Accounting Release No. 146

See discussion beginning at page 44.

RULE 146. TRANSACTIONS BY AN ISSUER DEEMED NOT TO INVOLVE ANY PUBLIC OFFERING

Preliminary Notes

1. The Commission recognizes that no one rule can adequately cover all legitimate private offers and sales of securities. Transactions by an issuer which do not satisfy all of the conditions of this rule shall not raise any presumption that the exemption provided by Section 4(2) of the Act is not available for such transactions. Issuers wanting to rely on that exemption may do so by complying with administrative and judicial interpretations in effect at the time of the transactions. Attempted compliance with this rule does not act as an election; the issuer can also claim the availability of Section 4(2) outside the rule.

2. Nothing in this rule obviates the need for compliance with any applicable state law relating to the offer and sale of securities.

3. Section 5 of the Act requires that all securities offered by the use of mails or other channels of interstate commerce be registered with the Commission. Congress, however, provided certain exemptions in the Act from such registration provisions where there was no practical need for registration or where the public benefits of registration were too remote. Among these exemptions is that provided by Section 4(2) of the Act for transactions by an issuer not involving any public offering. The courts and the Commission have interpreted the Section 4(2) exemption to be available for offerings to persons who have access to the same kind of information that registration would provide and who are able to fend for themselves. The indefiniteness of such terms as "public offering", "access" and "fend for themselves" has led to uncertainties with respect to the availability of the Section 4(2) exemption. Rule 146 is designed to provide, to the extent feasible, objective standards upon which responsible businessmen may rely in raising capital under claim of the Section 4(2) exemption and also to deter reliance on that exemption for offerings of securities to persons who need the protections afforded by the registration process.

In order to obtain the protection of the rule, all its conditions must be satisfied and the issuer claiming the availability of the rule has the burden of establishing, in an appropriate forum, that it has satisfied them. The burden of proof applies with respect to each offeree as well as each purchaser. *See Lively v. Hirschfeld,* 440 F.2d 631 (10th Cir. 1971). Broadly speaking, the conditions of the rule relate to limitations on the manner of the offering, the nature of the offerees, access to or furnishing of information, the number of purchasers, and limitations on disposition.

The term "offering" is not defined in the rule. The determination as to whether offers, offers to sell, offers for sale, or sales of securities are part of an offering (i.e., are deemed to be "integrated") depends on the particular facts and circumstances. *See* Securities Act Release No. 4552 (November 6, 1962). All offers, offers to sell, offers for sale, or sales which are part of an offering must meet all of the conditions of Rule 146 for the rule to be available. Release 33-4552 indicates that in determining whether offers and sales should be regarded as a part of a larger offering and thus should be integrated, the following factors should be considered:

(a) whether the offerings are part of a single plan of financing;
(b) whether the offerings involve issuance of the same class of security;
(c) whether the offerings are made at or about the same time;
(d) whether the same type of consideration is to be received; and
(e) whether the offerings are made for the same general purpose.

4. Rule 146 relates to transactions exempted from Section 5 by Section 4(2) of the Act. It does not provide an exemption from the anti-fraud provisions of the securities laws or the civil

liability provisions of Section 12(2) of the Act or other provisions of the securities laws, including the Investment Company Act of 1940.

5. Clients of an investment adviser, customers of a broker or dealer, trusts administered by a bank trust department or persons with similar relationships shall be considered to be the "offerees" or "purchasers" for purposes of the rule regardless of the amount of discretion given to the investment adviser, broker or dealer, bank trust department or other person to act on behalf of the client, customer or trust.

6. The rule is available only to the issuer of the securities and is not available to affiliates or other persons for sales of the issuer's securities.

7. Finally, in view of the objectives of the rule and the purposes and policies underlying the Act, the rule is not available to any issuer with respect to any transactions which, although in technical compliance with the rule, are part of a plan or scheme to evade the registration provisions of the Act. In such cases registration pursuant to the Act is required.

Rule 146.

(a) *Definitions*. The following definitions shall apply for purposes of this rule.

(1) *Offeree Representative*. The term "offeree representative" shall mean any person or persons, each of whom the issuer and any person acting on its behalf, after making reasonable inquiry, have reasonable grounds to believe and believe satisfies all of the following conditions:

(i) is not an affiliate, director, officer or other employee of the issuer, or beneficial owner of 10 percent or more of any class of the equity securities or 10 percent or more of the equity interest in the issuer, except where the offeree is:

   a) related to such person by blood, marriage or adoption, no more remotely than as first cousin;
   b) any trust or estate in which such person or any persons related to him as specified in subdivision (a) or (c) collectively have 100 percent of the beneficial interest (excluding contingent interests) or of which any such person serves as trustee, executor, or in any similar capacity; or
   c) any corporation or other organization in which such person or any persons related to him as specified in paragraph (a)(1)(i)(a) or (b) of this section collectively are the beneficial owners of 100 percent of the equity securities (excluding directors' qualifying shares) or equity interest;

(ii) has such knowledge and experience in financial and business matters that he, either alone, or together with other offeree representatives or the offeree, is capable of evaluating the merits and risks of the prospective investment;
(iii) is acknowledged by the offeree, in writing, during the course of the transaction, to be his offeree representative in connection with evaluating the merits and risks of the prospective investment; and
(iv) discloses to the offeree, in writing, prior to the acknowledgment specified in paragraph (a)(1)(iii) of this section, any material relationship between such person or its affiliates and the issuer or its affiliates, which then exists or is mutually understood to be contemplated or which has existed at any time during the previous two years, and any compensation received or to be received as a result of such relationship.

Note 1: Persons acting as offeree representatives should consider the applicability of the registration and anti-fraud provisions relating to brokers and dealers under the Securities Exchange Act of 1934 and relating to investment advisers under the Investment Advisers Act of 1940.

Note 2: The acknowledgment required by paragraph (a)(1)(iii) of this section and the disclosure required by paragraph (a)(1)(iv) of this section must be made with specific reference to each prospective investment. Advance blanket acknowledgment, such as for "all securities transactions" or "all private placements", is not sufficient.

Note 3: Disclosure of any material relationships between the offeree representative or its affiliates and the issuer or its affiliates does not relieve the offeree representative of its obligation to act in the interest of the offeree.

(2) *Issuer*. The definition of the term "issuer" in Section 2(4) of the Act shall apply, provided that notwithstanding that definition, in the case of a proceeding under the Bankruptcy Act, the trustee, receiver, or debtor in possession shall be deemed to be the issuer in an offering for purposes of a plan of reorganization or arrangement, if the securities offered are to be issued pursuant to the plan, whether or not other like securities are offered under the plan in exchange for securities of, or claims against, the debtor.

(3) *Affiliate*. The term "affiliate" of a person means a person that directly or indirectly through one or more intermediaries, controls, or is controlled by, or is under common control with such person.

(4) *Material*. The term "material" when used to modify "relationship" means any relationship that a reasonable investor might consider important in the making of the decision whether to acknowledge a person as his offeree representative.

(b) *Conditions to be Met*. Transactions by an issuer involving the offer, offer to sell, offer for sale or sale of securities of the issuer that are part of an offering that is made in accordance with all the conditions of this rule shall be deemed to be transactions not involving any public offering within the meaning of Section 4(2) of the Act.

(1) For purposes of this rule only, an offering shall be deemed not to include offers, offers to sell, offers for sale or sales of securities of the issuer pursuant to the exemptions provided by Section 3 or Section 4(2) of the Act or pursuant to a registration statement filed under the Act, that take place prior to the six-month period immediately preceding or after the six-month period immediately following any offers, offers for sale or sales pursuant to this rule, *Provided,* That there are during neither of said six-month periods any offers, offers for sale or sales of securities by or for the issuer of the same or similar class as those offered, offered for sale or sold pursuant to the rule.

Note: In the event that securities of the same or similar class as those offered pursuant to the rule are offered, offered for sale or sold less than six months prior to or subsequent to any offer, offer for sale or sale pursuant to the rule, *see* Preliminary Note 3 hereof as to which offers, offers to sell, offers for sale or sales may be deemed to be part of the offering.

(2) Transactions by an issuer which do not satisfy all of the conditions of this rule shall not raise any presumption that the exemption provided by Section 4(2) of the Act is not available for such transactions.

(c) *Limitation on Manner of Offering*. Neither the issuer nor any person acting on its behalf shall offer, offer to sell, offer for sale, or sell the securities by means of any form of general solicitation or general advertising, including but not limited to, the following:

(1) Any advertisement, article, notice or other communication published in any newspaper, magazine or similar medium or broadcast over television or radio;

(2) Any seminar or meeting, *except* that if paragraph (d)(1) of this section is satisfied as to each person invited to or attending such seminar or meeting, and, as to persons qualifying only under paragraph (d)(1)(ii) of this section, such persons are accompanied by their offeree representative(s), then such seminar or meeting shall be deemed not to be a form of general solicitation or general advertising; and

(3) Any letter, circular, notice or other written communication, *except* that if paragraph (d)(1) of this section is satisfied as to each person to whom the communication is directed, such communication shall be deemed not to be a form of general solicitation or general advertising.

(d) *Nature of offerees*. The issuer and any person acting on its behalf who offer, offer to sell, offer for sale or sell the securities shall have reasonable grounds to believe and shall believe:

(1) Immediately prior to making any offer, either:

(i) that the offeree has such knowledge and experience in financial and business matters that he is capable of evaluating the merits and risks of the prospective investment, or

(ii) that the offeree is a person who is able to bear the economic risk of the investment; and

(2) Immediately prior to making any sale, after making reasonable inquiry, either:

(i) that the offeree has such knowledge and experience in financial and business matters that he is capable of evaluating the merits and risks of the prospective investment, or

(ii) that the offeree and his offeree representative(s) together have such knowledge and experience in financial and business matters that they are capable of evaluating the merits and risks of the prospective investment and that the offeree is able to bear the economic risk of the investment.

(e) *Access to or Furnishing of Information.*
Note: Access can only exist by reason of the offeree's position with respect to the issuer. Position means an employment or family relationship or economic bargaining power that enables the offeree to obtain information from the issuer in order to evaluate the merits and risks of the prospective investment.
(1) Either

(i) each offeree shall have access during the course of the transaction and prior to the sale to the same kind of information that is specified in Schedule A of the Act, to the extent that the issuer possesses such information or can acquire it without unreasonable effort or expense; or

(ii) each offeree or his offeree representative(s), or both, shall have been furnished during the course of the transaction and prior to sale, by the issuer or any person acting on its behalf, the same kind of information that is specified in Schedule A of the Act, to the extent that the issuer possesses such information or can acquire it without unreasonable effort or expense. This condition shall be deemed to be satisfied as to an offeree if the offeree or his offeree representative is furnished with information, either in the form of documents actually filed with the Commission or otherwise, as follows:

(a) in the case of an issuer that is subject to the reporting requirements of Section 13 or 15(d) of the Securities Exchange Act of 1934:

(1) the information contained in the annual report required to be filed under the Exchange Act or a registration statement on Form S-1 under the Act or on Form 10 under the Exchange Act, whichever filing is the most recent required to be filed, and the information contained in any definitive proxy statement required to be filed pursuant to section 14 of the Exchange Act and in any reports or documents required to be filed by the issuer pursuant to Section 13(a) or 15(d) of the Exchange Act, since the filing of such annual report or registration statement, and

(2) a brief description of the securities being offered, the use of the proceeds from the offering, and any material changes in the issuer's affairs which are not disclosed in the documents furnished;

(b) in the case of all other issuers, the information that would be required to be included in a registration statement filed under the Act on the form which the issuer would be entitled to use, provided, however, that:

A. the issuer may omit details or employ condensation of information if, under the circumstances, the omitted information is not material or the condensation of information does not render the statements made misleading.

Note: The issuer would have the burden of proof to show that, under the circumstances, the omitted information is not material and that any condensation does not render the statements made misleading.

B. if the issuer does not have the audited financial statements required by such form and cannot obtain them without unreasonable effort or expense, such financial statements may be furnished on an unaudited basis, provided that if such unaudited financial statements are not available and cannot be obtained without unreasonable effort or expense, the financial statements required by Regulation Act under the Act may be furnished.

C. if the financial schedules required by Part II of the registration statement have not been prepared, they need not be furnished.

(c) notwithstanding paragraph (e)(1)(ii)(a) and (b) of this section exhibits required to be filed with the Commission as part of a registration statement or report need not be furnished to each offeree or offeree representative if the contents of the exhibits are identified and such exhibits are available pursuant to paragraph (e)(2) of this section;

(d) if the aggregate sales price of all securities offered in reliance upon this rule does not exceed $1,500,000, the information requirements of paragraph (e)(1)(ii) may be satisfied by furnishing the disclosure required by Schedule 1 of the Act; and

(2) the issuer shall make available, during the course of the transaction and prior to sale, to each offeree or his offeree representative(s) or both, the opportunity to ask questions of, and receive answers from, the issuer or any person acting on its behalf concerning the terms and conditions of the offering and to obtain any additional information, to the extent the issuer possesses such information or can acquire it without unreasonable effort or expense, necessary to verify the accuracy of the information obtained pursuant to paragraph (e)(1) of this section; and

(3) the issuer or any person acting on its behalf shall disclose to each offeree, in writing, prior to sale:

(i) any material relationship between his offeree representative(s) or its affiliates and the issuer or its affiliates, which then exists or mutually is understood to be contemplated or which has existed at any time during the previous two years, and any compensation received or to be received as a result of such relationship;

(ii) that a purchaser of the securities must bear the economic risk of the investment for an indefinite period of time because the securities have not been registered under the Act and, therefore, cannot be sold unless they are subsequently registered under the Act or an exemption from such registration is available; and

(iii) the limitations on disposition of the securities set forth in paragraph (h)(2), (3), and (4) of this section.

Note: Information need not be provided and opportunity to obtain additional information need not be continued to be provided to any offeree or offeree representative who, during the course of the transaction, indicates that he is not interested in purchasing the securities offered, or to whom the issuer or any person acting on its behalf has determined not to sell the securities.

(f) *Business Combinations.*

(1) The term "business combination" shall mean any transaction of the type specified in paragraph (a) of Rule 145 under the Act and any transaction involving the acquisition by one issuer, in exchange solely for all or a part of its own or its parent's voting stock, of stock of another issuer if, immediately after the acquisition, the acquiring issuer has control of the other issuer (whether or not it had control before the acquisition)

(2) All the conditions of this rule except paragraph (d) and paragraph (h)(4) of this section shall apply to business combinations.

Note: Notwithstanding the absence of a written agreement pursuant to paragraph (h)(4), any securities acquired in an offering pursuant to paragraph (f) are restricted and may not be resold without registration under the Act or an exemption therefrom.

(3) For purposes of paragraph (f) only, the issuer and any person acting on its behalf, after making reasonable inquiry, shall have reasonable grounds to believe, and shall believe, at the time that any plan for a business combination is submitted to security holders for their approval, or in the case of an exchange, immediately prior to the sale, that each offeree either alone or with his offeree representative(s) has such knowledge and experience in financial and business matters that he is or they are capable of evaluating the merits and risks of the prospective investment.

(4) In addition to information required by paragraphs (e) and (f)(2), the issuer shall provide, in writing, to each offeree at the time the plan is submitted to security holders, or in the case of an exchange, during the course of the transaction and prior to the sale, information about any terms or arrangements of the proposed transaction relating to any security holder that are not identical to those relating to all other security holders.

(g) *Number of Purchasers.*

(1) The issuer shall have reasonable grounds to believe, and after making reasonable inquiry, shall believe, that there are no more than thirty-five purchasers of the securities of the issuer from the issuer in any offering pursuant to the rule.

Note: See paragraph (b)(1) of this section, the note thereto and the Preliminary Notes as to what may or may not constitute an offering pursuant to the rule.

(2) For purposes of computing the number of purchasers for paragraph (g)(1) of this section only:

(i) the following purchasers shall be excluded:

(a) any relative or spouse of a purchaser and any relative of such spouse, who has the same home as such purchaser; and

(b) any trust or estate in which a purchaser or any of the persons related to him as specified in paragraph (g)(2)(i)(a) or (c) of this section collectively have 100 percent of the beneficial interest (excluding contingent interests);

(c) any corporation or other organization of which a purchaser or any of the persons related to him as specified in paragraph (g)(2)(i)(a) or (b) of this section collectively are the beneficial owners of all the equity securities (excluding directors' qualifying shares) or equity interests; and

(d) any person who purchases or agrees in writing to purchase for cash in a single payment or installment, securities of the issuer in the aggregate amount of $150,000 or more.

Note: The issuer has to satisfy all the other provisions of the rule with respect to all purchasers whether or not they are included in computing the number of purchasers under Subdivision (g)(2)(i).

(ii) there shall be counted as one purchaser any corporation, partnership, association, joint stock company, trust or unincorporated organization, *except* that if such entity was organized for the specific purpose of acquiring the securities offered, each beneficial owner of equity interests or equity securities in such entity shall count as a separate purchaser.

Note: See Preliminary Note 5 as to other persons who are considered to be purchasers.

(h) *Limitations on Disposition.* The issuer and any person acting on its behalf shall exercise reasonable care to assure that the purchasers of the securities in the offering are not underwriters within the meaning of section 2(11) of the Act. Such reasonable care shall include, but not necessarily be limited to, the following:

(1) making reasonable inquiry to determine if the purchaser is acquiring the securities for his own account or on behalf of other persons;

(2) placing a legend on the certificate or other document evidencing the securities stating that the securities have not been registered under the Act and setting forth or referring to the restrictions on transferability and sale of the securities;

(3) issuing stop transfer instructions to the issuer's transfer agent, if any, with respect to the securities, or, if the issuer transfers its own securities, making a notation in the appropriate records of the issuer; and

(4) obtaining from the purchaser a signed written agreement that the securities will not be sold without registration under the Act or exemption therefrom.

Note: Paragraph (h)(4) of this section does not apply to business combinations as described in paragraph (f) of this section. Notwithstanding the absence of a written agreement, the securities are restricted and may not be resold without registration under the Act or an exemption therefrom. The issuer for its own protection should consider, however, obtaining such written agreement even in business combinations.

(i) Report of offering. At the time of the first sale of securities in any offering effected in reliance on this rule the issuer shall file three copies of a report on Form 146 with the Commission at the Commission's Regional Office for the region in which the issuer's principal business operations are conducted or proposed to be conducted in the United States. The copies of such report with respect to an issuer having or proposing to have its principal business operations outside the United States shall be filed with the Regional Office for the region in which the offering is primarily conducted or proposed to be conducted. No report need be filed for any offering or offerings in reliance on Rule 146 the proceeds of which total, cumulatively, less than $50,000 during any twelve-month period. If any material change occurs in the facts set forth on the report on Form 146 filed with the Commission, the person who filed the statement shall promptly file with the Commission, at the Regional Office of the Commission in which the original report on Form 146 was filed, three copies of an amended Form 146 disclosing such change.

SECURITIES AND EXCHANGE COMMISSION
Washington, D.C. 20549
FORM 146

REPORT OF OFFERING MADE IN RELIANCE UPON RULE 146

1. (a) Name, address, and telephone number (including area code) and date and state (or other jurisdiction) of incorporation or organization of the issuer of the securities offered and sold;

(b) Type of business (check one).

_____ Oil/Gas _____ Real Estate _____ Other (specify)

(c) Full name of chief executive officer, general partner(s), promoter(s) and controlling person(s).

Instruction: If the general partner(s), promoter(s) or controlling person(s) is (are) not a natural person(s), so state and provide similar information for a natural person(s) having primary responsibility for the affairs of the issuer.

(d) Names and addresses of all organizers, promoters and sponsors of, and of all offeree representatives (as that term is defined in Rule 146(a)(1)) involved in, the offering reported on this form, indicating the capacity in which they acted.

2. With respect to securities sold or to be sold in this offering in reliance upon Rule 146, state the title of the class and the aggregate dollar amount of sales to date and sales to be made in the future in this offering.

Instruction: As to any securities sold or to be sold other than for cash or partly for cash and partly for other consideration, state the nature of the transaction and the source and aggregate amount of consideration received or to be received by the issuer.

3. Has the issuer made any previous filing with the Securities and Exchange Commission under Rule 146 (if so, specify the number of such filings)?

_____ Yes   _____ No

The Securities Act of 1933 or the Securities Exchange Act of 1934 as an issuer of securities?

_____ Yes   _____ No

Pursuant to the requirements of Rule 146 under the Securities Act of 1933, the issuer has duly caused this report to be signed on its behalf by the undersigned officer or person acting in a similar capacity.

Date of Report _____   _____
                                                                                              (Issuer)

                                                                                       _____
                                                                                              (Signature)

Instruction: Print the name and title of the signing representative under his signature. At least one copy of the report shall be manually signed. Any copies not manually signed shall bear typed or printed signatures.

Attention: Intentional misstatements or omissions of facts constitute Federal criminal violations (See 18 U.S.C. 1001).

Appendix M

Letter of Intent

See discussion beginning at page 83.

LETTER OF INTENT

The letter of intent is discussed in some detail in Section A of Chapter 4, "How to Negotiate and Evaluate Your Deal," page 79.

It should be emphasized that the letter of intent should have no legal effect, but merely set the deal on a "handshake" basis.

The precise form of transaction should be set forth early in the letter of intent. Here the parties contemplate that assets will be transferred to the acquiring corporation, and those assets are specified.

The precise consideration, here either cash or stock, should be specified.

Since, with a publicly traded stock, there is often a delay between the agreement and the closing, it is wise to have a provision clarifying how valuation is to be made of the publicly traded stock at the time of the exchange.

In an assets deal, the liabilities to be assumed should be clarified. Problems of collective bargaining (labor union) agreements and pension plans as well as office leases and other items should be specified.

Dear _____.

Ditton is interested in acquiring a portion of the assets and business of Tilson in exchange for a total purchase price as hereinafter set forth payable in Ditton convertible preference stock, participating series (preference stock), or in cash, all in accordance with the following proposal:

1) On the closing of the transaction, Tilson will transfer, assign, and deliver to Ditton the business of Tilson, including the vessels comprising the existing U.S. registered fleet of Tilson, the stock of Steamship Company, and all floating, fleet management, office lease, and other contracts pertaining to the operation of the vessels or to the operation of ore vessels owned by the corporation (but excluding working capital, prepaid insurance, the ore sales agency, tax credits, and all other corporate stocks). The vessels to be transferred to Ditton pursuant to this proposal consist of the following:

[precise description of each vessel included]

Said vessels are hereinafter referred to as "The Vessels" and will be transferred to Ditton at the closing in their present condition subject to reasonable wear and tear in the interim and as otherwise provided in this letter.

2) On the closing of the transaction, Ditton will issue and deliver to Tilson, at Tilson's option to be exercised at least forty-five (45) days prior thereto, that number of shares of Ditton preference stock that will be equal in value (when valued as hereinafter set forth) to $4,900,000 or $4,900,000 itself in cash.

3) In the event Ditton preference stock is to be delivered, it shall be valued at the average of the closing prices of such stock on the New York Stock Exchange as recorded by the *Wall Street Journal* for those days on the first 10 of the 13 trading days immediately preceding December 31, on which such stock was traded.

4) Ditton (or its wholly owned subsidiary, as hereinafter set forth) will assume and agree to perform the mortgage obligations of Tilson with respect to the _____ and the _____, aggregating as of the closing date a sum not to exceed $2,475,000. Further, Ditton will assume such of the liabilities and obligations of the Lakes shipping business as arise from the transfer to Ditton of the floating, fleet management, office lease, collective bargaining agreements, and employee pension plans (with the benefit of all existing pension funds to inure to Ditton); provided that such liabilities and obligations are disclosed to and are acceptable to Ditton.

This proposal is subject to the following conditions:

1) Tilson shall have obtained and can transfer to Ditton without restriction at the closing, a contract or contracts obligating to

Even though the letter of intent is not legally binding, it is very helpful to specify the known contingencies since it is likely that the letter of intent will serve as a checklist utilized by all parties in the future as the transaction progresses. Here in (1) and (2) there are specified certain practical business contingencies which were not resolved at the time of the "handshake"

Many contracts from customers require approval prior to assignment.

Later financial analysis is often required by the acquiring corporation.

The physical assets must be inspected.

Provision must be made for the execution of the formal contract of acquisition. It is a good idea from the acquiring corporation's standpoint to specify the chief warranties and indemnifications at this point in order to minimize trading at some later time.

These provisions are self-explanatory, but are important to any well thought out deal. From the attorneys' standpoint, it is important to have such provisions in a let-

place with the Ditton fleet not less than 20 percent of its iron ore hauling requirements on the Lakes during the calendar year ending December 31, 19———. The hauling rates specified in such contract or contracts shall be in an amount not less than the prevailing rates applicable to iron ore carriage on the Lakes during the periods specified.

2) Ditton, within 180 days following the execution of a definitive agreement by the parties in accordance with this proposal, shall have concluded such arrangement, contractual or otherwise, with such of Tilson's customers, existing or potential, as to the sole satisfaction of Ditton demonstrates the financial practicability of operating the vessels to be acquired pursuant to this proposal in the iron ore and coal hauling business.

3) Tilson shall have obtained the consent of all necessary third parties to the assignment by it of the contracts to be transferred to Ditton pursuant to this proposal.

4) Ditton shall be satisfied that the vessel financial operating statements of Tilson as at December 31, for the 12 months then ended present fairly the financial operating capabilities of Tilson's shipping business in conformity with generally accepted accounting principles applied on a basis consistent with that for prior periods and that there have been no material adverse changes in the shipping business of Tilson or the financial condition thereof since December 31.

5) As soon as is practicable after the execution of a definitive agreement, Tilson shall at its expense cause a survey of each of the vessels to be made and the results to be delivered to Ditton. Such survey must establish to Ditton's satisfaction that each of the vessels is in a seaworthy condition.

6) There shall be executed between Tilson and Ditton a definitive agreement covering the transaction upon the terms and conditions herein set forth and containing further terms and provisions satisfactory to the parties, which shall include, among other things, (a) provisions for an audit of Tilson by Ditton's auditors which will confirm the facts set forth in the vessel financial operating statements above referred to and that there has been no material adverse change in Tilson's shipping business or the financial condition thereof since December 31, (b) general warranties as to its shipping business and assets, (c) special warranties as to loss contracts, commitments, and sales proposals, and (d) representations, indemnifications, and restrictive convenants, commitments, and sales proposals, and (d) representations, indemnifications, and restrictive covenants (to include a covenant by Tilson not to compete with Ditton in the iron ore and coal hauling business on the Lakes for a period of five (5) years), all to survive the closing of the transaction, and all of which will in the opinion of the parties be adequate to protect their respective interests.

7) Ditton must be satisfied as to the terms of any leases of real and personal property to Tilson which cannot be performed or concluded within one year from the closing of the transaction.

8) That there are no material adverse changes in the (a) physical condition of the vessels, or (b) general business outlook for bulk movement of iron ore and coal on the Lakes by the vessels prior to

ter of intent in order to serve as a "flag" to both parties as they proceed with the transaction.

closing, a loss of not more than two of the vessels being deemed not such a change provided adequate insurance coverage is maintained and the proceeds thereof or replacement vessels are transferred to Ditton at the closing.

9) That the service cost of all of the pension plans to be transferred to Ditton, whether arising during the current period ending December 31, 19_____, or during any prior period, is paid by Tilson after first taking credit for the existing overfunding.

10) No legal fees, transfer taxes, brokers' or binders' fees, accountants' fees, or dissolution and winding-up expenses incurred by or properly chargeable to Tilson in connection with this transaction nor any sales or use taxes incurred in connection with this transaction will be assumed or paid by Ditton.

11) The ultimate acquisition of the assets and business of Tilson covered by this proposal may be made by Ditton or any one or more of its subsidiary or affiliated companies.

12) Tilson will use its best efforts (without making any commitments on behalf of Ditton) to preserve for Ditton the present relationships of Tilson with its employees, customers, and others having business relations with it.

13) As soon as is practicable after the closing, Tilson will change its corporate name to eliminate the word "Tilson" or any reference thereto.

The closing of the transaction shall take place between January 1 and January 3, 19_____, the date to be selected by Tilson, provided that Ditton is given fifteen (15) days prior notice of the closing date selected.

It is important that there be a paragraph stating that there is no binding obligation as a result of the letter of intent. Otherwise, future litigation may be invited if the deal never materializes.

In the interests of Tilson and Ditton, this proposal is not to be considered as an offer to purchase or a commitment to sell but rather as a tangible indication of our desire to acquire the Tilson shipping business and assets and of Tilson's desire to sell such a business and assets upon the terms and conditions generally outlined in this letter. Consequently, there shall be no binding obligation on the part of Ditton or Tilson in this regard until a definitive agreement covering the transaction herein outlined has been fully and properly executed by all parties concerned.

The existence of our proposal is to be kept confidential and not disclosed to any persons other than the officers and directors of Tilson.

Confidentiality should be dealt with after consultation with securities lawyers as to the requirements of disclosure.

If this proposal meets with your approval, we ask that you indicate such approval by returning the enclosed copy of this letter, appropriately signed. We will then immediately undertake the preparation of the proposed definitive agreement covering the transaction herein outlined.

Very truly yours,

Ditton Corporation
("Ditton")

The precise corporate names of the parties should be used and an authorized officer should execute the letter of intent.

By:_____
                    Vice President

Approved this _____ day of
_____, 19_____.

L.G. Tilson, Inc. (''Tilson'')

By:_____
    President

Appendix N

Memorandum of Closing

See discussion beginning at page 91.

MEMORANDUM OF CLOSING

MEMORANDUM TO: COLUMBIA CORPORATION

SUBJECT: Acquisition of Gordon, Inc.
Closing Memorandum

TIME: 10:00 A.M., Monday, December 19, 1980

PLACE: Offices of Management, Inc.
1747 Pennsylvania Avenue, N.W.
Washington, D.C. 20080

PRESENT: For Columbia Corporation:

                      S. R. Jones, President
                      B. C. Ramsgate, Secretary
                      J. D. Black, Esq., Counsel

          For Gordon, Inc.:

                      Albert G. Smith, President
                      Thomas Brown, Secretary
                      William Green, Esq., Counsel

          For Shareholders:

                      R. D. Founder, Sr.
                      R. D. Founder, Jr.
                      Sam Orange, Esq., Counsel

I. Prior to Closing:

The parties executed an Agreement dated November 29, 1980, and J. D. Black conferred with John Jackson, Esq., Mount Kisco, New York, concerning the present status of litigation matters involving Gordon, Inc., in that city.

II. At Closing:

All documents were delivered in escrow until the end of the Closing, at which time all documents were delivered simultaneously.

A. R. D. Founder, Sr. and R. D. Founder, Jr. delivered to Columbia Corporation the following:

1. Schedule of Stock Certificates and the Certificates.
2. Surrender of Options of R. D. Founder, Jr.
3. Release of R. D. Founder, Sr.
4. Release of R. D. Founder, Jr.

5. Assignment and Discharge of Indebtedness of R. D. Founder, Jr.
6. Covenant Not to Compete of R. D. Founder, Sr.
7. Employment Agreement with Covenant Not to Compete of R. D. Founder, Jr.
8. R. D. Founder, Sr. and R. D. Founder, Jr.'s Certificate of Warranty and Indemnification.
9. Certificate of Good Standing of Gordon, Inc.
10. Internal Revenue Service's letter Showing Qualification of Profit Sharing Plan of Gordon, Inc.
11. Certificate as to Offer to Minority Shareholders of Gordon, Inc.
12. Certified Copy of Profit Sharing Plan of Gordon, Inc. and Trust.
13. Resignations of all Directors of Gordon, Inc. and of all Officers of Gordon, Inc.
14. Certified Resolutions of the Shareholders and Board of Directors of Gordon, Inc.
15. Incumbency Certificate of Officers and Directors of Gordon, Inc.
16. Statement of The Orange Company, Broker.
17. Copy of Filings of Uniform Commercial Code with District of Columbia.
18. Letter Concerning Sick Leave Adjustment.
19. Opinion Letter of William Green, Esq.

B. Mr. Green delivered the Certificate of Title as to real property owned by Gordon, Inc.

C. Columbia Corporation and Gordon, Inc. delivered to R. D. Founder, Sr. and R. D. Founder, Jr. the following:

1. Note of Columbia Corporation to R. D. Founder, Sr. with Gordon, Inc. Guaranty.
2. Gordon, Inc. Note to R. D. Founder, Jr.
3. Security Agreement of Gordon, Inc.
4. Mortgage of Gordon, Inc.
5. Copies of Checks in Payment of Mortgage Tax by Gordon, Inc.
6. Columbia Corporation's Certificate of Warranty.
7. Certified Board Resolutions of Columbia Corporation.
8. Letter and Endorsements Concerning Continuation of Insurance.
9. Checks to R. D. Founder, Sr. and R. D. Founder, Jr. for Shares of Stock.
10. John Jackson, Esq. Delivered to J. D. Black, Esq. his Opinion as to certain matters of New York law.
11. Opinion of J. D. Black, Esq.

D. All remaining minority shareholders delivered their shares of common and preferred stock to Gordon, Inc. for cancellation upon payment in full pursuant to the Agreement of November 29, 1980.

III. After Closing:

A. A meeting of the Sole Shareholder of Gordon, Inc.
B. A meeting of the Director of Gordon, Inc. was held.
C. A meeting of the Trustees of the Profit Sharing Plan of Gordon, Inc. was held.

Appendix O

Employment Agreement

See discussion beginning at page 97.

EMPLOYMENT CONTRACT

THIS AGREEMENT made between Jones, Inc., a Georgia corporation (hereinafter called "Corporation") and Carter Horne (hereinafter called "Employee");

WHEREAS, Employee has been in the continuous employ of the Corporation since 1964, and during such time has developed and expanded the business of the Corporation with significant success; and

WHEREAS, the Board of Directors of the Corporation believes that the future services of Employee will be of great value to the Corporation; and

WHEREAS, Employee is willing to continue in the employ of the Corporation on a full-time basis for an additional five years.

NOW, THEREFORE, in consideration of the premises, the parties hereto have agreed as follows:

1. *Duties During Employment Period*. The Corporation hereby employs Employee, and Employee agrees to serve the Corporation as Chairman of the Board during the period (hereinafter called the "Employment Period") beginning April 16, 19____, and ending April 16, 19____. During this period, Employee shall devote such time, attention and energies to the business of the Corporation as shall be reasonably necessary to discharge his duties under this Agreement. Employee shall carry out such executive services and duties as shall be assigned to him from time to time by the Board of Directors provided such services and duties do not impose time demands on Employee which are unreasonably burdensome, and provided further that, only for purposes of determining whether there has been a violation under paragraph 7 below, Employee shall not be expected to perform duties substantially different from those performed by Employee prior to the date hereof.

2. *Restriction on Competition*. Employee is in the process of selling to an affiliate of Smith Corporation all of Employee's interest in the capital stock of the Corporation, and it is the intention of Smith Corporation to develop a nationwide business substantially similar to that conducted by the Corporation. Employee is a leader in the type of business conducted by the Corporation and has contacts which may prove useful in the expansion of the business. Based upon the foregoing, Employee hereby agrees that during the term of his employment and for a period of one (1) year thereafter, he will not, unless acting with the Corporation's prior written consent, directly or indirectly, own, manage, operate, join, control or participate in the ownership, management, operation or control of, or be connected as an officer, employee, partner with, any business engaged in the business of distributing building supplies and related products within those counties of the states of Alabama, Florida, Georgia, North Carolina, South Carolina and Tennessee shown on Schedule I, except the Employee may own up to 1% of the common stock of any company whose stock is traded in any stock exchange or over the counter. The Employee agrees that the remedy at law for any breach of the foregoing will be inadequate and that the Corporation shall be entitled to temporary and permanent injunctive relief without the necessity of proving actual damage to the Corporation.

3. *Compensation*. The Corporation shall pay to Employee, and Employee shall accept from the Corporation, for his services during the Employment Period, compensation at the minimum rate of $80,000.00 per annum, which shall be payable in equal installments no less often than monthly. Such compensation shall be reviewed annually.

4. *Disclosure of Information*. The Employee will not, during or for two years after the term of his employment, disclose the list of the Corporation's customers, sales arrangements, or other proprietary information of the Corporation, to any person, firm, corporation, association, or other entity for any reason or purpose whatsoever, except as such disclosure may be necessary or required in the ordinary course of business or in order to provide information to service agencies,

accountants, attorneys, or other consultants retained or employed by the Corporation. In the event of a breach or threatened breach by the Employee of the provisions of this paragraph, the Corporation shall be entitled to an injunction restraining the Employee from disclosing the information herein prohibited to be disclosed, or from rendering any service to any firm, person, corporation, association, or other entity to whom such information has been disclosed or is threatened to be disclosed. Nothing herein shall be construed as prohibiting the Corporation from pursuing any other remedies available to the Corporation for such breach or threatened breach, including the recovery of damages from the Employee.

5. *Expenses*. During the Employment Period, the Employee is authorized to incur reasonable expenses for promoting the business of the Corporation, including expenses for entertainment, travel (whether local or otherwise) and similar items. The Corporation will reimburse the Employee for all such expenses upon the presentation by the Employee of an itemized account of such expenditures in accordance with the Corporation's policy in effect from time to time.

6. *Physical Disability*. If by reason of illness or incapacity the Employee is unable fully to perform his duties during the Employment Period, his compensation shall be continued without modification until the expiration of three (3) months of such disability; should the disability continue beyond three months, but is not of sufficient severity to make the Employee eligible for disability retirement under the Corporation's Pension Plan, the Corporation shall continue pay to Employee at one-half (½) of his normal compensation in effect at that time, for the lesser of a period of one (1) year or until the Employee is once again able fully to perform his duties.

7. *Termination*. (a) If, during the Employment Period, the Board of Directors of the Corporation determines that the Employee is in violation of paragraphs 1, 2, or 4 of this Agreement, it shall inform the Employee of the violation by written notice. If, after 30 days of receipt of the notice by Employee, the Board of Directors and the Employee are not in agreement that the violation, if any, no longer exists, then the controversy shall, at the option of the Board be made the subject of an arbitration pursuant to paragraph 10 of this Agreement. If the award of arbitration is against the Employee, this employment shall be terminated as of the date of the award. (b) If the Employee's employment is terminated under subparagraph (a) of this paragraph 7, or if the Employee terminates this Agreement before its expiration, the Corporation shall only be obligated to pay the Employee compensation to the date of termination, and the Employee agrees that after such termination he will continue to comply with paragraphs 2 and 4 of this Agreement.

8. *Death During Employment*. If the Employee dies during the term of this Agreement, the Corporation shall pay to the estate of the Employee the compensation which would otherwise be payable to the Employee up to the end of the third (3) month following the month in which death occurs. Such payment shall be in addition to such other death benefits as are provided under the Corporation's Employees' Security Program.

9. *Fringe Benefits*. During the Employment Period, Employee shall be entitled to all benefits in effect from time to time which the Corporation provides to its executive officers, which fringe benefits (with the exception of cash bonuses) shall not be less than those fringe benefits provided by the Corporation to employees prior to January 1, 19_____.

10. *Arbitration*. Any controversy or claim arising out of or relating to this Agreement or the breach thereof shall be settled by arbitration to be held in Atlanta, Georgia, in accordance with the commercial rules then obtaining of the American Arbitration Association and the judgment upon the award rendered may be entered in any court having jurisdiction thereof.

11. *Notices*. Any notices required or permitted to be given under this Agreement shall be sufficient if in writing and if sent by Certified Mail to the Employee's residence in the case of the Employee, or to the principal office of the Corporation in the case of the Corporation.

12. *Waiver of Breach*. The waiver by the Corporation of a breach of any provision of this Agreement by the Employee shall not operate or be construed as a waiver of any subsequent breach by the Employee.

13. *Entire Agreement*. This instrument contains the entire Agreement of the parties. It may not be changed orally but only by an agreement in writing, signed by the party against whom enforcement of any waiver, change, modification, extent, or discharge is sought.

14. *Binding Effect.* This Agreement shall be binding upon and shall inure to the benefit of the heirs, executors, administrators, successors and assigns of the parties hereto.

IN WITNESS WHEREOF, the parties hereto have executed this Agreement this 5th day of May, 19_____.

JONES, INC.

By: _____

ATTEST:

_____
Alfred Jones, Employee

_____

Appendix P

Buy-Sell Agreement

See discussion beginning at page 100.

BUY-SELL AGREEMENT—AN INTRODUCTION

This form of agreement was tailor-made for a closely-held corporation owned by two brothers who wished to use life insurance to cover much of the corporation's obligation.

If two generations has been involved (such as father and child), then it would be best to consider a fixed price both for sales during life and at death. Such an agreement generally pegs the value of the parties' stock for estate tax purposes, if reasonable (see IRS Regulations § 20.2031-2(h)).

By providing that the corporation, instead of the other shareholder, is to purchase the stock, the remaining shareholder usually avoids paying for the ownership of the rest of the corporate stock with his own after tax dollars (see Rev. Rul. 69-608, 1969-2 C.B. 43).

BUY-SELL AGREEMENT

AGREEMENT by and between I.M. SHAREHOLDER, and U.R. SHAREHOLDER (hereinafter referred to as the Stockholders), and GOLIATH CORPORATION (hereinafter referred to as the Company), created and existing under the laws of the State of Delaware with its principal place of business at Atlanta, Georgia.

WHEREAS, Stockholders are the sole common stockholders of the Company, I.M. SHAREHOLDER owning 50% of the common stock thereof, and U.R. SHAREHOLDER owning 50%, and

WHEREAS, the parties to this Agreement believe that it is to their mutual best interests to provide for continuity and harmony in management and the policies of the Company, and

WHEREAS, therefore, it is their mutual purpose (a) to provide for the purchase by the Company of a decedent's stock interest therein, (b) to provide for the purchase by the Company of a stockholder's shares should he desire to dispose of any of this stock in the Company during his lifetime, and (c) to provide the funds necessary to carry out such purchase.

WITNESSETH:

NOW, THEREFORE, in consideration of the mutual agreements and covenants contained herein and for other valuable consideration, receipt of which is hereby acknowledged, it is mutually agreed and covenanted by and between the parties to this Agreement as follows:

ARTICLE 1. No stockholder shall during his lifetime transfer, encumber or dispose of any portion or all of his stock interest in the Company except that if a stockholder should desire to dispose of any of his stock in the Company during his lifetime, he shall first make a "buy or sell" offer to the other Stockholder. Such offer shall be in writing and shall state that the offering Stockholder wishes to either sell all of his stock to Company at a specified price and terms, or to cause Company to buy all of the other common Stockholder's stock at the same specified price and terms. Within 90 days of receipt of such notice, Company shall notify the offering Stockholder in writing that it will either buy out the offering Stockholder, or the other Stockholder, on such terms. The decision for Company shall be made solely by the other, non-offering Stockholder, and for purposes of enforcing this Article 1, such other Stockholder is hereby granted an irrevocable proxy to vote the offering Stockholder's shares of common stock. This provision shall also be interpreted as a Shareholder's Agreement under § 22-611 of the Georgia Business Corporation Code.

ARTICLE 2. Upon the death of any Stockholder, the Company shall purchase, and the estate of the decedent shall sell, all of the decedent's shares in the Company now owned or hereafter acquired. The purchase price of such stock shall be computed in accordance with the provisions of Article 3.

ARTICLE 3. Unless and until changed as provided hereinafter, it is agreed that, for the purpose of determining the purchase price to be paid for the interest of a deceased shareholder, the price for each share of Company stock is 5000 Dollars. This price has been agreed upon by the Stockholders and the Company as representing the fair value of the interest of each Stockholder, including his interest in the goodwill of the corporation. The Stockholders and the Company agree to redetermine the value of the Company and their respective interests therein within 120 days following the end of each fiscal year of Company. The value so agreed upon shall be endorsed on Schedule A attached hereto and made a part of this Agreement, and such endorsement shall take the following form: "The undersigned mutually agree on this _____ day of _____, A.D 19_____, that for the purposes of ¶3 of this Buy-Sell Agreement, each share of Company has a value of _____ Dollars. [signed I.M. SHAREHOLDER, U.R. SHAREHOLDER and GOLIATH CORPORATION]". If the Stockholders and the Company fail to make a redetermination of value for a particular year, the last previously stipulated value shall control, except that if the Stockholders and the Company have not so redetermined the value within the twenty-four months immediately preceding the death of a Stockholder, then the value of a Stockholder's interest shall be agreed upon by the representative of the deceased Stockholder and the Company through its surviving shareholders. If they do not agree upon a valuation within 90 days after the death of a Stockholder, the value of the deceased Stockholder's interest shall be determined by arbitration as follows: The Company and the surviving Stockholder shall each name one arbitrator; if the two arbitrators cannot agree upon a value within 30 days, they shall appoint a third arbitrator and the decision of the majority shall be binding upon all parties. In any determination of value made after the death of a Stockholder the value of insurance proceeds must not be taken into account.

ARTICLE 4. The Company is the applicant, owner and beneficiary of the following life insurance policies issued by the Large Life Insurance Company:

Policy #623842 insuring the life of I.M. SHAREHOLDER in the amount of $2,400,000.
Policy #623843 insuring the life of U.R. SHAREHOLDER in the amount of $2,400,000.

The Company agrees to pay premiums on the insurance policies taken out pursuant to this Agreement and shall give proof of payment of premiums to the Stockholders whenever anyone of them shall so request such proof. If a premium is not paid within 10 days after its due date, the insured shall have the right to pay such premium and be reimbursed therefor by the Company. The Company shall have the right to purchase additional insurance on the lives of any or all of its Stockholders; such additional policies shall be listed in Schedule B, attached hereto and made a part of this Agreement, along with any substitution or withdrawal of life insurance policies subject to this Agreement. In the event that the Company decides to purchase additional life insurance on any stockholder, each stockholder hereby agrees to cooperate fully by performing all the requirements of the life insurer which are necessary conditions precedent to the issuance of life insurance policies. The Company shall be the sole owner of the policies issued to it and it may apply any dividends toward the payment of premiums.

ARTICLE 5. If the purchase price exceeds the proceeds of the life insurance, the balance of the purchase price shall be paid in 24 consecutive quarterly payments beginning 6 months after the date of the stockholder's death. Such unpaid balance of the purchase price shall be evidenced by a series of negotiable promissory notes executed by the Company to the order of the estate of the deceased with interest at 97% per annum. Such notes shall provide for the acceleration of the due date of all unpaid notes in the series on default in the payment of any note or interest thereon and shall provide that upon the default of any payment of interest or principal, all notes shall become due and payable immediately, shall give Company the option of pre-payment in whole or in part at any time and shall be in such form as Company's counsel shall suggest.

ARTICLE 6. If any stockholder disposes of all of his stock in the Company during his lifetime or if this Agreement terminates before the death of a stockholder, then such stockholder shall have the right to purchase the insurance policy or policies on his life owned by the Company by paying an amount equal to the cash surrender value as of the date of transfer, less any existing indebtedness charged against the policy or policies. This right shall lapse if not exercised within 30 days after such disposal or termination.

ARTICLE 7. This Agreement may be altered, amended or terminated by a writing signed by all of the Stockholders and the Company.

ARTICLE 8. This Agreement shall terminate upon the occurrence of any of the following events:

1. Bankruptcy, receivership or dissolution of the Company, or
2. Death of Stockholders within a period of 30 days, or
3. When there is only one common shareholder in Company.

ARTICLE 9. The executor, administrator or personal representative of a deceased stockholder shall execute and deliver any and all documents or legal instruments necessary or desirable to carry out the provisions of this Agreement. This Agreement shall be binding upon the Stockholders, their heirs, legal representatives, successors or assigns, and upon the Company, its successors or assigns. This Agreement shall be governed by the laws of the State of Georgia.

ARTICLE 10. Notwithstanding the provisions of this Agreement, any life insurance company which has issued a policy of life insurance subject to provisions of this Agreement is hereby authorized to act in accordance with the terms of such policies as if the agreement did not exist, and the payment or other performance of its contractual obligations by any such insurance company in accordance with the terms of any such policy shall completely discharge such company from all claims, suits and demands of all persons whatsoever.

ARTICLE 11. If the Company is unable to make any purchase required of it hereunder because of the provisions of the applicable statutes or of its charter or by-laws, the Company agrees to take such action as may be necessary to permit it to make such purchases, and the Stockholders who are parties to this Agreement agree that they will also take such action as may be necessary for the Company to make such purchases.

ARTICLE 12. Notwithstanding any other provision of this Agreement, nothing herein shall prohibit transfer of shares of Company to the wife, any ascendant, or any descendant of a Stockholder, or trustee or custodian for any such persons, provided that any such transferee executes such documents and agreements as Company shall reasonably require in order to assure that such transferee shall be bound by all of the terms of this Agreement as if an original Stockholder signatory hereto.

ARTICLE 13. This Agreement supersedes all earlier agreements concerning the stock of Company among the parties or any of them.

ARTICLE 14. Stockholders shall cause Company to place on all certificates evidencing shares of common stock in Company a legend in such form as Company's counsel shall suggest to evidence the existence of this Agreement.

ARTICLE 15. Any notice hereunder shall be deemed given and received when personally delivered to a party, or on the third day after mailing U.S. Certified Mail, Return Receipt Requested, if to a Stockholder, to his then current address on the Company's books, and if to Company, to its registered office and agent. A copy of any notice to Company shall also be promptly given to both Stockholders.

IN WITNESS WHEREOF, the parties to this Buy-Sell Agreement have set their seals and caused this instrument to be executed this 30 day of January, 1980

_____(SEAL)
I.M. SHAREHOLDER

_____(SEAL)
U.R. SHAREHOLDER
("Stockholders")

                                                    GOLIATH CORPORATION
[Corporate Seal]   (the "Company")
Attest: By:_____
                                                           President

_____
Secretary

Appendix Q

FTC Franchising Rules

See discussion beginning at page 123.

PART 436—DISCLOSURE REQUIREMENTS AND PROHIBITIONS CONCERNING FRANCHISING AND BUSINESS OPPORTUNITY VENTURES

Sec.
436.1 The Rule.
436.2 Definitions.
436.3 Severability.
AUTHORITY: 38 Stat. 717, as amended, 15 U.S.C. 41-58.
SOURCE: 43 FR 59614, Dec. 21, 1978, unless otherwise noted.

§ 436.1 The Rule.

In connection with the advertising, offering, licensing, contracting, sale, or other promotion in or affecting commerce, as "commerce" is defined in the Federal Trade Commission Act, of any franchise, or any relationship which is represented either orally or in writing to be a franchise, it is an unfair or deceptive act or practice within the meaning of section 5 of that Act for any franchisor or franchise broker:

(a) To fail to furnish any prospective franchisee with the following information accurately, clearly, and concisely stated, in a legible, written document at the earlier of the "time for making of disclosures" or the first "personal meeting":

(1)(i) The official name and address and principal place of business of the franchisor, and of the parent firm or holding company of the franchisor, if any;

(ii) The name under which the franchisor is doing or intends to do business; and

(iii) The trademarks, trade names, service marks, advertising or other commercial symbols (hereinafter collectively referred to as "marks") which identify the goods, commodities, or services to be offered, sold, or distributed by the prospective franchisee, or under which the prospective franchisee will be operating.

(2) The business experience during the past 5 years, stated individually, of each of the franchisor's current directors and executive officers (including, and hereinafter to include, the chief executive and chief operating officer, financial, franchise marketing, training and service officers). With regard to each person listed, those persons' principal occupations and employers must be included.

(3) The business experience of the franchisor and the franchisor's parent firm (if any), including the length of time each: (i) has conducted a business of the type to be operated by the franchisee; (ii) has offered or sold a franchise for such business; (iii) has conducted a business or offered or sold a franchise for a business (A) operating under a name using any mark set forth under paragraph (a)(1)(iii), or (B) involving the sale, offering, or distribution of goods, commodities, or services which are identified by any mark set forth under paragraph (a)(1)(iii); and (iv) has offered for sale or sold franchises in other lines of business, together with a description of such other lines of business.

(4) A statement disclosing who, if any, of the persons listed in paragraphs (a)(2) and (a)(3) of this section:

(i) Has, at any time during the previous seven fiscal years, been convicted of a felony charge if the felony involved fraud (including violation of any franchise law, or unfair or deceptive practices law), embezzlement, fraudulent conversion, misappropriation of property, or restraint of trade;

(ii) Has, at any time during the previous seven fiscal years, been held liable in a civil action resulting in a final judgment or has settled out of court any civil action or is a party to any civil action (A) involving allegations of fraud (including violation of any franchise law, or unfair or deceptive practices law), embezzlement, fraudulent conversion, misappropriation of property, or restraint of trade, or (B) which was brought by a present or former franchisee or franchisees and which involves or involved the franchise relationship; *Provided, however,* That only material individual civil actions need be so listed pursuant to this subparagraph (4)(ii), including any group of civil actions which, irrespective of the materiality of any single such action, in the aggregate is material;

(iii) Is subject to any currently effective State or Federal agency or court injunctive or restrictive order, or is a party to a proceeding currently pending in which such order is sought, relating to or affecting franchise activities or the franchisor-franchisee relationship, or involving fraud (including violation of any franchise law, or unfair or deceptive practices law), embezzlement, fraudulent conversion, misappropriation of property, or restraint of trade.

Such statement shall set forth the identity and location of the court or agency; the date of conviction, judgment, or decision; the penalty imposed; the damages assessed; the terms of settlement or the terms of the order; and the date, nature, and issuer of each such order or ruling. A franchisor may include a summary opinion of counsel as to any pending litigation, but only if counsel's consent to the use of such opinion is included in the disclosure statement.

(5) A statement disclosing who, if any, of the persons listed in paragraphs (a)(2) and (a)(3) of this section at any time during the previous 7 fiscal years has:

(i) Filed in bankruptcy;

(ii) Been adjudged bankrupt;

(iii) Been reorganized due to insolvency; or

(iv) Been a principal, director, executive officer, or partner of any other person that has so filed or was so adjudged or reorganized, during or within 1 year after the period that such person held such position in such other person. If so, the name and location of the person having so filed, or having been so adjudged or reorganized, the date thereof, and any other material facts relating thereto, shall be set forth.

(6) A factual description of the franchise offered to be sold by the franchisor.

(7) A statement of the total funds which must be paid by the franchisee to the franchisor or to a person affiliated with the franchisor, or which the franchisor or such affiliated person imposes or collects in whole or in part on behalf of a third party, in order to obtain or commence the franchise operation, such as initial franchise fees, deposits, downpayments, prepaid rent, and equipment and inventory purchases. If all or part of these fees or deposits are returnable under certain conditions, these conditions shall be set forth; and if not returnable, such fact shall be disclosed.

(8) A statement describing any recurring funds required to be paid, in connection with carrying on the franchise business, by the franchisee to the franchisor or to a person affiliated with the franchisor, or which the franchisor or such affiliated person imposes or collects in whole or in part on behalf of a third party, including, but not limited to, royalty, lease, advertising, training, and sign rental fees, and equipment or inventory purchases.

(9) A statement setting forth the name of each person (including the franchisor) the franchisee is directly or indirectly required or advised to do business with by the franchisor, where such persons are affiliated with the franchisor.

(10) A statement describing any real estate, services, supplies, products, inventories, signs, fixtures, or equipment relating to the establishment or the operation of the franchise business which the franchisee is directly or indirectly required by the franchisor to purchase, lease or rent; and if such purchases, leases or rentals must be made from specific persons (including the franchisor), a list of the names and addresses of each such person. Such list may be made in a separate document delivered to the prospective franchisee with the prospectus if the existence of such separate document is disclosed in the prospectus.

(11) A description of the basis for calculating, and, if such information is readily available, the actual amount of, any revenue or other consideration to be received by the franchisor or persons affiliated with the franchisor from suppliers to the prospective franchisee in consideration for

goods or services which the franchisor requires or advises the franchisee to obtain from such suppliers.

(12)(i) A statement of all the material terms and conditions of any financing arrangement offered directly or indirectly by the franchisor, or any person affiliated with the franchisor, to the prospective franchisee; and

(ii) A description of the terms by which any payment is to be received by the franchisor from (A) any person offering financing to a prospective franchisee; and (B) any person arranging for financing for a prospective franchisee.

(13) A statement describing the material facts of whether, by the terms of the franchise agreement or other device or practice, the franchisee is:

(i) Limited in the goods or services he or she may offer for sale;

(ii) Limited in the customers to whom he or she may sell such goods or services;

(iii) Limited in the geographic area in which he or she may offer for sale or sell goods or services; or

(iv) Granted territorial protection by the franchisor, by which, with respect to a territory or area, (A) the franchisor will not establish another, or more than any fixed number of, franchises or company-owned outlets, either operating under, or selling, offering, or distributing goods, commodities or services, identified by any mark set forth under paragraph (a)(1)(iii) of this section; or (B) the franchisor or its parent will not establish other franchises or company-owned outlets selling or leasing the same or similar products or services under a different trade name, trademark, service mark, advertising or other commercial symbol.

(14) A statement of the extent to which the franchisor requires the franchisee (or, if the franchisee is a corporation, any person affiliated with the franchisee) to participate personally in the direct operation of the franchise.

(15) A statement disclosing, with respect to the franchise agreement and any related agreements:

(i) The term (i.e., duration of arrangement), if any, of such agreement, and whether such term is or may be affected by any agreement (including leases or subleases) other than the one from which such term arises;

(ii) The conditions under which the franchisee may renew or extend;

(iii) The conditions under which the franchisor may refuse to renew or extend;

(iv) The conditions under which the franchisee may terminate;

(v) The conditions under which the franchisor may terminate;

(vi) The obligations (including lease or sublease obligations) of the franchisee after termination of the franchise by the franchisor, and the obligations of the franchisee (including lease or sublease obligations) after termination of the franchise by the franchisee and after the expiration of the franchise;

(vii) The franchisee's interest upon termination of the franchise, or upon refusal to renew or extend the franchise, whether by the franchisor or by the franchisee;

(viii) The conditions under which the franchisor may repurchase, whether by right of first refusal or at the option of the franchisor (and if the franchisor has the option to repurchase the franchise, whether there will be an independent appraisal of the franchise, whether the repurchase price will be determined by a predetermined formula and whether there will be a recognition of goodwill or other intangibles associated therewith in the repurchase price to be given the franchisee);

(ix) The conditions under which the franchisee may sell or assign all or any interest in the ownership of the franchise, or of the assets of the franchise business;

(x) The conditions under which the franchisor may sell or assign, in whole or in part, its interest under such agreements;

(xi) The conditions under which the franchisee may modify;

(xii) The conditions under which the franchisor may modify;

(xii) The rights of the franchisee's heirs or personal representative upon the death or incapacity of the franchisee; and

(xiv) The provisions of any covenant not to compete.

(16) A statement disclosing, with respect to the franchisor and as to the particular named business being offered:

(i) The total number of franchises operating at the end of the preceding fiscal year;

(ii) The total number of company-owned outlets operating at the end of the preceding fiscal year;

(iii) The names, addresses, and telephone numbers of (A) The 10 franchised outlets of the named franchise business nearest the prospective franchisee's intended location; or (B) all franchisees of the franchisor, or (C) all franchisees of the franchisor in the State in which the prospective franchisee lives or where the proposed franchise is to be located, *Provided, however,* That there are more than 10 such franchisees. If the number of franchisees to be disclosed pursuant to paragraph (a)(16)(iii)(B) or (C) of this section exceeds 50, such listing may be made in a separate document delivered to the prospective franchisee with the prospectus if the existence of such separate document is disclosed in the prospectus;

(iv) The number of franchises voluntarily terminated or not renewed by franchisees within, or at the conclusion of, the term of the franchise agreement, during the preceding fiscal year;

(v) The number of franchises reacquired by purchase by the franchisor during the term of the franchise agreement, and upon the conclusion of the term of the franchise agreement, during the preceding fiscal year;

(vi) The number of franchises otherwise reacquired by the franchisor during the term of the franchise agreement, and upon the conclusion of the term of the franchise agreement, during the preceding fiscal year;

(vii) The number of franchises for which the franchisor refused renewal of the franchise agreement or other agreements relating to the franchise during the preceding fiscal year; and

(viii) The number of franchises that were canceled or terminated by the franchisor during the term of the franchise agreement, and upon conclusion of the term of the franchise agreement, during the preceding fiscal year.

With respect to the disclosures required by paragraphs (a)(16) (v), (vi), (vii), and (viii) of this section, the disclosure statement shall also include a general categorization of the reasons for such reacquisitions, refusals to renew or terminations, and the number falling within each such category, including but not limited to the following: failure to comply with quality control standards, failure to make sufficient sales, and other breaches of contract.

(17) (i) If site selection or approval thereof by the franchisor is involved in the franchise relationship, a statement disclosing the range of time that has elapsed between signing of franchise agreements or other agreements relating to the franchise and site selection, for agreements entered into during the preceding fiscal year; and

(ii) If operating franchise outlets are to be provided by the franchisor, a statement disclosing the range of time that has elapsed between the signing of franchise agreements or other agreements relating to the franchise and the commencement of the franchisee's business, for agreements entered into during the preceding fiscal year.

With respect to the disclosures required by paragraphs (a)(17) (i) and (ii) of this section, a franchisor may at its option also provide a distribution chart using meaningful classifications with respect to such ranges of time.

(18) If the franchisor offers an initial training program or informs the prospective franchisee that it intends to provide such person with initial training, a statement disclosing:

(i) The type and nature of such training;

(ii) The minimum amount, if any, of training that will be provided to a franchisee; and

(iii) The cost, if any, to be borne by the franchisee for the training to be provided, or for obtaining such training.

(19) If the name of a public figure is used in connection with a recommendation to purchase a franchise, or as a part of the name of the franchise operation, or if the public figure is stated to be involved with the management of the franchisor, a statement disclosing:

(i) The nature and extent of the public figure's involvement and obligations to the franchisor, including but not limited to the promotional assistance the public figure will provide to the franchisor and to the franchisee;

(ii) The total investment of the public figure in the franchise operation; and

(iii) The amount of any fee or fees the franchisee will be obligated to pay for such involvement or assistance provided by the public figure.

(20) (i) A balance sheet (statement of financial position) for the franchisor for the most recent fiscal year, and an income statement (statement of results of operations) and statement of changes in financial position for the franchisor for the most recent 3 fiscal years. Such statements are required to have been examined in accordance with generally accepted auditing standards by an independent certified or licensed public accountant. *Provided, however,* That where a franchisor is a subsidiary of another corporation which is permitted under generally accepted accounting principles to prepare financial statements on a consolidated or combined statement basis, the above information may be submitted for the parent if (A) the corresponding unaudited financial statements of the franchisor are also provided, and (B) the parent absolutely and irrevocably has agreed to guarantee all obligations of the subsidiary;

(ii) Unaudited statements shall be used only to the extent that audited statements have not been made, and provided that such statements are accompanied by a clear and conspicuous disclosure that they are unaudited. Statements shall be prepared on an audited basis as soon as practicable, but, at a minimum, financial statements for the first full fiscal year following the date on which the franchisor must first comply with this part shall contain a balance sheet opinion prepared by an independent certified or licensed public accountant, and financial statements for the following fiscal year shall be fully audited.

(21) All of the foregoing information in paragraph (a) (1) through (20) of this section shall be contained in a single disclosure statement or prospectus, which shall not contain any materials or information other than that required by this part or by State law not preempted by this part. This does not preclude franchisor or franchise brokers from giving other nondeceptive information orally, visually, or in separate literature so long as such information is not contradictory to the information in the disclosure statement required by paragraph (a) of this section. This disclosure statement shall carry a cover sheet distinctively and conspicuously showing the name of the franchisor, the date of issuance of the disclosure statement, and the following notice imprinted thereon in upper and lower case bold-face type of not less than 12 point size:

Information for Prospective Franchisees Required by Federal Trade Commission

* * * * *

To protect you, we've required your franchisor to give you this information. *We haven't checked it, and don't know if it's correct.* It should help you make up your mind. Study it carefully. While it includes some information about your contract, don't rely on it alone to understand your contract. Read all of your contract carefully. Buying a franchise is a complicated investment. Take your time to decide. If possible show your contract and this information to an advisor, like a lawyer or an accountant. If you find anything you think may be wrong or anything important that's been left out, you should let us know about it. It may be against the law.

There may also be laws on franchising in your state. Ask your state agencies about them.

FEDERAL TRADE COMMISSION,
Washington, D.C.

Provided, That the obligation to furnish such disclosure statement shall be deemed to have been met for both the franchisor and the franchise broker if either such party furnishes the prospective franchisee with such disclosure statement.

(22) All information contained in the disclosure statement shall be current as of the close of the franchisor's most recent fiscal year. After the close of each fiscal year, the franchisor shall be given a period not exceeding 90 days to prepare a revised disclosure statement and, following such 90 days, may distribute only the revised prospectus and no other. The franchisor shall, within a reasonable time after the close of each quarter of the fiscal year, prepare revisions to be attached to the disclosure statement to reflect any material change in the franchisor or relating to the franchise business of the franchisor, about which the franchisor or franchise broker, or any agent, representative, or employee thereof, knows or should know. Each prospective franchisee shall have in his or her possession, at the "time for making of disclosures," the disclosure statement and quarterly revision for the period most recent to the "time for making of disclosures" and available at that time. Information which is required to be audited pursuant to paragraph (a)(20) of this section is not required to be audited for quarterly revisions. *Provided, however,* That the unaudited information be accompanied by a statement in immediate conjunction therewith that clearly and conspicuously discloses that such information has not been audited.

(23) A table of contents shall be included within the disclosure statement.

(24) The disclosure statement shall include a comment which either positively or negatively responds to each disclosure item required to be in the disclosure statement, by use of a statement which fully incorporates the information required by the item. Each disclosure item therein must be preceded by the appropriate heading, as set forth in Note 3 of this part.

(b) To make any oral, written, or visual representation to a prospective franchisee which states a specific level of potential sales, income, gross or net profit for that prospective franchisee, or which states other facts which suggest such a specific level, unless:

(1) At the time such representation is made, such representation is relevant to the geographic market in which the franchise is to be located;

(2) At the time such representation is made, a reasonable basis exists for such representation and the franchisor has in its possession material which constitutes a reasonable basis for such representation, and such material is made available to any prospective franchisee and to the Commission or its staff upon reasonable demand. *Provided, further,* That in immediate conjunction with such representation, the franchisor shall disclose in a clear and conspicuous manner that such material is available to the prospective franchisee; and *Provided, however,* That no provision within paragraph (b) of this section shall be construed as requiring the disclosure to any prospective franchisee of the identity of any specific franchisee or of information reasonably likely to lead to the disclosure of such person's identity; and *Provided, further,* That no additional franchisee's potential sales, income, or profits may be made later than the "time for making of disclosures";

(3) Such representation is set forth in detail along with the material bases and assumptions therefor in a single legible written document whose text accurately, clearly and concisely discloses such information, and none other than that provided for by this part or by State law not preempted by this part. Each prospective franchisee to whom the representation is made shall be furnished with such document no later than the "time for making of disclosures"; *Provided, however,* That if the representation is made at or prior to a "personal meeting" and such meeting occurs before the "time for making of disclosures", the document shall be furnished to the prospective franchisee to whom the representation is made at that "personal meeting";

(4) The following statement is clearly and conspicuously disclosed in the document described by paragraph (b(3) of this section in immediate conjunction with such representation and in not less than twelve point upper and lower-case boldface type:

Caution

These figures are only estimates of what we think you may earn. There is no assurance you'll do as well. If you rely upon our figures, you must accept the risk of not doing as well.

(5) The following information is clearly and conspicuously disclosed in the document described by paragraph (b)(3) of this section in immediate conjunction with such representation:

(i) The number and percentage of outlets of the named franchise business which are located in the geographic markets that form the basis for any such representation and which are known to the franchisor or franchise broker to have earned or made at least the same sales, income, or profits during a period of corresponding length in the immediate past as those potential sales, income, or profits represented; and

(ii) The beginning and ending dates for the corresponding time period referred to by paragraph (b)(5)(i) of this section, *Provided, however,* That any franchisor without prior franchising experience as to the named franchise business so indicate such lack of experience in the document described in paragraph (b)(3) of this section.

Except, That representations of the sales, income or profits of existing franchise outlets need not comply with this paragraph (b).

(c) To make any oral, written or visual representation to a prospective franchisee which states a specific level of sales, income, gross or net profits of existing outlets (whether franchised or company-owned) of the named franchise business, or which states other facts which suggest such a specificl level, unless:

(1) At the time such representation is made, such representation is relevant to the geographic market in which the franchise is to be located;

(2) At the time such representation is made, a reasonable basis exists for such representation and the franchisor has in its possession material which constitutes a reasonable basis for such representation, and such material is made available to any prospective franchisee and to the Commission or its staff upon reasonable demand, *Provided, however,* That in immediate conjunction with such representation, the franchisor discloses in a clear and conspicuous manner that such material is available to the prospective franchisee; and *Provided, further,* That no provision within paragraph (c) of this section shall be construed as requiring the disclosure to any prospective franchisee of the identity of any specific franchisee or of information reasonably likely to read to the disclosure of such person's identity; and *Provided, further,* That no additional representation as to the sales, income, or gross or net profits of existing outlets (whether franchised or company-owned) of the named franchise business may be made later than the "time for making of disclosures";

(3) Such representation is set forth in detail along with the material bases and assumptions therefor in a single legible written document which accurately, clearly and concisely discloses such information, and none other than that provided for by this part or by State law not preempted by this part. Each prospective franchisee to whom the representation is made shall be furnished with such document no later than the "time for making of disclosures", *Provided, however,* That if the representation is made at or prior to a "personal meeting" and such meeting occurs before the "time for making of disclosures," the document shall be furnished to the prospective franchisee to whom the representation is made at that "personal meeting";

(4) The underlying data on which the representation is based have been prepared in accordance with generally accepted accounting principles;

(5) The following statement is clearly and conspicuously disclosed in the document described by paragraph (c)(3) of this section in immediate conjunction with such representation, and in not less than twelve point upper and lower case boldface type:

Caution

Some outlets have [sold] [earned] this amount. There is no assurance you'll do as well. If you rely upon our figures, you must accept the risk of not doing as well.

(6) The following information is clearly and conspicuously disclosed in the document described by paragraph (c)(3) of this section in immediate conjunction with such representation:

(i) The number and percentage of outlets of the named franchise business which are located in the geographic markets that form the basis for any such representation and which are known to the franchisor or franchise broker to have earned or made at least the same sales, income, or profits during a period of corresponding length in the immediate past as those sales, income, or profits represented; and

(ii) The beginning and ending dates for the corresponding time period referred to by subparagraph (6)(i), *Provided, however,* That any franchisor without prior franchising experience as to the named franchise business so indicate such lack of experience in the document described in paragraph (c)(3) of this section.

(d) To fail to provide the following information within the document(s) required by paragraphs (b)(3) and (c)(3) of this section whenever any representation is made to a prospective franchisee regarding its potential sales, income, or profits, or the sales, income, gross or net profits of existing outlets (whether franchised or company-owned) of the named franchise business:

(1) A cover sheet distinctively and conspicuously showing the name of the franchisor, the date of issuance of the document and the following notice imprinted thereon in upper and lower case boldface type of not less than twelve point size:

Information For Prospective Franchisees About Franchise [Sales] [Income] [Profit] Required by the Federal Trade Commission.

To protect you, we've required the franchisor to give you this information. *We haven't checked it and don't know if it's correct.* Study these facts and figures carefully. If possible, show them to someone who can advise you, like a lawyer or an accountant. Then take your time and think it over.

If you find anything you think may be wrong or anything important that's been left out, let us know about it. It may be against the law.

There may also be laws on franchising in your State. Ask your State agencies about them.

FEDERAL TRADE COMMISSION,
Washington, D.C.

(2) A table of contents.

Provided, however, That each prospective franchisee to whom the representation is made shall be notified at the "time for making of disclosures" of any material change (about which the franchisor, franchise broker, or any of the agents, representatives, or employees thereof, knows or should know) in the information contained in the document(s) described by paragraphs (b)(3) and (c)(3) of this section.

(e) To make any oral, written, or visual representation for general dissemination (not otherwise covered by paragraphs (b) or (c) of this section) which states a specific level of sales, income, gross or net profits, either actual or potential, of existing or prospective outlets (whether franchised or company-owned) of the named franchise business or which states other facts which suggest such a specific level, unless:

(1) At the time such representation is made, a reasonable basis exists for such representation and the franchisor has in its possession material which constitutes a reasonable basis for such representation and which is made available to the Commission or its staff upon reasonable demand;

(2) The underlying data on which each representation of sales, income or profit for existing outlets is based have been prepared in accordance with generally accepted accounting principles;

(3) In immediate conjunction with such representation, there shall be clearly and conspicuously disclosed the number and percentage of outlets of the named franchise business which the franchisor or the franchise broker knows to have earned or made at least the same sales, income, or profits during a period of corresponding length in the immediate past as those sales, income, or profits represented, and the beginning and ending dates for said time period;

(4) In immediate conjunction with each such representation of potential sales, income or profits, the following statement shall be clearly and conspicuously disclosed:

Caution

These figures are only estimates; there is no assurance you'll do as well. If you rely upon our figures, you must accept the risk of not doing as well.

Provided, however, That if such representation is not based on actual experience of existing outlets of the named franchise business, that fact also should be disclosed;

(5) No later than the earlier of the first "personal meeting" or the "time for making of disclosures," each prospective franchisee shall be given a single, legible written document which accurately, clearly and concisely sets forth the following information and materials (and none other than that provided for by this part or by State law not preempted by this part):

(i) The representation, set forth in detail along with the material bases and assumptions therefor;

(ii) The number and percentage of outlets of the named franchise business which the franchisor or the franchise broker knows to have earned or made at least the same sales, income or profits during a period of corresponding length in the immediate past as those sales, income, or profits represented, and the beginning and ending dates for said time period;

(iii) With respect to each such representation of sales, income, or profits of existing outlets, the following statement shall be clearly and conspicuously disclosed in immediate conjunction therewith, printed in not less than 12 point upper and lower case boldface type:

Caution

Some outlets have [sold] [earned] this amount. There is no assurance you'll do as well. If you rely upon our figures, you must accept the risk of not doing as well.

(iv) With respect to each such representation of potential sales, income, or profits, the following statement shall be clearly and conspicuously disclosed in immediate conjunction therewith, printed in not less than 12 point upper and lower case boldface type:

Caution

These figures are only estimates. There is no assurance that you'll do as well. If you rely upon our figures, you must accept the risk of not doing as well.

(v) If applicable, a statement clearly and conspicuously disclosing that the franchisor lacks prior franchising experience as to the named franchise business;

(vi) If applicable, a statement clearly and conspicuously dislcosing that the franchisor has not been in business long enough to have actual business data;

(vii) A cover sheet, distinctively and conspicuously showing the name of the franchisor, the date of issuance of the document, and the following notice printed thereon in not less than 12 point upper and lower case boldface type:

Information For Prospective Franchisees About Franchise [Sales] [Income] [Profit] Required by the Federal Trade Commission

To protect you, we've required the franchisor to give you this information. *We haven't checked it and don't know if it's correct.* Study these facts and figures carefully. If possible, show them to someone who can advise you, like a lawyer or an accountant. If you find anything you think may be wrong or anything important that's been left out, let us know about it. It may be against the law. There may also be laws about franchising in your State. Ask your State agencies about them.

FEDERAL TRADE COMMISSION,
Washington, D.C.

(viii) A table of contents;

(6) Each prospective franchisee shall be notified at the "time for making of disclosures" of any material changes that have occurred in the information contained in this document.

(f) To make any claim or representation which is contradictory to the information required to be disclosed by this part.

(g) To fail to furnish the prospective franchisee with a copy of the franchisor's franchise agreement and related agreements with the document, and a copy of the completed franchise and related agreements intended to be executed by the parties at least 5 business days prior to the date the agreements are to be executed.

Provided, however, That the obligations defined in paragraphs (b) through (g) of this section shall be deemed to have been met for both the franchisor and the franchise broker if either such person furnishes the prospective franchisee with the written disclosures required thereby.

(h) To fail to return any funds or deposits in accordance with any conditions disclosed pursuant to paragraph (a)(7) of this section.

§ 436.2 Definitions.

As used in this part, the following definitions shall apply:

(a) The term "franchise" means any continuing commercial relationship created by any arrangement or arrangements whereby:

(1)(i)(A) a person (hereinafter "franchisee") offers, sells, or distributes to any person other than a "franchisor" (as hereinafter defined), goods, commodities, or services which are:

(*1*) Identified by a trademark, service mark, trade name, advertising or other commercial symbol designating another person (hereinafter "franchisor"); or

(*2*) Indirectly or directly required or advised to meet the quality standards prescribed by another person (hereinafter "franchisor") where the franchisee operates under a name using the trademark, service mark, trade name, advertising or other commercial symbol designating the franchisor; and

(B)(*1*) The franchisor exerts or has authority to exert a significant degree of control over the franchisee's method of operation, including but not limited to, the franchisee's business organization, promotional activities, management, marketing plan or business affairs; or

(*2*) The franchisor gives significant assistance to the franchisee in the latter's method of operation, including, but not limited to, the franchisee's business organization, management, marketing plan, promotional activities, or business affairs; *Provided, however,* That assistance in the franchisee's promotional activities shall not, in the absence of assistance in other areas of the franchisee's method of operation, constitute significant assistance; or

(ii)(a) A person (hereinafter "franchisee") offers, sells, or distributes to any person other than a "franchisor" (as hereinafter defined), goods, commodities, or services which are:

(*1*) Supplied by another person (hereinafter "franchisor"), or

(*2*) Supplied by a third person (e.g., a supplier) with whom the franchisee is directly or indirectly required to do business by another person (hereinafter "franchisor"); or

(*3*) Supplied by a third person (e.g., a supplier) with whom the franchisee is directly or indirectly advised to do business by another person (hereinafter "franchisor") where such third person is affiliated with the franchisor; and

(B) The franchisor:

(*1*) Secures for the franchisee retail outlets or accounts for said goods, commodities, or services; or

(*2*) Secures for the franchisee locations or sites for vending machines, rack displays, or any other product sales display used by the franchisee in the offering, sale, or distribution of said goods, commodities, or services; or

(*3*) Provides to the franchisee the services of a person able to secure the retail oulets, accounts, sites or locations referred to in paragraph (a)(1)(ii)(B)(*1*) and (2) above; and

(2) The franchisee is required as a condition of obtaining or commencing the franchise operation to make a payment or a commitment to pay to the franchisor, or to a person affiliated with the franchisor.

(3) Exemptions. The provisions of this part shall not apply to a franchise:

(i) Which is a "fractional franchise"; or

(ii) Where pursuant to a lease, license, or similar agreement, a person offers, sells, or distributes goods, commodities, or services on or about premises occupied by a retailer-grantor primarily for the retailer-grantor's own merchandising activities, which goods, commodities, or services are not purchased from the retailer-grantor or persons whom the lessee is directly or indirectly (A) required to do business with by the retailer-grantor or (B) advised to do business with by the retailer-grantor where such person is affiliated with the retailer-grantor; or

(iii) Where the total of the payments referred to in paragraph (a)(2) of this section made during a period from any time before to within 6 months after commencing operation of the franchisee's business, is less than $500; or

(iv) Where there is no writing which evidences any material term or aspect of the relationship or arrangement.

(4) Exclusions. The term "franchise" shall not be deemed to include any continuing commercial relationship created solely by:

(i) The relationship between an employer and an employee, or among general business partners; or

(ii) Membership in a bona fide "cooperative association"; or

(iii) An agreement for the use of a trademark, service mark, the trade name, seal, advertising, or other commercial symbol designating a person who offers on a general basis, for a fee or otherwise, a bona fide service for the evaluation, testing, or certification of goods, commodities, or services;

(iv) An agreement between a licensor and a single licensee to license a trademark, trade name, service mark, advertising or other commercial symbol where such license is the only one of its general nature and type to be granted by the licensor with respect to that trademark, trade name, service mark, advertising, or other commercial symbol.

(5) Any relationship which is represented either orally or in writing to be a franchise (as defined in this paragraph (a)(1) and (2) of this section) is subject to the requirements of this part.

(b) The term "person" means any individual, group, association, limited or general partnership, corporation, or any other business entity.

(c) The term "franchisor" means any person who participates in a franchise relationship as a franchisor, as denoted in paragraph (a) of this section.

(d) The term "franchisee" means any person (1) who participates in a franchise relationship as a franchisee, as denoted in paragraph (a) of this section, or (2) to whom an interest in a franchise is sold.

(e) The term "prospective franchisee" includes any person, including any representative, agent, or employee of that person, who approaches or is approached by a franchisor or franchise broker, or any representative, agent, or employee thereof, for the purpose of discussing the establishment, or possible establishment, of a franchise relationship involving such a person.

(f) The term "business day" means any day other than Saturday, Sunday, or the following national holidays: New Year's Day, Washington's Birthday, Memorial Day, Independence Day, Labor Day, Columbus Day, Veterans' Day, Thanksgiving, and Christmas.

(g) The term "time for making of disclosures" means ten (10) business days prior to the earlier of (1) the execution by a prospective franchisee of any franchise agreement or any other agreement imposing a binding legal obligation on such prospective franchisee, about which the franchisor, franchise broker, or any agent, representative, or employee thereof, knows or should know, in connection with the sale or proposed sale of a franchise, or (2) the payment by a prospective franchisee, about which the franchisor, franchise broker, or any agent, representative, or employee thereof, knows or should know, of any consideration in connection with the sale or proposed sale of a franchise.

(h) The term "fractional franchise" means any relationship, as denoted by paragraph (a) of this section, in which the person described therein as a franchisee, or any of the current directors or executive officers thereof, has been in the type of business represented by the franchise relationship for more than 2 years and the parties anticipated, or should have anticipated, at the time the agreement establishing the franchise relationship was reached, that the sales arising from the relationship would represent no more than 20 percent of the sales in dollar volume of the franchisee.

(i) The term "affiliated person" means a person (as defined in paragraph (b) of this section):

(1) Which directly or indirectly controls, is controlled by, or is under common control with, a franchisor; or

(2) Which directly or indirectly owns, controls, or holds with power to vote, 10 percent or more of the outstanding voting securities of a franchisor; or

(3) Which has, in common with a franchisor, one or more partners, officers, directors, trustees, branch managers, or other persons occupying similar status or performing similar functions.

(j) The term "franchise broker" means any person other than a franchisor or a franchisee who sells, offers for sale, or arranges for the sale of a franchise.

(k) The term "sale of a franchise" includes a contract or agreement whereby a person obtains a franchise or interest in a franchise for value by purchase, license, or otherwise. This term shall not be deemed to include the renewal or extension of an existing franchise where there is no interruption in the operation of the franchised business by the franchisee, unless the new contracts or agreements contain material changes from those in effect between the franchisor and franchisee prior thereto.

(l) A "cooperative association" is either (1) an association of producers of agricultural products authorized by section 1 of the Capper-Volstead Act, 7 U.S.C. 291; or (2) an organization operated on a cooperative basis by and for independent retailers which wholesales goods or furnishes services primarily to its member-retailers.

(m) The term "fiscal year" means the franchisor's fiscal year.

(n) The terms "material," "material fact," and "material change" shall include any fact, circumstance, or set of conditions which has a substantial likelihood of influencing a reasonable franchisee or a reasonable prospective franchisee in the making of a significant decision relating to a named franchise business or which has any significant financial impact on a franchisee or prospective franchisee.

(o) The term "personal meeting" means a face-to-face meeting between a franchisor or franchise broker (or any agent, representative, or employee thereof) and a prospective franchisee which is held for the purpose of discussing the sale or possible sale of a franchise.

§ 436.3 Severability.

If any provision of this part or its application to any person, act, or practice is held invalid, the remainder of the part or the application of its provisions to any person, act, or practice shall not be affected thereby.

NOTE 1.—The Commission expresses no opinion as to the legality of any practice mentioned in this part. A provision for disclosure should not be construed as condonation or approval with respect to the matter required to be disclosed, nor as an indication of the Commission's intention not to enforce any applicable statute.

NOTE 2.—By taking action in this area, the Federal Trade Commission does not intend to annul, alter, or affect, or exempt any person subject to the provisions of this part from complying with the laws or regulations of any State, municipality, or other local government with respect to franchising practices, except to the extent that those laws or regulations are inconsistent with any provision of this part, and then only to the extent of the inconsistency. For the purposes of this part, a law or regulation of any State, municipality, or other local government is not inconsistent with this part if the protection such law or regulation affords any prospective franchisee is equal to or greater than that provided by this part. Examples of provisions which provide protection equal to or greater than that provided by this part include laws or regulations which require more complete record keeping by the franchisor or the disclosure of more complete information to the franchisee.

NOTE 3.—[As per § 436.1(a)(24) of this part]:

Disclosure Statement

Pursuant to 16 CFR 436.1 et seq., a Trade Regulation Rule of the Federal Trade Commission regarding Disclosure Requirements and Prohibitions Concerning Franchising and Business Opportunity Ventures, the following information is set forth on [name of franchisor] for your examination:

1. Identifying information as to franchisor.
2. Business experience of franchisor's directors and executive officers.
3. Business experience of the franchisor.
4. Litigation history.
5. Bankruptcy history.
6. Description of franchise.
7. Initial funds required to be paid by a franchisee.
8. Recurring funds required to be paid by a franchisee.
9. Affiliated persons the franchisee is required or advised to do business with by the franchisor.
10. Obligations to purchase.
11. Revenues received by the franchisor in consideration of purchases by a franchisee.
12. Financing arrangements.
13. Restriction of sales.
14. Personal participation required of the franchisee in the operation of the franchise.
15. Termination, cancellation, and renewal of the franchise.
16. Statistical information concerning the number of franchises (and company-owned outlets).
17. Site selection.
18. Training programs.
19. Public figure involvement in the franchise.
20. Financial information concerning the franchisor.

Index